Theatre never exists in a

it is not its own island,

nor an empire carving out borders;

it is not the center of its universe.

Instead, the theatre is the **essential center** to and for the universe. It does not stand apart, defiant, in contrast, indifferent. **It is a sum total of its surroundings,** its neighbors.

Through its artists, the theatre is in service, connected to its communities.

Through its art, it is in constant and meaningful dialogue with its myriad citizens.

The theatre throws open its door, sets the proverbial table, inviting everyone to a seat.

On that table is a sumptuous feast of stories that reflect, that represent the collective and individual histories of the human race, whether traditional or contemporary, whether **epic** or intimate; stories that explore, dissect and affirm our beliefs, ideas and rituals, this, our timeless chronicle of the people.

This is the theatre's heart.

this theatre seeds, nurtures and produces
bold, relevant and innovative theatre work
created by bold, relevant and imaginative artists.

The work challenges and inspires audiences
to embrace familiar situations anew,
consider different perspectives from different worlds;
ignites a raging fire in them to ask hard questions,
in hope that they will furnish their own answers
for individual, communal or global change.

The work **ENTERTAINS**, documents, *celebrates* their **complex**, contradictory humanity;

it # astounds,

mesmerizes them

with the *magic* of their own imaginations, and reminds them of the simple enchantments of

a spoken word,

a moment,

a *gesture* in their daily lives.

This theatre must demand and encourage its playwrights, its generative and collaborative artists, designers and crew, its staff and board to always be courageous, to dare, to dream. Never opt for the safe, the sure nor the easiest path. Be fearless. Write, direct and produce the play as if it's your last play. It's better to having a brilliant failure than a boring success. Start a fire and jump into it; for others will leap with you.

Artists, be unafraid of politics and fight for social justice. You give voice to the voiceless, visibility to the invisible. You articulate what others can't. So, capture your generation's howl, your community's song, your country's cry. Fashion a harsh mirror for the audience to see themselves through beauty, through flaws. Weave new stories, myths and narratives for the present, for the ages.

You are our master storyteller, following a tradition born from millennia and civilizations past, gathering people around a fire, under stars and sky. Your Gilgamesh, your Iliad, your Ramayana and Orphan of Zhao, your King Lear and Raisin in the Sun, your Angels in America and How I Learned to Drive, your work will live in the now and forever. You are our Homer, Moliere, our Lorca and Churchill, our Fornes and our Wilson. You are a descendent of storytellers who told the hakawati in cool desert nights, who painted the animals in dim Lascaux caves, and recited Tlinglit legends about ravens and coyotes under the tallest redwoods.

It is your turn.

Tell your story.

Share your voice in this theatre
made of fire and fearlessness.

This is the people's theatre.

A public theatre.

Our theatre.

Set it aflame.

man·i·fes·to (man-*uh*-fes-to) A public declaration
of principles, policies, or intentions,
especially of a political nature.

MANIFESTO series

edited by
Chay Yew

Volume 4

Samuel D. Hunter

Trieu Tran with Robert Egan

Keri Healey

Dan O'Brien

Holly Arsenault

UNIVERSES

CONTENTS

ACKNOWLEDGEMENTS

The editors wish to thank the following for their assistance
in compiling this volume.

CULTURE
KING COUNTY LODGING TAX

Annex Theatre

Theater Off Jackson

Elliott Bay Books

Jennifer, Brontë & Rowan Neel

Pruzan Abode

Rain City Projects is an Associated Program of Shunpike, shunpike.org.

FOREWARD

For over two decades, Rain City Projects has been proud to be a member of a community that embraces the risky endeavor of new theater work. In the Pacific Northwest, it is possible for a playwright to create a piece, pull together a reading or two, take advantage of a community workshop, and then to present their work on their own dime or under the umbrella of one of our many new works theaters. The bold failures become a learning ground for everyone involved. And the successes? What of the successes?

One hopes that a success in our community will go on to other productions, in other places, and will help develop playwrights on a national level. But that doesn't always happen.

In 2006, Rain City Projects decided to sing the praises of our successes, of our playwrights who are talented and bold and risky and funny, artists who are being shaped in the Northwest. The goal is to expose them to a wider audience and encourage the world to take notice.

So, we launched the **Manifesto Series**.

We begin with an endorser, a playwright with roots in the Pacific Northwest who has a national voice and presence. We ask them to write a manifesto of what theater is, what it should be. Then we let them choose scripts by Northwest playwrights which fulfill that manifesto. And then we publish the collection in an anthology and widely disperse the anthology with a thumbs-up.

With this, our fourth collection, we are certain we are on the right track. We are delighted with Chay Yew's manifesto and in awe of the quality of scripts in the collection he chose. Read them with our blessings. Love them with the knowledge that we do, too.

Becky Bruhn
Rain City Projects

SAMUEL D. HUNTER's plays include *The Whale* (2013 Drama Desk Award, 2013 Lucille Lortel Award for Outstanding Play, 2013 GLAAD Media Award, Drama League and Outer Critics Circle nominations for Best Play), *A Bright New Boise* (2011 Obie Award for Playwriting, 2011 Drama Desk nomination for Best Play), and his newest plays, *The Few, A Great Wilderness, Rest*, and *Pocatello*. His plays have been produced by such theaters as Playwrights Horizons, Rattlestick Playwrights Theater, Seattle Rep, Victory Gardens, South Coast Rep, Williamstown Theater Festival, The Old Globe, Woolly Mammoth Theatre Company, Denver Center Theatre Company, Clubbed Thumb, and Page 73. His work has been developed at the O'Neill Playwrights Conference, the Ojai Playwrights Conference, Seven Devils, and elsewhere. Sam is the winner of a 2012 Whiting Writers Award, the 2013 Otis Guernsey New Voices Award, the 2011 Sky Cooper Prize, and the 2008–2009 PONY Fellowship. He is a member of New Dramatists, an Ensemble Playwright at Victory Gardens, a Core Member of The Playwrights' Center, a member of Partial Comfort Productions, and was a 2013 Resident Playwright at Arena Stage. A native of northern Idaho, Sam lives in NYC. He holds degrees in playwriting from NYU, The Iowa Playwrights Workshop, and Juilliard.

Samuel D. Hunter

The Whale

CHARACTERS:

CHARLIE   Early to mid forties, male, weighing around 600 lbs

LIZ   Mid to late thirties, female

ELDER THOMAS   19, male

ELLIE   17, female

MARY   Early to mid forties, female

SETTING:

Northern Idaho, the present.

The main room of a small, white-walled, desolate apartment in a cheaply constructed two story building. The room is dominated by a large couch that sags in the middle, re-enforced by several cinder blocks.

Within arm's reach of the couch are: a small computer desk on rollers with a laptop on top, a large pile of papers, a walker, a claw for reaching, and a whole universe of full, empty, and half empty food containers (donuts, candy bars, fried chicken, burgers, two liter soda bottles, etc.). Little effort has been made to clean up trash or organize.

A small kitchen is off to one corner of the stage, a bathroom and bedroom offstage.

NOTES: The play is served much better by being performed without an intermission (running time is roughly 1 hour, 50 minutes). However, if absolutely necessary, an intermission can be taken in between Wednesday night and Thursday morning.

Dialogue written in *italics* is emphatic, deliberate; dialogue written in ALL CAPS is impulsive, explosive.

A "/" indicates an overlap in dialogue.

MONDAY
MORNING.

> *Charlie, a morbidly obese man in his early forties, dressed in oversized sweatpants and an oversized sweatshirt, sits on the couch in front of his laptop, speaking into a small microphone hooked up to his computer.*

CHARLIE: This is from a paper I got from a student last year, a freshman at UC Santa Barbara. He was writing this for an American Lit class. It's a paper about *The Great Gatsby. (pulling out an essay)* "There were many aspects to the book *The Great Gatsby*. But I was bored by it because it was about people that I don't care about and they do things I don't understand. In conclusion, *The Great Gatsby* wasn't so great, LOL." *(stops reading)* The problems with this essay are painfully obvious. The student has no discernible thesis, almost no analysis whatsoever . . . I'll be posting the paper in it's entirety, what I want you to do is read through it a few times, and then post a three to four paragraph response providing concrete ideas for revision. Also, those of you who haven't given me paper four, I need it by five o'clock, *no exceptions.* And remember—the more revision you guys do on these papers, the better. The more you can change, chances are the stronger these papers will be. Alright?

AFTERNOON.

> *Charlie, in the same position before, in front of his computer, masturbating to gay porn.*
>
> *After a few moments, his breathing becomes more and more shallow. He pushes the computer desk away from him. He feels some sharp pain in his chest.*
>
> *He reaches toward his cell phone, but accidentally knocks it onto the floor. The pain becomes worse. All the while, the gay porn is still playing in the background.*
>
> *Charlie takes some deep breaths, wheezing loudly, trying to calm himself down.*
>
> *A knock at the door.*

CHARLIE: Liz?!

> *Another knock.*

CHARLIE: *It's not locked, just come in! I need help, I—!*

> *Elder Thomas enters, wearing a white shirt, black tie, and black slacks. He holds some books and a bike helmet.*

ELDER THOMAS: Oh, my God. Oh, Gosh, are you—? *(pause)* I should call an ambulance. Should I call an ambulance?

Elder Thomas notices the gay porn, still playing. Charlie quickly reaches over and shuts his laptop.

ELDER THOMAS: I don't have a phone, do you have—?

Charlie pulls out a few sheets of paper, hands them to Elder Thomas.

CHARLIE: Read this to me.

ELDER THOMAS: Wait, what?

CHARLIE: Read it to me, *please.*

ELDER THOMAS: I have to call you an ambulance! I don't know what to do, I'm just—

CHARLIE: I don't know what's going to happen in the next five minutes. Please, read it to me. PLEASE JUST READ IT TO ME.

ELDER THOMAS: OKAY! OKAY, I JUST— *(reading, quickly)* "In the amazing book *Moby Dick* by the author Herman Melville, the author recounts his story of being at sea. In the first part of his book, the author, calling himself Ishmael, is in a small sea-side town and he is sharing a bed with a man named Queequeg—" *(stops)* What is this?! Why am I reading this?! I need to call someone—!

CHARLIE: *(pleading)* PLEASE JUST READ IT. *ANY OF IT.*

ELDER THOMAS: *(reading)* "I was very saddened by this book, and I felt many emotions for the characters. And I felt saddest of all when I read the boring chapters that were only descriptions of whales, because I knew that the author was just trying to save us from his own sad story, just for a little while. This book made me think about my own life, and then it . . . It made me feel . . ."

Charlie's breathing starts to become normal. He takes a few deep breaths, calming himself down.

ELDER THOMAS: Did that—help?

CHARLIE: Yes. Yes, it did.

ELDER THOMAS: I'm calling an ambulance, where's your phone?

CHARLIE: I don't go to hospitals.

ELDER THOMAS: I can't help you, I don't even know CPR—!

CHARLIE: *I don't go to hospitals. (pause)* I'm sorry. Excuse me, I'm sorry. You can go if you want, I . . . Thank you for reading that to me.

Pause. Elder Thomas doesn't move.

ELDER THOMAS: Are you feeling better?

CHARLIE: Yes.

ELDER THOMAS: Are you sure?

CHARLIE: Yes.

ELDER THOMAS: Okay. Um. I— *(pause)* I represent the Church of Jesus Christ of Latter Day Saints? We're sharing a message for all faiths?

3

CHARLIE: Oh.

ELDER THOMAS: Yeah. *(pause)* Would you—like to hear about the Church?

    Pause.

CHARLIE: Okay.

ELDER THOMAS: Really?

CHARLIE: Yes. Actually, yes. *(pause)* But I should call my friend. My friend is a nurse. She should come over. She knows what to do, she—takes care of me.

ELDER THOMAS: Okay, good, where's your—?

CHARLIE: My cell phone is over there, can you get it for me?

    Charlie points to a cell phone on the other side of the room. Elder Thomas picks up the cell phone and hands it to Charlie.

ELDER THOMAS: Do you want me to— . . .?

CHARLIE: Stay with me.

    Pause.

ELDER THOMAS: I really should—

CHARLIE: I'm not sure what's going to happen right now. I'd—rather there was someone here with me. If that's alright.

ELDER THOMAS: Yeah, okay.

CHARLIE: Thank you.

    Pause.

ELDER THOMAS: What was—? That thing I read to you about *Moby Dick*?

CHARLIE: It was an essay. It's my job, I do online tutoring, online classes on expository writing.

ELDER THOMAS: But why did you want me to read that to you?

CHARLIE: Because I thought I was dying. And I wanted to hear it one last time.

LATER THAT AFTERNOON.

    Charlie sits on the couch, Liz stands over him, taking his blood pressure. Elder Thomas sits in the corner.

LIZ: You should have called an ambulance.

CHARLIE: With no health insurance?

LIZ: Being in debt is better than being dead. What's wrong with you? Why is there a Mormon here?

CHARLIE: Did I have a heart attack?

LIZ: No, you didn't have a heart attack. *(reading his blood pressure)* Huh.

CHARLIE: What is it?

Pause.

LIZ: Tell me what you felt.

CHARLIE: Pain, in my chest. It was hard to breathe, I felt like I couldn't intake air.

LIZ: How are you sleeping?

CHARLIE: I'm tired all the time. I'm sleeping on the couch now actually, I can breathe better.

Liz takes out a stethoscope. She checks his breathing.

LIZ: You're wheezing.

CHARLIE: I always wheeze, Liz.

LIZ: You're wheezing more. Take a deep breath.

Charlie takes a deep breath.

LIZ: Did that hurt?

CHARLIE: A little. What was my blood pressure?

LIZ: 238 over 134.

Pause. Liz puts the stethoscope away.

CHARLIE: Oh.

LIZ: Yeah. Oh.

Pause.

CHARLIE: Could you hand me my walker? I haven't been to the bathroom all day, I'm ready to explode.

Liz hands him his walker, Charlie gets up with some effort. It's obvious he's having chest pain. Liz watches him.

LIZ: You want help?

CHARLIE: No, I'm fine. Just—. Sorry.

LIZ: What are you sorry about?

CHARLIE: Sorry. I don't know. Sorry.

CHARLIE makes his way to the bathroom, wheezing loudly.

Elder Thomas and Liz look at one another.

ELDER THOMAS: I should go.

LIZ: Thank you. For helping him. *(pause)* You on your mission?

ELDER THOMAS: What?

LIZ: Is this your mission? You're on your mission now?

ELDER THOMAS: Oh—yeah.

LIZ: Where are you from?

ELDER THOMAS: Iowa.

LIZ: You grew up in Iowa and they sent you to *Idaho* on your mission?

ELDER THOMAS: Yeah, I don't know. Some of my friends got to go to Los Angeles. A few went to Africa. It's—fine. *(pause)* Is he going to be—?

LIZ: No. No, he's not.

ELDER THOMAS: He's sick?

LIZ: He's very, very, very sick. *(pause)* I grew up Mormon.

ELDER THOMAS: Really? Oh, that's—that's actually nice to hear, I actually haven't run into a lot of others. Surprising, small town in Idaho, you'd think you'd . . . Do you go to the church over near the highway, or the—?

LIZ: I fucking hate Mormons. *(small pause)* I shouldn't say that, I don't fucking hate Mormons, I fucking hate Mormon*ism*. How can you believe in a God like that? He gives us the Old Testament, fine, we'll all be Jews. Then Jesus shows up and he's like, "Hey so, I'm the son of God, stop being Jewish, here's the New Testament, sorry." And then he shows up a *second* time, and he's like, "Oh, shit, sorry! Here's this other thing, it's called the Book of Mormon." And after all that, we're still supposed to wait around for him to come back a *third fucking time* to kill us all with holy fire and dragons and—

ELDER THOMAS: That's a really unfair summary of my beliefs.

LIZ: I'm just saying, why would God not just give us all the right answers to begin with?

ELDER THOMAS: He has a plan.

LIZ: A plan that he's constantly revising.

ELDER THOMAS: I guess.

> *Pause.*

LIZ: Look—it was good of you to stay with him. But if you're waiting around to convert him, or—

ELDER THOMAS: We don't "convert people." Our message is a message of hope for/people of all faiths—

LIZ: People of all faiths, I know, you're sweet. But he's not interested in what you have to say. It's the last thing he wants to hear. *(lights up a cigarette)* Listen, you can go if you want. I know Charlie appreciates what you did.

ELDER THOMAS: He said he wanted to hear about the church.

> *Pause.*

LIZ: Charlie said he wanted to hear about the church?

ELDER THOMAS: Yes.

> *Pause.*

LIZ: No, he doesn't.

ELDER THOMAS: Why not?

LIZ: I just know.

ELDER THOMAS: How?

LIZ: Because it's caused him a lot of pain.

ELDER THOMAS: How?

LIZ: It killed his boyfriend.

> *Pause.*

ELDER THOMAS: You're saying the church—

LIZ: —killed his boyfriend. Yes, the Church of Jesus Christ of Latter Day Saints killed Charlie's boyfriend.

> *Pause.*

> And I should add that, personally, the Mormon Church has caused *me* a lot of pain in *my* life. That guy in there is the only person I have any more that even resembles a friend, and I am not letting you come over here to talk to him. Especially not now, not this week.

ELDER THOMAS: Why not this week?

LIZ: Because he's probably not going to be here next week.

ELDER THOMAS: Where is he going?

> *Charlie comes back out from the bathroom on his walker, moves toward the couch.*

CHARLIE: I'm sorry you had to come over, Liz. And I'm sorry—

LIZ: It's alright.

CHARLIE: I'm sorry that I always think I'm dying.

> *Pause.*

LIZ: Charlie, your blood pressure is 238 over 134.

CHARLIE: That's not much more than it usually is.

LIZ: Yes, it is. And your normal blood pressure is at near-fatal levels as it is.

> *Pause.*

CHARLIE: I'm sorry, I'm feeling better now. You can go back to—

LIZ: Go to the hospital.

CHARLIE: I'm sorry.

LIZ: Stop saying you're sorry. Go to the hospital.

CHARLIE: Liz—I'm sorry—

LIZ: I'm calling an ambulance and they're going to take you to the hospital!

CHARLIE: I can't!

LIZ: You're going to die, Charlie. You have congestive heart failure. If you don't go to the hospital, you will die. Probably before the weekend. You. Will. Die.

> *Pause.*

CHARLIE: Then I should probably keep working, I have a lot of essays this week.

7

LIZ: GODAMMIT CHARLIE.

CHARLIE: I'm sorry. I'm sorry. I know, I'm—an awful person. I know. I'm sorry.

> *Pause.*

ELDER THOMAS: Do you still want to hear about the church?

LIZ: NO. HE DOES NOT.

ELDER THOMAS: Okay. That's fine, I'm sorry, I—I'll go. *(pause)* I still don't understand why you wanted me to read that essay to you.

> *Pause.*

CHARLIE: It's a really good essay.

ELDER THOMAS: I actually thought it was pretty bad.

CHARLIE: It got a bad grade. But—it's a really, really good essay.

> *Elder Thomas exits. A few beats pass.*

LIZ: Did you tell him you wanted to hear about the Church?

CHARLIE: He's just a kid, Liz. He helped me out.

> *Charlie grunts in pain, holding his chest a bit.*

LIZ: What?

CHARLIE: I'm fine.

LIZ: No, you're not.

> *Pause.*

CHARLIE: I think—I need to call Ellie.

LIZ: Ellie?

CHARLIE: Yeah.

> *Pause.*

LIZ: What, so you're like—giving up?

CHARLIE: What else am I supposed to do?

LIZ: Go to the hospital!

CHARLIE: Okay, I could go to the hospital. Get a bypass operation or whatever. Rack up several hundred thousand dollars of hospital bills that I won't be able to pay back, ever. Then I'll come back home, maybe, and last—what? A year? At the most? All so I could spend another year in what I'm sure is no small amount of pain.

LIZ: Nice positive thinking, Charlie. This affects me too, you know? You're my *friend*.

CHARLIE: I know. I'm sorry.

LIZ: You say you're sorry again, I'm going to shove a knife right into you, I swear to—

CHARLIE: Go ahead, what's it gonna do? My internal organs are two feet in at least.

8

Pause. Liz laughs.

LIZ: Fuck you.

Charlie smiles. They look at one another.

Pause. Finally Liz sighs, goes to the couch, grabbing the remote. She sits next to Charlie, puts her head on his shoulder. She turns on the television, flips through the channels absentmindedly.

LIZ: I've been telling you that this was gonna happen.

CHARLIE: Yeah.

LIZ: Haven't I been telling you—?

CHARLIE: Yes, I know. You have.

Pause.

LIZ: Well I'm not letting you just *die*. I don't care what you think, I'm not letting it happen.

Liz continues to flip through the channels. Silence.

CHARLIE: Did you bring food?

Silence. Liz continues to flip channels.

CHARLIE: Liz.

Liz flips a few more channels. Silence.

CHARLIE: I'm really hungry.

A few more channels. Silence. Then, without looking at Charlie, Liz goes to her bag and pulls out a large bucket of fried chicken. She goes to Charlie and puts it in his lap, keeping her eyes on the TV.

CHARLIE: Thank you.

Charlie opens the bucket, eats. Liz continues to flip channels, then lands on one

LIZ: Judge Judy, I've seen this one. It's good.

Charlie continues to eat, Liz watches the television.

NIGHT.

Charlie, alone, much later that night, eating the last piece of chicken from the bucket. The TV is on at a low level. As he finishes, he turns off the TV, staring forward silently for a moment.

CHARLIE: *(soft)* In the first part of his book, the author, calling himself Ishmael, is in a small sea-side town and he is sharing a bed with a man named Queequeg.

Charlie takes a breath, tries to make himself comfortable on the couch.

CHARLIE: The author and Queequeg go to church and hear a sermon about Jonah, and later set out on a ship captained by the pirate named Ahab, who is missing a leg, and very much wants to kill the whale which is named Moby Dick, and which is white.

Charlie breathes. He shifts on the couch, the movement causing pain in his chest.

CHARLIE: In the course of the book, the pirate Ahab encounters many hardships. His entire life is set around trying to kill a certain whale. I think this is sad because this whale doesn't have any emotions, and doesn't know how bad Ahab wants to kill him.

Charlie settles into the couch, closes his eyes.

CHARLIE: He's just a poor big animal. And I feel bad for Ahab as well, because he thinks that his life will be better if he can kill this whale, but in reality it won't help him at all. This book me made think about my own life. This book made me think about my own life. This book made me—

Lights quickly snap to black.

In the darkness, there is the faint sound of waves lapping against the shore— so quiet that it's nearly inaudible. The sound continues for a moment, rising just a bit in volume, becoming a bit more discernible, before lights rise on:

TUESDAY
MORNING.

Charlie sits on the couch. Ellie stands near the door. There is an awkward silence.

ELLIE: How much?

CHARLIE: I haven't been able to weigh myself in years, it's hard to know. Five-fifty? Six hundred?

ELLIE: That's disgusting.

CHARLIE: I know. It is disgusting, I'm sorry.

ELLIE: Does this mean I'm going to get fat?

CHARLIE: No, it doesn't. I was always big, but I just—let it get out of control.

Pause.

ELLIE: Who was the woman?

CHARLIE: What woman?

ELLIE: There was a woman in the background, when you called me.

CHARLIE: Oh, that's—my friend, Liz.

ELLIE: You have a friend?

CHARLIE: Yeah. She's a nurse, she used to do in-house calls for the hospice—

ELLIE: Is she, like, your fag hag? Because it seems like she could do a lot better.

    Pause.

CHARLIE: Was your mom okay with you coming here?

ELLIE: I didn't tell her. She would've freaked out. *(pause)* Why don't you just go to the hospital?

CHARLIE: I don't have health insurance.

ELLIE: But you might die.

CHARLIE: It's not worth it. *(pause)* It's really good to see you. You look beautiful. How's school going? You're a senior, right?

ELLIE: You actually care?

CHARLIE: Of course I care. I pester your mom for information as often as she'll give it to me. *(pause)* So why aren't—don't you have school?

ELLIE: Suspended until Friday.

CHARLIE: Oh. Why?

ELLIE: I blogged about my stupid bitch lab partner. She told her stupid bitch mom and the vice principal said it was "vaguely threatening."

CHARLIE: You don't like high school?

ELLIE: Only retards like high school.

CHARLIE: But—you're going to pass, right?

ELLIE: I'm failing most of my classes. My dumbass counselor says I might not graduate. I'm a smart person, I never forget anything. But high school is such bullshit. Busywork.

CHARLIE: It's important.

ELLIE: How would you know? *(pause)* So, what? You want me to like help you clean yourself or go to the bathroom or something? Because if you need someone to help you do that stuff, then you need to find someone else.

CHARLIE: You don't need to do anything disgusting, I promise.

ELLIE: Just being around you is disgusting. You smell disgusting. Your apartment is disgusting. You look disgusting. The last time I saw you, you were disgusting.

CHARLIE: There's no way you could remember that. You were two years old.

ELLIE: I'm a smart person, I never forget anything. In the living room, with that old red couch and the TV with the wood frame. And you were on the floor, and mom was screaming at you and you were just apologizing over and over, you were so pathetic. I remember that. Can I have one of those donuts?

    Small pause.

CHARLIE: Yeah, sure.

11

Ellie grabs a donut from a package sitting near the kitchen.

ELLIE: You weren't all that heavy back then. I mean, you were fat, but not like this.

CHARLIE: Yeah.

ELLIE: Why did you gain all that weight?

Pause.

CHARLIE: I'd like us to spend some time together this week.

ELLIE: Why?

CHARLIE: We don't even know one another.

ELLIE: So?

Pause.

CHARLIE: I can pay you.

ELLIE: You want to pay me to spend time with you?

CHARLIE: And I can help you with your work. It's what I do for my job, I help people edit their essays—

ELLIE: Are you serious?

CHARLIE picks up some essays sitting next to him.

CHARLIE: It's what I do all day long. I can help you pass your classes.

ELLIE: How are you like, qualified to edit essays?

CHARLIE: I have a masters degree. In English, from the U of I. I teach online classes, it's my job.

ELLIE: You teach online?

CHARLIE: Yes.

ELLIE: Your students know what you look like?

Pause.

CHARLIE: I don't use a camera. Just a microphone.

ELLIE: That's probably a good idea. *(pause)* Counselor dumbass says that if I show a lot of improvement in one subject that I might be able to pass. I can rewrite my old essays for credit, so you have to rewrite all of those, and write every other essay for the rest of the semester. And they have to be really good.

CHARLIE: I really shouldn't write them for you.

ELLIE: Well, it's what you're gonna do if you want me around. How much can you pay me?

CHARLIE: Whatever I have. All the money I have in the bank.

ELLIE: How much money do you have in the bank?

Pause.

CHARLIE: A hundred and twenty—

ELLIE: You want me to be here all week for a hundred and twenty dollars?

CHARLIE: Thousand. A hundred and twenty thousand dollars. *(pause)* I never go out, I don't have health insurance, all I pay for is food, internet, three-fifty a month in rent. And I work all the time.

ELLIE: You'd give all that money to *me*? Not my mom, to *me*?

CHARLIE: Yes. All of it. Just—don't mention it to your mom. Okay? *(pause)* Also . . . I'll write the essays for you, but I'd like you to do some writing yourself. Just for me. They don't have to be perfect, I'd just like you to write an essay or two for me.

ELLIE: Why?

CHARLIE: You're a smart person, I bet you're a strong writer. I want to know what you have to say. Plus, I'm a teacher. I want to make sure you're getting something out of this.

ELLIE: I don't even understand you. *(silence)* Stand up and walk over to me.

CHARLIE: What?

ELLIE: Come over here. Walk toward me. Come over here, beside me.

Charlie pauses for a second, then reaches for his walker.

ELLIE: Without that thing. Just stand up, and come over here.

CHARLIE: Ellie, I can't really—

ELLIE: Shut up. Come over here.

Charlie takes a few deep breaths, then tries to stand on his feet.

He is unsuccessful at getting off the couch, and he begins to have severe chest pains. His breathing becomes quicker.

He tries again, this time he nearly gets up on his feet, but falls backward when the pain becomes unbearable. He is wincing from the pain, lying back on the couch, wheezing loudly.

Ellie stares at him, unmoved.

NIGHT.

Charlie sits on the couch. Liz is standing near Charlie fiddling with a small machine with electrodes attached to it.

Liz has brought various bulk-sized groceries, they sit near the door still in bags.

LIZ: I don't remember what it's called, something ridiculous, I don't remember. But it's for you, it's going to help you out. This machine here, it senses perspiration. It's an indicator of stress. So the idea is, if you know what makes your stress level go up, you can learn to control it. And that'll reduce your heart rate, lower your blood pressure.

Liz starts attaching the machine to Charlie's hand.

CHARLIE: Where did you get this thing?

LIZ: Ginny, from the hospital, she's into this stuff.

CHARLIE: Do you know how to use it?

LIZ: If Ginny can figure it out, I'm sure it's not that hard. Here. *(turns on the machine)* You see that number right there? That's how much you're sweating. You wanna try and make that number go down.

> *Pause.*

CHARLIE: So what do I—?

LIZ: I don't know, just—relax. Take a deep breath. You're calm. You're very, very calm.

> *Charlie takes a deep breath. Liz rubs his shoulders a bit, watching the machine.*

LIZ: There, the number's going down. Isn't that better? It's about establishing a relationship between your brain and your body. Now you know you're calming yourself down because the little machine is telling you so.

CHARLIE: You really think this is going to help?

LIZ: Yes! It'll help, you just—need to do this all the time.

> *Pause. Liz continues to rub his shoulders and watch the machine.*

CHARLIE: Ellie came over.

> *Pause.*

LIZ: She did?

CHARLIE: Yes. *(pause)* She's—amazing.

LIZ: Yeah?

CHARLIE: And—angry. Very angry. She's coming back tomorrow. I'm writing her essays for her, for school. She's failing most of her classes, I think. She's smart, I can tell she's smart, she just doesn't—

LIZ: Charlie, do you really—? You really think this is a good idea?

CHARLIE: What do you mean?

LIZ: Sorry, but you haven't seen this girl since she was two years old, and *now* you want to reconnect with her? By doing her homework for her?

CHARLIE: It's fine. It'll be fine.

LIZ: What is she gonna do if something happens to you, if you need help?

CHARLIE: I just want to spend some time with her, get to know her. I'm— worried about her.

LIZ: Why?

CHARLIE: She has this—website.

> *Charlie takes the machine off of his hand. He opens up his laptop, pulls up a website. Liz looks at the computer.*

LIZ: I don't understand, what am I looking at?

14

CHARLIE: She calls it a "hate blog." She posts pictures of her friends, her mom even, and she just—insults them. The only thing she ever talks about is how much she doesn't like people.

LIZ: Huh. She's an angry little girl.

CHARLIE: Yes, she is. And I'm worried.

LIZ: She's just being a teenager. She'll be fine, she's got her mom to look out for her.

Liz goes to her shopping bags, puts the food away in the kitchen as she talks.

LIZ: Listen, you shouldn't worry about her. When I was a kid—when my dad would really piss me off—I used to go to the supermarket over on Johnson, you remember that big place that used to be out there?

CHARLIE: Sure.

LIZ: I used to just—*trash* the place. And I was really good at it, I never got caught. I'd walk in really normally, wait until I was in an aisle with no one in it, and then I'd—very quietly—destroy it. Open all the jars and boxes, spill everything on the floor. Pour out the milk, smash the produce under my feet. By the time I was done, they didn't know what hit them. Like this silent tornado had swept through the whole store. I was one angry little girl.

CHARLIE: You never told me about that.

LIZ: Yeah, well, it's not exactly a time in my life I love to think about, or—. *(pause)* I'm just saying, you should be thankful that Ellie's doing this shit on the internet and not getting herself into real trouble.

Liz takes an extra large meatball sub out of a shopping bag, brings it to Charlie. Charlie starts eating it, fairly quickly.

LIZ: Just don't get too worked up about this. You don't need anything stressing you out right now.

Liz heads back to the kitchen.

CHARLIE: I just want to make sure she's doing okay.

LIZ: She has a mother, Charlie. She's not alone, she has her mom.

CHARLIE: Well, she—

Charlie stops, choking on the meatball sub. Liz remains in the kitchen, not noticing him.

Pause. Charlie starts to panic.

LIZ: What? *(no response)* Charlie, you okay?

Liz comes out of the kitchen, sees Charlie.

LIZ: Oh God. Oh God, are you choking?! You're choking?!

Charlie leans forward as best he can, Liz hits his back a few times. It doesn't help.

LIZ: Okay, okay—lean over the arm!

15

Charlie struggles to lean over the arm of the couch, stomach down. As best as she can, Liz pushes on Charlie's back, attempting the Heimlich Maneuver. Finally, she puts all her weight into it, and Charlie spits out the piece of food.

LIZ: *Shit.* Oh, shit, Charlie.

CHARLIE: *(breathing heavily)* I'm okay. I'm okay.

Liz breathes. Charlie rolls back into a sitting position on the couch.
Long pause.

LIZ: GODDAMMIT CHARLIE, WHAT IS WRONG WITH YOU?

CHARLIE: I'm sorry—

LIZ: Chew your food like a normal human being! You could have choked to death just then, you realize that?! *You could have died right in front of me, you could have just—!*

Silence. Liz breathes.

CHARLIE: I'm sorry, Liz.

Another silence. Liz calms down. She looks at her watch, then grabs the remote control, turning on the television.

LIZ: *House* is on. Preview looked good, a guy whose arm has a mind of its own, something like that. *(pause)* You want a Dr. Pepper?

Pause.

CHARLIE: *(quiet)* I'm sorry, Liz.

LIZ: I asked if you want a Dr. Pepper.

Pause.

CHARLIE: *(quieter)* I'm sorry.

Lights quickly snap to black.

The sound of waves returns, this time just a bit louder, rising in volume until lights rise on:

WEDNESDAY
MORNING.

Charlie sits in front of the computer, as before, speaking into a microphone.

CHARLIE: A lot of you had some questions about my most recent assignment, so I just wanted to clear up some misconceptions. This is a new teaching strategy I'm trying out, so please bear with me. First, when I asked you to "make it more personal," I was not being "creepy" as Tina436 recently commented. And when I asked you to "not edit your bad grammar or potentially subjective, unspecific, or just plain stupid ideas," I had not gone "apeshit insane yo" as UNCMark45 recently commented. Do you all realize that I can access the class discussion

16

forum? (*pause*) Listen, at this point in this class, I've given you all I can in terms of structure, building a thesis, paragraph organization. But for once—just write it. See what happens. It won't count toward your final grade, you can rewrite it later if you want, I just—I want to know what you really think. Okay?

AFTERNOON.

> *Charlie sits on the couch, Ellie sits in a chair on the other side of the room, typing on her iPhone. Charlie is reading an essay.*

CHARLIE: This is . . . (*pause*) You say here that Walt Whitman wrote "Song *For* Myself."

ELLIE: (*not looking up*) Yeah?

CHARLIE: It's called "Song *of* Myself."

ELLIE: My title's better.

> *Pause.*

CHARLIE: Yeah, well, it—. . . Okay, I'll just change it.

CHARLIE writes something in the essay. He keeps reading.

CHARLIE: Okay. "In the poem 'Song of Myself' by Walt Whitman, the author tells us how amazing he is. He tells us that he is better than everyone else, and that people should listen to what he says, because he is so wonderful."

ELLIE: You don't need to read it out loud. Just correct it.

CHARLIE: But it's not—. . . This really isn't what the poem is about.

ELLIE: Yes it is. I read it. It was really long and boring and it was about how great he thinks he is.

CHARLIE: But he's not really talking about himself, he's using the metaphor of "I" to refer to something a lot more universal. That's what's so amazing about the poem, on the surface it seems really self-involved and narcissistic, but actually it's about exploding the entire definition of the "self" in favor of this all-encompassing—

ELLIE: Oh my God I don't care.

> *Pause.*

CHARLIE: You just want me to write it for you?

ELLIE: Yes.

CHARLIE: You don't want to understand the poem at all?

ELLIE finally looks up from her iPhone.

ELLIE: You think I don't understand it?

CHARLIE: Well—

17

ELLIE: You're just like my idiot teachers. You think because I don't go nuts over some stupid little poem, it's because I'm too stupid to understand it.

CHARLIE: I didn't say that—

ELLIE: Maybe I *do* understand it. Maybe I understand *exactly* what this poem is about, but I just don't care. Because it was written by some self-involved moron, and even though he thinks that his "metaphor for the self" is deep and shit, it doesn't mean anything because he's just some worthless nineteenth-century faggot. How about that?

Pause. They stare at one another.

CHARLIE: That's an interesting perspective.

ELLIE: You think you're funny?

CHARLIE: It could make for an interesting essay.

ELLIE: Oh my God shut up. Just fix it, okay? Write that thing about "exploding the definition of self," my English teacher will love that.

Ellie goes back to her iPhone. Charlie stares at her.

CHARLIE: How's your mom doing?

ELLIE: Oh my God.

CHARLIE: I just thought we could—talk. A little.

ELLIE: If you're not going to write these essays for me, then I'm not gonna—

CHARLIE: Look, Ellie, I don't need you here to write this for you. I could write this essay in my sleep. And it's not fair of me to force you to stay here. If you really don't want to be here, you can go. You can still have the money.

Pause. Ellie looks at Charlie.

ELLIE: You'd let me have the money anyway?

CHARLIE: Yes.

ELLIE: I thought you wanted to get to know me.

CHARLIE: I do. But I don't want to force you to be here, that's not fair. It's up to you.

Ellie looks at him for a moment, then puts away the iPhone.

ELLIE: She's fine. Mom. I guess.

CHARLIE: Have you told her that you're coming over here?

ELLIE: No. She'd be pretty angry. Plus, she'd want the money.

CHARLIE: Is she—happy?

ELLIE: When she drinks.

CHARLIE: Oh. (*pause*) Do you guys still live over in the duplex over on Orchard?

ELLIE: You don't even know where we live? How'd you get my cell-phone number?

CHARLIE: Facebook.

ELLIE: Creepy. You don't stay in touch with mom?

CHARLIE: Sometimes. She really only tells me things about you.

ELLIE: Why?

CHARLIE: Because that's all I ask about.

    Pause.

ELLIE: When I was little we moved to an apartment on the other side of town, near the Circle K.

CHARLIE: Is your mother—with anyone now?

ELLIE: No. Why, you interested?

CHARLIE: Oh, no, I was just—

ELLIE: I'm kidding, Jesus. How could you be with anyone? (*pause*) Why did you gain all that weight?

CHARLIE: Oh, that doesn't—

ELLIE: If you're gonna interrogate me, I get to do the same thing. Why did you gain all that weight?

    Pause.

CHARLIE: Someone very close to me passed away, and it—had an effect on me.

ELLIE: Who was it?

CHARLIE: My . . .

    Charlie hesitates.

ELLIE: Your boyfriend?

CHARLIE: Yes, my boyfriend. My partner.

ELLIE: What was his name?

CHARLIE: Alan.

ELLIE: How'd he die?

CHARLIE: He sort of . . . Slowly killed himself. (*pause*) He had the flu, and it developed into pneumonia, but he got that sick because he—just sort of shut down. Stopped taking care of himself, stopped eating.

ELLIE: Why did he do that?

CHARLIE: He felt guilty. (*quick pause*) I'd rather not talk about this right now, is that alright with you?

ELLIE: Whatever.

    Pause.

CHARLIE: I'll fix this essay for you before you leave, but I'd like you to do a little writing for me. Alright?

ELLIE: You were serious about that?

CHARLIE: Yes. Here.

Charlie pulls out a notebook and a pen, hands them to Ellie.

ELLIE: I hate writing essays.

CHARLIE: I know, just—be honest. Just think about the poem for a while, and write something. Write what you really think.

ELLIE: You want me to write what I really think?

CHARLIE: Yes. Don't worry about it being good, I'm the only person who will see it. *(short pause)* Okay, I'm going to be in the bathroom for a while, but I'll start working on your essay after—

ELLIE: I'm not helping you to the bathroom.

CHARLIE: I didn't ask you to help.

With a lot of effort, Charlie manages to stand up with his walker. He makes his way to the bathroom. Ellie starts writing absent-mindedly. After a sentence or so, she gets bored. She opens up Charlie's laptop and starts looking around.

A knock at the door.

Ellie is about to call for Charlie, then stops. She thinks for a moment.

Ellie goes to the door, opening it. Elder Thomas stands in the doorway.

ELDER THOMAS: Oh, hi—uh. I'm… I was looking for Charlie?

ELLIE: He's in the bathroom.

ELDER THOMAS: Oh, okay. *(short pause)* I can come back, if he—

ELLIE: No, it's fine. Come in.

Elder Thomas comes inside, Ellie shuts the door behind him.

ELDER THOMAS: Are you his—friend?

ELLIE: I'm his daughter.

ELDER THOMAS: Oh. Wow, I… I didn't know that.

ELLIE: You surprised?

ELDER THOMAS: Yes.

ELLIE: What's more surprising? That a gay guy has a daughter, or that someone found his penis?

ELDER THOMAS: I really should go.

ELLIE: Don't be a pussy. That nametag makes you look like a retard.

ELDER THOMAS: We—have to wear them.

ELLIE: I don't care. What are you doing here again? Who are you?

ELDER THOMAS: Charlie said he—wanted to hear about the church. I'm with the Church of Jesus Christ of Latter Day Saints. I came by the other day, he wasn't feeling well, I thought I'd try him again. I brought some reading materials, and I thought we could talk about—

ELLIE: I'm bored.

ELDER THOMAS: Oh.

20

Pause.

ELLIE: I'll tell you one thing I like about religion. What I like about religion is that it assumes everyone is an idiot and that they're incapable of saving themselves. I think they got something right with that.

ELDER THOMAS: That's not really what I—

ELLIE: I'm not finished talking. I'm saying that I appreciate how religion makes people realize that, I appreciate that. But what I don't like about religion is that once people accept Jesus or whatever, they think they're more enlightened than everyone else. Like, by accepting the fact that they're stupid sinners, they've become better than everyone else. And they turn into assholes.

> *Pause.*

ELDER THOMAS: I don't really know what to say. I have some pamphlets—

ELLIE: Hold still.

ELDER THOMAS: What?

> *Ellie takes out her iPhone, takes a picture of Elder Thomas.*

ELDER THOMAS: Why did you just do that?

ELLIE: Are you coming back tomorrow?

ELDER THOMAS: I don't—I'm not sure—

ELLIE: Come back tomorrow, I'll be here around the same time.

ELDER THOMAS: I'm sorry, what's happening?

> *Charlie comes out of the bathroom with his walker, sees Elder Thomas.*

CHARLIE: Oh.

ELDER THOMAS: Hi, Charlie. I was just—

> *Ellie takes a picture of Charlie, then puts the iPhone back in her bag.*

ELLIE: Will you have that done by tomorrow?

CHARLIE: Sure.

ELLIE: Five page minimum.

CHARLIE: I know. It'll be good, I promise.

> *Ellie extends a hand to Elder Thomas.*

ELLIE: I'm Ellie.

ELDER THOMAS: *(shaking her hand)* Elder Thomas.

ELLIE: Weird. See you later.

> *Ellie exits. Charlie and Elder Thomas look at one another.*

ELDER THOMAS: Are you ready to hear about the Church?

> *Pause.*

CHARLIE: Yes.

21

LATER THAT AFTERNOON.

Charlie sits in the same position as before, Elder Thomas holds some pamphlets. Charlie is glancing through one of them absent-mindedly.

ELDER THOMAS: It was written by prophets, pretty much in the same way that the Bible was written. Through revelation and prophecy by the Nephite prophet Mormon, who lived in the Americas in the fourth century. He transcribed the history of his people onto a set of golden plates, and then hundreds of years later Joseph Smith, a man from upstate New York, translated the book from the gold plates in about sixty-five days or so—

CHARLIE: You go to the church near the highway, right? The older one, the one by the U-haul?

ELDER THOMAS: Um—yeah. And to translate this book in sixty-five days is pretty remarkable because it means he had to translate the equivalent of about eight single-spaced pages per day—

CHARLIE: What's your name?

Pause.

ELDER THOMAS: I told you. It's Elder Thomas.

CHARLIE: But what's your real name?

ELDER THOMAS: Thomas.

CHARLIE: That's your last name, right? What's your first name?

ELDER THOMAS: You don't need to know my first name.

CHARLIE: Oh.

Pause.

ELDER THOMAS: What's also really incredible is that the Book of Mormon actually contains many distinct literary styles, including ancient Hebrew poetry and—

CHARLIE: Why is that incredible?

ELDER THOMAS: Well, it—how would some farm boy living in upstate New York have known how to write in the style of ancient Hebrew poetry? It's living proof of God's intervention.

CHARLIE: Hm. *(pause)* You know, actually—I know all this.

ELDER THOMAS: What do you mean?

CHARLIE: I've read just about every Wikipedia article about Mormonism—

ELDER THOMAS: I don't know if Wikipedia is the best source for—

CHARLIE: I also read the Book of Mormon.

ELDER THOMAS: The whole thing?

CHARLIE: Sure. A couple times.

Pause.

22

ELDER THOMAS: Did you—like it?

CHARLIE: I thought it was . . . Devastating.

ELDER THOMAS: Huh. Okay. I don't know about that.

CHARLIE: That one story about—Sherem? Sherem was questioning whether Jesus was actually God, so God struck Sherem down. And Sherem repented as he was dying, said that he was wrong, and so everyone believed in Jesus. God killed this man to—prove a point. That story, it's—devastating.

ELDER THOMAS: Yeah, that—I never thought about it like that, but— (*pause*) You know what I think is amazing? The Bible is great and everything, I mean—it's a really great way to come to understand God. But it's so—distant. This thing written thousands of years ago, on the other side of the planet, in languages we don't speak. It's been translated and translated, probably rewritten over and over and over. But the Book of Mormon—it's like, a *direct link* to God's word. One translator, writing in English, right here in America, just a few generations ago. It's—

CHARLIE: Devastating.

ELDER THOMAS: No. No, it's—hopeful. It makes you feel like there's some meaning to being here, right now, in America. Do you see that? (*pause*) You're so close in time and space to God's revelation, Charlie, that should make you feel proud. It should inspire you. It should keep you from doing this to yourself.

> Pause.

CHARLIE: I'm not interested in converting, Elder Thomas. I don't find the Mormon Church hopeful. I don't find it amazing, and I don't find the proof convincing.

ELDER THOMAS: Wait so why did you want me to—? (*pause*) Um. I want to just make sure that—. I want to make sure you know that I'm just coming over here to talk about the church. That's it.

CHARLIE: Well, yeah. What?

ELDER THOMAS: I just . . . I don't know if— (*pause, then suddenly*) You're not attracted to me, right?

CHARLIE: Oh my God.

ELDER THOMAS: It's just, with the—. What you were watching, the first time I came in here—

CHARLIE: I am not attracted to you. Please, understand me when I say that. *I am not attracted to you. You're a fetus.* (*pause*) Is that what you really think of me?

ELDER THOMAS: *No, I*—

CHARLIE: No, really. Tell me the truth. Do you find me disgusting?

> Pause.

23

ELDER THOMAS: No. (pause) It's just that—you said you wanted to hear about the church.

CHARLIE: I did want to hear about the church. Your church, the one by the U-Haul, near the highway. I wanted to hear about *that* church.

ELDER THOMAS: I don't understand.

CHARLIE: You can go now, I'm sorry if I—

ELDER THOMAS: Is this about your—? Your domestic—. . .

CHARLIE: How do you know about—?

ELDER THOMAS: Your friend, Liz—she told me, she said that your—whatever, he had gone to the church?

CHARLIE: Look, you don't want to hear about this, you're just a kid—

ELDER THOMAS: I'm not a kid, I'm nineteen. (pause) Charlie—I've been going door to door for a while, you know? But no one understands that—I want to get to know them. The good and the bad, everything. How are we supposed to talk about your spiritual life if I don't know anything about who you are?

Pause. Charlie considers for a moment.

CHARLIE: His name—my partner's name, it was Alan. (pause) It sounds strange, but he was actually a student of mine. He was only a couple years younger than me, he had gone back to school after his mission. His parents were trying to get him to marry someone from the church, I think he barely knew her. But he was gonna go through with it—until he met me. It was ridiculous, he was the engaged son of a Mormon bishop, I had a wife and kid at home. But we just—couldn't stand to be apart. (pause) You really want me to keep going?

ELDER THOMAS: Yes. Really, yes.

CHARLIE: I thought he'd be able to get over all this religious stuff, but—
. . . It got worse and worse, to the point where every time we'd drive by that church near the highway he'd start to hyperventilate. His parents had abandoned him, refused to talk to him at all. But one night, about ten years ago, his father showed up here and told Alan he just wanted him to go to church the next day. He said, "I'm giving the talk tomorrow and I've written it for you. If you never come again—just come to church tomorrow." I told Alan not to go, but . . . The next morning he came home afterward, and he was just—hollow. It took him over, and he just—stopped everything. He stopped bathing, he stopped eating, he stopped sleeping. And a few months later, he was gone.

ELDER THOMAS: What happened? At the service?

CHARLIE: I don't know. Alan wouldn't tell me what they did to him. I guess—I was hoping you could find out.

Pause.

24

ELDER THOMAS: I don't—I'm not even from here, I don't know if—

CHARLIE: I know—never mind. It's ridiculous.

> *Pause.*

ELDER THOMAS: I'm going to ask around, alright? I'll see if anyone remembers that day, the last day he was there. Who knows, someone might remember.

CHARLIE: You'd do that?

ELDER THOMAS: Of course. I just want to help. That's why I'm on a mission in the first place, right?

> *Liz enters through the door with an extra wide wheelchair and a shopping bag.*

LIZ: Alright, I got you something. I did some asking around, and this doctor said—

> *Liz notices Elder Thomas.*

LIZ: What the hell, Charlie?

ELDER THOMAS: I was just—

LIZ: *Charlie?*

CHARLIE: It's fine, Liz.

LIZ: What did I say about your stress level? You don't need someone coming over and telling you that you're going to hell.

ELDER THOMAS: I never said that, I would never say that.

LIZ: Leave.

CHARLIE: Liz—

LIZ: *Get out.*

ELDER THOMAS: Okay.

> *Elder Thomas heads for the door.*

CHARLIE: Liz, stop it. He didn't do anything to you, for Christ's sake. He's just a kid.

ELDER THOMAS: I'm nineteen. *(pause)* I'll just go—

LIZ: Actually—stay. We'll have a chat. *(to Charlie)* I brought you this.

CHARLIE: Thank you. What is it?

LIZ: What the fuck does it look like? It's a fat guy wheelchair.

CHARLIE: Why do I need a wheelchair?

LIZ: I was talking to one of the E.R. doctors, he told me that moderate activity would be a good idea. That a sense of independence would help you keep your spirits up. Now you don't have to sit on that couch all day long.

CHARLIE: How much did you pay for this thing?

25

LIZ: Nothing. We ordered it specially for a patient a few months ago, it's just been sitting around.

CHARLIE: What happened to the patient?

LIZ: Try it out. Now you can go to the bedroom by yourself, get to the bathroom more easily.

Liz moves the wheelchair next to Charlie.

Charlie braces himself on his walker and manages to pull himself up.

Liz positions the wheelchair behind Charlie, Charlie starts slowly backing into the wheelchair.

LIZ: *(like a truck backing up)* Beep. Beep. Beep. Beep.

Charlie stops, looks back at her. Liz smiles.

Charlie continues, then sits in the wheelchair, wheezing loudly. He tries it out, wheeling himself a few feet.

LIZ: Good?

CHARLIE: Yeah, it's——. It's actually nice. *(rolls a few more feet)* Thank you, Liz, it's really—

LIZ: Why don't you see if it fits through the bedroom door, you probably haven't been in there for days, right?

ELDER THOMAS: I should probably go—

LIZ: Not before we have our little chat.

ELDER THOMAS: Oh, I. What?

CHARLIE: Liz—

LIZ: *(to Charlie)* Give us a few minutes.

Liz pushes him toward the bedroom, out of the room. Liz turns back to Elder Thomas, stares at him.

LIZ: Take a seat.

Elder Thomas sits down.

LIZ: So. Iowa?

ELDER THOMAS: What?

LIZ: You're from Iowa.

ELDER THOMAS: Uh. Yes.

LIZ: What part?

ELDER THOMAS: Waterloo?

LIZ: You asking me?

ELDER THOMAS: No, I— I'm from Waterloo.

Pause. Liz smokes.

LIZ: So listen. You're just a kid, you don't know anything. But I want to be very clear with you about a few things if you're going to keep coming over here. *(pause)* I know this is fun for you. You get to travel around,

26

act superior to everyone else. Plus you get to go home, get married, get some boring job, have tons of kids, and when you die you get your own planet. It all sounds pretty awesome. But, there are other kinds of people. People like Charlie, for whom this amazing plan doesn't fit. You can't fit a round peg in a square hole, and you certainly can't fit a morbidly obese gay peg in a Mormon hole. That came out wrong. *(pause)* Point is—you're a sweet kid, but he doesn't need this right now.

ELDER THOMAS: I disagree.

Pause.

LIZ: Excuse me?

ELDER THOMAS: Sorry, I just—I think this is exactly what he needs right now. He's refusing to go to the hospital, he's dying—what he needs is some spiritual guidance.

LIZ: And you're gonna give him that?

ELDER THOMAS: No. God will.

LIZ: I see. *(pause)* My big brother went on a mission. Went to Switzerland.

ELDER THOMAS: Oh.

LIZ: Yeah. He was the good kid. I however was the black sheep—by the time I was thirteen, I refused to go to church, told my dad I didn't believe in God. Even had to move out of the house, went to live with my aunt and uncle in Boise until I graduated. But not my big brother—he was a good Mormon. He wrote me a letter a few months into his mission, he told me he was cold all the time. That he was cold all the time, and lonely, but he preferred being out there in Switzerland because he didn't want to come back and get married.

ELDER THOMAS: He didn't want to—?

LIZ: Dad had set it all up, pushed him into getting engaged to this girl from the church he barely knew. When he came back, he refused to go through with the wedding. Fell in love with someone else, started a whole new life. Until one day, when he went back to the church—I don't know what the hell they did to him that day, but it sure fucked him up. And after that he just started wasting away until he was just—gone. *(pause)* That was my brother. Alan. My big brother who was *crushed* under the church that you think can save Charlie.

ELDER THOMAS: Oh.

Silence. Liz stares at him, smoking.

ELDER THOMAS: I'm sorry.

LIZ: What the fuck are you sorry about? *(pause)* Where's your companion?

ELDER THOMAS: What?

LIZ: You always have to be in pairs. I know that. It's sort of a big deal for you to be out here alone, isn't it?

27

Pause.

ELDER THOMAS: Elder Johnson. He's—not feeling well.

LIZ: Not feeling well?

ELDER THOMAS: Why does it matter?

LIZ: It's a pretty big deal for you guys not to—

ELDER THOMAS: Well, to be honest, he's having some—problems and he's pretty useless right now, but I thought I could do some good. By myself. Help just *one* person.

LIZ: And that one person is Charlie.

ELDER THOMAS: Yes.

Charlie comes out of the bedroom. Liz doesn't notice him.

LIZ: Listen to me. He doesn't need your help, he doesn't want saving. In a few days he's probably going to be dead, and right now what he needs is for you to leave him alone. I am the only person who knows how to take care of him, do you understand? *I am the only one who can save him.*

CHARLIE: Liz.

Liz turns around, sees Charlie. Elder Thomas quickly gathers his things and exits. Liz forces a smile.

LIZ: Everything go alright in there? *(no response)* I've got an hour or so before I need to get back, we could watch some Maury. Wheel yourself over here, c'mon.

Liz turns on the television. Charlie stares at her, not moving.

NIGHT.

Charlie, alone, in his wheelchair. He is laying some blankets out for the night onto the couch. He's about to move onto the couch when he notices Ellie's notebook. He wheels himself over to it, picks it up, opens it.

CHARLIE: *(reading)* "This apartment smells. This notebook is retarded. I hate everyone."

Charlie looks at it for a moment, smiling.

CHARLIE: "This apartment smells. This notebook is retarded. I hate everyone."

Charlie laughs a little. The laugh quickly turns into a cough, which produces pain in his chest. He takes a few breaths, trying to calm himself down.

CHARLIE: *(soft)* I felt saddest of all when I read the boring chapters that were only descriptions of whales, because I knew that the author was just trying to save us from his own sad story, just for a little while. This apartment smells.

Charlie takes a few deep breaths, wheezing. The pain starts to subside.

28

CHARLIE: This apartment smells. This notebook is retarded. I hate everyone. The author was just trying to save us from his own sad story, just for a little while. I hate everyone. The author was just trying to—

Lights quickly snap to black.

In the darkness, once again we hear the sound of waves—louder now, and more distinct, building a little in volume before lights rise on:

THURSDAY
MORNING.

Charlie sits on the wheelchair, in front of his laptop, speaking into the microphone.

CHARLIE: KimmyBallz429, I read your recent post on the discussion forum about strategies for coming up with a good thesis. You said that I want you to "just pick a sentence from the book and say it's good or some shit." *(pause)* I think I owe you all an apology. I've been teaching you all to rewrite and rewrite and rewrite, to edit your thoughts and change them and make them clearer, more precise, more objective. And I'm starting to realize that that's horseshit. You don't have any true reaction to these books because I've taught you to edit your reactions, to reshape them and reconfigure them over and over. And after all that, you don't even have a reaction at all. You just end up hating it. *(pause)* How about this? Don't write about the book. Forget the assignment, forget the readings. Hell, forget everything you know about what makes a good essay and just—write. Just sit down, and write me something. Just give me something honest. Okay?

LATER THAT MORNING.

Ellie stands by the door, holding an essay.

ELLIE: So it's good?

CHARLIE: It's really, really good.

ELLIE: What grade am I gonna get?

CHARLIE: It's a really good essay.

ELLIE: Yeah, whatever. Okay bye.

Ellie turns to the door.

CHARLIE: I was hoping you could write a little more in your notebook.

ELLIE: Oh my God.

CHARLIE: You've only written a couple sentences so far—could you write me some more?

29

ELLIE: I kind of hate you.

CHARLIE: Yeah, but you hate everyone. *(pause)* Look, just keep going with what you were doing. Forget the poem, forget about writing an essay. Just keep going, write about whatever you want, whatever you're thinking—

ELLIE: Shut up, just give me the notebook.

Charlie hands Ellie the notebook. She sits down, opening it. She is about to write, then looks at Charlie.

ELLIE: My mom found out. That I'm coming here.

Pause.

CHARLIE: How?

ELLIE: Small town bullshit. Her friend Judy saw the car parked outside here. *(pause)* She asked me how big you were.

CHARLIE: She knows that I—?

ELLIE: She just heard you gained weight. She doesn't know you're a monster. *(pause)* She made me promise to stop coming over.

CHARLIE: Did you tell her about the money?

ELLIE: I'm not retarded.

Pause. Ellie writes a bit, Charlie watches her.

CHARLIE: I was in a strange place in my life when I married your mom.

ELLIE: Did I fucking ask?

CHARLIE: Sorry. I just thought you . . . I'm sure your mom has told you the whole story anyway.

ELLIE: No, she hasn't, she doesn't like talking about you. Ever. But I'm pretty sure I know the story anyway. You come home one day, "Oh, honey, I'm so repressed, I need to self-actualize or some stupid shit." And mom starts screaming, then you're on the floor, just like I remember, looking pathetic and fat. Is that it?

Pause.

CHARLIE: I understand that you're angry.

ELLIE: Oh my God.

CHARLIE: But you don't need to be angry at the entire world. I'm the asshole, just be angry at me, don't take it out on—

ELLIE: You think you're the only person who's ever fucked me over? Trust me, I have a list. And you're no more important than any other asshole that's treated me like dirt.

Ellie goes back to writing. Charlie watches her. A few moments pass.

ELLIE: You could have sent her money, you know.

CHARLIE: What?

ELLIE: If you have all that money. You could have been sending money to my mom.

CHARLIE: I did.

ELLIE: I mean more than just child support.

> *Long silence.*

CHARLIE: I did. *(pause)* I'm so sorry, Ellie. I'm so, so sorry.

> *Ellie looks up at Charlie for a second, then goes back to writing.*
> *A few moments pass. Ellie puts the pen down, looks at Charlie.*

ELLIE: I'm hungry.

> *Pause.*

CHARLIE: There's stuff for sandwiches in the kitchen.

ELLIE: Okay. *(pause)* I'll make you one, but it's going to be small. And I'm only using turkey or chicken, and no mayonnaise.

> *Pause.*

CHARLIE: Thank you.

> *Ellie gets up, goes into the kitchen.*

CHARLIE: What were you writing about?

ELLIE: I was writing about how when you die, you won't fit through the door or the windows. So they'll probably have to take you out in pieces.

> *Ellie exits into the kitchen.*

AFTERNOON.

> *Charlie is asleep in his wheelchair. Ellie is sitting on the couch typing on Charlie's laptop, smoking pot from a small glass pipe.*
> *A knock at the door.*
> *Ellie puts the pipe in Charlie's hand. Charlie doesn't wake up.*

ELLIE: Yeah?

ELDER THOMAS: *(from outside)* I, uh—hello?

> *Ellie pauses for a second, recognizing the voice, then takes the pipe out of Charlie's hand. She goes to the door, opening it. Elder Thomas stands in the doorway holding his bicycle helmet.*

ELLIE: What?

ELDER THOMAS: Oh, I—

ELLIE: What?

ELDER THOMAS: Hi. *(sees the pipe)* Are you—?

ELLIE: I'm bored. Come inside.

ELDER THOMAS: Maybe I should—

ELLIE: Oh my God stop talking. Take that nametag off, I told you, you look like a retard.

Ellie closes the door behind Elder Thomas.

ELDER THOMAS: *(seeing Charlie)* Is he . . .?

ELLIE: Do you ever finish sentences? He's asleep.

ELDER THOMAS: I can come back.

ELLIE: He'll be asleep for a while.

ELDER THOMAS: Oh. Is he okay?

ELLIE: I don't know. I ground up some Ambien and put it in his sandwich.

ELDER THOMAS: Oh my God, is he—?

ELLIE: I only gave him a couple, he's fine. I can take three at a time.

ELDER THOMAS: Why did you—? You have Ambien? Where did you get Ambien?

ELLIE: I had sex with a pharmacist. Just kidding, gross. My mom eats them like tic tacs. Do you ever wear anything different?

ELDER THOMAS: Should he be taking sleeping pills? He's sort of sick and—

ELLIE: Yeah, anyway. Why is your name "Elder"?

ELDER THOMAS: It's not my real . . . During the mission, we all get called "Elder." My last name is Thomas, so—I'm Elder Thomas.

ELLIE: It makes you sound, like, important. Which you're not.

Ellie takes a hit from the pipe. Elder Thomas watches.

ELDER THOMAS: No, I'm not.

ELLIE: Does this make you nervous?

ELDER THOMAS: No, I—. Well, yeah, it does.

ELLIE: It's just pot, it's not like I'm smoking crack or anything. You probably have no idea what I'm talking about.

ELDER THOMAS: Don't—. I know what you're talking about. I know what drugs are.

ELLIE: You only think you know what drugs are because your parents told you a whole bunch of lies about them. You probably think that smoking pot will turn you into a homeless person or something.

ELDER THOMAS: You know, I'm not an idiot. I've smoked pot before.

ELLIE: Oo, I'm so impressed.

ELDER THOMAS: I'm not trying to impress you, I'm just saying—

ELLIE: You have not smoked pot.

ELDER THOMAS: Yes, I have. It was—kind of a problem.

ELLIE: A "problem"?

ELDER THOMAS: My bishop told me I had an addiction.

ELLIE: That is the stupidest fucking thing I have ever heard in my entire life.

Ellie takes a hit, holds it in.

ELDER THOMAS: I was doing it every day. I had a problem.

ELLIE: You were a stoner. You had a hobby.

Ellie exhales, blowing the hit in Elder Thomas' face.

ELDER THOMAS: Okay, I'm leaving.

Elder Thomas gets up.

ELLIE: If you leave, I'll feed him the rest of the pills I have in the bottle.

Elder Thomas stops.

ELDER THOMAS: What?

ELLIE: There's probably twenty or thirty more. I'll crush them up and mix them into some water and pour it down his throat.

ELDER THOMAS: Why would you say something like that?

ELLIE: Sit down.

ELDER THOMAS: You wouldn't really do that, would you?

ELLIE: Oh my God sit down.

Elder Thomas pauses, then comes back to the couch and sits down.

ELLIE: Why do you keep coming back here?

ELDER THOMAS: He wants me to come over, he told me. He needs help.

ELLIE: That's a stupid reason. Take a hit.

ELDER THOMAS: What? No.

ELLIE: You've never smoked before.

ELDER THOMAS: Yes, I have.

ELLIE: You're some sheltered little Mormon boy, you haven't done anything. You don't know anything. God, I can't even look at you.

ELDER THOMAS: Why do you talk like that, is this how you treat everyone?

ELLIE: Yeah. Why does he want to talk to you?

ELDER THOMAS: I think he needs God to be in his life right now.

ELLIE: That's an even stupider reason. Do you think he wants to have sex with you? That's so gross, oh my God. Take a hit.

ELDER THOMAS: He doesn't want to—! I don't want to take a hit!

ELLIE: Why are you such a *pussy*? You wear a *bicycle helmet*. Take a hit.

Ellie shoves the pipe into Elder Thomas' chest.

ELDER THOMAS: I told you—

ELLIE: If you don't take a hit, I'm going to call the police and tell them you tried to rape me. Take a hit.

Pause.

ELDER THOMAS: I don't understand you at all.

ELLIE: Oh my God.

Elder Thomas takes the pipe.

ELDER THOMAS: Is there a carb on this?

ELLIE: Oo, I'm so impressed.

ELDER THOMAS: I wasn't trying to—

ELLIE: There isn't a carb.

> *Elder Thomas takes a hit. He exhales.*
>
> *Ellie takes out her iPhone and snaps a quick picture Elder Thomas as he exhales.*

ELDER THOMAS: *(coughing)* What are you doing? Why did you just—?

ELLIE: Calm down. Take another hit.

ELDER THOMAS: What are you going to do with that picture?

ELLIE: I'm gonna masturbate to it, is that what you want me to say? You're a pervert. Take another hit.

> *No response. Elder Thomas stares at her.*

ELLIE: Look, I'm just fucking with you, alright? I'm not gonna kill anyone, I'm not gonna tell anyone you raped me. I don't understand why people believe everything I say. People are such idiots, it's so easy, it's ridiculous.

ELDER THOMAS: You aren't going to feed him more Ambien?

ELLIE: No.

ELDER THOMAS: Did you really put some in his sandwich?

ELLIE: That I did. Just a couple. So he'd stop bugging me.

ELDER THOMAS: Why don't you just leave?

ELLIE: I don't know.

ELDER THOMAS: If you hate him so much why do you keep coming over?

ELLIE: I'm done answering questions now.

ELDER THOMAS: Okay. *(silence)* Can I have another hit?

ELLIE: It goes against your religion, and that makes you a hypocrite. Go ahead.

> *Elder Thomas takes another hit—a big one.*

ELDER THOMAS: I never really thought I had a problem. I did it every day for a while, then I stopped. If I was able to stop then how is it a problem?

ELLIE: That's the only smart thing you've said since you came in here.

ELDER THOMAS: This is really good weed.

ELLIE: No it's not. You just haven't smoked in a while.

> *Ellie takes another picture of him.*

ELDER THOMAS: I really wish you wouldn't do that.

ELLIE: Yeah, I heard you the first time. Do you find me attractive?

34

ELDER THOMAS: I—

ELLIE: Because I'm not attracted to you at all, just to let you know.

    Pause.

ELDER THOMAS: Okay.

ELLIE: I'm not trying to be mean or anything. But I just don't think you're good looking or interesting. Or intelligent.

ELDER THOMAS: *(a little hurt)* Oh.

ELLIE: Oh my God grow up. Maybe someone else finds you attractive, just not me. Maybe my dad finds you attractive.

ELDER THOMAS: I really wish you wouldn't say that.

ELLIE: It's so easy to make you uncomfortable, it's a little sad. You can cash that out.

ELDER THOMAS: You don't mind?

ELLIE: No.

    Elder Thomas takes another big hit from the pipe. He's pretty high by this point.

ELDER THOMAS: I don't know if I'm going to be able to bike back to my apartment.

ELLIE: Wow, you're pretty high, aren't you?

ELDER THOMAS: Yes. Yes, I am. And if my parents knew I was getting high, that I was getting high while I was on my *mission*—

ELLIE: You're not on a mission.

    Pause.

ELDER THOMAS: What?

ELLIE: I said you're not on a mission. Jesus. *(pause)* I remembered your name from your name-tag. The Mormon website has a search engine for, like, everything. Anyway, there was a list of twelve people on missions in northern Idaho, and you're not one of them.

    Pause.

ELDER THOMAS: They didn't update the website.

ELLIE: I'm not a retard.

    Pause.

ELDER THOMAS: I need to go.

ELLIE: You keep saying that. Why are you pretending to be a Mormon missionary?

ELDER THOMAS: I'm not—I *am* on a mission—

ELLIE: Oh my God.

ELDER THOMAS: I mean I—*was.* I was on a mission.

ELLIE: Here?

35

ELDER THOMAS: I have to go.

Elder Thomas stands up, a little shaky on his feet.

ELLIE: What happened?

ELDER THOMAS: *Why do you care?!*

ELLIE: Because I think we have a blossoming friendship.

Pause. Elder Thomas looks at her.

ELDER THOMAS: I thought you said I wasn't attractive or interesting or intelligent.

ELLIE: So?

ELDER THOMAS: So why would you want to be my friend?

ELLIE: Because everyone else I know is even less attractive, interesting, and intelligent than you.

Pause.

ELDER THOMAS: You won't tell anyone?

ELLIE: Who am I gonna tell?

Pause. Elder Thomas goes back to the couch, sitting next to Ellie.

ELDER THOMAS: I was in Eastern Oregon, in Pendleton. It's where they do that big annual rodeo, the famous one—

ELLIE: I really, really don't care about that.

ELDER THOMAS: Anyway, I was on my mission there. Last year.

ELLIE: What happened?

ELDER THOMAS: I left. I didn't want to do it anymore. *(pause)* We just kept trying to talk to people, really *engage* with them, but most of the time they'd just talk to us for a little while, say "thank you", and we'd never hear from them again. So after a while, it was like—what am I *actually doing* here? Am I really, like, really *helping* people?

ELLIE: No you were not.

ELDER THOMAS: I started to feel that way, too.

ELLIE: I don't *feel* that way, I *know* that you weren't helping people. Like, for a fact. It doesn't help people to tell them how to believe in God. Why would that help people?

ELDER THOMAS: It might bring them eternal salvation.

ELLIE: Oh my God you actually think that?

ELDER THOMAS: Yeah . . . Maybe.

ELLIE: "Maybe"? You're shitty at being a religious person.

ELDER THOMAS: I just—I *want* to believe it. My family, all my friends, they seem like—totally happy. I wanna be like that.

ELLIE: So why did you come to Idaho?

ELDER THOMAS: I got kicked off the mission.

36

ELLIE: For smoking pot?

ELDER THOMAS: For assaulting my companion.

> *Pause.*

ELLIE: You're full of shit.

ELDER THOMAS: No, I'm not.

ELLIE: Oh my God you so are.

ELDER THOMAS: Seriously.

ELLIE: So what, like, you went on a "pot bender"?

ELDER THOMAS: I wasn't smoking at all. The moment I stepped foot in Oregon, I made a promise to myself that I wouldn't smoke any more. And I didn't.

ELLIE: Which is a shame if it's your first time in Oregon. So why did you beat him up?

ELDER THOMAS: He just . . . He didn't care. About anything. We'd go out every day, we'd try to talk to people, and no one would listen, and he *didn't even care.* I tried to talk to him about different sections of town we could go to, different ways to engage them, different ways to *help* these people . . . But you could tell, if we spent our whole mission there ministering and hadn't helped *one single person*, he wouldn't have cared. His faith was just—. He didn't need to earn it or prove it *at all.* And one day, we were out in this little farming community, and we weren't helping anyone, and he kept complaining about being hungry, and how hot it was out that day, and—I just lost it. I went nuts. *(pause)* He told me his parents would sue me, that I'd go to jail. All I wanted to do was finish this mission, I wanted to see Mormonism help *one person.* So, I just got on a bus. I still have a few thousand dollars left in my checking account. I went to the church here in town a couple times, I found this nametag in the common room.

ELLIE: You have like *huge* pores on your face, did you know you have huge pores?

ELDER THOMAS: Were you listening to me? Why did you just say that?

ELLIE: So what's your real name?

ELDER THOMAS: Why do you want to know?

ELLIE: Because we're friends now.

> *Pause.*

ELDER THOMAS: Joseph Paulson.

> *Ellie takes a picture of him.*

ELLIE: You're slightly more interesting now.

ELDER THOMAS: Thank you.

The door bursts open revealing Mary, a woman of about forty but who looks considerably older.

ELLIE: Shit.

Mary pushes past Ellie, sees Charlie. She stops immediately.
Long silence as she stares at Charlie. She moves toward him slowly.

ELLIE: Mom—

MARY: Shut up.

She stands next to Charlie, looking down at him.

MARY: Charlie.

Charlie doesn't move.

MARY: *Charlie.*

No response. Mary looks at Ellie. Ellie looks away.

ELLIE: Yeah okay sorry.

LATE AFTERNOON.

Charlie sits in his wheelchair, awake but very groggy. Liz is attaching an oxygen tank to the wheelchair and running a hose over his ears and under his nose. Mary sits on the couch smoking a cigarette. Ellie stands by the door, Elder Thomas in the opposite corner.

Throughout the scene, Charlie's breathing is much more shallow, and his wheezing is much worse.

LIZ: *(to Mary)* You know, he's not breathing so good. Second-hand smoke isn't really a great idea.

CHARLIE: She's fine, Liz.

LIZ: What, are you a doctor?

MARY: No, and neither are you.

Mary puts out the cigarette in an empty soda can. She stares at Charlie.

LIZ: Are you having more pain?

CHARLIE: Yes. Wheezing's getting worse.

LIZ: How easy is it to move?

CHARLIE: Not very.

LIZ: How about any confusion? Have you felt disoriented, confused, forgotten where you are or what you're doing?

CHARLIE: No. Would that be bad?

LIZ: Yes. That would be very bad.

CHARLIE: So—am I okay?

LIZ: No, you're not "okay." But as far as the sleeping pills, you're fine. I think she only gave you a couple.

ELLIE: Yeah, that's what I told you.

Liz takes off the stethoscope, moves toward Ellie.

LIZ: Listen to me. I was a very angry, very stupid little girl once too, but this goes beyond smoking pot and posting shit on the internet. If you would have given him more pills than that, you could have—

ELLIE: Yeah, except I didn't give him more than that, I gave him *two pills.*

MARY: *(to Ellie)* Ellie, how much money did he offer you?

CHARLIE: Mary. Don't.

MARY: *(to Charlie)* All of it? It would have to be all of it. It would take quite a lot of money to make that girl do something she doesn't want to do.

ELLIE: How do you know about—?

MARY: *(to Ellie)* You think I'm an idiot? You think for one second I would believe that you were coming here out of the kindness of your heart?

ELLIE: You're not getting any of it. He said I could have all of it.

LIZ: Charlie doesn't have any money. I do all his shopping, I know exactly how much is in his checking account.

Pause.

MARY: *(to Charlie)* She doesn't know?

CHARLIE: Mary—

MARY: *(to Liz)* Where do you think all the money from his teaching has been going? The account for Ellie—by now it has to be huge. *(to Charlie)* Over a hundred thousand at least, right?

LIZ: *(to Charlie)* That isn't true, is it? *(pause)* Charlie, we could have gotten you anything you needed—special beds, physical therapists, fucking *health insurance*— . . . Last year when my car broke down, and I had to walk through the snow to get your groceries—

CHARLIE: I offered to get your car fixed—

LIZ: And I refused because I thought you had seven hundred dollars in your bank account. *(pause)* You had all that money that you were keeping a *secret* from me? Why were you doing that? What, you think I would try and *take* it from you?

CHARLIE: No, of course not, I . . . It's for Ellie. It's always been for Ellie. *(pause)* If there was ever some kind of emergency, I would have given you money—

LIZ: Would you? You've been keeping this from me for years, you really think I can trust you?

Pause. Liz starts grabbing her things.

CHARLIE: Please don't go.

Liz exits. Pause.

ELLIE: Mom—you're not getting any of my money.

MARY: Oh, shut up, Ellie. *(pause)* Both of you, leave. Right now.

> *Pause.*

ELLIE: I need the car keys.

MARY: You can walk.

ELLIE: It's like two miles!

MARY: Do you really think that I care?

ELLIE: I hate you.

> *Ellie exits. Elder Thomas moves out of the corner, moving toward Charlie.*

ELDER THOMAS: I'll come back.

> *Charlie looks at him.*

CHARLIE: Yeah, okay.

> *Elder Thomas exits. A long moment of silence.*
>
> *Mary stares at Charlie. She stands up, still looking at him. She circles his wheelchair, looking at him from all sides.*

MARY: Jesus, Charlie.

> *Pause. Mary looks away. She takes a cigarette out of her purse, lights it up.*

MARY: So this—heart thing. It's serious, yeah?

CHARLIE: Pretty serious.

MARY: You gonna be okay?

> *Pause.*

CHARLIE: I'll be fine.

> *Pause.*

MARY: Do you have anything?

CHARLIE: What? *(pause)* Oh, uh—maybe, in the kitchen. There might be something in the cabinet over the stove, the highest shelf on the right.

> *Mary exits momentarily, returning with a bottle of vodka and a glass. She pours a large drink for herself, drinks.*

MARY: Our deal was we'd wait until she was out of the house to give her the money.

CHARLIE: What's the difference?

MARY: The difference is she's seventeen and in high school. She's going to spend it on ponies or marijuana or something.

CHARLIE: I think she's a little smarter than that.

MARY: I really wish you wouldn't have done this, Charlie. This is the last thing I need right now. *(taking a long drink)* How has it been? Getting to know her.

CHARLIE: She's—amazing.

40

Mary chuckles.

MARY: You still do that.

CHARLIE: What?

MARY: That positivity. It's so annoying.

CHARLIE: *(smiling)* Well, you're a complete cynic, I was just trying to balance us out.

MARY: I guess I do miss that. That one thing.

CHARLIE: Just that?

MARY: That, and the cooking. Last month I tried to make a pie and I nearly set the entire apartment building on fire, Ellie threw all our pots and pans into the dumpster so I'd never try to do it again. You still cook?

CHARLIE: Not for years now. It's—hard for me to get into the kitchen.

Pause.

MARY: Charlie, I . . . I never knew you were doing this to yourself.

CHARLIE: You never asked me how I was doing.

MARY: You never asked me how I was doing either. Every month it's just, "how much money do you need?" and "how's Ellie?"

CHARLIE: You didn't tell me she was failing out of high school.

MARY: Well, now you know. I guess I just didn't need the lecture from you about my involvement in her education.

CHARLIE: That's not what I— *(long pause)* How are you doing, Mary?

Pause.

MARY: Fine.

CHARLIE: Are you working?

MARY: No.

CHARLIE: Do you need me to send more money?

MARY: *No.*

Pause.

CHARLIE: It's good to see you. *(pause)* Mary, I know that I screwed everything up. I know it must have been terrible. And humiliating. And I know that I'm not supposed to be around her—hell, you could call the police if you want to—

MARY: Christ, you really think I'd do that?

CHARLIE: You fought me pretty hard for full custody. And I don't blame you, after what I did. But I just want to see her—I've *always* just wanted to see her. Is it so awful that she has a gay father?

MARY: No, actually, it's not. *(pause)* She's—awful, isn't she?

CHARLIE: What?

MARY: Ellie. She's awful. She's a terror.

41

CHARLIE: No, she's—she has a strong personality, but—

MARY: Charlie, she doesn't even have any *friends*. Not a single one. She's so cruel that no one at school will even *talk* to her. *(pause)* When she was nine, ten, I thought—I'm not giving him the satisfaction. I'm not letting him see this awful little girl and blame it all on me. No way.

CHARLIE: Wait, is that why you've been keeping her from me all this time? You thought I would think you were a bad mother?

MARY: At first. But later on—when she was fifteen, sixteen. I was worried she would hurt you.

CHARLIE: "Hurt" me? That's ridiculous—

MARY: You've been around her for two days now, and already she's almost killed you. *(pause)* I was protecting you, Charlie. You've always been so fucking sensitive, ready to break down over anything . . . And here's this girl—this girl who takes *pleasure* in hurting people, this *terrible* girl. *(pause)* Believe me Charlie, I don't take any pleasure in admitting it, I'm her mother for Christ's sake. I spent way too many years saying to myself, she's just rebellious, she's just difficult. Charlie—she's evil.

CHARLIE: *She is not evil.*

> Pause. Mary goes to Charlie's laptop, types.

CHARLIE: What are you doing?

MARY: Just—.

CHARLIE: If you're gonna show me Ellie's site, I've already seen it—

MARY: Did you see what she posted this morning?

> Mary brings the computer to Charlie. Charlie looks at the screen.

MARY: When I saw this picture of you . . . I thought I should come over.

> Charlie continues looking at the computer.

CHARLIE: *(reading)* "There'll be a grease fire in Hell when he starts to burn."

> Pause.

MARY: Don't feel bad, I've made quite a few appearances on that little site of hers. *(pause)* You okay?

> Pause.

CHARLIE: She's a strong writer.

MARY: *That's* your response?

CHARLIE: This isn't evil, this is honesty. Do you know how much bullshit I've read in my life?

MARY: My God, things never change. I don't understand you, Charlie.

CHARLIE: Every time I called you, I'd ask about her and you'd tell me she was doing fine. If she's so evil, why didn't you ever—

MARY: What was I supposed to tell you? That she was off treating her friends like dirt and slashing her teachers' tires? You didn't want to hear about that stuff.

CHARLIE: I could have helped her!

MARY: She doesn't want your help! She doesn't want anyone!

Mary gets up, wandering aimlessly around the room, drunk by this point and a little shaky on her feet.

CHARLIE: Mary, sit down.

MARY: You think I didn't want her to have a dad? She *adored* you. The only reason you married me in the first place was to have a kid, I know that.

CHARLIE: *Mary. Please.*

Mary stops, gets her drink and sits back down.

MARY: This brings back memories, doesn't it? *(pause)* Listen. I . . . I never got to say that I was sorry.

CHARLIE: What would you have to be sorry about?

MARY: That's not what I mean, I . . . I mean about your—friend.

CHARLIE: Oh. *(pause)* His name was Alan.

MARY: I know his fucking name, Charlie. *(pause)* I saw him once, after you left. In the K-mart parking lot. I should have wanted to run him over, or punch him in the face, but when I went up to him, he was so—
. . . He was carrying these bags, he could barely lift them, he was so thin. Looked like he was about to fall over. I went up to him with all these amazing things I was going to say, hurl at him like bricks. And I looked at him, and I—asked him if he wanted some help. He let me carry a couple of bags to his car for him, he said thank you, and I left. I never even told him who I was. *(pause)* When I heard what happened, I thought about coming by. Bringing Ellie to see you. I should have done that, I guess, and I'm sorry.

CHARLIE: It's okay. I'd be angry at me too. *(pause)* But thank you. For saying that.

Pause.

MARY: You're wheezing.

CHARLIE: Yeah. It's gotten worse.

MARY: Are you having trouble breathing? Should I call someone?

CHARLIE: No, it's—

MARY: Let me hear.

Mary puts her ear to Charlie's chest, listening to him breathe.

CHARLIE: How do I sound? *(no response)* Today was the first time we were all together in fifteen years, you realize that? *(pause)* Back when Ellie was first born, we did that road trip to the Oregon Coast together. And we stayed in Newport, and Ellie loved the sand so much. You and I layed on the beach together, and Ellie played in the surf, and later that day I went swimming in the ocean. Last time I ever went swimming, actually. And I kept cutting my legs on the rocks, and the water was so cold, and you were so mad that my legs bled and stained the seats in the minivan. And you said for days after that I smelled like seawater. You remember that?

Charlie puts his hand on Mary's back as she listens. Silence.

MARY: You sound awful.

CHARLIE: I'm dying, Mary.

Mary looks at him.

MARY: Fuck you.

CHARLIE: I'm sorry.

MARY: *Fuck you. (pause)* For sure?

CHARLIE: Yeah. For sure. *(pause)* Listen to me. I need to make certain that Ellie's going to be okay. Beyond the money. She has to have someone around who won't give up on her.

Pause.

MARY: You've been eating yourself to death for fifteen years and you're saying that *I* gave up on her?

CHARLIE: I wanted to see her, Mary, I wanted to be a part of your life—both of your lives—

MARY: Go to the hospital, Charlie! You have money, go to the hospital!

CHARLIE: We both know that money is for Ellie. But beyond that, I have to make sure that she's going to be alright, I have to be sure that she's going to have a decent life, where people care for her and she cares for other people— . . . She doesn't have anyone else, Mary.

MARY: *(grabbing her things)* I have to . . . I need to go.

CHARLIE: I need to know I did *one thing* right in my life.

Mary heads to the door. She opens the door and then stops, not looking at Charlie.

MARY: We both did our parts. I raised her, you're giving her the money. It's the best we could do. *(pause, still not looking at him)* Do you need anything before I leave? Water, or something?

Pause.

CHARLIE: No.

Pause.

MARY: Do you— . . . Do you want me to help you to the bathroom?

Charlie doesn't respond. Mary waits for a beat, then exits.

NIGHT.

Charlie is asleep in his wheelchair. His wheezing has gotten much worse, and his breathing is shallow enough that it starts to effect his speech; he often has to pause mid-sentence to take a breath.

There is a loud knock at the door, Charlie wakes up with start, the sudden movement producing pain in his chest. He winces. Another loud knock.

CHARLIE: Liz?

ELDER THOMAS: *(offstage)* Can I come inside?

CHARLIE: What the hell are you—? Are you okay?

ELDER THOMAS: *(offstage)* I'm fine, please let me come inside!

CHARLIE: Yes, just—!

Elder Thomas enters.

CHARLIE: Are you—? What's wrong?

ELDER THOMAS: I'm sorry, I'm really, really, really high.

CHARLIE: Why are you high?

ELDER THOMAS: My parents called me tonight.

CHARLIE: So?

ELDER THOMAS: My parents found out where I am. They found out that I'm in Idaho.

CHARLIE: I don't understand.

ELDER THOMAS: Your daughter, she sent pictures of me smoking pot to the mission in Oregon, and told them where I was. And my parents saw the pictures, and they called the church here in town, and they told them where I was staying, and I can't figure out if she was trying to help me or hurt me. Do you ever get that feeling with her?

CHARLIE: I don't. Really understand—

ELDER THOMAS: I thought my parents were going to disown me, and you know what they said? They said they *loved* me, they *cared* about me, and they wanted me to come home. How *awful* is that?

Charlie feels a sharp pain in his chest, he bends his head down in pain.

ELDER THOMAS: What's wrong?

CHARLIE: I'm fine.

ELDER THOMAS: No, you're not.

CHARLIE: It's just . . . It's going to go away, it just hurts—

ELDER THOMAS: I just want to help. I know I can help you.

CHARLIE: I'm not going to the hospital—

ELDER THOMAS: I know. I won't make you go. But I can help you.

CHARLIE: Look, just go home to your family, if you need money for a bus or something—

45

ELDER THOMAS: I know what happened to Alan.

Pause.

CHARLIE: What?

ELDER THOMAS: I know what happened that day, at church, the last time he was there. *(pause)* I got an e-mail tonight, from Cindy Miller, from the church. She remembers. I had to come tell you right away.

Silence.

CHARLIE: What did they do to him?

Short pause.

ELDER THOMAS: The talk that day, the talk that his father gave—it was about *Jonah.*

Pause.

CHARLIE: What?

ELDER THOMAS: *Jonah and the whale. (pause)* Don't you see? That essay you had me read to you—the one you like so much, the one about *Moby Dick . . .* Charlie, I get it now, I understand what God's been doing with me here, I understand why he sent me to you, right when you needed help. This isn't just a coincidence, when I read that e-mail—I knew I was helping you talk with God. It re-affirmed my faith. *(pause)* Jonah—it's about refusing the call of God, you know? Jonah tries to escape from God's will, he gets swallowed by a whale, and when he prays to God for help, God saves him by making the whale spit him out onto shore.

Silence.

Charlie laughs a little bit, the laughter causing pain in his chest.

CHARLIE: Is this what it fucking comes down to? I always thought, whatever they did to him that day must have been so awful, so cruel . . . A story? Some stupid *story*, that's what killed him?

ELDER THOMAS: No, it's *not* a just a story—

CHARLIE: Look, I appreciate what you're trying to do, but this doesn't mean anything, it—. I don't even know what I was expecting to find out, it's not—

ELDER THOMAS: *Listen to me. (short pause)* Charlie, your boyfriend—he tried to escape God's will, he chose his lifestyle with you over God. And when he heard this story, when he heard *God's word*, he knew. He knew the *truth*. He never prayed for salvation—but it's not too late for you.

Pause.

CHARLIE: You think Alan died—because he chose to be with me? You think God turned his back on him because he and I were in love?

ELDER THOMAS: *Yes.*

Silence. Charlie stares at him.

CHARLIE: You know, I wasn't always this big.

> *Short pause.*

ELDER THOMAS: Yeah, I know—

CHARLIE: I mean, I was never the best looking guy in the room, but—Alan still loved me. He still thought I was beautiful.

ELDER THOMAS: Okay—

CHARLIE: Halfway through the semester, he started meeting me during my office hours—we were both crazy about one another, but we waited until the course was done before we . . .

ELDER THOMAS: This isn't important—

CHARLIE: It was just after classes had ended for the year, it was a perfect temperature, and we went for a walk in the arboretum. And we kissed.

ELDER THOMAS: Charlie, stop.

CHARLIE: Listen to me. We used to spend entire nights lying next to one another, naked—

ELDER THOMAS: Stop.

CHARLIE: We would make love—

ELDER THOMAS: I don't want to hear about—

CHARLIE: *We would make love.* Do you find that disgusting?

ELDER THOMAS: Charlie, God is ready to help you, you don't have to—

CHARLIE: *I hope there isn't a God. (pause)* I hope there isn't a God because I hate thinking that there's an afterlife, that Alan can see what I've done to myself, that he can see my swollen feet, the sores on my skin, the patches of mold in between the flaps—

ELDER THOMAS: Okay, *stop—*

CHARLIE: —the infected ulcers on my ass, the sack of fat on my back that turned brown last year—

ELDER THOMAS: *Stop.*

CHARLIE: This is disgusting?

ELDER THOMAS: YES.

CHARLIE: *I'm* disgusting?

ELDER THOMAS: YES, YOU'RE DISGUSTING, YOU'RE— . . .

> *Elder Thomas stops himself.*
>
> *Long silence. Charlie stares at him.*

CHARLIE: Go home to your family.

> *Pause. Elder Thomas exits. Charlie breathes heavily, wheezing, trying to calm himself down.*
>
> *The lights quickly snap to black.*

In the darkness, the waves are heard once again—this time definite, sharp, and aggressive, rising quickly in volume until lights rise on:

FRIDAY
MORNING.

Charlie, at his computer, speaking into a microphone. A small web cam rests next to his laptop, not hooked up. Charlie is noticeably weaker, and is having trouble maintaining his line of thought.

CHARLIE: So, here we are. Your complaints have been heard. The powers that be have decided to replace me with someone else—someone more "stable" and "traditional" as the e-mail to me said. This person will no doubt make you rewrite and rewrite and rewrite, just like I did for seventeen years, analyzing every word, every punctuation mark for clarity and precision of meaning, and . . . *(pause)* You all sent me your essays. Your new essays, the ones you didn't rewrite. The ones you didn't think about, and . . .

Charlie types for a second, pulling up something on his computer.

CHARLIE: KristyStar9, you wrote: "My parents want me to be a radiologist, but I don't even know what that is." Peter6969, you wrote: "I'm sick of people telling me that I have promise." AdamD567, about two pages in, you wrote: "I think I need to accept that my life isn't going to be very exciting." You all wrote these—*amazing*, things, I just— *(pause)* I want to be honest with you now. I've been just a voice to all of you all semester, and now you've been so honest with me, I just . . .

Charlie pauses, then plugs the web cam into his computer. He stares at it for a second. He moves the camera away from him, then tilts it down, filming his body. He brings the camera back up to his face.

CHARLIE: These assignments—they don't matter. This course doesn't matter. College doesn't matter. These beautiful, honest things you wrote—they matter.

Charlie pauses a second, then throws his computer and the camera across the room. They crash against the wall.

48

AFTERNOON.

Charlie is sitting in his wheelchair. Liz stands in the doorway, staring at the broken computer, holding her bag.

CHARLIE: I'm sorry.

LIZ: Don't.

Liz makes her way inside, closes the door slowly. She moves over to Charlie.

CHARLIE: Liz—

LIZ: I said don't.

Liz stares at him for a second. She reaches into her bag, pulling out a stethoscope. She puts it on, then moves toward Charlie, putting it on his chest. She gently adjusts the oxygen tube underneath his nose.

LIZ: Breathe in.

Charlie breathes in.

LIZ: More.

CHARLIE: I can't. Hurts.

Liz takes the stethoscope off, puts it back in her bag. She looks at Charlie.

LIZ: I really hate you for putting me through this again, you know that? (*pause*) Those last few months before Alan . . . And I'd come over here, and I'd scream at him, shake him. For God's sake, eat something! You stupid piece of shit, you just need to eat something! (*pause*) I'd come back and the food would be gone. Not because he ate it—but because he hid it somewhere. Threw it out the window, fed it to the neighbor's dog. You were beside yourself, had no idea what to do . . . God, that was awful.

CHARLIE: It was awful for me, too.

LIZ: Well, you weren't the one who found him. In your bed, underneath the covers, curled up like a fetus. God, you think you only see things like that in documentaries.

Liz reaches into her bag, taking out two sub sandwiches.

LIZ: I got you two meatball subs. Extra cheese. I don't know what I'm doing. (*pause*) You have money. You need to go to the hospital.

Pause.

CHARLIE: No.

LIZ: For me. Go to the hospital for me.

CHARLIE: No.

Pause.

LIZ: How *dare* you do this to me again?!

Silence. Charlie's breathing is increasingly shallow.

The sound of waves from before is heard at a very low level, steadily increasing in volume as the scene progresses.

CHARLIE: She helped him.

LIZ: What?

CHARLIE: She wasn't trying to hurt him. She was trying to help him.

LIZ: Who are you talking about?

CHARLIE: The Mormon kid. He's going home. She did that. She wasn't trying to hurt him.

LIZ: Oh, God, Charlie?

CHARLIE: She didn't do it to hurt him, she did it to send him home.

LIZ: Do you feel light-headed? Charlie, look at me.

CHARLIE: She was trying to help him!

LIZ: Who?!

CHARLIE: Ellie. She was trying to help him, she just wanted him to go home.

LIZ: Oh my God. You need—. I don't know what to do, I can't help you!

Charlie looks at Liz.

CHARLIE: Do you ever get the feeling. That people. Are incapable. Of not caring? People. Are. Amazing.

Ellie charges in through the front door holding the essay from before. She stops when she sees Charlie, looking at him for a brief moment.

ELLIE: What's wrong with him?

LIZ: He's dying.

Pause.

ELLIE: So call someone.

CHARLIE: No.

ELLIE: Call an ambulance.

CHARLIE: No. Liz. Please don't.

ELLIE: Call a fucking ambulance!

Liz takes out her cell phone.

CHARLIE: Liz. Please.

LIZ: No. I'm not letting this go on any more, I'm calling an ambulance. I'm not going through this again!

ELLIE: I need to talk to him.

Liz starts dialing.

LIZ: So talk.

ELLIE: Alone.

LIZ: I'm not leaving you alone with him.

ELLIE: I need to talk to him alone!

CHARLIE: Liz. Please.

Liz looks at him. Pause.

LIZ: Fine. I'm calling an ambulance, and I'm waiting downstairs. We'll get you to the hospital, and you're *going to be fine*. You understand me?

Liz exits.

ELLIE: What's wrong with you?

CHARLIE: I can't. Breathe very well.

Pause.

ELLIE: The ambulance is coming. They'll take you to the hospital, you should have gone a while ago. *(pause)* Why did you do that?!

CHARLIE: What?

Ellie holds up the essay.

ELLIE: I failed.

CHARLIE: It's. A really good essay.

ELLIE: No, it's not a really good essay! I failed! *(pause)* Are you just trying to screw me over one last time before you die? I don't care that you're dying! I don't care about you! Do you want me to fail out of high school, is that why you did this?

CHARLIE: I didn't. Write it.

ELLIE: This is the essay you gave me yesterday.

CHARLIE: You didn't. Read it.

ELLIE: I don't need to read it, it got an F!

CHARLIE: Read it.

Ellie looks at the paper for a second.

ELLIE: This is . . . I know what this is.

CHARLIE: I knew you would. You never. Forget anything.

ELLIE: I wrote this. *(pause)* I wrote this in eighth grade for English, why do you—?

CHARLIE: And I felt saddest of all. When I read the boring chapters. That were only descriptions of whales. Because I knew. That the author was just trying to save us. From his own sad story. Just for a little while.

ELLIE: Why do you have this?

CHARLIE: Your mother. She sent it to me. Four years ago. I wanted to know how you were doing. In school. So she sent it. And it's the best essay. I've ever read.

Pause.

ELLIE: Why are you fucking with me like this?

CHARLIE: I'm not. *(pause)* You're so beautiful. Ellie, you're beautiful.

ELLIE: Stop saying that.

CHARLIE: You're amazing. This essay. Is amazing.

ELLIE: Stop saying that!

CHARLIE: You're the best thing. I've ever done.

Charlie has a severe chest pain, he doubles over. Ellie is frantic.

ELLIE: What's the matter?!

CHARLIE: Ellie.

ELLIE: I can't be here right now, I have to go, I can't—

CHARLIE: You're perfect. You'll be happy. You'll care for people.

ELLIE: The ambulance is coming, they'll help you!

CHARLIE: No. They won't.

Pause.

ELLIE: *You're going to the hospital.*

CHARLIE: No.

ELLIE: You just need surgery or something!

CHARLIE: Read it to me.

ELLIE: What?!

CHARLIE: If you want to help. Read it to me. You can help me. If you read it.

Ellie is holding back tears at this point.

ELLIE: You asshole. You fat fucking asshole!

CHARLIE: You'll help. If you read it.

ELLIE: Fuck you.

CHARLIE: Please.

ELLIE: Fuck you!

CHARLIE: Ellie.

ELLIE: Dad, *please.*

Pause. Ellie looks at Charlie, pleading. Ellie and Charlie are in the same position as they were in their first scene together. The sound of waves gets louder and louder.

ELLIE: *(reading)* "In the amazing book *Moby Dick* by the author Herman Melville, the author recounts his story of being at sea. In the first part of his book, the author, calling himself Ishmael, is in a small sea-side town and he is sharing a bed with a man named Queequeg."

Charlie smiles at Ellie through the pain. He reaches up and takes the oxygen tube out of his nose.

ELLIE: "The author and Queequeg go to church and hear a sermon about Jonah, and later set out on a ship captained by the pirate named Ahab, who is missing a leg, and very much wants to kill the whale which is named Moby Dick, and which is white."

Charlie braces himself on his wheelchair.

ELLIE: "In the course of the book, the pirate Ahab encounters many hardships. His entire life is set around trying to kill a certain whale."

Wheezing heavily and with a huge amount of effort and pain, Charlie manages to stand up.

ELLIE: "I think this is sad because this whale doesn't have any emotions, and doesn't know how bad Ahab wants to kill him."

> *Charlie, staring at Ellie, manages to take one step forward. His breathing becomes quicker. The waves are louder still.*

ELLIE: "He's just a poor big animal. And I feel bad for Ahab as well, because he thinks that his life will be better if he can kill this whale, but in reality it won't help him at all."

> *Charlie takes another step. His breathing is more and more rapid.*

ELLIE: "I was very saddened by this book, and I felt many emotions for the characters."

> *Another step.*

ELLIE: "And I felt saddest of all when I read the boring chapters that were only descriptions of whales, because I knew that the author was just trying to save us from his own sad story, just for a little while."

> *Charlie takes one last step toward Ellie. The waves reach their loudest level.*

ELLIE: "This book made me think about my own life, and then it made me feel glad for my—"

> *Charlie looks up. The waves cut off.*

> *A sharp intake of breath. The lights snap to black.*

> *END OF PLAY.*

TRIEU TRAN is a remarkably talented actor with a fast-rising career. Trieu earned his BA in Performing Arts from American University. He has appeared in numerous theatrical productions through the years. Notably, the role of Alan Strang in *Equus* (LADCC Nomination) with George Takei @EWP, and the title role in *Oedipus The King, The Legacy Codes* (Dean Goodman Award) with TheatreWorks. Other favorites include: *Rashomon, As You Like It, Henry IV, Part One (Hotspur)*, and the title role in *Richard III*. Film: *Trade of Innocents, How High, Hancock, Desperation, Tropic Thunder*. Trieu reoccurs as "Joey Phan" on the HBO series *The Newsroom*. He also reoccurs on the Hulu original series *Quickdraw*, as well as on the upcoming series *Intruders* for BBC America. *Uncle Ho To Uncle Sam* is his first play written with co-author Robert Egan (current Artistic Director of Ojai Playwrights Conference, former Artistic Director of The Mark Taper Forum and Seattle Rep). *Uncle Ho to Uncle Sam* was first developed at the Ojai Playwrights Conference in 2011. It had its world premiere in Seattle at ACT in fall 2012. *Uncle Ho to Uncle Sam* also had a run at The Kirk Douglas Theatre in 2013, and a run at Shubert Theatre in Boston in fall 2014.

ROBERT EGAN is an award winning producer, director and dramaturge. He is the Artistic Director/Producer of the Ojai Playwrights Conference and was the Producing Artistic Director of the Mark Taper Forum and Founding Artistic Director of its New Work Festival in which he produced and developed Pulitzer Prize winners *Angels in America* and *Kentucky Cycle*. Robert was the Associate Artistic Director of the Seattle Repertory Theatre and created their new play program, The Other Season. He also created Home Productions. Robert is the Founder/President of RHEgan Productions LLC and Eye Street Media. Directing and producing credits include productions at theatres in the U.S. including Kirk Douglas; South Coast Rep; La Jolla Playhouse; Berkeley Rep; Public Theatre; Playwrights Horizons; Naked Angels; Hip Hop Theatre Festival; A Contemporary Theatre; the Empty Space; Signature Theatre; Kennedy Center; and Europe in England at Oxford Playhouse and Oxford University Drama Society among others. He produced/directed a national Hip-Hop Tour for Norman Lear, and developed/directed a production for the HBO Aspen Comedy Festival. For television he has directed episodes of *Frasier* and *Stark Raving Mad*, among others. Education: Boston College, Oxford University, and Stanford University.

Trieu Tran
with Robert Egan

Uncle Ho to Uncle Sam

Trieu Tran enters wrapped in a South Vietnamese Flag.

The day of my birth, April 20—1975, began a chain reaction of events that forever transformed my home, my Viet Nam. Within moments of my birth, the skies unexpectedly fill with thunder and lightening. *(Thunder.)* Within days of my birth—the cowardly, drunken President Thieu of South Viet Nam flees Saigon for foreign shores with a suitcase of gold bars bought with American aid dollars. Settling on the shores of Massachusetts, his troubled memory is pounded clean by the relentless waves of money. Within two weeks of my birth—American Armed Forces Radio broadcasts Bing Crosby's *White Christmas.* Upon hearing this secret warning, US citizens gather at prearranged pickup points to abandon my homeland. America's goodbye statement carefully crafted by President Nixon and Henry Kissinger—simply states—"We have achieved peace with honor."

How do I discover my birth is the catalyst for this tragedy? Throughout my childhood and eventually throughout my dreams my father, Thuan Ngoc Tran, rages, "Uncle Ho Chi Minh told me, 'All men are created equal—you have the right to Life, the right to be Free, and the right to achieve Happiness.' And Uncle Sam from JFK to LBJ to Richard Millhouse Nixon told me, 'America will support any friend, oppose any foe, and bear any burden in defense of your liberty.' First, my 'liberty' got buried in fields made fertile with the blood of simple Vietnamese families. Then, my 'liberty' got buried again in foreign fields sown

with the bitter seeds of exclusion. I knew there were two Viet Nams—
Communist and Capitalist. I did not know there were two America's—
the Caucasians and the rest of us. Trieu Tran, God cursed the day that
you were born. The night that forced you from your mother's womb." To
the day my father died he held on to this disturbed, dark belief that the
day of my birth, April 20, 1975, was a catalyst for his demise and that of
my country.

RE-EDUCATION OF THE TRAN FAMILY:

Dense jungle images. Vietnamese Lullaby plays.

As I wipe the drool off my groggy, mud-stained face—I wake to the
sounds of birds in a nearby bamboo grove. My mother, under a banyan
tree in her white *ao dai,* talks to a beetle-nut tooth-stained old woman.
Sitting on a straw mat, the old lady sells sugarcane and rambutans. She
points towards the green fields to one side and the dark jungle ahead.
"Fields good. Jungles bad."

"Trieu di," mom beckons me to continue our journey. My grandfather's
voice echoes in my head, "Keep your eyes out for Viet Congs. They eat
dogs and little boys. And they smile right before they do it." Grandpa
is my King. And I—his mighty warrior. My dad is the middle son of
12 children. And he is the only one who has produced a boy—me, Trieu
Tran. At the tender age of 4, I am the family's greatest treasure. My
Grandpa named me Trieu, after Lady Trieu—a great Vietnamese warrior
who defeated China long, long ago. Grandpa says she had breasts three
feet long that she threw over her shoulders and tied down as she led her
men to victory. "You are that fearless warrior! You will bring us respect
and riches. No grandson—a Buddhist curse. You—a Buddhist blessing!!"

My mother leads us deep into the jungle. I imagine the Viet Congs
sneaking out of tunnels and attacking us. Energized by the sun
streaming through the banyan trees, I see a dragonfly buzzing nearby.
This is how I will outsmart the Viet Congs. Slowly, slowly, I reach out
and strike. YES! Its wings between my fingers, I show mom, "Look I
caught a Viet Cong! Mom, will dad remember me?" "A father never
forgets his only son."

"I was just a baby when he left." "Your father did not leave, he was taken
away to be re-educated. It's time for you to meet him."

Six hours pass and the straw grass reaches up to my skinny waist. The
lush green rice paddies transform into deep muddy ditches and barbwire
fences. Black smoke smothers the treetops. Mother becomes tense as
a man with a big gun suddenly appears. "Is that father?" "No, he's a

teacher." "Why does he have a gun?" "It's dangerous in the jungle." "Why does father go to school in the jungle?" "America abandoned us. He had new things to learn."

Mom walks to the teacher with the gun. She hands him cigarettes she's brought along. He shakes his head and shoves her to the ground. Mom crawls to him and pushes money into his hands. I defiantly walk to the teacher with the big gun. "Caio Chu"—I greet him. The teacher has a thin, angry face. "Do you love your Uncle Ho? Do you love your Uncle Ho!" I help my mother off the ground. Then I turn to him, "I love all my Uncles, Uncle." The teacher nods with a sickening smile.

The teacher leads us to a group of men. They are tied to bamboo stakes, covered in dirt, blood oozing from cuts, skin burnt like roasted duck. Mom reaches out to one of the men. He is gagged, hands tied behind his back. Telephone wires hold him upright against his bamboo pole—they cut through his flesh—mosquitoes hover over him in a huge swarm.

The teacher rips off his gag, "Your father does not respect Uncle Ho, like you. He lies in his confessions. He loves the Americans." My father's eyes meet mine—he studies my face, here before him—is his only son. Tears begin to trickle down his bloodstained cheeks. I realize these are not teachers. These are the Viet Congs. I start to cry. My father's face grows fierce—his tears cease instantly. With a sudden narrowing of his eyes he says without words, "This is not the time. This is not the time." I hold back my flood of tears and do nothing. "Forgive me father. Someday I will be your warrior! I promise!"

Mom's touch breaks me out of this trance. She pulls me up to her bosom. Armies of mosquitoes chase us—chase us away from this—my first memory of my father.

O CANADA: OUR HOME AND NATIVE LAND:

Snow. Ice. Canadian Anthem. Frozen bridges across a river.

I arrive in Saskatoon, Saskatchewan, Canada. The winter of 1982. Strange white flakes fall from the winter skies. Riding down the dragon-necked escalator, I see a group of Vietnamese wearing fur-hats, ear-muffs, and thick-scarves—more clothes than I've ever seen on anybody. At the bottom of the dragon-necked, people-mover—white parents are hugging their kids. They look happy. My first impression of this new land—a pale-white winter sky with pale-white snow and pale-white families— all smiling.

Saskatoon, Saskatchewan is an endless province of nothingness—a vastness of ice and snow flooding the earth that keeps my family hibernating for months. Running through the middle of my new city, is a frozen, lifeless river. Crossing this wide expanse are seven bridges. The locals call it Bridge City. We are crammed into a tiny nest of a two-bedroom house—duplex 33-C on Regina Court. Throngs of relatives live here. It's much warmer huddled together. Lots of body heat and lots of alcohol to soothe this—their winter of discontent. They are not really blood relatives, but in this new world anyone who looks and sounds like a Viet is considered family—by my dad.

Dad interacts with whites—only out of necessity—like the various Christian Church groups who continually come to our house recruiting. The Jehovah Witnesses are the worst. They come to our door and scold me for watching "The Dukes of Hazard" on TV. Dad confronts them, "My son learning the American way—fast cars, money, big boobs and sex." That scares them away. I decide I want to be a Catholic. Jesus had a loving mother. And his father was not around very much. Plus, the Catholics always bring great gifts at Christmas. Even though we can't afford the batteries to make their toys work, I say, "A battery-less toy is better than no toy at all."

Fun logos. Sesame Street. McDonalds. Christmas.

Outside this tiny nest, I am free at last. Free to find satisfaction with "Big Whoppers" at Burger King and Happy Meals at McDonalds. Prizes in the Happy Meals! Skinny 7½ year-old boat-boy getting rewarded for eating! My appetite for all things Caucasian grows every day. Sesame Street, Wayne Gretzky, The A-Team, Ice Skating, Peanut Butter and Jelly, Cheerios, Christmas. Let It Snow, Let It Snow, Let it Snow!

On this particular Christmas Eve I wake up to the overture to our Yuletide festivities—a distant phone rings, muffled voices outside my bedroom door. Then dad's booming voice, "I go where I want, do what I want. I will not sacrifice everything for you!"

"You have no idea what sacrifice is. I brought our children here on boat of death. You look at me as stupid country girl, but I am good wife. You will not leave our children alone on Christmas Eve!"

"You disrespectful bitch! I survived the Viet Cong for this?"

A slap. A scream. A door slams. I am at the window. Mom in the icy storm. Lights from a nearby house flicker on. "Fuckin' chinks, shut the fuck up!" Mom disappears into the frozen darkness. Dad suddenly rages into my room. "Trieu, get away from that window." I refuse to look at him. I clasp my hands and pray like the Catholics. I ask Jesus to punish him. "Sonofabitch, you disrespect me? Trieu Tran! You are my son. Look at me! You choose her over me? Momma's boy. I am blessed with three girls. First born son turns out to be—pussy!"

I turn to face him—defiance in my eyes. Dad violently attacks my dresser. Knocks everything off. Then suddenly—silence. Thunder and lightening—outside. He lays down on my mattress—"Our war was fought on rice fields, because it was a war to save our souls. We escaped hell and what have we found? Nothing. Except that hell is the only living truth. I know your mother misses home. She looks into the shadowed waters of memory and what does she see? Viet Nam—the grassy smell of rice fields, the scent of mango, guava, papaya. Me kissing her, my beautiful peasant girl, under the banana tree. That was freedom. Your mother wants to believe everything stays beautiful all the time. But within those shadowed waters lies something deeper, something so terrible—it can explode everything into tiny fragments. This—your mother does not see."

Every time dad's 'other wife' phones here—this nightmare erupts. We've never met her. But we know—she's out there. Cause dad runs to her when she calls—escapes into his secret life. I wonder what's going on right now in white people's homes. They don't have these problems. They are happy watching TV laughing at Johnny Carson late into the night. Beneath my shadowed waters is my mom—like a wounded dove wandering the frozen banks of the Saskatchewan River. Who will comfort her in this pale-white land?

SOUTH CHINA SEA:

Deep blue seas. Ocean waves. Moon Festival music.

Darkness—me, my mother, and my two sisters—quietly crawl through a field—near a river where we've hidden a canoe to take us to the big fishing boat in the bay. A large Moon Festival takes place nearby. Music echoes as we climb into our canoe. Three flashes of light from the big fishing boat. "Children, swallow these pills. You must be very quiet. It's very dangerous. These pills will give you sleep and good dreams." Without hesitation, mom paddles into the darkness.

Lady Trieu carries me through a vast rice paddy. I am cradled in her 3-foot bosoms strapped across her chest. We are now racing, racing through the muddy, green waters when suddenly Viet Congs spring up ahead spraying us with machine gun fire. Bullets explode all around, but bounce off Lady Trieu and me. We trample and scatter the Viet Congs. And there in the distance tied to a bamboo stake is my dad. I race to him and lift him up in the crook of my right arm . . . and we fly to the moon.

I awake from this dream back in the canoe drifting, all alone, away from the big fishing boat. Something moves in the water nearby. My Uncle

Pham emerges from the darkness, "Sshhhh! We must paddle back to the big boat. Quiet." Faces dimly visible in the moonlight—stare at me. I get wedged between relatives I have never met. My uncle shakes his head. "Your mother is careless bitch, many lives risked to get you in this boat." An ancient woman with long silver hair gleaming in the moonlight hisses, "Your careless uncles forgot you. In their rush to unload canoe, they did not see you asleep under your blanket. Your mother threatened, 'Unless you get my son. I will scream and wake the Viet Cong.' Your mother saved you."

I wake to the warmth of the sun. This 6-year-old Boat Boy longs to swim with the dolphins skimming through the calm seas. I follow their path to a shadow on the horizon! "BOAT!" The ship gets closer. These boatmen look like my uncles, only darker. They wear sarongs and headbands. They board our boat. Without warning one of them pulls out a machete. The rest turn our boat upside down searching for treasure. These are pirates!

A big, burly pirate gropes my two teenage cousins. He carries them onto the pirate boat. Women wail as my shrieking cousins are attacked. One of my cousins hemorrhages . . . rivers of blood. An old, feeble man is attacked. He points to my Uncle Pham and shouts, "He has gold in his mouth!" Uncle Pham is knocked to the floor, his mouth forced open. The pirates twist his gold teeth out with rusty pliers. Blood explodes everywhere.

One skinny pirate pushes my mother down! He rips and tears at her pants. She screams as his boney fingers penetrate places she does not like. I jump on his back. Someone hits me hard. A pirate holds my legs and dangles me like a rag doll over the side of the boat. The silvery haired old woman cuts through the terror and into the soul of the Pirate Captain: "I know you understand Vietnamese. Stop your men and God will forgive you. If not, you will have a lifetime of darkness. No god will forgive you for violating a pregnant woman. God has put the life of an unborn child in your hands for a reason. Choose carefully what you do now."

I know my mother is not pregnant but I also know we are about to be killed. So I welcome this lie. The Pirate Captain stops his men: "My wife and I have failed to conceive male child. I will not kill unborn. But in your prayers you must promise me, beg—God grants me a son."

"Save the boy too. And save the girls on your boat."

The Captain takes back the power and the respect of his pirate crew: "I saved the pregnant woman. You can have the boy—or—the girls. God has put their lives in your hands for a reason, old woman. You choose." We hear the screams and cries of my cousins as the pirate boat

60

sails away. Mom covers me with kisses. "You are my warrior-prince. Thank you for saving me." "No, mother, that old woman saved us." I crawl over to thank her. "Life is never fair for people like you and me. There will always be blood. When your time comes, choose carefully. I know you—you can save the many, not just one."

DANCING WITH MICHAEL JACKSON:

TRIEU begins to dance like Michael Jackson.

Finally, we have a new house. "A Section 8 Duplex." After three years in Canada, I have my own bedroom—and a stereo where I listen to Michael Jackson. I want to be the "King of Pop." My daily diet here at 1049 Madison Drive consists of eggs with rice, eggs with ramen, eggs with soy sauce, eggs with ketchup, all courtesy of dad's new job as an assembly worker at—The Star Egg Factory. Lots of eggs mixed with Canadian beer have made my dad a big burly man. Arriving immigrants flock to him like helpless broken birds. They all answer to dad—the vengeful, unyielding GOD. Inside our growing community—he is king.

Today, we celebrate our new home and honor the anniversary of my grandpa's death. And here we go again. The red-blotchy-faced adults begin their drunken dance of unfulfilled promises in the new land.

"I am soldier without a country!"

"I speak French to these Canadians, they don't understand what I'm saying. DUMA!"

"Learn English, LAUCA!"

"I had servants in Vietnam, now I'm at the mercy of welfare!"

My dad stands tall from his newspaper-trashed throne. "We Vietnamese must be one. Rivers go dry, mountains wear away, but we will live on! No trust to outsiders! We may not be living the American dream, but no white motherfuckers can say we can't dream the American way!" Then the phone rings. Dad answers it. And suddenly clears the room.

"Pham! I work in an egg factory. I cannot pay you $30,000 for bringing my children out of Viet Nam! While your belly was full, I begged like a dog for a single grain of rice from the Viet Cong. Where were you then, my brother? No money, Pham."

Mom can't help herself, "We owe your brother for trip on boat of death? He's disgrace. He is coward."

"Dingu! Shut your mouth. You don't talk about my brother. Freedom has a price tag for everyone now!"

61

Mom finally reveals what's deep in her heart. "I'm tired pretending. Pretending—this new beginning. I am first-wife, but I am non-person. Everywhere I go—silent stares. While you sneak off to 'the bitch.' Get boom-boom—while I cook, clean, take care of our children. This not freedom. I cry not for me, I cry for them. I am ashamed to be their mother."

The sound of dad's fist on mom's face, then the whhoosshh of a butcher knife missing her head and chipping the plaster on our duplex wall. The sight of my mother bleeding from a broken nose and my bloodshot-eyed father standing there, no shirt, exposing a new bald eagle tattooed across his chest. Clenched fist in one hand, a butcher knife in the other.

Our white neighbor, Keith, drives us to the Emergency Room. I fear dad will know I betrayed him by calling Keith. Snow falls and Bing Crosby's *White Christmas* comes on the car radio. Can we just keep driving and never come back? While we wait at the hospital, characters on TV, the X-Men, keep me company. Mother finally emerges her loving eyes discolored, swollen, a bandaged nose. "Hey there Trieu, how's my brave little warrior?" "I'm fine, mom."

We walk through a labyrinth of corridors to Keith's car. Another cold ride to another cold place—called home. Entering the house with great caution, mom disappears into my sisters' bedroom. Guitar music drifts from the living room. Dad strums his guitar, cigarette dangling from his mouth. No whiskey or beer in sight. (*TRIEU sings.*) "You escape Viet Nam with gold, you own restaurants here. No gold, you are a fuck. Tell me, who am I?"

"Immigrant . . ."

"No, immigrants choose to go somewhere. We are refugees. Understand!"

"Yes."

"Now, what's this I hear about Keith taking you to the hospital tonight? What'd you tell him?"

"Nothing."

"Don't lie. You told him I beat your mother, didn't you?"

Suddenly dad heads upstairs. I follow him. I enter my parent's bedroom. No sign of dad. Naked people on the TV—breathing heavy and moaning. I hear something from the bathroom. I go in. In the dark, dad sobs, naked in the tub. The bathroom mirror—shattered. Dad's hand wrapped in a bloody wash-cloth. His eyes lift to meet mine.

"Don't turn on the lights. Come here. Take your clothes off. You're filthy." (*Beat.*) I do not move. He gets out of the tub. I see him reflected behind me in the shattered bathroom mirror. His face looks so terrible, so full of pain. "I'm your father. You never complain when your mother washes you. Get in the tub. We must wash her blood off!"

I take off my blood-stained clothes and—we—get in the tub. Dad obsessively scrubs the blood off my body. This is not right. But intimate moments like this—I so long for. I know it won't last long. "How many times do I have to beat you before you believe—I love you?"

My face distorts in the shadowy waters of this bathtub. The intense rhythms of my heart—beat like a broken drum with each rough touch of my father. My body is like an oven. Salty tears engulf my face. Am I dreaming? No, it's my own father—pulsing veins in his neck, blood-red eyes. "Trieu, it's hard to be a man in America. Wash away the sorrow—wash away the pain—wash away the shame." This is not right. I am drowning. I am drowning. I am drowning. *(Water ritual.)*

THAI CAMPS:

Sound of waves. Children's voices. Announcement in Thai.

I have been living in Songhkla Refugee Camp in Thailand for 9 months. When will the voice on the camp speakers announce the name of the Tran family—calling us to France, Hong Kong, Germany or "America." I'm 7—my sisters 5 and 3. Families with young children are supposed to go first.

But here we are! Stop #1 for us Boat People! Thousands of Vietnamese packed into squalid, shanty shacks on a tiny strip of beach. Homes made out of cardboard and tin sheets. I have learned to be alert, listen to gossip—and know who's got what and how much they got. I love hanging with my Cousin Duc. He's 11. We have a secret "begging business" that gets us money to buy candy. Having lost a lot of weight, I'm small and frail, so I get more sympathy than Duc. He needs me to be the face of our operation. This really pisses him off, "You may be the face. But I'm the brain. I run this shit, little shit."

We know who all the wealthy Vietnamese are. Today our last begging stop—is Great Aunt Nguyen. Duc commands—"Grab her bag of rice if she won't give you any." "We don't need to steal. Stand back and watch the master work." I walk toward her shanty shack with my plastic bag. "Ma'am, I'm hungry, do you have any left over rice for my little brothers and sisters?" "And how many are there?" "Only 14 of us since baby Kim Cuc died." The old lady dumps handfuls of rice into my bag. Mission accomplished! I hand the bag to Duc. He then sells our rice to the Thai guards—who feed it to their pigs. Duc hands me my share of the money.

"That's all? C'mon Duc!"

"Your fault, the master didn't look sad enough today."

A slap stings my face. My mother catches us in the midst of our negotiation. "How many times do I have to tell you, we don't beg. Your sisters starve and you buy candy? Selfish! You disgrace me!"

Now I spend all my time on the beach. I have never tried to swim in the ocean like the other kids. I don't want to disappear like my dad. Last time I saw him was 3½ years ago. Mother bribed his Viet Cong guards to let him out for one day to attend his father's funeral. And then—he vanished. I know he's out there somewhere. Waiting for me. I slowly step towards the sea, each step finds a bit more courage. I feel a hand on my shoulder. There is Cousin Duc.

"Your dad is alive. He is with a new wife, in a place called—Canada."

I race to mom. She holds a letter. "Is dad still my father?"

"He always be your father."

"Am I gonna have another mom?"

"Your father thought we never make it out. But we did, Trieu. Almost there. Almost there. We will get him back."

Announcement to come to the buses in Thai.

A few days later, we are called to a row of buses waiting to take us and other refugees to the airport. My dad with help of the Ebenezer Baptist Church is sponsoring our little family to this big place called—Canada. On the bus everyone talks about the new life that awaits us:

"Canada? Couldn't the US accept us out of guilt?"

"America, I heard they give everyone two sets of keys when you step off the plane. One for new car and one for new house."

"My brother in Australia—he never mention that."

"I say America, not Australia."

Voices begin to celebrate. "Khong go gi quy hon doc lap tu do!!!"— "Nothing is more precious than independence and freedom." This is their chant. I chant with them—not aloud—but in my heart.

CANADA: THE FINAL PARTY:

Eerie night in rural Canada. Coldness. Druggy music plays.

Into dens of alcoholism, drugs, and prostitution, my sisters and I are now always along for the ride with dad in his big blue Lincoln

Continental. Only 10 years old—wherever he goes I go. If I keep my mouth shut, dad rewards me. I got a BMX bike and a new stereo system. Dad quit his job at the egg factory. But with his new, secret employment activities, we are finally living like white Canadians.

Tonight we are with dad's small army of underworld enforcers at the apartment of his right hand man, Bao. This is command central for all of dad's business operations. This clique of Viet hoodlums raise their glasses in drunken uniformity to my father—"THOUNG, TIEN, TU, TOI!" The 4T's is their slogan—which means—Love, money, prison, crime!—"Bui Doi!" (Dust of Life).

On the stove black tar burns—their number one money-maker. Heroin. Dad calls it, "Black gold." Dad's cigarette dangles beneath his disapproving eyes. That look he always gives me right before he beats me. But dad's look is not intended for me. It is for Vu—"The Bull." I wish he would go back to Edmonton. Vu just got out of prison for beating up a cop. He is the same size as dad but with bigger muscles. He has been around for weeks and he and my dad are always competing. Tonight Vu is making Tiet Canh—raw duck blood with finely chopped innards, sprinkled with peanuts and mint—then you refrigerate to coagulate. Vu asks me to kill the duck in the kitchen sink. He holds the knife out to me, "Come on, little pussy!" I refuse. Vu slits the duck's neck. He drains the blood into a bowl and squirts some on my cheek.

My father's eyes are storms, "No one calls my son—a pussy!" Dad stares straight at Vu "The Bull"—hands at his side—a bottle in each fist. Vu laughs, "You left your balls back at that Viet Cong camp!" Vu "The Bull" has finally crossed the line. Dad looks at me. His eyes say, "Now is the time. Now is the time!" Dad, my dad, is finally my protector. He loves his first-born son. "Vu has a knife!" someone screams. My sisters and I are shoved into a side room. I try to open the door. Someone holds it shut. I want to defend my dad. Chaos. My sisters scream. They help me pull the door open.

(In Vietnamese.) "Oh, God, Vu stab me too deep!"

The air is deathly still. I turn to my right. Vu "The Bull" laying there, blood covering his head, dripping down his neck, down his arm to the knife in his hand. I turn to my left. Dad lies on the kitchen floor. I kneel down next to him. No blood. "Dad, you saved your first-born son. You won. Get up. Please get up." His eyes meet mine. Tender and loving for once. We are suspended. Floating, floating.

65

I stare at a cotton ball hanging from dad's stomach. Who placed it there? There is blood now on the cotton ball. I peel it off to see if dad is hurt. It just keeps coming and coming—it's my father's guts uncoiling from his stomach. Dad's eyes are now barely open. "Trieu, promise me . . ."

"Dad, what? Promise what? Tell me. Please, tell me! Jesus, don't let my dad die. Jesus, are you listening? Jesus, are you listening?"

BODY TAKEN / SPIRIT SHAKEN:

TRIEU in white cloth headband. Funeral music. Ritual feel.

Look at my stupid Uncle Pham taking pictures next to dad's coffin. Take your pictures. I'll sit back here—in the back of the temple. My dad always insisted, "Do not cremate me, I want to be buried in the dirt where I die. This will bring me peace." I don't belong to this cursed family. Uncle Pham keeps saying, "Don't be disrespectful, you should be standing by your dad's coffin!" Who does he think he is? He's the one who has no respect. He only talked to dad when he wanted $30,000 for the trip on boat of death. He hasn't even seen him since Vietnam. Now dad's dead, he shows up. And he demands my dad be cremated. I don't care if he is my uncle. I'll sit here. I know my father's spirit will not be happy.

At the airport I see my dad's plastic urn for the first time. Uncle Pham is holding it. As he walks to the gate he turns, "I am taking your dad with me to Seattle, to the United States. His mother wants him there. She will take care of him. You are the man of the family now. See if you can at least take care . . . of your mother and sisters." And he is gone. And my dad is gone. I wave goodbye to him as the plane takes off for Seattle. *(TRIEU bows three times then rips off funeral wear.)* One good thing—my mother and I are free now to live without fear. We are free to find the real America. Free to find liberty at last.

USA: BOSTON AND BEYOND:

Copeland's "Fanfare for a Common Man" plays. TRIEU: "I pledge allegiance to the flag of the United States of America, and to the republic for which it stands, one nation under God, indivisible, with liberty and justice for . . ."

Ellis Island is not my port of entry, no goddess of liberty in sight. We don't land on no Plymouth Rock, we land on a hot humid tarmac in inner-city Boston—by way of Northwest Airlines via Saskatoon, Saskatchewan. My saga continues from Logan airport straight to—PJ's Inner City Housing Project.

Tonight's heat reminds me of Vietnam. Our 22-inch fan blows hot sticky wind. Johnny Carson plays on our 13-inch TV. My mom serves freshly cooked food to grandpa and dad's fading pictures on our homemade altar. She struggles to keep their spirits content. I have to admit I am growing a little resentful. Being the new man of the family, I am forced to go through puberty in a small bedroom with mom and my two sisters. But mom refuses to let my spirit weaken. Working double shifts as a waitress, she puts food on the table and remains intensely proud of our Vietnamese roots. Our first Thanksgiving—an American turkey stuffed with raw mango, guava and rambutans with accents of lemon and ginger grass. She is a good mother, so I work to be the good Asian son—straight A's, the model minority with MIT and Harvard ambitions. I do this out of love and respect for this woman who has made this ghetto tenement— a home.

But outside our home, I am the rabid chameleon, soaking up everything American. I am not an ABC, an American Born Chinese, nor am I—an FOB—Fresh off the Boat. I am a first generation Vietnamese-AMERICAN. From the Viet Cong infested jungle to the concrete jungle, from the Ho Chi Minh Trail to the Freedom Trail. I see African-Americans, Latino-Americans, Italian-Americans and Irish-Americans. I don't get the Asian kids. My sisters and the other Viets only run with other Asians. Their Walkmans blast only Vietnamese New Wave sounds of Bad Boy Blue and Modern Talking. Asian kids all wear the same cheap suits from Tellos or Structure, and blow dry their hair, spraying an entire bottle of Aqua Net for that forever hair blowing in the wind look. They all wanna look the same, wanna act the same, wanna be the same. Not me! I want to be a part of this new world!

There goes Rick. He is the leader of the Dopeland Posse and he is Puerto Rican. Just out of prison. He beat up some white townie for trying to steal his Caddie. "Hey Rick, what's up, my dog?" He cruises on by without so much as a glance. There goes T-Bone! The #1 Man of the Black Magics. They walk with a swagger, a strut—like they own these streets. "Yo T-Bone, what's up, my brother?" And T-Bone floats on by like I'm not even there. There's Jimmy Adessa. The youngest member of the Irish Mo's—only 10-years-old. He's with his mom. She loves her vodka more than her little Jimmy, "Jimmy get in the fuckin' cah. Don't be a smahtass ass, Jimmy. Get in the fuckin' cah!" And he says, "Get the fuck outa here, ma!" I want to belong to this America! Tough like Rick, proud like T-Bone and bold like Jimmy! I want to cross-over. One nation under god. But there are so many borders!

America—the melting pot that has yet to really melt! But I soon discover there is a big movement happening out there that's gonna make this melting pot finally melt—the Hip-Hop Nation!! The hip-hop sounds of Public Enemy, Run DMC, Slick Rick and NWA become "my" sound. No more grooving to the sounds of Michael Jackson. Hip-hop gives me—a voice. With verbal defiance I can express the frustration of being denied—inclusion, respect. Tupac's words speak to my heart! "I see no changes, all I see is racist faces, misplaced hate makes disgrace the racist—I wonder what it takes to make this one better place." Hip-hop is colorless! I see my way to fit in. If you Swagger with baggy pants, drink 40s of Old English, and smoke blunts—you are considered down. But I'm not down. Not here. Not in East Boston. I remain an outsider. An American ghost.

BOSTON LATIN HIGH:

Inner city Boston school—we see lockers and hallways.

My freshman year at Boston Latin High School, I get into a fight with some senior. He comes up to me at lunch while I'm sitting alone at an empty table, "Get up Gook. That's my seat!" I've heard chink, I've heard jap, but never "gook." This Italian kid, Michael Amato, reveals the true meaning of the "G" word. I know he wants to see me get my ass kicked. But I walk over to the 'Gook Calling' white kid and I kick his ass with a metal lunch tray. My reputation for being my own man—quickly grows. This demystifies the Asian stereotype of—Trieu Tran.

That first sharp whack of cold, hard metal on pale, white skull cracks open a door. For this is when my friendship with Michael Amato begins. I earn his respect. And this allows me to infiltrate white culture. I get introduced to cannoli, lasagna, and the North End. This is a neighborhood where every Grandpa Sal likes a crack at a gook's head with his grandson's hockey stick. At Mike's house I would hear, "These fuckin' chinks and niggas are taking over our neighborhood. Go down to the Italian festival on Saratoga and nuttin' but a bunch of spicks and gooks!" Realizing I'm there, I get Rocky Balboa air jabs followed by, "You're different, you're our friend."

My Cousin Duc, my business associate from the Thai camps, confronts me, "They not your friends, White-boy. Join my posse."

"Duc, no, I won't join your posse. I mean you robbed Cousin Kim's house? How can you guys rob our own people?"

"Asian people don't use banks. All that gold they bring from Vietnam. Fast cash, American way—bitch! Look in the mirror. White people gonna keep you down man. Live fast, die young—American Dream baby."

Being in an Italian gang causes resentment for a lot of Asians. Especially at Boston Latin High. They think I think I'm better than them. To them I'm—a banana—yellow on the outside, white on the inside. A Cambodian gang, the "Khmer Reds," the most violent, vicious posse in Boston, waits after school to jump me for being a Benedict Arnold. My Italian buddies quickly have my back. I step forward, "Fuck you! I'd rather drink beer and steal cars with Michael Amato—than get stuck in an Asian gang. You're stuck. Stuck together. Like fucking sticky rice! Melt muthafuckers!"

> *Announcement interrupts the scene—"Trieu Tran come to Headmaster Connelly's Office." Interior space at school.*

"Premium est esse, quam esse tale." This is on the wall above Headmaster Connelly's desk. "Before you become something, you have to exist first." I am trying to do just that—exist. Not imprisoned by race, by facial aspect—none of that bullshit. This is America for fucksakes. This is Boston. "Mr. Tran, you apparently were involved in a very serious altercation last week on the front steps of my school."

"You have no idea what happened."

"The police report: 'An eye-witness says they saw Trieu Tran shatter the orbital socket of a young Asian male with a blow to the left side of his face—causing permanent blindness'."

"What witness?"

"The police report goes on, "Trieu Tran threatened to have his Chinese gang shoot the young man and he defended himself."

"First of all, I belong to an Italian gang. Second of all, they threatened to shoot me, and I defended myself."

"I don't understand. Straight A's and you're in my office every other week. Conduct yourself like a good Asian student should."

"Headmaster Connelly, what happened on the steps of this school was with one of those 'good Asian students,' Phirun Vanni, who is a 'Khmer Red.' He happens to be the younger brother of their boss-man, Sovann Vanni. I made the mistake of telling them to "Melt Mutherfuckers!" So Phirun pulls a gun and tries to kill me on your school steps. Click, click. It jams. So I hit him. Like any 'good Asian student should'."

"Mr. Tran, I think you'll be a better off—at East Boston High."

EAST BOSTON HIGH:

> *Rap song plays harsh and loud—NWA "Gangsta! Gangsta!"*

At my next school—East Boston High—in AP History—I am taught the Revolutionary War up to World War II, even though the library has a few books on Vietnam. Or should I say, the Vietnam War, from the GI's perspective. I go to my home room teacher, Don: "If I wanted that version of the war I could stick in the VHS of Apocalypse Now, Platoon, Hamburger Hill, and Full Metal Jacket—the lies of "Me Love You Long Time." Where is my father's story? Where are the boat people? And the real Ho Chi Minh? Nowhere to be found."

The next week there are new books in the library and Don personally hands me a biography of Ho Chi Minh. "Trieu, you should join my group of young immigrant men called "The Disciples." "Most of them are 'fatherless' just like you. They know first-hand the struggles of 'refugees.' Maybe you can open up and figure a few things out with these guys. Find some peace." I join the group. For a teacher, Don turns out to be unbelievably cool. An ex-college football star, a brilliant guy and a true friend—he lets us use his house as a haven for open discussion. We can say and feel—whatever we want.

Don re-introduces me to Jesus Christ. We attend mass together. He teaches me the world is full of imperfect people. Everyone, I mean everyone, falls short. After six months of this comforting spiritual journey, Don confides—"Your father speaks to me at night. He begs me, help Trieu, his spirit is troubled. Your dad hurt you—didn't he? That's why you act out and hurt others. *(Kneels.)* Jesus doesn't care what happened yesterday. Relatives are relative. Jesus does not hold grudges nor should you. Forgive your father."

Don takes my hands, "Close your eyes. Lord, this is Trieu. He comes to you tonight, a sinner. Blackness in his heart, he opens it to let you in. Heal him, Lord. Take away his pain. Good, Trieu. Good. Cry. Let it go. That's it—my son. Jesus loves you and . . . your father loves you." Don leans in. He kisses my forehead. So tender. Like the father I never knew. He embraces me. Then he suddenly bear hugs me. Now on top of me and choking me he pants: "I've never done this with anyone before. Nothing in the Bible about two guys—I mean, Jesus never said anything?"

"What are you talking about? I have been fucked with enough. Stop or I swear to fuckin' God! Stop! Please, stop!"

"Trieu. Jesus kissed the apostles. Jesus kissed the apostles. Jesus kissed the apostles."

I shove him away. I hit him. His head cracks back. And hits the floor. I run like I've never run before. I hear my father's voice so vividly, so clearly, like he's running right beside me—he rages, "Stick to your own kind. Stand up and fight, pussy. Kill him! It's hard to be a man in America, isn't it!"

Life at East Boston High becomes a living hell. Don has the balls to persecute me. He tells school security I'm selling drugs so I get harassed everyday. He calls my home and leaves messages trying to entice me back into his house. I'm having a nervous breakdown, so I go to the school counselor—"I am shocked you would fabricate such accusations against a trusted teacher." Desperate, I go to an outside psychologist—"There have been rumors about Don sexually abusing immigrant boys. Boys like you don't have a voice in this world. It's up to you to speak for them." I tell my mom. She says, "This stops now!" We press charges against Don.

In court, it's my word against his. He—denies everything. As word gets out about the case, former students, all refugee boys like me, come forward to accuse Don of sexual abuse. Don is offered a plea bargain, quietly resigns and walks away free. And it becomes clear to me there are two races in America—the Caucasians and the rest of us. I am forced out of East Boston High and on to my next school.

NINA, SHAKESPEARE, AND TUAN:

We soon transform to the beautiful feeling of Nina.

So Buh-bye to Jesus, and fake-fathers. Buh-bye to the streets, and fake-warriors. My future—stares me square in the face. I apply to Boston College High—a Jesuit Prep School. I get in. One last stand. I gotta make this one work. I become obsessed with survivors and survival. I go to hear lots of lectures. Tonight I am at one by Elie Wiesel on his experience while imprisoned in Nazi concentration camps. He says, "Because I remember, I despair. Because I remember, I have the duty to reject despair." Ironically, it's here I meet Nina.

She ushers in a pretty great time in my life. For I fall in love. Not once, but three times. All in the same year. This is highly unusual for me. My ability to maintain a consistent relationship with anyone but my mother is a challenge. I began to think I am really named after the Vietnamese word—'trieu,' meaning 'tide.' Restless and uncertain. Coming into people's lives—only to rush out again. Until Nina . . .

An older woman, she's 19, a freshman at Boston University. She's educated, a beautiful spirit—with the most soulful eyes, turquoise-emerald, like a sky after a violent storm. Peaceful and radiant. Calm, she brings me calm, for the first time in my life. And she introduces me to my second great love, William Shakespeare. Nina is an English major so she's constantly reading his plays. And she asks me to read with her—out loud.

Her vast knowledge of the writer and his work—opens a door into the magical world of language. One afternoon we read "Romeo and Juliet."

The words are powerful. They capture my longing for Nina but also capture my feelings about being caught between clashing cultures that will not let lovers be lovers. That night, I inevitably try and push Nina away, "Nina, I can't do this anymore. You see how people look at us. Even your own family. They look at us with that 'Nina can do better!'— look. Someday you'll find a rich white boy from Chestnut Hill to rescue you from me." She patiently says, "Trieu, Sonnet 109. You can't underestimate the power of these words. Just say the words."

O! never say that I was false of heart,
As easy might I from my self depart
As from my soul which in thy breast doth lie:
That is my home of love

Nina leans into me, "All is well. I'm here. I'm not going anywhere. Live right here—right now, Trieu." Sonnet 109 is our poetic bridge to passionate make-up sex. Nina then takes me to see Henry VI Part 3. I am blown away by the multicultural casting. My face, my voice is there on the stage, present in the greatest struggles of history. I am particularly fascinated by Gloucester. The son fighting for his family, for their blood, their honor at all cost.

And I—like one lost in a thorny wood,
Seeking a way and straying from the way;
Not knowing how to find the open air . . .
But toiling desperately to find it out—

That night, lying in Nina's arms, it hits me. There is purpose in all she does. Every play, every sonnet, every poem she has me read—she wants me to confront something. Nina helps me see my father's life, like Henry VI, speaks to the cycle of blood that can consume the best of men if they get caught in its grasp. My father was suffocated by rivers of blood. I cannot get caught in his current.

Shortly after, I meet my third great love, Tuan. He is an immigrant from Vietnam. FOB—fresh off the boat. But damn, is he smart. We have classes together. Hardly knows the language, and hardly says a word—but he gets straight A's. He is a loner at Boston College High. Not by choice but by his immigrant status. I watch him sit in the cafeteria. And he looks over at me. His loneliness and fear reminds me of me in Canada. But I stay away.

Nina says, "You opened up to me, you can open up to Tuan." "Nina, I just can't take on anyone's troubles right now. Life is too good." "Trieu, do not be afraid of shadows." With the calming voice of Nina in my head—I decide to sit with Tuan at lunch. Tuan can't believe I am dating a white girl. It's beyond his comprehension. See, Tuan is a bit old

72

fashioned, still influenced by traditional thinking. I actually envy his simplicity, but, most of all, his incredible kindness.

I learn Tuan doesn't go home directly after school to his Dorchester Housing Project. "Trieu, only thing waiting for me is my war-torn father. He haunted by terrible demons. We never speak. All is silence. All the time." We have a lot in common. He quickly becomes the brother I never had. So I take it as my task to educate him—on how to live a borderless existence with "skyscraper dreams in the Hip-Hop Nation!" Tuan and I start walking all over Boston. We take to sitting at bus stops—philosophizing.

"There's certain American phrases you're gonna have to learn, Tuan. I can't really explain why being a Red Sox fan is—'like a religion.' It just is."

"Trieu, they always losing man. Why we always on the losing side? I'm tired of being on losing side. I want to win once."

"I know. I'm tired of losing too."

"Trieu, knowledge is key. We must be smarter than everyone just to be in this American game."

"You're right, Tuan. Knowledge! Is our way to win! Tonight, Nina is taking us to see a play. She says this play—is our play!"

That night Nina takes us to see Richard the III. Tuan and I are overwhelmed. We are shocked to find we both identify with Richard. We both are ambitious, but no matter what we do, how much we achieve, how hard we work—we are seen as "abortive rooting hogs, rudely stamped, unfinished." But knowledge will set us free. We decide to memorize the whole play. Tuan and I are sitting at one of our favorite bus stops waiting . . . for what? We have no idea as usual. We recite some "Richard the III" and philosophize.

True hope is swift, and flies with swallows' wings
Kings it makes gods, and meaner creatures kings.

"Tuan, I believe we can reinvent ourselves here, dude. The Irish experienced the same damn bullshit we're going through, and look at them, they run this town!"

"Trieu, I think you right. I will stay here. I'm going to Harvard, be a doctor, so I can bring my family from Vietnam to Boston."

"Dude, check this out. American refugee via Saigon, am I wrong, my skin's yellow my eyes long . . . "

BANG! BANG! Tuan is shot right through the head. His body slumps to the ground. The car reverses and smashes into Tuan.

(Thunder and music.) I should have only taken half of this acid tablet.

73

Calm down, this is the only way Tuan's spirit will speak to me. I must get Tuan's forgiveness. The bullets were meant for me. "The Khmer Reds" settling old gang scores. "Melt mutherfuckers!" I am watching the world move in slow mo'. Maverick Square, East Boston. Waiting for the bus to take me to Tuan's funeral. I love the Red Sox. I love America. I don't want to be like other Viets—isolated and disconnected. I want to be part of this world. But it doesn't want me. The cycle of blood goes on and on. My father's voice pierces through my acid haze, "God cursed the day that you were born. The night that forced you from your mother's womb." If I could drain this damned blood within me—I would. I want to Tu Thu. No! I will avenge your death Tuan. I promise—you will rest in peace.

I run to Cousin Duc's house. His bloodshot eyes are like those of a hunted animal. I avoid watching Duc's new ritual of needle and spoon. He offers me heroin. "No. Duc, I need your car and a gun."

"Hey, you ever seen the pictures of your dad's funeral? Look. Everyone's wearing white and crying. Fuckin' Asians, man, always time for a Kodak moment. Your dad's face always kills my high, man. He definitely a bad ass ghost."

Duc sticks himself with the needle. I look down at Duc's photo album. What's this? In the back is a picture of VU 'THE BULL'!?" There he is with my Uncle Pham in the Thai Refugee Camp when I was there as a kid. Pham knows the man who killed my father. All these years, Pham knows VU and where to find him! And he's the guardian of my dad's ashes! I close my eyes and my father comes to me. Bare-chested, rage in his eyes, an eagle tattoo emblazoned across his chest. Butcher knife in one hand and—now—gun in the other. "You should be the protector of my ashes. Bring me home. Then Kill 'The Bull.' Unless you do this— I will never rest. And nor will you."

"Duc, wake up, man. Take me to the airport! I going to Grandma's to get dad's ashes. Look at this picture. My father's ghost torments me. I must get Uncle Pham to tell me where Vu is. And I must kill 'The Bull' to put an end to all this bullshit!"

Duc grabs me, "Dude, kill Vu, but, please, don't bring your dad's ashes to Boston. He'll kick my ass."

SEATTLE AT LAST:

Puget Sound, Space Needle, mountains.

This first born son, arrives in the Northwest of the United States, Seattle. And I get a dose of petty, fucked-up, Vietnamese dysfunction from my dad's family:

"What happened that night?"

"We wanted to kill that motherfucker, Vu 'The Bull'—grandma stopped us!"

"He only got five years, no justice!"

"In America, he'd get the electric chair!"

"Why didn't you save him. Every little boy can dial 911!"

"STOP! I WILL FIND VU 'THE BULL' and kill him myself! Look at this picture—Uncle Pham. You and Vu. You've known where he's been all along. And you never did a goddamn thing. You coward!"

Uncle Pham breaks the deadly stillness, "Your father comes to us in our dreams—drowning in blood. The priest says your father's soul brings blackness and death. No one wants his ashes. Doesn't matter if I kill Vu. Never did! Only the first-born son can stop this. Only you can end this. Take him. He's yours now."

"Trieu!" Grandma's voice stops me. "It's all big circle. Karma. What price you willing to pay for your father's peace? Your own? You can't drain my son's blood from your veins. It's your legacy. Comets extinguish themselves but memory refuses to die. You can honor you father with a few flowers on his grave. But you can't waste your life tending faded flowers. Someone must die for this to end. Blood for blood. Choose carefully."

FINALLY HOME IN BOSTON:

TRIEU carries the ashes to his mother. Tupac tribute plays.

"Mother, dad is finally home."

"Trieu, your grandma called. I beg you—do not kill Vu 'the Bull.' Be thankful for the things you have. I love you. You helped me endure all these years. That is your gift. I'm begging you, bury this hatred in your heart."

"It's not me. It's him. Death is all around me."

"No, you're angry. Dat Khach que nguoi. 'Lost and lonely in a hostile land.' Your father muttered that in his sleep. Losing Vietnam cost your dad. It cost him—his self. The Vietcong and the Americans cut off his balls. He didn't know how to love you. Forget him."

"I can't. His spirit haunts me. His voice inside me. Tuan is dead. Vu must die for this to end."

"All over the world people know American burgers, blue jeans, luxury

75

cars! We, Vietnamese, we beat the Chinese, the French, the Americans! What are we known for? WAR. BLOOD. Trieu, remember the silvery haired old woman on boat of death, 'Life is never fair. There is always blood. When your choice comes—you save the many. Not just one.' Save us. Live, son."

That night, with my father's ashes by my side, I have this dream. I am in a bathtub, naked, my body stained with blood. In the shadowy waters I see Tuan's face begging for help. I reach for him . . . BANG! BANG! Sitting in the bloody tub across from me—naked—is my father.

It is now dead midnight.
Alack. I love myself. Wherefore? for any good
That I myself have done unto myself?
O, no! alas, I rather hate myself
For hateful deeds committed by myself!
I am a villain: yet I lie. I am not.
My conscience hath a thousand several tongues,
And every tongue brings in a several tale,
And every tale condemns me for a villain.
I shall despair. There is no creature loves me.
It's hard to be a man in America.
Peace with honor—is all I sought in life
Help me find it in the next.

My father holds out a knife to me. I take the knife. *(TRIEU takes knife.)* Kill the rage/the resentment/Silence the thunder/the lightning/In my head/my heart/my soul/that is my father.

RITUAL OF ENDING AND BEGINNING:

> *TRIEU holds the urn out to the audience. Ritual space.*

That dream has vanished but no matter how hard I try: my father remains—a perpetual memory that perpetually takes flight—the caterpillar becoming the butterfly again and again and again.
"Father, the day of my birth, April 20, 1975, did begin a chain reaction of events that forever transformed my life. I hear your voice but I refuse to live in your shadow. Now I carry the voice of Tuan, 'I want to win for once.' Nina, 'Live right here—right now.' Mother and the Silvery Haired Old Woman, 'Save the many, not just one.' Shakespeare, 'We hath long been mad, and scarr'd ourselves/The father rashly slaughter'd his own son/The son, compell'd been butcher to the sire.' Father, I will not continue to kill—to achieve peace with honor."

But I need your help. Let us all embrace the vast, shadowy waters—the ocean—that connects each and every one of us. The same salt is in our tears, the same buoyancy of birth in our hearts—the same darkness in our souls—ashes to ashes—connects each and every one of us.

So I look to the West and seek your blessing. America, free me from rigid Confucian Mores that imprison generation upon generation in ancient rituals of vengeance and violence. America, you seduce me deeper than any French kiss—you wrap my native tongue and leave me butt-naked, delighted with optimism. Teach me to suppress the rage when I hear Jap, Chink, Nip, and Gook. Don't let me lose the hope that this is my home. America—bless me.

I look to the East and seek your blessing. Asia, your sacred blood flows through my veins—free me to love both who I am and who I am becoming. Asia, help embrace new beginnings with the dawning of every sun. Teach me to navigate a world where Uncle Ho's photo is replaced by RUN DMC. Asia, our mothers and fathers labor in kitchens where roaches eat like kings off the plates they serve—let me light the way to give them the respect and compassion they deserve. Asia—bless me.

From "Uncle Ho to Uncle Sam." Now we're in your hands. Now we're your history too. Put us somewhere safe and sacred. Give us peace. Bless us. Bless us all with the belief that we can finally achieve "peace with honor."

THE END

KERI HEALEY's plays include *Torso*, *Cherry Cherry Lemon*, *Penetralia*, *The Ikea Cycle: Tiny Domestic Dramas*, *Parrot Fever (Or, Lies I've Told In Chat Rooms)*, and *Don't You Dare Love Me*. She is currently working on a new script called *T.B.I. (Traumatic Brain Injury)*. A member of Printer's Devil Theater and Seattle Repertory Theatre's Writers Group, Keri has been awarded new works grants by 4Culture, the Seattle Office of Arts & Culture, and Artist Trust, and was shortlisted for The Stranger's 2012 Genius Award in Theater. Keri received the American Theater Critics Association's 2013 M. Elizabeth Osborn New Play Award for *Torso*.

Keri Healey

Torso

Evil is unspectacular and always human, and shares our bed and eats at our own table.
—W. H. Auden

CHARACTERS:

DAPHNE MAAS	female, mid-40s, office worker and sometime writer
EDDIE CAMPILLO	male, 40-50-ish, taxi driver. Also plays TED DANIELS (attorney), PALMER PREWITT (Daphne's former brother-in-law), and DR. BRANDENBURG (the surgeon sued by Daphne's family)
MARLO ROY	female, same age as DAPHNE, former childhood friend, aspiring actor. Also plays ELEANOR STONE (attorney)
DOMINICK ROY	male, mid-30s, MARLO's younger brother, owns a small landscape company, stoner. Also plays DIRECTOR, SAMMY (Daphne's 16-year-old nephew), DR. MELLIS (consulting physician to the lawsuit), and CHRIS JACOBS (teenager, classmate of DAPHNE and MARLO)
TINA SHACKLEY	female, late 20s-early 30s, DOMINICK's girlfriend. Also plays CEIL (Daphne's sister), REPORTER, and WAITRESS

SETTINGS:

Seattle: Motel room, Seattle-Tacoma International Airport taxi stand, Inside of Eddie's taxi, Daphne's apartment front entrance (exterior), Various restaurants and bars, City streets (exterior)

Minnesota: Fringe theater stage, Nana's house (interiors & garage), Dom & Tina's farm (exterior), Interrogation rooms at Sheriff's office

ACT I

SCENE I

This morning. The room is dark. About five A.M. Daphne is asleep on the bed. The light comes on in the adjoining bathroom briefly, but then the door is shut and the room goes back to dark.

ATTORNEY (VOICEOVER): Hello Daphne?

DAPHNE (VO): Hello.

Sound of toilet flushing in adjoining bathroom.

ATTORNEY (VO): This is Eleanor Stone. I want to thank you for participating in this deposition today.

DAPHNE (VO): Of course.

ATTORNEY (VO): On the line with us are Ms. Pearson who will be recording your responses to my questions and your attorney, Ted Daniels.

Sound of water running in adjoining bathroom.

Mr. Daniels will not be asking any questions, but he will be allowed to raise an objection to any question being asked of you.

DAPHNE (VO): I understand.

ATTORNEY (VO): I'm hoping there'll be no need for that, though.

DAPHNE: OK.

ATTORNEY (VO): No need to be nervous.

DAPHNE: OK.

ATTORNEY (VO): I'll try to keep this as simple as possible, OK?

DAPHNE (VO): OK. I'm ready.

The bathroom door opens, spilling light into the room. Eddie emerges, turning off the light as he exits the bathroom. He comes back toward the bed, but does not get into it. He stands by the side of the bed watching Daphne sleep. He picks up a watch from the nightstand, puts it on, tries not to wake her. He plays with the watch, thinks about it, takes it off. Not yet. Can't decide whether to stay or go. Daphne rustles. He watches.

DAPHNE: *(waking up slowly, bleary)* Wha–
    (confused) Who–?
    Ah! *(suddenly terrified)* Oh, God. SHIT!

EDDIE: Hey.

DAPHNE: Please—

EDDIE: Hey, it's me.

DAPHNE: What's—

EDDIE: It's just me. Eddie.

DAPHNE: How did you—
    No. Don't.
    Please, please don't—
EDDIE: Hey, hon. What's the matter?
DAPHNE: Don't hurt me. I won't say any—
EDDIE: Hurt you?
DAPHNE: Just, please, please leave—
EDDIE: Hold on—
DAPHNE: Who are—
    Oh God.
    WHO THE FUCK ARE YOU?!

SCENE 2

The night before. At the Seattle-Tacoma International Airport. Eddie is at the wheel of a taxi. He gets out of the car to open the back passenger side door for Daphne.

EDDIE: No bags?

DAPHNE: Nope. *(She is drunk, a kind of thoughtful, self-amused drunk.)* No . . . baggage.

    Eddie closes the door after Daphne gets into the car. He walks around to the driver's side and gets in. Picks up a log book and makes a note in it.

EDDIE: *(in the mirror)* Where we going, hon?

DAPHNE: Oh. *(thinks)* Uhh, north. Take highway ninety-nine north.
    To Bitter Lake.

EDDIE: And where?

DAPHNE: I moved to BITTER Lake. My ex thinks that's hilarious.

EDDIE: You got an intersection there?

DAPHNE: It's right off of ninety-nine. I'll tell you where to turn when we're close.

    They take off.

DAPHNE: Busy night?

EDDIE: Not really.

DAPHNE: Not yet, huh? Not quite holiday time, huh? Bet you're busy then. I don't go home much for the holidays anymore. To see my family. Do you go home for the holidays?

EDDIE: This IS home.

DAPHNE: Ah. Me, I'm not a big . . . holiday traveler.
    Pause.

I send them gifts, though. You know. For Christmas? I do.

Beat.

Are there, like, busier times of day, though? For you.

EDDIE: Sure.

DAPHNE: What are they?

EDDIE: Specifically?

DAPHNE: Yeah.

EDDIE: The specific hours, you want to know?

DAPHNE: Yes.

EDDIE: Why do you want to know this?

DAPHNE: What do you mean?

EDDIE: How is it helpful for you to know this information?

DAPHNE: I'm. Interested. In your job.

EDDIE: Why?

DAPHNE: It's. Interesting.

EDDIE: No. It's not.

DAPHNE: Sure, it is.

EDDIE: How so?

DAPHNE: You know. It's. People. YOU get to meet people. All kinds of people.

EDDIE: Yeah?

DAPHNE: Hear their stories.

EDDIE: Oh, right.

DAPHNE: What, so you don't like hearing other people's stories?

EDDIE: Not really.

Pause.

DAPHNE: Not very talkative, are ya?

EDDIE: Have you ever thought you're maybe too talkative?

DAPHNE: I'll let that one slide because you might be onto something. But seriously, you're stuck in a car with a stranger for twenty, thirty minutes . . . you don't have anything at all to say them? You're not at all curious about anything about this person?

EDDIE: Ok, how's this: *(feigns interest)* you coming home from anywhere fun?

DAPHNE: See? How hard was that? No, as a matter of fact, I am NOT coming home from anywhere fun. I was actually on my way somewhere tonight.

EDDIE: Oh yeah?

82

DAPHNE: Going outta town. You ever do that? Just take off outta town on the spur of the moment?

EDDIE: Not much.

DAPHNE: Aw, where's your adventurous spirit, huh? Grab your bathing suit, sunglasses, head to Ma-zat-lan. What would you . . . would you bring your . . . wife? Girlfriend? What?

EDDIE: Where were you headed?

DAPHNE: Minnesota.

EDDIE: I'll bite. What's in Minnesota?

DAPHNE: Only life and death matters.

EDDIE: So, why aren't you there now?

DAPHNE: Well, there's a little story behind that. *(almost to self:)* About the quote unquote SAFETY of other passengers. But, then, YOU don't like to hear other people's stories.

EDDIE: Bingo.

DAPHNE: Apparently, the airlines prefer that you consume only THEIR alcoholic beverages. Only after you have boarded THEIR flights. Forget trying to board a plane a little, let's say, "pre-relaxed."

EDDIE: Fear of flying?

DAPHNE: Let's just say, I had a very bad day.

EDDIE: Take a number, lady.

> *Daphne recognizes something about Eddie.*

DAPHNE: Hey. What's your name?

EDDIE: Eddie.

DAPHNE: Eddie.

EDDIE: Yup.

DAPHNE: Eddieeeee. I know you.

EDDIE: Oh yeah?

DAPHNE: Oh my God. I KNOW you.

EDDIE: I don't think so.

DAPHNE: About a year ago.

EDDIE: Not ringing any bells.

DAPHNE: The Elysian? YA-HOO?

> *Flashback to a year ago: Eddie is sitting in a restaurant booth, a half finished beer in front of him. Daphne approaches him at his table.*

DAPHNE: Are you Eddie?

EDDIE: I am.

DAPHNE: I'm Daphne. Hi. I'm glad you found the place.

Daphne slides into the booth across from him.

EDDIE: You come here a lot?

DAPHNE: Sometimes. They've got good soup.

EDDIE: Well, they got shit for beer.

DAPHNE: Huh. Well. The soup's good at least. *(Pause.)* What's that you're drinking?

EDDIE: *(He lifts his bottle, looks at it, and dismisses her question.)* I wanted Salitos.

DAPHNE: I don't know that one.

EDDIE: Something I used to drink when I was growing up.

The WAITRESS stops by.

WAITRESS: *(to Daphne)* Did you want to see a menu?

DAPHNE: No, I . . . hey, do you guys still have that pumpkin flavored ale you were doing a while ago?

WAITRESS: Yup.

DAPHNE: Good. I'll have that.

WAITRESS: I'll be right back.

EDDIE: *(impatient)* Hey. Could we get some chips or something?

WAITRESS: All right. Did you want to order any other food?

DAPHNE: Not right now, thanks.

Waitress leaves. Daphne gives Eddie a polite, first date smile.

So.

They watch each other and the room for a bit, she looking around a little more than he. After a moment:

EDDIE: *(He is looking her over. Not unpleased. His beer is kicking in.)* Mmm . . . mmm . . . mmh.

DAPHNE: What?

EDDIE: A guy sees something. Maybe he likes it.

DAPHNE: Huh.

EDDIE: Am I not supposed to compliment you?

DAPHNE: You just called me "it."

EDDIE: You look different than your picture.

DAPHNE: It was an old picture. I don't keep that many photos of myself lying around.

EDDIE: You oughta get one of them camera phones.

DAPHNE: Maybe. Sometime.

EDDIE: I got one. *(He reaches into his pocket.)* We could take a picture—

DAPHNE: No, don't worry about it.

EDDIE: Come on, it's no big deal. I'll come over there— (*He starts to get up out of his seat and come over to her side of the booth.*)

DAPHNE: No, it's OK.

EDDIE: You don't want a souvenir?

DAPHNE: No. (*She didn't mean to sound so abrupt.*) Not right now.

EDDIE: (*sits back down*) OK. OK. Maybe later. (*Fiddles with his camera a little. Pause. He holds camera up and snaps a quick picture of her.*) Here. See? I'll email this to you so you have a fresh one.

DAPHNE: Great.

EDDIE: So that's how it's gonna be with Eddie, huh?

> Waitress drops off Daphne's drink and a basket of chips and salsa. Awkward silence.

DAPHNE: In your email you said that you work with kids, right? Teenagers?

EDDIE: Street outreach.

DAPHNE: And what does that mean, exactly?

EDDIE: Oh, are we talking "exactly" now?

DAPHNE: I'm interested.

EDDIE: OK. I counsel kids living on the street.

DAPHNE: That's interesting.

EDDIE: It is what it is.

DAPHNE: What's that like?

EDDIE: Drugs, booze, gangs, jail. Most of these kids got no future unless someone steps in.

DAPHNE: And that's you.

EDDIE: Somebody's gotta.

DAPHNE: And how do you help them?

EDDIE: Tell them the truth.

DAPHNE: Which is?

EDDIE: They're worth saving.

DAPHNE: How'd you get into that?

EDDIE: Used to be one of 'em. I was lucky, though. Probably should be dead by now.

DAPHNE: Were you ever in prison?

> He looks at her.

EDDIE: Drink up. You don't get to ask that until your third beer.

> Pause. Daphne is not sure whether he's serious or teasing her.

EDDIE: So, you "write," huh? See, I remembered something from your profile.

DAPHNE: Right.

EDDIE: I'm not as dumb as I look.

DAPHNE: Um, I like to write. I used to do it more. I used to write professionally, I mean.

EDDIE: And now you . . . what? Write unprofessionally?

DAPHNE: There wasn't enough money it. The pay's not regular.

EDDIE: Regular pay. Sounds nice.

DAPHNE: Now I just work in an office.

EDDIE: I should write. I have seen stuff in my life. Whoo. So what did you write? You ever write anything I've seen on TV?

DAPHNE: I never wrote for TV.

EDDIE: So you were never famous?

DAPHNE: Not even close.

EDDIE: Damn. For a minute there, I thought I was gonna be able to brush up next to fame.

DAPHNE: Sorry.

EDDIE: You gotta let me read some of that sometime. What you wrote. *(Eddie flags down the Waitress. Referring to their drinks.)* Two more.

DAPHNE: No, I'm OK.

EDDIE: Bring it. I'll drink it.

DAPHNE: You like to read?

EDDIE: Not much.

DAPHNE: So what do you like to do?

EDDIE: I'm curious. Why'd you pick this place to meet?

DAPHNE: It's close to where I live. It's convenient. And not too crowded.

EDDIE: Everyone's really young here.

DAPHNE: Not so much. You think so?

EDDIE: This is not my neighborhood. Not my people.

DAPHNE: I just thought this would be a nice place to talk and get to know each other a little better.

EDDIE: I want to take you out for a big steak somewhere. Somewhere they got bottles of wine. And dancing.

DAPHNE: That seems like a lot for a first meeting, don't you think?

EDDIE: But it's nice, right? Steak? Lots of music and people smiling, forgetting about their problems. Look around here, everybody looks like they got a bus to catch. No one's relaxed.

DAPHNE: I don't know what you're talking about.

EDDIE: You can see it in their eyes.

DAPHNE: *(giving it another try)* Do you have any family around here?

86

EDDIE: How many of these Yahoo dates you been on?

DAPHNE: Three.

EDDIE: And you always bring them to this same place, right? Close to your house? Convenient?

DAPHNE: You'd think that way too if you were a woman. You'd make sure you're in a place that's familiar and—

EDDIE: Safe.

DAPHNE: And safe.

EDDIE: Like I'm gonna hurt you.

DAPHNE: Women get hurt. It's a fact of life.

EDDIE: Men get hurt, too.

DAPHNE: Statistically, less often than women do.

EDDIE: I got shot once.

DAPHNE: By a date?

EDDIE: I'm just saying, no one's ever safe.

DAPHNE: Have I pissed you off or something?

EDDIE: (mimicking her) Where were you born and what was your father like and when did you have your first wet dream and how much money did you make in your last job . . . What are you doing, treating this like it's your job? Question, question.

DAPHNE: This is what people do on dates. They ask questions. How else am I supposed to learn who you are?

EDDIE: I'm a man, you're a woman.

DAPHNE: So?

EDDIE: You're not gonna learn about me like that.

DAPHNE: Huh.

EDDIE: Look at me. I'm smiling at you. Letting you be. Just relax.

DAPHNE: I AM relaxed.

EDDIE: Let's go somewhere. Get a steak.

DAPHNE: How does one of us think this night is going to end with steak, huh?

EDDIE: Don't be that way.

DAPHNE: I think I'm gonna go to the bathroom, Eddie, and then . . . I'm going home. This was a good try. It's not really a . . . connection, though. Right? You stay and finish your beers.

EDDIE: (by now, pretty buzzed) Fair enough, fair enough. But wait, I'll give you a ride home.

DAPHNE: No thanks, I live nearby.

EDDIE: No, no come on. Let me at least walk you outside.

87

They both get up, Daphne reaching into her purse for money.

No, no, I'll get that. I got it.

She lets him pay. He counts out some bills to leave on the table. They walk out of the restaurant, sort of together, Daphne walking a little bit ahead of Eddie. He is a bit wobbly. At some point, they stop and Daphne turns to Eddie, making it clear that this is where they say goodbye.

DAPHNE: OK. Well, thanks.

EDDIE: *(making some sort of gesture with his hands as if to say "ta-daa")* Safety first.

DAPHNE: Right.

EDDIE: Which way you going?

Daphne makes a sort of non-committal head nod in a vague direction.

Well. That. Is. That.

DAPHNE: *(waiting for him to start walking away first)* You take it easy, OK?

EDDIE: *(tired and a little sad)* Hey now. Don't say 'take it easy' like that. Like it's the last time you're gonna be seeing Eddie.

Daphne watches Eddie walking off, whistling or singing a little song to himself, pulling out his keys and jangling them, trying to hold onto his dignity.

Back to the present, in the taxi.

EDDIE: That was you?

DAPHNE: That was me.

EDDIE: Huh. Well. This day just keeps getting better, don't it?

DAPHNE: Oh, you had a bad day, huh? Did YOU get denied boarding onto a flight you really needed to catch? Did YOU get escorted out of the airport, in front of people and the CHILDREN, like a criminal, just because some uptight airline employee felt that you needed to SOBER UP? And THAT, Eddie, that was just FROSTING on the delicious cupcake-made-of-crap that was today. And now this. YOU.

EDDIE: We're getting kinda close to Bitter Lake. Why don't you give me that address now? Get you home.

DAPHNE: Sure. Whatever. Turn left when you get to 125th, it'll be three blocks and then we'll take a right.

EDDIE: When did you move?

DAPHNE: Huh?

EDDIE: Didn't you use to live over on the other side of town? Over by that place we met at?

DAPHNE: So you do remember.

EDDIE: It's coming back to me.

DAPHNE: Oh, yeah. Moved this year. New place. New life. *(Beat.)* Whatever happened to your street outreach . . . thing? You still do that?

88

EDDIE: You read the papers? Thirty percent cuts in state funding means thirty percent less street outreach.

DAPHNE: Oh.

EDDIE: Yeah. Oh.

DAPHNE: I'm sorry about that. It sounded really . . . int—

EDDIE: Interesting. Yeah. Sure. Everything's interesting.

> *Daphne watches the road out of the taxi's window.*

DAPHNE: (*quietly*) No, that really was.

SCENE 3

> *Marlo is on a stage in Minneapolis. She is just finishing up her delivery of an audition monologue. A Director is seated in the actual audience.*

MARLO: Look up the answers.
Find out what they want to hear and tell it to them.
The doctors, the lawyers, the whole goddamn lot of them.
Learn to lie and live with it.

> *Intentional beat.*

Thank you.

DIRECTOR: Interesting.

MARLO: Yeah?

DIRECTOR: Interesting choice, Marlo.

MARLO: Well, you saw that thing I did at Pegasus Theater, right?

DIRECTOR: Which?

MARLO: Back in May.

DIRECTOR: I'm not sure.

MARLO: "Enough About Me"?

DIRECTOR: Huh?

MARLO: The title.

DIRECTOR: Oh. Yeah.

MARLO: The baby play. All the women are pregnant . . . the childbirth thing.

DIRECTOR: Yeah, yeah. No. I didn't catch that one.

MARLO: Oh.

DIRECTOR: I heard it was pretty—

MARLO: It was good, it was OK. It was–

DIRECTOR: Hal directed that one, right?

MARLO: Hal?

DIRECTOR: Slaughter.

89

MARLO: Oh, no, it was Susan deLile.

DIRECTOR: Oh yeah, yeah. Right. She any good?

MARLO: I liked her, yeah.

DIRECTOR: I haven't seen her stuff.

MARLO: Yeah, well she definitely helped me, you know, take some new approaches to, uh, scene work. But that script was—

DIRECTOR: Yeah, I heard it wasn't great.

MARLO: Well, it was—no it was *fine*. It just. It just was . . . limiting.

DIRECTOR: Right.

MARLO: For me. Acting-wise. So I'm trying some new things out.

DIRECTOR: So, you picked this one.

MARLO: I really related to this character's sense of loss. Powerlessness. She's grieving, but she's so angry by the end of it—

DIRECTOR: So she . . . TELLS us about her anger.

MARLO: Well. She describes what it's doing to her.

DIRECTOR: I'm not interested in people DESCRIBING things to me.

MARLO: But it's internal.

DIRECTOR: Internal doesn't move us forward, Marlo. It doesn't get us to action.

MARLO: I wanted to show you . . . my emotional range.

DIRECTOR: Here's what I'm interested in. Something happens on page one and then something happens on page two and then something happens on page three. The rest is bullshit.

MARLO: OK. I totally get what you're saying.

DIRECTOR: Do you agree?

MARLO: Um. I guess it's sort of a matter of taste.

DIRECTOR: No it isn't, Marlo. It's a matter of boredom.

MARLO: OK.

DIRECTOR: No person on earth wants to hear about someone else's grief. They wanna SEE it. Watch it happen.

MARLO: But not everything's about—

DIRECTOR: Can I be honest with you?

MARLO: Please.

DIRECTOR: I've seen your work.

MARLO: OK.

DIRECTOR: You work hard.

MARLO: Thanks.

DIRECTOR: You're a good team player.

90

MARLO: That's my goal.

DIRECTOR: I'm . . . not looking for a team player.

MARLO: What are you looking for?

DIRECTOR: Meat.

MARLO: I mean, I've done some Mamet stuff in some workshops . . .

DIRECTOR: Not Mamet meat.

MARLO: If you tell me what you want, I can totally go there...

DIRECTOR: Are you the person who lights the match and then runs away?

MARLO: What?

DIRECTOR: Or are you the person who lights the match and then stays to watch the house go up in flames?

MARLO: Oh.

DIRECTOR: Are you THAT person?

MARLO: I've never thought about that.

DIRECTOR: Cuz I see you as the person who THINKS about lighting the match but then makes the sensible choice and puts the match away. Maybe you finger the matchbook in your pocket. Maybe for years. Am I right?

Marlo can't respond.

Of course, I'm just talking about your acting. Rethink this monologue maybe.

MARLO: All right.

DIRECTOR: Make something happen. Strike that match. Put a fucking exclamation point on it.

MARLO: I see what you mean.

DIRECTOR: I'm just giving you my perspective, Marlo. Meat. MEAT. You do what you want.

MARLO: Sure. OK. *Meat.*

Pause.

Um, Shawn, do you think you'll be doing callbacks?

DIRECTOR: Ah. We'll see.

MARLO: OK. Well, when do—Nevermind. Uh. Thank you.

DIRECTOR: No problem. Good to see you.

Marlo starts to leave the stage.

Hey and if you know anyone who's interested, we just lost our stage manager, so send me any phone numbers or just hit me up on Facebook, OK?

MARLO: *(leaving)* OK. All right.

91

SCENE 4

Earlier yesterday. Seattle. Daphne is in her apartment. She is sitting down at a table or on a couch or on the floor, sipping a glass of wine and reading a piece of mail. It is a letter from her attorney accompanied by a settlement check. Open near her is a copy of a deposition. Nearby is a stack of another six depositions; each is several hundred pages long.

DAPHNE: *(To herself. Musing. As if from memory.)* It was line eight-hundred-forty-seven . . . Line eight-hundred-forty-seven . . . It says "She didn't have a wedding."

The phone rings several times. Daphne is confused by the sound and does not get up to answer it right away.

TED DANIELS (VO): Hello, Daphne.

DAPHNE: *(guessing)* Hi, Ted?

Daphne picks up the phone and brings it to her ear.

TED DANIELS (VO): How ya doing? Feel ready for your deposition?

Now Daphne understands what's going on. She is having a flashback. It is six months ago, in this same room, at this same phone. She paces around a bit, with phone in hand.

DAPHNE: Guess so.

TED DANIELS (VO): Ah, it'll go fine.

DAPHNE: What if they ask me about—

TED DANIELS (VO): Just take your time. Breathe. Don't rush.

DAPHNE: OK, I won't. What if I forget things? Dates and . . . I do that.

TED DANIELS (VO): Say you don't remember.

DAPHNE: Have they talked to everybody else already?

TED DANIELS (VO): Yep, they got the whole family.

DAPHNE: And how'd they sound?

TED DANIELS (VO): It's going fine, don't worry.

DAPHNE: My mom? Was she a mess? She didn't go off about Palmer too much, did she?

TED DANIELS (VO): She held up all right.

DAPHNE: And if they ask me about him, what should I say? I want to be honest . . . but I don't want to lose us the case.

TED DANIELS (VO): Go ahead and be honest. But not TOO honest. You don't have to offer up details. I'm going to call Ms. Stone now, OK? Talk to you soon. *(Beat.)* Oh and Daphne, she's going to be very nice to you. Just remember, she's not your friend.

Daphne fidgets around her apartment nervously, readying herself for the phone call. She finally sits down at her dining table, steadying her breath. After a few long moments, the phone rings.

Both the Attorney's and Ted Daniel's lines are voiceovers.

ATTORNEY: Hello Daphne?

DAPHNE: Hello.

ATTORNEY: This is Eleanor Stone. I want to thank you for participating in this deposition today.

DAPHNE: Of course.

ATTORNEY: On the line with us are Ms. Pearson who will be recording your responses to my questions and your attorney, Ted Daniels. Mr. Daniels will not be asking any questions, but he will be allowed to raise an objection to any question being asked of you.

DAPHNE: I understand.

ATTORNEY: I'm hoping there'll be no need for that, though.

DAPHNE: OK.

ATTORNEY: No need to be nervous.

DAPHNE: OK.

ATTORNEY: I'll try to keep this as simple as possible, all right?

DAPHNE: OK. I'm ready.

ATTORNEY: Do you have any questions at this point?

DAPHNE: I don't think so.

ATTORNEY: Good.

DAPHNE: Actually, though, I might be a little nervous.

ATTORNEY: That's pretty natural.

DAPHNE: I don't talk about this much. About her. Not with other people. I might cry.

ATTORNEY: That's understandable.

DAPHNE: I hope I don't. But I might.

ATTORNEY: Why don't we start with something simple then?

DR. BRANDENBURG (VO): Where did the pain start?

ATTORNEY: You are living in Seattle now, correct?

DAPHNE: Yes.

ATTORNEY: When did you move there?

93

DAPHNE: *(careful, trying to be sure to get the date right)* Nineteen-ninety-three.

ATTORNEY: We heard from some of your family members that you moved out there to pursue your writing. Are you still writing?

DAPHNE: I did that for a while. But. It's. Not anymore. I mean, I have a . . . blog. But. No.

ATTORNEY: Growing up, you lived with your family in Minnesota, is that right?

DAPHNE: We moved away during my senior year of high school.

ATTORNEY: What year was that?

DAPHNE: *(careful)* Nineteen-eighty…six. No—five. It was five.

ATTORNEY: To Texas.

DAPHNE: Right.

ATTORNEY: Was your sister, Cecilia, the only one in your family to move back to Minnesota?

DAPHNE: Ceil.

ATTORNEY: Pardon?

DAPHNE: That's what we call her. Ceil. For short.

ATTORNEY: All right.

DAPHNE: Cecilia was too . . . fancy . . . for her. And, yes. She moved back to Minnesota. Years later. She missed it.

ATTORNEY: And your parents and your other siblings all remained living in Texas until the time of Ceil's death, correct?

> *Sound of a heart beating. Sammy appears beside Ceil who sits atop a hospital examination table. Dr. Brandenburg is checking her over.*
> *She is wheezing.*

SAMMY: Can't you SEE my mom is DYING?!

DR. BRANDENBURG: Your mother isn't dying.

SAMMY: She's crying. She never cries. And she can barely sit up.

DR. BRANDENBURG: Ma'am, can you tell me, where did the pain start?

> *They disappear.*

ATTORNEY: Can you tell us about your relationship with your sister, Ceil?

> *Ceil appears.*

CEIL: Hey, dufus.

ATTORNEY: Were the two of you close?

DAPHNE: *(to CEIL)* It's Daffy.

CEIL: OK, dufus.

DAPHNE: Stop calling me that.

CEIL: Whatever you say, dufus.

> *Ceil disappears.*

DAPHNE: *(back in deposition)* My dad nicknamed me "Daffy."

ATTORNEY: Excuse me?

DAPHNE: Yes, we were. Close.

ATTORNEY: Even after you moved to Seattle, you remained close?

DAPHNE: I would say so.

ATTORNEY: You would talk on the phone . . .

> *Ceil appears.*

CEIL: Hey you.

ATTORNEY: . . .visit her . . .

CEIL: I can't sleep. Tell me a story.

Ceil disappears.

ATTORNEY: . . .how often, would you say?

No response from Daphne.

ATTORNEY: Daphne?

DAPHNE: Is there a special number?

ATTORNEY: Pardon?

DAPHNE: Is there a specific number of phone calls that tells you we were close?

ATTORNEY: Of course not.

DAPHNE: Because write THAT number down. Whatever it is. Because I don't remember how many times we called.

TED DANIELS: It's all right, Daphne. To the best of your recollection.

Pause.

DAPHNE: Once a week. Sometimes more, sometimes less.

ATTORNEY: Did you visit your sister in Minnesota much?

DAPHNE: Just one time.

ATTORNEY: And did she ever travel to Seattle to visit you?

DAPHNE: She never got the chance.

ATTORNEY: Was there ever a time in your relationship with your sister that you didn't communicate frequently? When you didn't remain close?

A memory.

DAPHNE: You can't just leave Sammy at mom and dad's like that, Ceil.

CEIL: They don't have a problem with that.

DAPHNE: They didn't know where you were.

CEIL: They said it's OK, they would watch him.

DAPHNE: They had no idea where you were. For THREE DAYS. That's not babysitting. That's child abandonment.

CEIL: I didn't abandon anything.

DAPHNE: Mom had me calling hospitals. Jesus.

CEIL: For chrissake, I'm here now. I'm taking care of him. You don't know what it feels like.

DAPHNE: Just don't take off like that again. Call them if you get tied up at work. Or stay out all night.

CEIL: Cuz you know everything, right? You come in and tell me what to do then go right back to college and know NOTHING about what I have to deal with.

95

DAPHNE: You chose this.

CEIL: So what?

DAPHNE: You CHOSE this, so don't bitch about me being in school. Don't bitch about me getting to do whatever because I'm working for what I get.

CEIL: Oh, cuz you're so responsible, aren't you?

DAPHNE: Maybe. Yeah.

CEIL: And I'm just a fuckup.

DAPHNE: Don't start.

CEIL: Yep, I'm the fuckup.

DAPHNE: You have a kid. Be mad at me and blame me and hate me, I don't care. You have a kid. And I didn't tell you to have a kid. When you told me you were having a baby, what did I say, huh?

CEIL: Yeah, you would love it if Sammy didn't exist.

DAPHNE: But he does. Does that matter to you at all?

CEIL: You don't know. You have no idea what I have to deal with.

DAPHNE: Get that asshole boyfriend of yours to help.

CEIL: Shut up.

DAPHNE: Just. *(exasperated)* Fucking grow up.

    Memory dissolves.

ATTORNEY: How long was it before you spoke to your sister again?

DAPHNE: Maybe a year. *(Beat.)* Maybe more.

ATTORNEY: Would you say your sister took a lot of risks in the way she lived her life?

DAPHNE: Do you mean, is this her fault? That she died?

ATTORNEY: That's not what I'm asking.

DAPHNE: Because it's SOMEONE's fault.

ATTORNEY: Let's go back—

DAPHNE: No, she didn't take risks. She just took longer. To grow up. She settled down, though, and things got more stable with Sammy and . . . she was doing well.

ATTORNEY: And it was then that you moved to Seattle? After things . . . stabilized?

DAPHNE: Yeah. *(correcting:)* Yes.

ATTORNEY: Let's talk a little bit about Cecilia's home life. She eventually got married.

DAPHNE: Right.

ATTORNEY: Did you ever spend much time with her husband, Palmer Prewitt?

DAPHNE: *(She considers how to word this.)* I never got to know him very well.

ATTORNEY: Did you understand their marriage to be a good one?

 PALMER appears.

PALMER: *(forcefully.)* Hey, get back here and fold these fucking sheets!

 PALMER disappears.

DAPHNE: I didn't spend that much time with them. Together.

ATTORNEY: Your sister never talked about their relationship with you?

DAPHNE: Not really.

ATTORNEY: Not on those weekly phone calls you shared?

DAPHNE: We mostly talked about Sammy.

ATTORNEY: Did you attend their wedding?

DAPHNE: No.

ATTORNEY: Were you and Cecilia still estranged at that point?

DAPHNE: There WAS no "estrangement." It was—

ATTORNEY: Why didn't you attend your sister's wedding?

DAPHNE: She didn't HAVE a wedding.

ATTORNEY: Could you repeat that?

DAPHNE: *(In a fantasy sequence, she tries to explain what she actually meant. These words are not heard by the attorneys. Perhaps the lights can shift to indicate a heightened, in-Daphne's-mind-only moment.)* Not a WEDDING-wedding, it was just gonna be a, you know, a little get together after she and Palmer got back from the justice of the peace, with some drinks and chips and salsa and a cake and all that. It was all so spur of the moment. Ceil didn't EXPECT that we'd all be able make it. She only gave us a week's notice and even if I had wanted to be there, I couldn't afford to get a plane ticket at that point. She understood this. And, I sent her a crockpot afterwards. And she loved that. And so, yeah, I didn't go. I didn't watch her get married. But, I promise you, it wasn't a big deal.

 Back to reality.

ATTORNEY: Daphne?

TED DANIELS: Daphne, are you still there?

ATTORNEY: We didn't get your last response. Do you need me to repeat the question?

DAPHNE: Huh?

ATTORNEY: The question was: why didn't you attend your sister's wedding?

DAPHNE: Oh. *(Pause.)* She didn't have a wedding.

ATTORNEY: Did you say she didn't have a wedding?

TED DANIELS: Can we take a break now?

ATTORNEY: Can you clarify that answer please?

TED DANIELS: Ms. Stone, my client needs to take a break now. Daphne? Daphne?

> *Daphne just stares. Lights change to indicate an end of the flashback and a return to the present. Daphne is absolutely alone in this. She looks back at the printed deposition copy in front of her.*

DAPHNE: *(bereft)* Line eight-hundred-forty-six. *(reading)* "Ms. Stone: Why didn't you attend you sister's wedding?" . . . and then I said . . . line eight-hundred-forty-seven . . . I said that she . . . I thought I said . . . but it just says . . . *(Beat. Reads.)* "She didn't have a wedding." *(Beat.)* That's all I said.

SCENE 5

> *In Dominick and Tina's bedroom, at Nana's house.*

DOMINICK: *(Looking out the window of his bedroom. Quietly, to himself.)* Motherfuck. Thinks nobody's watching him. *(calling to TINA who's in another room)* See that kid out there, Tina? Whaddaya think he's up to? Just pacing out there?

TINA: *(comes into the bedroom, brushing her teeth)* What are you talking about?

DOMINICK: Punk on the cell phone. Out there.

TINA: We gotta get in to work, Dominick.

DOMINICK: Whaddaya think he thinks he's gonna pull off?

TINA: *(She comes over to window and looks out quickly.)* I dunno. Just looks like a dumb high school kid.

DOMINICK: He's casing.

TINA: Nah.

DOMINICK: He's checking that place out. See? Standing there. Then walking up and down.

TINA: You're paranoid.

DOMINICK: He's just pacing and waiting.

TINA: You always think that shit.

DOMINICK: Nobody's good these days.

TINA: *(laughs)* Shut up.

DOMINICK: [If] you're not at school and you're not at work, you're no place. And no place is a place you're gonna find trouble. You WANT trouble.

TINA: C'mon. Get ready.

DOMINICK: I'm telling you.

TINA: You sound like your grandma.

DOMINICK: She should know. This place got broke into twice before I moved in.

TINA: (teasing him) You're like her sexy little pitbull.

DOMINICK: Stop it.

TINA: (tickling him) Guard dog!

DOMINICK: Get off.

TINA: Aw, I think it's nice you look after your grandma.

DOMINICK: Look at him. Hoodie. Cell phone. He's checking who's home, who's in their yard, who's got babies and dogs. Who's old. Who's gonna open the door. He's looking for cars. Looking over his cell phone into the back seats of cars. Just peeking like he thinks no one suspects what he's doing. I see you, buddy. Right here. Looking for laptops and UPS boxes. Anything you can take, right. Ain't got no respect that somebody earned that stuff. He never earned nothing himself.

TINA: Good thing you don't got shit here for him to steal.

DOMINICK: Doesn't matter. You don't got shit, they'll still take it.

TINA: Dom, you are getting totally paranoid. As if you never stole nothing outta the back of someone's car. (laughs) I'm sure!

DOMINICK: You grow up, though, Tina. He don't even care. This guy. Doesn't even know about showing up on time, clocking in. Look, he's laughing. Motherfuck on the other end of the phone probably made some stupid joke. Ten years from now, you think he's gonna remember that joke? Think it's gonna make one single difference in the way he gets to conduct his life? Right now, though, that stupid fuck is laughing like that joke's as important as his first day of kindergarten. Like it's a classic. Motherfuck doesn't even know anything about real life.

TINA: Then call the police.

DOMINICK: What're THEY gonna do?

TINA: If you're worried, you should call the police.

DOMINICK: Tina?

TINA: What?

DOMINICK: C'mere. (She comes close to him and wraps her arms around his waist.)

TINA: What, baby?

DOMINICK: You see me as good father material, don't you?

TINA: Sure.

DOMINICK: I could make a good father figure to someone, right?

TINA: Sure, baby.

DOMINICK: You never tell me that no more.

TINA: But I think it.

DOMINICK: You promise?

TINA: I see you at every Christmas, baby, carving turkey for everybody.

DOMINICK: Ham. Ham for Christmas.

TINA: Sure, ham.

DOMINICK: And I'll always have enough presents for all our kids, right?

TINA: We're gonna have at least three or four.

DOMINICK: All of them get ten presents each.

TINA: You know it, baby.

DOMINICK: *(to himself)* I can do this. Keep telling me that, Tina. Don't stop telling me, OK?

TINA: C'mon, Dom, we gotta get going. Jimmy'll be all over your ass if you're late getting out to Woodland Creek. He says the leaves are getting bad out there.

DOMINICK: Yeah. OK. Go start the car.

Tina leaves. Dominick stares out the window a little longer. Makes a gun with his hand, aims it at the kid outside, and mouths "pop" as he fires it at the boy. Then he saunters out of the bedroom.

SCENE 6

Eddie's cab. In front of Daphne's apartment building.

EDDIE: That's sixty-one-ten.

Daphne pulls a bunch of bills from her bag and gives them to Eddie. He makes change. She tries to figure out the tip.

DAPHNE: You mind, uh, waiting till I get inside? That girl that was stabbed last year? In the doorway? That was right over on that block over there.

EDDIE: All right.

DAPHNE: I mean, I might not be your favorite person, but you certainly don't want me to get stabbed in my doorway. Or maybe . . .

EDDIE: I'll wait.

DAPHNE: I wish I had something more . . . SOMETHING . . . to say to you—

EDDIE: Overtalking again.

DAPHNE: But. Thanks. You know. For the ride.

Eddie waits and watches as Daphne walks to her door. She digs down into her large handbag, rifling for her keys. Can't find them. This goes on for a while. Frustrated, she finally dumps her purse on the ground and sifts through all the junk.

EDDIE: Everything OK?

Daphne shakes her head and keeps sifting.

EDDIE: What's the trouble?

DAPHNE: Keys.

Eddie gets out of the cab and walks over to her.

DAPHNE: I can't find my keys.

EDDIE: You gonna be able to get in?

DAPHNE: They gotta be here.

EDDIE: Maybe you can ring a neighbor?

DAPHNE: I don't—Goddamn it.

EDDIE: Look, I, uh...I gotta get back to the airport.

DAPHNE: I know, I know. Can you just please wait here a second till I— Goddamn it. I know I had . . . *(starts retracing her steps aloud)* . . . I had them at the airport. I was at the counter and then . . . I—with my boarding pass—I went . . . OK to the—no, I stopped, first I stopped at the bathroom, and then to get something to drink, no, before that, some magazines at the newsstand and—

EDDIE: I GOTTA get going.

DAPHNE: No, wait wait wait! I think, I think, no I can't remember, I mean I'm pretty sure they were with me but now that I'm actually thinking about it, I don't remember for sure whether I dumped them into that tray thingy at security. I mean, I don't remember actually seeing them. In there. Of course, those security guys could've taken them—

EDDIE: Think. Could you have lost the keys somewhere else BEFORE you got to the airport?

DAPHNE: Well, Eddie, I made a few stops this evening on my way to the airport.

EDDIE: Oh, jeez.

DAPHNE: I left here after I got the mail. In my car. Went to the bank. Drove over to Becky's to drop off—

EDDIE: Short version.

DAPHNE: I'm thinking! *(She thinks.)* Pizza! I got a slice of pizza.

EDDIE: OK, you wanna call that place?

DAPHNE: That was my FIRST stop.

EDDIE: Oh, Jesus.

DAPHNE: Take me there?

EDDIE: Nah, I gotta get back.

DAPHNE: Could you take me there and I'll look around?

EDDIE: Just call them.

DAPHNE: You'd still need to take me over there to pick them up if they have 'em.

EDDIE: You call 'em now, they say they got the keys. You pick them up in the morning. Go sleep this off.

DAPHNE: Who knows where those keys'll be by morning, Eddie? Plus my car. I left it over there.

EDDIE: Over where?

DAPHNE: Capitol Hill.

EDDIE: Oh man.

DAPHNE: I took a cab from the Hill to the airport.

EDDIE: Why'd ya do that?

DAPHNE: This trip was all very . . . impromptu, Eddie! C'mon, I have money. I'll pay you just as much as the airport people would. More.

EDDIE: I don't need to be running drunks all over hell and back tonight.

DAPHNE: Hey.

EDDIE: Tonight's just not the night, hon.

DAPHNE: You say that like this is me all the time. Like this is the way I just am. I'm not.

EDDIE: Look here—

DAPHNE: What you see here tonight, this isn't me. This . . . state I'm in, there's a good reason.

EDDIE: There always is.

DAPHNE: Now, I'm not saying you don't have problems. But today, today was—

EDDIE: Look, I feel for ya, but I think you're gonna be a hell of a lot better off if we can get you inside.

Daphne sinks down onto the ground and considers herself, surrounded in the detritus of her belongings. Starts to cry a very tired cry.

DAPHNE: Look at me. I can explain this. So much has happened.

After a moment, Eddie crouches down on the ground near her.

EDDIE: It doesn't matter.

DAPHNE: Right. Cuz why would you care?

EDDIE: Tomorrow, you'll start fresh. You'll feel better. You can find your keys. You can go back to the airport and get on that plane.

DAPHNE: It'll be too late.

EDDIE: Too late for what?

DAPHNE: To solve it.

EDDIE: What are you trying to solve tonight, huh?

DAPHNE: A murder.

EDDIE: You a detective now?

DAPHNE: No.

EDDIE: A reporter?

DAPHNE: More of a . . . concerned citizen.

EDDIE: Who was murdered?

DAPHNE: This guy in Minnesota.

EDDIE: And you are very *concerned* about this guy?

DAPHNE: It's not who was killed that matters. It's who DID the killing.

EDDIE: And who was that?

DAPHNE: I can't tell you that.

EDDIE: Why not?

DAPHNE: Because it's just speculation right now.

EDDIE: Oh.

DAPHNE: It's "alleged."

EDDIE: I see.

DAPHNE: But I don't think she did it.

    Beat.

EDDIE: Why not?

DAPHNE: Cuz the guy was her brother.

EDDIE: The guy she killed?

DAPHNE: And her accomplice was her other brother.

EDDIE: That's fucked up.

DAPHNE: And see, she wouldn't do that.

EDDIE: People can do a lot of shitty things.

DAPHNE: Normal people just don't kill their brothers.

EDDIE: Some do.

DAPHNE: But I know her.

EDDIE: Like personally?

DAPHNE: We grew up together.

EDDIE: I know a lot of people—[could] surprise you what they're capable of.

DAPHNE: But murder?

EDDIE: And worse.

DAPHNE: What's worse than murder?

EDDIE: Leaving your victim alive.

DAPHNE: *(horrified)* Eddie. God.

    Beat. Thinks about it.

  Huh. That's what my mom said, too.

EDDIE: Yeah?

DAPHNE: When my sister died. My mom said the only thing worse she could imagine was if my sister was kept alive on machines. Death was kind, she said.

> *Pause.*

EDDIE: You lost your sister, huh?

DAPHNE: Yeah.

EDDIE: Mine's gone, too.

> *Pause.*

DAPHNE: It's a hell of club, ain't it?

> *Pause.*

EDDIE: And that's all that needs to be said about that.

> *They sit there for a long quiet moment.*

EDDIE: So, this murderer—

DAPHNE: Alleged.

EDDIE: You think she didn't do it.

DAPHNE: If she did, there's gotta be a good reason, right?

EDDIE: There are good reasons for that sort of thing?

DAPHNE: I have to find out why.

EDDIE: What does it matter to you?

DAPHNE: It just does.

EDDIE: This is important to you?

DAPHNE: Very.

EDDIE: So, you gotta go to Minnesota.

DAPHNE: Yes.

EDDIE: Tonight.

DAPHNE: I need to go there and talk to her. Face to face.

> *Pause.*

EDDIE: Then we better find those keys.

> *Slowly, Eddie helps Daphne up from the ground and they gather the stuff from her bag and get into his cab.*

104

SCENE 7

REPORTER (VOICEOVER): The brother and sister of a missing Hennepin County man have been arrested and accused of killing him and burning his body in a dispute over a family business. Anson Roy's body was found in a fire at a farm located in rural Redwood County. Siblings Dominick and Marlo Roy of Minneapolis were booked into the

Hennepin County jail Friday on suspicion of second-degree murder. Dominick Roy's girlfriend, Tina Shackley, was also arrested and is suspected of participating in the murder.

Dominick is sitting at a table in a police interrogation room.

DOMINICK: Can I get a glass of water?

Pause.

Or something? Mountain Dew? No, no water's probably better. I'm real dry. My throat.

Pause.

How long's this gonna take, you think?

Beat.

No, no. I don't gotta get anywhere, I got medicine to take. I gotta stay on schedule.

Beat.

Yeah, well I wanna be helpful, but—thing is—I just don't know what happened out there. I was, I wasn't there.

Beat.

Is that what this is about? A fire?

Beat.

I dunno why anyone was out there having a fire so late. I can't tell you cuz I wasn't there. Have you talked to Marlo yet?

Beat.

She's my sister. Have you talked to her yet? Marlo can tell you what, what, whatever happened. She was out there at the farm, wasn't she?

On another area of the stage, Marlo is being interrogated.

MARLO: Oh yeah, that. Well, the thing about that restraining order was, it was totally unnecessary. It was something my brother Anson cooked up to throw suspicion off of himself. HE was the one breaking the law, see? So he had to make me and Dominick look bad.

DOMINICK: I can give you Marlo's cell. Call her .

MARLO: We never harassed Anson. Never. I never violated that restraining order.

DOMINICK: She can straighten this out. I was not there. She'll tell you that.

MARLO: Of COURSE, I was angry about it at first.

DOMINICK: Give me a pencil, k? I'll write down her number.

MARLO: No, I wasn't even angry. I was UPSET. I was hurt.

DOMINICK: Come on, ask her. I'm telling you, I wasn't there.

MARLO: I mean, this is a FAMILY MEMBER.

DOMINICK: Well, yes, EARLIER. I was there earlier. Like, yesterday. But not when you say she had this fire going. I don't know about that. I had to leave.

MARLO: How do you think YOU'D respond to a complete and utterly unexpected betrayal by your BROTHER?

DOMINICK: I had to leave to get back to the city. I had to get to work today. I mean, I'm supposed to be at work right now, but I'm . . . here.

MARLO: See, the thing about Anson—we found out—is, he isn't as honest as he had everyone believing. He comes off like this family man, like this guy you could trust, and we TRUSTED him. But he's smart. He just has a sense for what people want to hear, what they want to believe. And he played us. He played everybody. Now, maybe you could say that's how the game is played. That's how life works. Maybe you could say we could all learn something from my brother. But I don't want to live in that kind of cynical world.

Lights off on Marlo.

DOMINICK: Look, no, yeah I told Marlo . . . she was, well she was out there anyway, you know, picking up some things . . . from the farm, we had some furniture she was gonna take, and . . . so I told her if she was gonna be there, she might as well . . . I told her I had a bunch of leaves I had to get rid of. And I told her if she was gonna be there anyway, could she burn these leaves? I wasn't aware that the fire was illegal. That's my bad. If I steered her wrong, telling her to burn those leaves, that's on me. Totally.

Beat.

Yeah, leaves. If she was burning anything else, I don't know about it. Leaves is all I know was in that fire. I told Tina, she's my girlfriend, I said can you just make sure that if Marlo makes a fire that it's totally out before you go to bed? And then I left.

Beat.

Yeah, Tina was staying there. Just for the night. She was getting, like I said, the furniture—

Beat.

For Marlo.

Beat.

Marlo was there WITH Tina.

Beat.

Huh? What truck?

Beat.

No, I took my car back to the city. What TRUCK?

Beat.

Oh, the Silverado? That, that's Tina's truck. What about it?

Beat.

SHIT, I don't know anything about NO blood in NO truck. Can someone please tell me what the FUCK is going on here?!

Daphne and Eddie are in the pizza joint. Eddie is reading aloud from Daphne's phone.

EDDIE: *Blood was found on the driveway of the exterior of the victim's house, on the trees, and on property landscaping.* Geez, on the TREES?

DAPHNE: I told you. Keep reading.

EDDIE: *Within the pool of blood, authorities found a pair of pants consistent in size to Anson Roy, a latex glove, and the broadhead from an arrow.* What the fuck?

DAPHNE: *(taking the phone from him) Two bottles of bleach and cans of black spray paint were found in the Chevy Silverado pick-up truck that Tina Shackley was driving when she was later arrested.*

EDDIE: I don't get the black paint.

DAPHNE: *In a wood pile near Anson Roy's house, authorities found a crossbow and a bloody baseball bat. Both items were painted black.*

EDDIE: What's that? Like camouflage?

DAPHNE: *The suspects allegedly drove Anson Roy's body to a farm owned by Tina Shackley in Jackson County, about two hundred miles from the scene of the Twin Cities murder.*

EDDIE: So, this guy is killed at his house but then the body is found way out in the country?

DAPHNE: *The Jackson County sheriff's office got a call to investigate an illegal fire after midnight at the Shackley farm.* Probably a neighbor calling that in, right?

EDDIE: *At about one A.M., the sheriff arrived at the farm and found Marlo Roy alone, tending the fire.* This is the one that's your friend, right? This Marlo person.

DAPHNE: *(overriding him) When asked about the fire, Marlo allegedly told police . . .*

MARLO: That's not my brother. That's not my brother...in there.

DAPHNE: *It was at that moment that police spotted in the fire what appeared to be...a human torso.*

ACT 2

SCENE I

Eddie and Daphne are in his taxi, Eddie is driving. Daphne is in the back seat.

DAPHNE: OK, but what I'm saying is, in order to kill someone—I'm talking about KILLING someone here—someone in your family, someone that you LOVE—

EDDIE: This guy was shot with a crossbow. That's a hunter's weapon, you know.

DAPHNE: Well, they're in Minnesota.

EDDIE: Are you saying it was just "handy"?

DAPHNE: I'm saying I bet people in Minnesota HAVE crossbows. It's not that unusual.

EDDIE: Plus he was beaten to death with a baseball bat. AND run over by a Volkswagon Passat. *(Beat.)* Before being burned in a fire.

DAPHNE: Your point?

EDDIE: And we won't even get into how his head and limbs got disconnected from his body before he got put into that fire.

She is quiet. Just stares at him. He looks back at her, either in the taxi's mirror or leaning back over the seat.

EDDIE: And you're convinced that these are people who love each other.

DAPHNE: I went to school with them.

EDDIE: But did you go home with them every night?

DAPHNE: Their family wasn't one of those families.

EDDIE: You don't know that.

DAPHNE: I do know.

EDDIE: You CAN'T know the shit that people are capable of. Lots of 'em can show up the next day with a smile on their face.

DAPHNE: I don't have my head in the sand, I know how dysfunctional families work.

EDDIE: Yeah, but you think this happens to other people, not people like you and your friends.

DAPHNE: I don't think that.

EDDIE: You're a snob.

DAPHNE: No.

EDDIE: Face it, you're a snob. But you can unlearn that.

DAPHNE: Simmer down, Dr. Phil. I just don't think that you change that much, that . . . that your moral code changes that fundamentally during your life. If a kid is lighting fire to cats' tails at seven years old, I think we can all agree where that's headed. But to go from here waaaaay over to THERE in terms of your basic, moral compass in the course of twenty or thirty years . . . I just don't believe that.

EDDIE: Hey, even nice people snap. How long has it been since you've seen these folks?

DAPHNE: It's been a while.

EDDIE: What, like, five years?

DAPHNE: More than that.

EDDIE: Ten?

DAPHNE: We haven't been in touch since I moved away. *(noticing something outside her window)* Hey, that's the place, right there. Just pull over and I'll run in.

EDDIE: How long ago was that?

Daphne gets out of the taxi.

DAPHNE: I was seventeen.

Eddie turns on the radio in the taxi. Lights up on Marlo.

MARLO: That house over there—the dark green one—that's where Scott Parvey used to bury frog bodies. This was back when they were just building it, back when it was just a cement foundation and some lumber. We'd come out here on our bikes and watch the construction workers pour the cement and after they'd leave for dinner, we'd sneak onto the site and try to find some patches of wet concrete to stick our hands into. Sometimes we'd stick in some leaves or stones. Just to leave a mark. Well, Scott Parvey used to catch frogs and keep 'em in jars in his mom's laundry room. Every once in a while, you know, a frog would die. And he'd bring 'em over here while we were playing. He'd bury 'em right up against the foundation. This was gonna be the biggest house in the neighborhood and we didn't know who was gonna live here yet. We were all excited to find out if the new people had kids. Don't you remember being a kid and knowing every single person who moved in and out of our neighborhood? I can't even imagine that anymore.

Daphne returns to the taxi and gets into the front passenger seat.

EDDIE: Back seat.

DAPHNE: Aw, come on.

EDDIE: Get in the back. You find the keys?

DAPHNE: They didn't have them either.

EDDIE: Jesus. Did you look around yourself? Or did you just ask some asshole up front if they found some keys?

DAPHNE: I looked around.

EDDIE: Because they could be on the floor and no one noticed. Or prolly wound up between some seat cushions somewhere.

DAPHNE: I told you, I looked.

EDDIE: Didn't take you very long.

DAPHNE: I didn't want to keep you waiting.

EDDIE: Well, I want you to be thorough.

DAPHNE: OK, so now what?

EDDIE: Hon, we've been to four places and no keys have turned up.

DAPHNE: They have to be somewhere.

EDDIE: Don't focus on the keys, focus on—

DAPHNE: We need to get out of this car is what we need to do.

EDDIE: What?

DAPHNE: We need to walk.

EDDIE: Why?

DAPHNE: Because that's how I think. Walk with me and we'll look around and we'll see signs and people and cracks in the sidewalk and I'll remember what I'm forgetting.

> *They get out of the car and start to walk. As they exit the cab, Eddie reaches under his seat to pull out a gun and tuck it into his belt. Daphne catches this.*
>
> *After a moment:*

EDDIE: You mind if I ask—

DAPHNE: Oh, now you grew a politeness gene? *(mimics him)* 'Mind if I ask?'

EDDIE: You finished?

DAPHNE: Go on.

EDDIE: What were you doing going to all these places tonight? I mean, we're talking about bars here—

DAPHNE: One place was just for pizza.

EDDIE: OK. So. None of my business, but . . . what the fuck, how many bars you need to hit before you get on an airplane?

DAPHNE: It wasn't about the plane.

EDDIE: No? Was it about your friend?

DAPHNE: No.

EDDIE: What was it? You get dumped? Fired? Evicted? What?

DAPHNE: I got a check.

EDDIE: What?

DAPHNE: In the mail today. Four thousand two hundred and twelve dollars.

EDDIE: So you were drinking to celebrate?

DAPHNE: Quite the opposite.

EDDIE: Sounds like a happy thing to me.

DAPHNE: You'd think, right? But it comes with a story.

EDDIE: Naturally.

DAPHNE: And I know you don't like to hear those.

EDDIE: Right.

DAPHNE: But maybe if there's blood and guts and everything, maybe you'd be willing to listen?

EDDIE: Try me.

>   *Lights change.*

DAPHNE: My sister Ceil had a little boy who was five years old by the time she met Palmer Prewitt. They were seated next to each other at the blackjack table at the Little Six Casino in Prior Lake, Minnesota. He was showing a Three and a Seven on the table when she split her Tens and, miraculously, got dealt two Aces right before his next turn, breaking the only rule of etiquette that ever mattered to that man.

>   *Ceil and Palmer are sitting at a blackjack table.*

PALMER: You don't do that, you know. You're never supposed to split your Tens.

CEIL: I don't know 'bout that. Seems to have worked out all right for me.

DAPHNE: And that's the story Palmer and Ceil would tell for the next decade, about how their romance started. How they met like people in the movies do. How they winked and laughed and told each other their stories over drinks—how she was

CEIL: an up-by-my-bootstraps single mom studying to be a dental assistant

DAPHNE: and how he was

PALMER: an entrepreneur with a saw and a hammer and a pickup truck

DAPHNE: who took one look at all of those tudor-esque suburban mega-houses peppering the Twin Cities and saw buckets and buckets of gold. They dated. They moved in together. Got married. One day, Ceil felt sick. Went to the emergency room out near their place in Shakopee, her teenage son, Sammy, driving her there. She and Sammy sat in the waiting room for three hours before someone finally examined her.

SAMMY: Can't you SEE my mom is DYING?!

DR.BRANDEBURG: Your mother isn't dying.

SAMMY: She's crying. She never cries. And she can barely sit up.

DR.BRANDENBURG: Ma'am, can you tell me, where did the pain start?

DAPHNE: *(to Ceil)* And that is the question I beg you to consider carefully when it's asked of you.

DR. BRANDENBURG: *Where did the pain start?*

DAPHNE: Because if you try to paint an honest picture of your pain . . . if you try to be accurate—

CEIL: It started out small, like a stomachache—

DAPHNE: If you try to tell them that your pain became sharper and more defined as the day went on, causing you to lose concentration and mix up names and forget how to answer the phones, and then—

CEIL: Moved up, into my chest, it pounded and became warm—

DAPHNE: Flushing your upper chest with a lava-like feeling, a blood explosion, before once again turning into sharpness, into tiny edges of broken glass that cut at your tissue—

CEIL: Stabbing from the inside over and over again—

DAPHNE: If you tell them things happened in this way, you risk being shooed away, misdiagnosed. They might misread your pain, this pain that—

CEIL: Started in my *belly*—

DAPHNE: Might assume it to be—

DR. BRANDENBURG: Indigestion.

DAPHNE: *Because* it started in your belly and not in your chest. Might believe that you are a hypochondriac and might tell you that you're overreacting. Maybe they'll jack you up on lidocaine to take away some of that pain, and send you home, tell you to just go to bed and—

DR. BRANDENBURG: Call tomorrow if you don't feel better.

DAPHNE: Just because you told them it started in your belly and not in your heart. Learn to lie. Look up the answers. Find out what they want to hear and tell it to them. The doctors, the lawyers, the whole goddamn lot of them. Learn to lie and live with it.

> *Lights change. Ceil is gone.*

It took four years. We sued that doctor. Me, my family, and good old Palmer Prewitt. Four years. A dissecting aortic aneurysm. Her heart just split in two.

> *Lights up on Dr. Mellis.*

DR. MELLIS: I have reviewed autopsy findings for Ceil Prewitt and hold the opinion that Dr. Brandenburg departed from accepted standards of care in discharging Mrs. Prewitt from the hospital.

> *Dr. Mellis's voice continues, but becomes a background murmur as Daphne punctuates key words for Eddie, as if reading from the autopsy.)*

DR. MELLIS: Despite the medical history obtained by the paramedics and the triage nurse documenting the chief complaint of sudden and sharp onset of chest pain, Dr. Brandenburg used an "abdominal pain" form versus a "chest pain" form when he started his evaluation of Mrs. Prewitt.

> DAPHNE: Chief complaint
>
> chest pain
> ABDOMINAL pain form—
> VERSUS

DAPHNE: He used the wrong form.

DR. MELLIS: I will testify . . .

> DAPHNE:

that had Dr. Brandenburg ordered a chest CT scan with IV contrast, the aortic arch dissection would have very likely been diagnosed. Cardiovascular surgeons would have been able to perform timely surgery for Mrs. Prewitt. I hold the opinion that had Dr. Brandenburg complied with accepted standards of care, Mrs. Prewitt would be— *(overlapping)* Alive today.

> Would have
> Been diagnosed
> Would have
> Perform surgery
>
> If he complied
>
> Would be
> *(overlapping)* Alive today.

Light out on Dr. Mellis.

DAPHNE: So, today, the check arrives. Four thousand two hundred and twelve dollars. The sum total of the value of my sister's life. I mean, the real sum total, the big magoo, was three hundred thirty-seven thousand dollars. But there's lawyers. And Palmer. THEY each took forty percent. Ten percent went to Sammy. Of course, now he's over in Afghanistan hunting IEDs, so there's no telling whether HIS check will ever be cashed. Of the rest, five percent went to my parents. And the remaining five percent was divided among her four siblings. So, a sister is ultimately worth one point two five percent.

EDDIE: That's a . . . really shitty story.

DAPHNE: Yeah, but you gotta admit it's rich with violence, intrigue, and heroes and villains. So I get this check and I'm thinking: it's over, this is all over. The doctor gets spanked and now we can move on with our lives. And then it hits me: We HAVE TO move on with our lives. And I'm not ready to. So, I went out for a drink.

EDDIE: But don't you think—

DAPHNE: Buh buh buh . . . walking. So I went out for a drink. And another. And while I'm drinking, I get an email on my phone. From an old high school buddy. Did you know, she says, that Marlo Roy was just arrested? Here's the link, she says. You're not going to believe this, she says.

EDDIE: And so you, sitting there with pockets stuffed with fresh dollar bills—

DAPHNE: Fresh HUNDRED dollar bills—

EDDIE: You see a new mission for yourself. You're gonna go sort this thing out.

DAPHNE: That actually took hours to occur to me. In the meantime, I read every article I could find online. It's just kind of . . . surreal. Why does something like this happen?

EDDIE: Love or money.

DAPHNE: It's that simple?

EDDIE: Nothing simple about love OR money.

Daphne and Eddie continue their walk off stage as the next scene begins.

Lights up on Marlo and Dominick, sitting in a car in Minnesota, just a block away from Anson's house. Marlo is sitting in the driver's seat.

MARLO: I thought I'd grow up and have a house just like that one, Dominick. *(Beat.)* I thought we'd live in this neighborhood for the rest of our lives.

DOMINICK: You always think that when you're a kid.

MARLO: When you think about living in a shitty apartment, you think about a shitty apartment in Paris, France. How'd I wind up in a shitty apartment just ten miles from the town I grew up in, huh?

DOMINICK: Why are we here, Marlo?

Marlo pulls an envelope out of the glove compartment. She opens it and removes a folded letter. She reads it until she finds the passage she is looking for.

MARLO: It says: "I find this behavior to be harassing, inappropriate, and threatening. Respondent's emails"—"respondent," that's me—"to my home email address are disturbing, rambling, and at times unintelligible, and they suggest that she means harm to me and/or my family. She has made unfounded accusations against me. She has, on at least three occasions, entered my property . . ." I was on his LAWN, fer chrissakes . . . respondent, respondent, wait, here it is: "I believe that without a harassment restraining order, respondent will continue to harass me both at my place of work and at home and . . . blah blah . . . could escalate—ESCALATE—into physical confrontation and, potentially, violent behavior." Do you see what he's done, Dominick? Our brother has essentially invented this fairy tale to put a target on our backs. We're the ones the police will be looking at. We can't come within (*she looks*) a hundred yards of him. This is a motherfucking piece of fiction, Dominick. This is Moby Dick. THIS. THING.

DOMINICK: Well.

MARLO: Well.

DOMINICK: Well.

MARLO: What do you mean "well"?

DOMINICK: What am I supposed to say?

MARLO: Dom.

DOMINICK: Well what?

MARLO: It's time to get serious here, Dom. Anson is winning this fight. You and me—we're out. We're done. Now we can't even walk across his front lawn without getting arrested. Do you understand this?

DOMINICK: Yeah.

MARLO: If I inch this car down this street a little farther and we happen to drive by his house real slow, BOOM! we're in violation of this restraining order.

DOMINICK: I get it.

MARLO: It's not just my name on this thing. Dom. You understand that, right? Your name is on here, too. Here's a record of us, of our family, that Anson has created out of thin air.

DOMINICK: Shut up. Shut up.

MARLO: He paints us as the abusive ones. You and me. Says we're the ones who stole and frittered away the earnings from the business. We're the ones trying to deflect the blame onto HIM.

DOMINICK: SHUT UP. I gotta think.

MARLO: Thinking time is over, Dom. It's time to ACT. How long before Roy Lawn Service can't pay its bills, huh?

DOMINICK: Tina says we got, like, two months covered in savings.

MARLO: But then comes winter and your work slows down.

DOMINICK: I know.

MARLO: And Anson took away, what, like half of your regular clients when he left to go work with R.J.? He's filling their minds with terrible shit about you that's not gonna stop spreading until you do something about it.

He doesn't respond.

What are you gonna do, Dom . . . bag groceries? And me? I've got one industrial coming up. That's it. I had to turn down a play in order to take extra hours at Crate and Barrel.

Dominick is quiet. She waits for a response from him.

MARLO: I don't understand your reaction, Dom.

DOMINICK: What do you want me to say?

MARLO: I want you to be angry.

DOMINICK: I AM angry.

MARLO: I want you to understand how fucked up we are.

DOMINICK: Maybe Tina and I should go to Wisconsin. Her folks are there.

MARLO: Dom, Roy Lawn belongs to you more than it ever belonged to Anson. You started that business.

DOMINICK: I don't know what I can fucking do, Marlo! He knew how to hide the money he was taking. He knows how to get people to believe him. What have I got, huh? You tell me. I'm never gonna get all that back. You—what the fuck does it matter to you? You can move. You can be in plays anywhere. I got nothing left here. NOTHING.

MARLO: You don't start over at my age, Dom. I've built something here, too, you know. I don't WANT to move. And Nana's house . . . that was gonna be ours to split. All of ours. I needed that.

DOMINICK: Well, it's all HIS now.

MARLO: Dom! There is one thing that can happen that will put everything in the universe back in order. Do you know what that one thing is?

DOMINICK: No.

MARLO: Yes, you do. Think about it. Something . . . happens.

DOMINICK: Like what?

MARLO: Like . . . for instance, an earthquake.

DOMINICK: But, we don't—

MARLO: Nobody can argue with an earthquake, right? It happens. And it's a tragedy, right?

DOMINICK: Yeah.

MARLO: Or a tornado. *(Beat.)* Or cancer. *(Beat.)* Or lightning storm. Or overdose. Or—

    Pause.

DOMINICK: Car crash?

MARLO: *(affirming him)* Or car crash.

DOMINICK: What about when Jerry Conover's house got blown up because of that gas line?

MARLO: Bad things happen to people, Dom. They do.

DOMINICK: *(trying to digest what she's saying)* He's our brother.

MARLO: That's right. He's your brother. And now he's taking the one thing in your life you built up into something good and he's taking a humongous dump all over it.

Dominick slowly makes the transition from being shocked by Marlo's suggestion to digesting it.

DOMINICK: Hunting accident.

MARLO: Something we could never see coming.

DOMINICK: Can't avoid something like that, can we? And it's nobody's fault, really.

MARLO: What a fucking tragedy.

They are quiet for a moment. Lights out on Marlo and Dominick.

Daphne & Eddie have ducked into a bar and are sitting. There are drinks in front of them. Hers is a coffee.

DAPHNE: Sounds like more than money problems to me. Sounds worse than that.

EDDIE: Spoken like someone with no money problems.

DAPHNE: No one kills for the kind of money these people likely had.

EDDIE: Kids kill each other for sneakers, hon.

DAPHNE: I'm not rich, you know.

EDDIE: You got four thousand dollars in your pocket. You're sure not poor.

Beat.

DAPHNE: You want it?

EDDIE: Sure.

Daphne takes an envelope out of her purse and from it, pulls out a one hundred dollar bill and hands it to Eddie.

DAPHNE: Here.

EDDIE: I was kidding.

DAPHNE: It's for being my driver.

After thinking it over, he takes it.

DAPHNE: And here. *(She hands him another one.)* This is for keeping me company.

EDDIE: I'm not taking that one.

DAPHNE: I mean for helping me solve the mystery.

EDDIE: There's no mystery here to solve.

DAPHNE: There's always a "why" to be figured out. Take it.

EDDIE: I sense disappointment coming your way.

DAPHNE: I'm used to that. Take it. It's like you're my writing partner.

EDDIE: But you don't write no more. You said.

DAPHNE: I don't. I said it's 'like.'

He takes the bill from her.

EDDIE: You see, this is where you people with money get perverse.

Daphne rolls her eyes at him.

DAPHNE: How did your sister die, Eddie?

EDDIE: You gonna give me another hundred for that?

DAPHNE: Can I ask that?

EDDIE: It was an accident.

DAPHNE: Car?

EDDIE: Nah.

DAPHNE: How?

EDDIE: It was . . . a neighborhood thing.

DAPHNE: A what?

EDDIE: A disagreement.

DAPHNE: A what? Like a fight? *(He nods.)* When?

EDDIE: She was fourteen.

DAPHNE: And you were?

EDDIE: I was there.

DAPHNE: I meant . . . how old?

EDDIE: Sixteen.

DAPHNE: That would be sad. Not knowing your sister as an adult, I mean.

EDDIE: That would have been nice.

DAPHNE: I remember Ceil as a kid. She was pretty badass, even then.

Lights change. A flashback. CHRIS JACOBS' basement.

CHRIS JACOBS: Truth or dare time, douchebags.

DAPHNE: *(to EDDIE)* Choice A is to answer a question truthfully.

CHRIS JACOBS: Have you ever stolen something? Have you ever cheated on a test? Who in this room would you do it with?

DAPHNE: *(to EDDIE)* Choice B is to *do* something, do whatever the person whose turn it is asks you to. I am fourteen and after a childhood of hiding behind Truth, I pick Dare. When you're fourteen, the Dares generally consist of kissing someone, making a prank phone call, or vandalizing something. I am prepared to do any of these things.

Daphne gets up from her chair to participate in the scene, while also continuing to relay the tale to Eddie who remains seated at the bar.

Chris Jacobs is the one who gets to pick my Dare, though, and he tells me he wants me to

CHRIS JACOBS: get fingered by Matty Devlin.

DAPHNE: (to CHRIS) No. Then I pick truth.

CHRIS JACOBS: You already picked Dare, too bad.

DAPHNE: Well, I take it back. I pick Truth.

CHRIS JACOBS: You'd only lie.

DAPHNE: No. I'll tell you something good.

CHRIS JACOBS: No, you picked Dare, you do Dare.

DAPHNE: It's not fair. Everyone else just had to kiss somebody.

CHRIS JACOBS: Nobody here wants to kiss you, skank.

    Chris laughs stupidly. Ceil and Marlo enter.

CEIL: Kiss ME then.

DAPHNE: Ceil was just a year younger than me, but she was completely unafraid of all those things that kept me up in my room reading books every night. She busts into Chris's basement right at that moment. She's got Marlo with her. Those girls are tough as nails and they wear makeup and they scare the hell outta boys.

CEIL: I'll trade ya. Give her Truth and you can kiss me instead, asswipe.

    The memory dissolves. Daphne returns to her seat at the bar.

DAPHNE: I never once rescued her the way she rescued me.

    Pause.

    What was your sister's name, Eddie?

EDDIE: Marie.

DAPHNE: Well. Here's to Marie. Marie and Ceil.

    They toast.

EDDIE: Yeah. She was a good kid.

DAPHNE: So. This "disagreement." Was someone, I mean, was there . . . someone who was . . . responsible . . . for Marie's death?

EDDIE: There's sure no doctor gonna pay me for it, that's all I know.

DAPHNE: I'm not talking about money.

EDDIE: Not everything can be blamed on someone, you know.

DAPHNE: Why not?

EDDIE: Cuz what's the point? Your doc got to cut a check and move on. And look at YOU.

DAPHNE: I'll get past this.

EDDIE: When, huh?

DAPHNE: Someday.

EDDIE: Seriously, when?

DAPHNE: When it's all done.

EDDIE: How much more done can it get?

119

DAPHNE: When Sammy's back from Afghanistan safe and sound. When Christmas doesn't feel bad. And when that bastard husband of hers chokes on a turkey leg and dies. Then. Then I'll get past this.

EDDIE: What did he do?

DAPHNE: Well, he sure as hell didn't take her to the hospital that night. Sammy did. It's line six hundred twenty nine on Sammy's deposition. They asked, *and where was your step-father on the night your mother died*?

EDDIE: Maybe he was working late.

DAPHNE: Sammy and Ceil didn't get home from the hospital till one A.M. Palmer's still not there. Ceil goes to sleep. *(Ceil crawls into the bed onstage. Falls asleep. Daphne watches this and directs Eddie's attention to it.)* Then he comes home, who knows when, comes home and sleeps next to her all night. WHILE SHE DIED.

EDDIE: When you're asleep, you don't—

DAPHNE: Why are you defending him?

EDDIE: Defending him? I never met the guy. I'm just saying—

DAPHNE: Could YOU sleep next to a woman whose body grew cold? Who stopped breathing? You'd feel that.

> Beat.

Sammy found her. Her kid found her in the morning. Dead in her bed. That FUCK Palmer got up and brushed his teeth and went to work with his dead wife still in his bed.

EDDIE: Yeah, that . . . that's real . . . unfortunate.

DAPHNE: It wasn't an accident, Eddie. It wasn't an oversight.

EDDIE: You can't know that.

DAPHNE: I saw them when they came home to my parents' every Christmas.

EDDIE: But didn't you say he sued the doctor with you all?

DAPHNE: I heard the way he ordered her around. She was never more than his housekeeper.

EDDIE: You must have been on good terms with him if you did that.

DAPHNE: That was forced on us by the judge, Eddie. There couldn't be TWO wrongful death suits, so the judge merged our two parties into one claim. So we could get SOMETHING for Sammy cuz that asshole sure wouldn't.

EDDIE: You're spinning, hon. The case is closed. You're hanging onto someone to blame. That's pretty natural.

DAPHNE: Fuck you that's-pretty-natural! He LEFT her there. He waited till the clock ran out. Till she was ice cold.

> Beat. Reigns herself in a little.

(*sarcastically*) Can't sue him for that, though.

EDDIE: (*teasing, trying to calm her down*) Yeah. Well, I guess you better just kill him. Seems to be the popular thing to do.

DAPHNE: (*in the same spirit*) Here's four thousand and change. YOU go kill him.

EDDIE: We'll need a plan.

> *Lights up on Marlo and Dominick at Nana's house.*

DOMINICK: I don't know why we couldn't do this at your apartment.

MARLO: I told you my roommate's there tonight.

DOMINICK: Well shit, Marlo, Nana's right in the next room.

MARLO: She's not coming out of there. Calm down.

DOMINICK: What if she hears something?

MARLO: Goddamn, Dom, she plays her TV so loud the wall shakes. (*shouts toward bedroom*) YOU DOING OK IN THERE, NANA? YOU WANT SOME RC COLA?

> *No response. Marlo looks at Dominick as if to say, 'You see?'*

MARLO: She's fine.

DOMINICK: Tina'll be home soon.

MARLO: So what?

DOMINICK: I don't want her to hear this.

MARLO: You haven't told her about it yet?

DOMINICK: No, and I don't want her to know.

MARLO: But we need her, Dom.

DOMINICK: No, we don't.

MARLO: She has to take you over there.

DOMINICK: No, she can't.

MARLO: She HAS TO drive you in her truck. If my car is spotted there, I'll be arrested. You know that.

DOMINICK: You can rent a car.

MARLO: Paper trail, Dom.

DOMINICK: Tina's not involved in this.

MARLO: What do you mean, she's not involved? She's the one that found Anson's second set of books. She KNOWS what he did. And if anything happens to him and the cops ask her about it and she puts two and two together, she's gonna know you did something.

DOMINICK: We did—

MARLO: Yeah yeah. You gotta tell her, Dom.

> *Tina enters the front door, carrying a box of fried chicken.*

121

TINA: Oh. Hey Marlo. I didn't know you were coming over.

DOMINICK: Hey baby, yeah Marlo needs me to help her out—

TINA: Oh, you need to go out? I thought we were—

DOMINICK: Yeah, I'm going over—

MARLO: No, that can wait, Dom.

DOMINICK: But you said—

MARLO: No. It can wait.

DOMINICK: *(Beat.)* OK.

MARLO: That smells good, Tina.

TINA: Yeah, if I knew you were coming over, I woulda got more chicken.

DOMINICK: She's not staying.

TINA: She could. *(Beat.)* I mean, I could make some spaghetti to go with. *(No one says anything.)* What's going on, you guys?

DOMINICK: What?

TINA: I walked in on something. What?

DOMINICK: Nothing.

> Quiet.

MARLO: Dom?

> He doesn't say anything.

TINA: Oh, don't scare me like this, baby. Just tell me.

MARLO: Dom. *(waits)* Tina, Dom and I, we've been talking about some things—

DOMINICK: *(shakes off Marlo)* Tina. This is something. Uh. I've been thinking over some options lately. You know, with things being what they are with the business . . .

TINA: Yeah, I know. And I was thinking I could totally go down to Target, maybe get like ten, fifteen hours a week there. It won't interfere with my schedule for you, I'll just do nights.

DOMINICK: No, that's not what I'm saying, Tina.

TINA: I wanna be a contributor, Dom.

DOMINICK: You are. That's not the thing.

MARLO: Dom, careful here.

TINA: Did I do something wrong?

> Dominick thinks before he starts this.

DOMINICK: Baby, my dad . . . a long time ago, I was, like, eleven, my dad he took off for a few days in our old trailer. Didn't say nothing to me, no goodbye, just jumped into the trailer with our old dog, Shotzi, and left. He comes home, like three days later. It's late at night and I'm in bed and he comes up to my room and he wakes me up and tells me that he had to take Shotzi up to the lake and he had to shoot him. And that was that. The dog had cancer and it was better this way, he said. It was just . . . done. (*Beat.*) Honey, when there's a cancer, you gotta get rid of it. Get rid of it clean. And it may hurt, but afterwards, things are gonna get better for everybody.

TINA: You have . . . cancer?

DOMINICK: And we gotta get rid of it, baby.

MARLO: Tina.

TINA: (*starts to cry*) Oh, Dom...

MARLO: Tina, Dom doesn't have cancer.

TINA: What?

MARLO: He's talking about Anson.

TINA: Huh?

DOMINICK: Marlo and I have gone over this—

MARLO: You know, since we—

DOMINICK: There's really nothing else we can do—

MARLO: When Nana dies, Tina, where are you two gonna go? Anson's gonna—

TINA: So what do—

MARLO: Tina, can you imagine—

DOMINICK: Let me, Marlo!—

MARLO: That a lot of the problems we're having would be solved if Anson—

DOMINICK: (*races to cut Marlo off*) Was gone.

TINA: What do you mean? (*No response.*) What? (*It dawns on her.*) No, you're not serious.

MARLO: He is.

TINA: Dominick, you can't be serious about this.

DOMINICK: This is what's gonna happen, Tina...

TINA: Dominick, nooo.

DOMINICK: We're gonna go out there, like we're just trying to talk with him one more time. Reason with him. He's not gonna want to. But we just gotta get him outside. And then—

MARLO: We're gonna get him in the car.

DOMINICK: We'll take him out, out, off the highway somewhere, leave him there—

MARLO: Probably need to drug him first or something, knock him out.

DOMINICK: A couple days go by. People notice he's missing. But it makes sense. We say, oh he's probably on a hunting trip.

MARLO: Totally plausible.

123

DOMINICK: But then maybe we get worried. Call it in. Missing persons or whatever.

MARLO: They'll find the car. It'll look like a carjacking gone bad.

DOMINICK: Our hands'll be clean, Tina.

TINA: You're just both upset.

DOMINICK: He has MY CAR.

TINA: What?

MARLO: The Passat.

TINA: So what?

DOMINICK: He drives it around. He acts like he owns it, but I'm still paying on that car still, Tina.

MARLO: You think that's fair?

TINA: But you're talking about . . . *killing* your brother for a car. This isn't YOU, Dom.

DOMINICK: If the car is *stolen*, then any money that comes back from that, any insurance . . . I get.

TINA: So, just STEAL the car. Don't hurt anybody.

DOMINICK: Yes, but, if the car disappears and Anson tries to get his hands on the insurance money—

MARLO: Or, if he tells the police that Dom took it—

DOMINICK: Tina, if Anson's still around after the car is stolen, we're screwed.

MARLO: Sooo . . .

DOMINICK: What if Anson . . . goes . . . WITH the car?

MARLO: It's totally natural.

TINA: I don't feel good.

MARLO: Dom.

DOMINICK: Tina.

MARLO: Dominick.

DOMINICK: Tina, it's me.

TINA: I don't know.

DOMINICK: It's still me, baby. You KNOW me.

TINA: This isn't . . .

MARLO: Look. We did this wrong. This is the wrong approach. You're not drunk enough to be saying these things and she's not drunk enough to be hearing them. We should be laughing our asses off about this.

TINA: It's not funny.

MARLO: We should have been drunk and making jokes about this until it got to be late . . . until we got to be so tired at laughing at our own

124

shithole predicament that the whole idea begins to make sense. Tell me. TELL ME that you haven't thought about it, Tina! You're a goddamn liar if you say you haven't.

DOMINICK: Hey—

MARLO: Here's our one chance. We don't know what he's gonna do next week or where he's gonna be the week after that. But we know where he is and how to get to him today. Right now. And it's not gonna get better. And it's not gonna go away. And he's never gonna pay for what he did.

TINA: But he's your blood, Marlo. Think about that.

MARLO: FUCK HIM! Did he think about blood when he stole Nana's life savings? Did YOUR father think about blood when he walked out on your mom?

TINA: That's not killing, though.

MARLO: Life is shit without money, and you know it. We just barely had enough to get by anyway, but it sure was more than we have now, wasn't it? So you tell me. How did he not kill us first?!

DOMINICK: Take it easy. OK. Just . . . calm down, Marlo, and take it easy. It'll be all right.

MARLO: She needs to decide, Dom. She needs to decide. In or out. And if you're out, you better fucking leave this state and never say a goddamn word.

DOMINICK: Marlo.

MARLO: In or out. Cuz we're doing this.

Lights out on Nana's house.

DAPHNE: You sit around and laugh about it enough, and killing a guy begins to make a lot of sense.

EDDIE: That's big talk for a nice girl from the suburbs.

DAPHNE: *(lightly)* You don't think I could do that, do you?

EDDIE: I'm just saying.

DAPHNE: I visited Ceil in Minnesota just one time. It was Christmas, the year after she and Palmer got married. Palmer was unhappy with how I folded the sheets on the couch I slept on. He yelled at me. Told me

We are in a memory.

PALMER: *(forcefully)* Hey, come on back here and refold these fucking sheets!

DAPHNE: And I laughed, not a laugh-laugh, but a kind of are-you-kidding-me laugh. I looked over at Ceil *(lights up on Ceil)*. She was cooking breakfast. I looked in her face for some kind of recognition that this was ridiculous, that *(to Ceil)* this was how insane people acted, *(back to Eddie)* that this was just . . . a joke. But she didn't smile, she didn't jump to my defense. She, uh, actually she flinched the tiniest bit.

Her head, not even her whole head, just her eyes twitched, begging me to

CEIL: *(very softly)* Be quiet, please, be quiet . . . please, please don't make him mad.

The memory disappears.

DAPHNE: Palmer married a cocktail waitress six months after my sister died. They had a baby a month later. Believe me. This world wouldn't miss that man.

EDDIE: *(humoring her)* And how exactly would you do the job?

DAPHNE: With a knife. A knife so sharp it would nick your finger from inches away. I wouldn't worry about being efficient or clean. I wouldn't worry about getting away with it. I would want to take nineteen deep chops into his gut while his eyes were open, watching me. And I would want to be dragged away by police in full view of the neighborhood with my bloody hands pulled behind my back. But I know that's not very practical. So, I'm thinking . . . gun.

EDDIE: Oh. You ever shoot anybody?

DAPHNE: No. But what's the big deal? Point and click, right?

EDDIE: *(laughs)* Yeah. That's about the size of it.

DAPHNE: You?

EDDIE: What?

DAPHNE: You've shot someone.

EDDIE: Who says?

DAPHNE: You have. I can tell. *(He just looks at her.)* You carry that gun. I saw it.

EDDIE: You saw what?

DAPHNE: You totally took it out from under the seat and put it in your jacket when we got out of the cab. I figure, you carry a gun, you must think you need to. Can I see it?

EDDIE: No.

DAPHNE: But you HAVE used it, right? On someone?

Silence.

How much would it take to get you to shoot someone again, huh? I mean, if someone had an envelope full of hundred dollar bills to offer? How many would it take?

He just looks at her.

I mean. Theoretically.

Beat.

EDDIE: C'mon. It's time to go.

Eddie picks up the check lying on the table amid all the glassware. Starts to leave. Daphne grabs his forearm.

DAPHNE: Cuz I could kill him, Eddie. If I saw him tonight. I could really kill him.

EDDIE: Well, then it's a pretty good thing you didn't make that flight.

Marlo, Dominick, and Tina are seated at tables in separate interrogations rooms.

TINA: Can I just tell you something? There's a lot you have to think about when you run a business. Dominick, see, he does all of the outdoor stuff, the lawn care and the tree trimming. He does fertilizing and mowing, weed maintenance. Summers are crazy, he can be out there twelve hours a day—easy—some days. Someone's gotta keep track of the billing and so forth. That's me. Well, and before me, it was Dominick's brother, Anson. That was back when, you know, Dominick and Anson ran the business together. Then, well, the whole thing blew up on account of, you know . . . a family "disagreement" sort of thing.

MARLO: So, yes, whether I agreed with it or not, I did not violate the terms of Anson's precious restraining order. I stayed away. Didn't call, didn't even drive by. But Dominick, well he's made of different stuff than me. I have this shell, see, I have to. I'm a professional actor. I think Dominick, on the other hand, took it a little more personal. He was. Injured. Insulted. And I know that maybe I should have tried harder to stop him when he told me about wanting to go over to Anson's, but honestly, when he wants something, he's going to get it, and I honestly thought that the best I could do, in my position, was to be ready to do some damage control. That's kind of my role in the family. Plus, well, I think that maybe I did believe that in the end, we really did deserve to at least get that car back.

DOMINICK: Anson could have turned the car over at any point, but he stopped returning any of our calls. I just wanted to get the car and leave.

MARLO: That's all we wanted. I was just gonna wait for Dominick's call, you know, in case he needed my help. I knew how to handle Anson best. He listens to me. All that money. Dom wasn't the only one who got duped. My grandmother, my mom and dad, they all asked him to watch over their accounts, too. We're talking close to a million dollars. Anson's the one they chose. HE's the one everyone trusted. That Passat was all we had left.

DOMINICK: I'm telling you, we SPOKE to lawyers. No lawyer would help us get back that money. Statue of limitations. STATUE OF FUCKING LIMITATIONS, we were told. Nothing they could do. So the thing we planned was, when I went over there if Anson showed any resistance to giving me back the keys, I was supposed to call my sister Marlo and then, see, I was gonna hand over the cell phone to Anson and Marlo would talk to him, distract him, and then I was just gonna grab the keys from him when he wasn't thinking straight and then I was gonna take off in the car. And, you know, in court, if he said I stole it I could always show the paperwork. Tina had those records. (*Pause.*) Um, am I gonna be needing a lawyer, you think?

TINA: You just never see it coming, I tell you, people taking advantage of that kind of power. Especially your family, right? He was just, you know, trying to save up. We were. We are. Me and Dom. We want to have kids. Get outta the city eventually. We got that little farm out there. Well . . . you know. Yeah, you just never see it coming. (*Pause.*) I'm not saying Dominick actually DID anything. But I'd be lying if I tried to tell you this was one big happy family.

Eddie and Daphne are walking.

DAPHNE: (*pointing to a building*) And that, over there, is my old apartment.

EDDIE: You don't think THEY might have an extra set of your keys lying around, do you?

DAPHNE: Aw c'mon, this hasn't been all bad, has it—hanging out with me?

EDDIE: Nah, you're a joy to be around.

DAPHNE: I'm gonna let that one go, Eddie, cuz I know you'll feel bad about your sarcasm in the morning. Besides, I feel I'm passably sober enough for you to take me back to the airport.

EDDIE: I'm not going back to the airport tonight, hon.

DAPHNE: But you have to.

EDDIE: I'm a little too buzzed to drive now.

DAPHNE: Well, walk it off. Come on.

EDDIE: Look.

DAPHNE: Where?

EDDIE: Up there.

DAPHNE: Ahh.

EDDIE: That's nice. That's a nice night up there.

They walk a bit more.

DAPHNE: So, lemme ask you something.

EDDIE: Shoot.

DAPHNE: You're gonna kill a guy.

EDDIE: Let's say.

DAPHNE: You've got a plan. You've got these partners to help you execute the plan. How does it all go so wrong?

EDDIE: (*Beat.*) Dissent.

DAPHNE: Someone gets greedy?

EDDIE: Maybe someone feels he's getting outvoted on decisions.

128

DAPHNE: A turf thing.

EDDIE: Could be he sees signs he shouldn't trust his partners. Not all sports are team sports.

DAPHNE: So, let's say—

EDDIE: *(notices where they are)* That's that place, isn't it?

DAPHNE: Which place?

EDDIE: Place we met.

DAPHNE: Oh. Yeah.

EDDIE: Our . . . date.

DAPHNE: First and last.

EDDIE: I'm pretty sure it ended right here on this very sidewalk. With me being sent on my way.

DAPHNE: That was your own doing, chief.

EDDIE: Whaddya mean? I was having a great time.

DAPHNE: That was NOT a great time.

EDDIE: I'm gonna bet you one of these shiny hundred dollar bills I now have in my pocket that I was the best Yahoo date you ever had.

DAPHNE: Ha!

EDDIE: How many guys in golf shirts answer your ad, huh?

DAPHNE: That date sucked.

EDDIE: Only cuz you wouldn't let it get great.

DAPHNE: What kills me is that you, you got to leave that date thinking you were the FUN guy with all this personality, and I was some uptight bitch. I had this speech written in my head that night, right after you stumbled down the street to your car—I was gonna write you this long email—

EDDIE: You should of.

DAPHNE: Ah. A day late and a dollar short. That's our story, Eddie.

EDDIE: Tell me off now.

DAPHNE: No. The moment's not there anymore.

EDDIE: I could of written you an email, too, you know.

DAPHNE: Yeah, yeah.

EDDIE: I have feelings, too.

DAPHNE: You know, I came to that date thinking great thoughts. I don't like dating, Eddie. But I figured, what could it hurt? I WANT to be happy. So I smiled and I told you about me and I asked about you because that's what people who want to be happy do, but of course you didn't care. I tried. You didn't. And I bet you told a completely different story to your friends the next day, didn't you?

EDDIE: I didn't tell—

129

DAPHNE: Oh, this one, she was a real bitch.

EDDIE: You know what I told my friends?

DAPHNE: What?

EDDIE: That when I met you, you were wearing a red dress and you had a great big flower in your hair—

DAPHNE: *(dismissive)* All right. Great.

EDDIE: And you were out in front of the Four Seasons coming from some swanky party in there, but you were leaving, you had enough of those people. Or maybe it was a wedding or something, you and the bride got into it cuz there you were, at her wedding, looking like a million bucks in that shiny red dress.

DAPHNE: Well, this was useful.

EDDIE: So you leave and the guy in the monkey suit outside, he calls for a cab for you.

DAPHNE: I didn't valet?

EDDIE: You came with someone.

DAPHNE: Oh, this is getting better.

EDDIE: But you're leaving without him.

DAPHNE: I piss him off, too?

EDDIE: So, you, the red dress, the flower—

DAPHNE: We're all waiting outside for a cab.

EDDIE: And who do you think walks on by?

DAPHNE: Let me guess.

EDDIE: I say, I know a place—

DAPHNE: I look like a girl could use a hot cuppa joe, huh?

EDDIE: You're that girl.

DAPHNE: And this is what you told your friends?

EDDIE: What friends?

DAPHNE: Oh.

EDDIE: Let me clue you in. A guy don't tell nobody about looking on the computer for someone to talk to. Maybe YOU went on that date cuz you're trying to get over the guy who left you or maybe cuz your shrink recommended it. I'm showed up cuz I thought you might like me. *(Beat.)* I think we can chalk it up to both of us had a bad day.

> Pause.

DAPHNE: Eddie?

EDDIE: It maybe wasn't the worst first date in the whole world, you know.

DAPHNE: I don't think you should drive anymore tonight.

EDDIE: How am I gonna get home?

130

DAPHNE: You shouldn't go home.

EDDIE: Where am I gonna go then?

DAPHNE: I know a place. *(Beat.)* You look like a guy could use a hot cuppa joe.

EDDIE: Hmm.

> *There, a decision is made. They linger a moment and then head off.*
>
> *Dominick is in bed. Tina is puttering around the room, walking in and out of the room, looking for mindless little chores to do to help her avoid getting into bed with Dominick.*

DOMINICK: You gotta come to bed sometime, Tina.

TINA: I got stuff I gotta clean up. One of us has to keep things straightened up, you know.

DOMINICK: You're not cleaning. You need sleep.

TINA: I'll sleep when I'm tired, Dom.

DOMINICK: You ARE tired.

TINA: You don't get to tell me when I'm tired, k? *(Beat.)* YOU go to sleep [if] you're so concerned about sleeping. How 'bout that?

DOMINICK: Come on, baby, sit down.

> *She ignores him.*

How long you gonna be mad at me, Tina? You can't stay mad forever.

TINA: Yes, I can.

DOMINICK: See, I told ya you were mad.

TINA: What am I supposed to do, Dom? Get in bed and lie down next to you and sleep all peaceful while I know what's going on in your head? I never knew this before about you. That you could lie there and think about killing someone.

DOMINICK: Not just anyone, Tina. I would NOT kill just anyone.

TINA: It's not even self-defense or—

DOMINICK: We could make it look like that if it would make you feel better, Tina, I swear.

TINA: That's not my point, Dom. It's in your head. It's in your heart. I thought I already knew what was in there, but I know nothing now.

DOMINICK: It's not—

TINA: How can I ever know what else is in there, Dom?

DOMINICK: Don't be mad at me, Tina, please.

> *A cell phone sitting on the floor next to their bed, on Dominick's side, rings. He picks it up, sees who's calling, and takes the call.*

DOMINICK: Hey.

MARLO: Hey, Dom.

DOMINICK: What's up?

MARLO: You talked some more to Tina yet?

DOMINICK: Yeah.

MARLO: And?

DOMINICK: Don't worry about it.

MARLO: You sure?

DOMINICK: It'll be fine.

MARLO: Oh. All right. That's good. Well, um, I gotta . . . I've been doing some thinking, and I think that we oughta . . . just slow down on this idea, Dom.

DOMINICK: What?

MARLO: For now.

DOMINICK: No.

MARLO: Yeah, I've been going over it in my head and, I know we both agreed it's the thing we WANT to do, and I still, I STILL think that. But man . . . I think . . . we should . . . NOT do it, you know what I mean?

DOMINICK: What the hell?

> *Dominick moves away from Tina and sits on the edge of the mattress, facing away from her.*

MARLO: Yeah, it's crazy, Dom. It's a crazy idea. You know, think about it. We're . . . we can't really go through with this.

DOMINICK: What are you talking about, yes we can.

MARLO: Let's just let things cool down a little.

DOMINICK: No—

MARLO: Dom, I'm not ready to risk this going bad. I can't. I got a job. Today. The one I auditioned for this week. It's out in Chanhassen and it's a supporting role, but it pays and it'll get me my Equity card and I have to take it. And I can't fuck it up by getting arrested or even questioned about somebody getting killed. I just can't bring that type of attention to myself at this point in my career. So we can't do this. We just can't do this, you hear me?

> *Beat.*

DOMINICK: I hear you.

MARLO: We could still try to get the car, though. You agree with me, right?

> *Nothing.*

Dom?

DOMINICK: *(Beat.)* It's a crazy idea.

MARLO: OK, good. Oh god, I feel so much better. Ahh. You'll see, I'll take this part and then it'll be your turn for something good to happen. I'll be there to make sure. I promise you. You hear me?

DOMINICK: Yeah, I hear ya.

MARLO: You trust me, right?

DOMINICK: Yeah.

MARLO: OK, well I'm gonna go to bed. You get some sleep, too, k?

DOMINICK: K.

MARLO: Bye.

> *He hangs up but sits on the bed with it in his hand, still.*

TINA: What was that about?

DOMINICK: Marlo. She called it off.

TINA: She did? Why?

DOMINICK: Just the Anson part.

TINA: Yeah?

DOMINICK: We're still gonna do the car.

TINA: Oh. *(She thinks.)* Ohh. *(She starts to cry.)* This is better.

DOMINICK: Yeah.

TINA: Oh, you'll see, Dom. This is so much better.

> *Tina calms down and eventually settles into bed. Dominick remains seated and alert on the edge of the bed. Tina watches him carefully and slowly realizes the awful truth that he is now disappointed not to be going ahead with the plan to kill Anson. As Dominick gradually settles in under the covers with her, Tina lies there uneasily. The lights dim.*

> *At some point, Dominick gets up off the bed and leaves the room, goes into Nana's garage and start assembling his spray paint project, pulling out boxes and objects, laying newspaper, shaking cans of black spray paint, etc. Dominick starts spray painting a bat, several arrows, and a crossbow that are laid out on the floor. At one point he lifts up the crossbow and sprays until it's coated in black. Stops spraying, lifts it up, and stares at it for a long moment.*

> *Garage doors close and Dominick exits stage as scene transitions into hotel room.*

> *When the lights come up, Eddie and Daphne are entering a motel room. Eddie's still got the key card in his hand. He lays it down on a table or night stand, hesitantly. They both are incredibly nervous to be here and approach each other cautiously.*

EDDIE: So maybe that's it.

DAPHNE: You think she just calls it off? Just like that.

EDDIE: She comes to her senses. She's thought about it. She's seen the darkest corner of herself. She realizes that committing to this—this act of violence—won't give her what she wants.

DAPHNE: You think she found clarity, huh? A union job offer made her see the light?

EDDIE: Sometimes that's all it takes.

DAPHNE: Eddie. Eddie Spaghetti.

EDDIE: It's the grief talking.

DAPHNE: You think that's why I'm here?

EDDIE: If it is, I don't mind.

DAPHNE: Cuz everyone is after something, ain't that right?

EDDIE: Otherwise the Habitrail stops spinning round and round.

> *There is a silence as they allow themselves to settle into the room, each placing their personal objects—handbag, jacket, etc. in a specific place, as if laying out a child's clothing for morning. Each one's awareness of the other is acute throughout this ritual. When they are both still again:*

DAPHNE: Show me where you got shot.

> *Eddie lifts his shirt. Daphne approaches him and lays her hand on the spot.*

And you shot back, didn't you?

> *Eddie nods.*

Where did you hit him?

EDDIE: *(He points to a place on his own body, somewhere in the stomach area.)* You wanna aim right at the chest, but you'll settle for hitting 'em anywhere in the torso. That's where all the critical organs are. Lungs, stomach, heart—

DAPHNE: What did it feel like?

EDDIE: There's a specific feeling to pulling a trigger to full release that your finger never forgets. You gotta isolate the impulse in your finger to pull every other muscle in your body along with it when you curl it around the trigger. You're gonna want to move other body parts with it. But you can't. You gotta just focus. As you squeeze the trigger, it'll get heavier, you'll wanna just jerk your finger fast, but you gotta stop yourself. You gotta commit to it. You gotta keep squeezing evenly until you feel it release.

> *Beat.*

DAPHNE: Show me.

> *Slowly, reluctantly, Eddie produces the gun he has been carrying. He unloads it, shows Daphne how to hold it, how to aim it, and in doing so, begins to hold her.*

EDDIE: You think you want to feel that feeling now, but you don't. It lives in your muscles too long.

DAPHNE: Does it drown out the other noise?

EDDIE: Some nights.

DAPHNE: Good enough.

Daphne and Eddie find their way into a kiss. Eddie lays the gun down on the nightstand. Throughout the following scene with the Roys, Daphne and Eddie remain seen as they make their way into bed, starting to have sex, and then settling into sleeping while the other scene goes on.

Lights up on Marlo and Tina watching TV in Nana's living room. It is nighttime and they watch in a darkened room. We can hear a competing TV playing, the sound coming from Nana's bedroom, offstage. We also hear a door quickly opening and closing, also offstage.

TINA: Dom? That you?

Another sound of a door shutting.

Dom? Everything OK?

Dominick comes out of the bathroom and into the living room, a towel in his hand is stained with blood. There is blood all over his clothing. The blood's been rinsed off his face and hands in part, but traces of it remain smeared on his skin and in his hair. He is a wreck—nervous, shaking, breathing heavily.

TINA: Oh my God!

MARLO: What the fuck happened?!

TINA: Get him out. Get him OUTSIDE!

The two women rush Dominick outside. Tina herds the trio to the side of the house, off to the side of the driveway where they are in low light from a streetlight. Tina grabs a hose and pulls Dominick's head down under it, turning on the water. The water is freezing and it's cold outside and Dominick reacts to this, shaking uncontrollably. Tina holds him steady as she washes him.

MARLO: Where's Anson?

TINA: Go get a clean towel and a blanket. AND SOME TRASH BAGS!

Marlo follows Tina's instructions and goes back inside the house. Tina pulls off Dominick's outer clothing, tossing it into a pile. Dominick follows Tina's lead and steps out of his clothing, struggling to stay warm. Throughout his monologue, Tina continues to undress him, hose him off, and wipe the blood off his body.

135

TINA: It's OK. It's OK.

Marlo comes back outside with a towel which Tina grabs from her and hands to Dominick.

MARLO: What happened?

DOMINICK: Tina. Tina dropped me off down the street from Anson's place. I walk up, try to get closer to the house. I wait outside, out by the road. The car's not there. I wait. I just wait. Then I can see the car coming up the road. He pulls into the driveway. I'm hiding out there, he can't see me. I got a bag with me. Brought some backup with me, just in case.

MARLO: Dom, we said JUST THE CAR.

DOMINICK: Shut up, Marlo! I said just in case. Anson gets out of the car and I start to walk up the drive toward him. He sees me. Starts pointing, telling me get back to the road, I gotta leave. Says he's gonna call the cops on account of the restraining order. But I keep going up to him. And we're both yelling now. And I charge at him, just throw my whole body at him and he swings at me. Swings at my face. Starts pushing me back, hitting me in the chest with his hands, like . . .

Dominick demonstrates each action with his hands as he describes it.

He keeps pushing me, and I'm going backwards, like, and we're heading back down the driveway to the road when he stops. Tells me to get the fuck outta his yard. Outta his life. Tells me I'm going to jail. He's going to the cops. And then he starts back to the car. He's taking out his keys and I dunno I just see him about to leave and ruin everything. So I run back and pick up my crossbow and before he can reach for the car door handle, I . . .

Dominick mimes picking up the crossbow and firing it.

But he doesn't go down. He's just spinning and clutching his chest, trying to hold onto something, coming at me still, so I throw down the crossbow and grab my bat and just start . . .

He does this.

. . . swinging at him. And I connect. And I connect. And the bat keeps hitting him. The shoulders first. And then again. And again. And the bat keeps on . . . hitting. And then I hit his head.

There is a sound effect to indicate Anson's head being smacked by a bat.

And he goes down.

Marlo is crying loudly inconsolably by this point, holding herself. Tina is focused on Dominick's story.

There's just so much blood. His head is . . . swollen. I can't even see him. I'm trying to think what to do and I gotta get him in that car. But I can't find the keys. He had 'em in his hand when I first shot at him. I scramble around a little and find 'em. They fell under the car a little, on the driveway, so I'm reaching under there to get 'em. Then I try dragging him over to the car, pulling him up under his arms, get him over there. I try to pull him up into the backseat, figure we can pose him later, but I can't get him in there. I just . . . can't. There's too much fucking stuff packed in his back seat, boxes and shit. So fuck it, I drag him over to the side of the house and cover him with a bunch of leaves and I take off. Came right here.

136

MARLO: You LEFT him there?

DOMINICK: Uh huh.

MARLO: Are you out of your mind?

TINA: Marlo, be quiet.

MARLO: His dead body is sitting out on his lawn—

DOMINICK: I'm not sure if he was dead yet, he was huffing and puffing pretty bad still.

MARLO: Sitting out there so anyone could find it?

DOMINICK: I put him under some stuff, I said.

MARLO: Fucking LEAVES!?

TINA: Marlo, shut up.

MARLO: God, you FUCKUP! This was supposed to be about a car!

TINA: Marlo, it's time for you to shut up. We need a plan to fix this now.

MARLO: Oh great, another plan. We HAD a plan.

TINA: Well, it's time for a new one.

MARLO: *(to Dominick)* You left the weapons just lying around, too?

TINA: Both of you. FUCKING FOCUS! *(She resumes cleaning the scene, tossing Dom's clothing into trashbags, etc.)* Now, we gotta get that Passat back to Anson's place so it looks like he's home. We gotta go over there now and clean up and we don't want anyone driving by seeing people wandering around while Anson's car is not even there.

MARLO: I'm not going over there.

TINA: Yeah. You ARE. We'll take my truck. *(Tina is thinking through these steps very quickly but is not at all haphazard about it. She delivers them in a firm and confident manner.)* Dom, we gotta get you dressed. I'm gonna bag up these clothes and we'll burn them later. Dom, you'll come with me and Marlo, you're gonna drive the Passat.

MARLO: I'm not—

TINA: *(overriding her)* You get there first and gather up anything you can see, anything that was left behind, and then we'll drive up and you can dump 'em in the back of the truck. We gotta stop off and get some bleach from the store, clean up some of that blood in the driveway. Then we gotta get his body up onto the truck.

MARLO: Where're we gonna take it, huh? Just gonna leave it somewhere? Where the FUCK are we gonna get rid of a body?!

Pause.

TINA: I got an idea for that.

The trio exits, wiping up all spilled water with their towels and taking the towels with them. Marlo re-enters, now dressed in a jacket, with a rake or

137

hoe in her hand. She is now at Dominick and Tina's farm where she tends a fire. She is calm. The burning body crackles in the fire. Daphne approaches her. This is Daphne's dream.

MARLO: *(without looking at Daphne)* That's not my brother. That's not my brother...in there.

DAPHNE: Where is he then?

MARLO: Dunno. He disappeared.

DAPHNE: Marlo.

MARLO: It doesn't matter, though. I can take care of things. I can get all the paperwork in order.

    Beat.

You here for the reunion? That's this year, you know. Twenty-five years since high school. You didn't even graduate from here, though, so—

DAPHNE: I'm here to see you.

MARLO: Yeah. Well. *(Beat.)* Lot's changed. *(Beat.)* You know, bringing the body out to the farm was the stupidest idea, in retrospect. That wasn't my idea. It was probably one of the damn neighbors called it in when they saw the smoke. I wanted to leave the body IN the Passat. I said to dump it somewhere along I-94 and then just report it stolen. But Dominick—GOD!—he just wouldn't let go of that motherfucking car. The cheap shit. I told him insurance would cover it. But hell if he was gonna trust insurance guys at this point.

DAPHNE: How would you have preferred to do it?

MARLO: Ultimately, I think poison works best.

    Beat.

DAPHNE: How are you doing?

MARLO: *(shrugs)* It's boring. It's more boring than you'd think.

    Beat.

Did you like Texas?

DAPHNE: It was OK.

MARLO: I was thinking about moving down there, maybe. Be good to try something new.

DAPHNE: Marlo, what happened?

MARLO: Why? You wanna write a book about it or something?

DAPHNE: I meant, what happened . . . to you?

MARLO: Cuz I could tell you some things would make a real good book. You know, I wrote a couple new monologues. Thought I'd use them for auditions. I could maybe read 'em to you? Sometime?

    Daphne doesn't say anything.

138

Oh, so you think the fact we sang in choir together makes us friends? You're just a girl who moved away. Why are you here?

DAPHNE: What did it feel like?

MARLO: That's what you want to know?

DAPHNE: Did it help you?

MARLO: It felt good.

DAPHNE: Really?

MARLO: He's a pile of bones and skin. There's no soul in there.

DAPHNE: It's that easy?

MARLO: Whether it was a good thing or a bad thing we did, it was . . . it's done. Doesn't have to burden my mind anymore.

> *Lights change. Marlo and the fire go away and Daphne is left alone. Ceil enters the stage, gasping for breath, and gets in bed with Eddie, in the empty space left by Daphne. She lies down, breathing with great effort, re-enacting her final moments, perhaps. Eddie, still undressed, gets up from the bed and exits into the hotel bathroom. Daphne watches this. Ceil's breathing stops.*

DAPHNE: You're not there, you know.

CEIL: *(referring to phantom MARLO)* Neither was she. You know.

> *Daphne sits down on the bed across from Ceil.*

DAPHNE: You stayed with him.

CEIL: *(sits up)* Yes.

DAPHNE: Why'd you do that? I coulda helped you. I woulda made you stay at that hospital all night.

CEIL: *(She doesn't know how to say this.)* I just—

> *Beat.*

Nah. Nothing you could do.

DAPHNE: Don't do that. You always did that. Always giving up and settling for—

> *Ceil is overcome.*

What happened to you?

> *Beat.*

I was telling this group . . . I was talking about you, uh, to this group. I went there to this grief thing—

CEIL: *(laughs)* You had therapy cuz of me?

DAPHNE: Sort of.

CEIL: That's priceless.

DAPHNE: Shut up. I told this story about you—you know, the one about that pumpkin painting contest back when—and I'm sobbing and these people are all patting me on the shoulder and rubbing my back. And the next woman in the circle, she's right next to me, she turns to me and she's nodding and tilting her head, saying there there, she understands. Says she felt exactly the same way when her dog died. Her DOG.

CEIL: Shit.

DAPHNE: Nobody says that when you lose your husband. Your daughter. Nobody compares them to a PET. But man, nobody knows what to do with siblings.

CEIL: I dunno. Dogs are pretty cool. I like 'em better than most people.

DAPHNE: After the meeting, I keyed her car.

CEIL: So much for therapy.

DAPHNE: Yeah.

> *There is a moment of peace. Then Daphne starts to cry.*

Forgive me. Please. Forgive me. Forgive me. You need to forgive me. Please. Please. Forgive me.

> *Ceil considers Daphne, but does not let her off the hook. She does not judge her, nor does she forgive her. Ceil gets up and exits the hotel room, concluding Daphne's dream and leaving her there in the present moment. In the hotel room. About five a.m. Eddie re-enters from the bathroom and approaches the bed, seeing Daphne tossing and turning. He tries to wake her.*

EDDIE: Hey.

DAPHNE: Please—

EDDIE: Hey, it's me.

DAPHNE: What's—

EDDIE: It's just me. Eddie.

DAPHNE: How did you—
No. Don't.
Please, please don't—

EDDIE: Hey, hon. What's the matter?

DAPHNE: Don't hurt me. I won't say any—

EDDIE: Hurt you?

DAPHNE: Just, please, please leave—

EDDIE: Hold on—

DAPHNE: Who are—
Oh God.
WHO THE FUCK ARE YOU?!

EDDIE: Wake up. You're having a nightmare.

DAPHNE: *(clutching her chest with both hands and breathing deeply and with great effort)* It's—I can't breathe. It's my heart. Call the nurse assist—

EDDIE: What?

DAPHNE: The NURSE ASSIST LINE. It's on the fridge. Call them.

EDDIE: You're not at home. You're here. You're in a hotel. You're safe. Everything will be OK.

DAPHNE: I think I'm having a heart attack.

EDDIE: You're not.

DAPHNE: I am. Call 9-1-1.

EDDIE: Just sit. Here, just sit. Sit back and, and just breathe. And I'll call . . . wait a minute and I'll call. But just breathe . . .

She does, slowly beginning to settle down.

Now, what does it feel like?

DAPHNE: Hot. And. Pressure. Like pushing, something's pushing down on it.

EDDIE: Any stabbing pains?

DAPHNE: Just burning.

EDDIE: OK, just breathe. I'm getting you some water.

He runs into the adjoining bathroom and returns with a glass of water. He rejoins her and sits or crouches close to her.

Do you remember where you are?

She looks around.

Do you remember who I am?

She looks at him.

It's gonna be all right.

DAPHNE: You can't promise me that.

EDDIE: Yes, I can.

DAPHNE: You're gonna be mad at me.

EDDIE: Why would I be mad at you?

DAPHNE: The keys.

EDDIE: Yeah?

DAPHNE: The keys. *(Beat.)* They're in my purse. I just—

EDDIE: You had 'em the whole time?

DAPHNE: I was afraid you'd leave me alone there. At my apartment. I couldn't be alone last night, Eddie. I can't be alone. Make it go away, Eddie. Make it GO AWAY.

EDDIE: It doesn't go away.

DAPHNE: Then I can't do this.

EDDIE: Not alone you can't.

DAPHNE: Don't fucking life-coach me.

EDDIE: I'm not. I'm saying you're not special, hon. There's a hundred million schmoes like you out here right now melting down. And we're all gonna be OK. Any day now.

DAPHNE: Her heart, Eddie, her heart just tore in two.

EDDIE: And there's nothing else you can do about that.

Beat.

Here. Drink some water.

He gets up.

DAPHNE: Are you leaving? Please don't go.

EDDIE: Do you want me to stay?

DAPHNE: Are you mad at me?

EDDIE: Do you want me to stay?

DAPHNE: Yes.

Beat.

We could. Get. Breakfast.

Pause.

EDDIE: I like eggs.

DAPHNE: I like eggs.

EDDIE: OK.

DAPHNE: OK then.

EDDIE: I'm gonna—I think I oughta take a shower. You. You stay there. Relax. Drink. Breathe.

He nods. She nods with him. He goes into the bathroom and the water is turned on. We hear the sound of the shower throughout the rest of the scene.

For a moment, Daphne has found relief, peace. She is here now and needs to face a new day. And maybe this will be OK. After settling down and considering her future, she gets up and begins getting dressed, slowly picking up pieces of her clothing from where they were left the night before.

Slowly, it begins to dawn on her. This won't be OK. And as she accepts this fact, Daphne's instincts take over. She completes the following actions: She finishes getting dressed. She takes the envelope full of money out of her purse and leaves it on the table. She walks over to Eddie's pile of clothing and rifles through his pockets, finding his keys and taking them. Then she walks over to the nightstand where Eddie left the gun. She picks it up, places it in her purse, gives the room one final once-over, then exits out the hotel room door, the shower waterfall still audible.

END OF PLAY

142

DAN O'BRIEN is a playwright and poet living in Los Angeles. His play, *The Body of an American*, received its European premiere in January 2014 in an extended run at the Gate Theatre in London, in co-production with Royal & Derngate Theatre in Northampton, England, directed by James Dacre. *The Body of an American* was commissioned by The Playwrights' Center's McKnight Commission and Residency Program (Minneapolis, MN), premiered at Portland Center Stage, directed by Bill Rauch, and received the inaugural Edward M. Kennedy Prize for Drama, the PEN Center USA Award for Drama, The Horton Foote Prize, and the L. Arnold Weissberger Award. O'Brien's award-winning debut poetry collection, *War Reporter*, is published by Hanging Loose Press in Brooklyn and CB editions in London.

Dan O'Brien

The Body of an American

Inspired in part by the book
Where War Lives by Paul Watson

CHARACTERS:

Two actors play all the roles here: ideally an actor in his 30s who plays **DAN** most of the time, and an actor around 50 to mostly play **PAUL**.

The older of these two actors has the first line of the play, and with each new character-heading—even when it's the same character—the actors alternate.

In the right-hand column of the script are suggestions of photographs, maps, moving images, etc., to be projected somewhere prominent onstage; as well as suggestions for occasional sound design. All of the photographs listed are by Paul Watson or the playwright or unknown, except where noted.

PLACE & TIME:

SCENES 1–7: various.

SCENES 8–10: the Arctic, the Present.

I do want to hear this because
you're another person in this story.
Um, and each, each person in this story
ends up telling his own story of what
I call—the working title for the book
I'm writing is Where War Lives. From a quote
of Albert Camus when he was keeping
his notebooks pre-World War Two. And a friend
wrote to him saying, you know, I'm grappling
with this philosophical question, Where
does this vile thing, war, live? And Camus said,
he's in Algiers at the time and he says,

I look at the bright blue sky and I think
of the guilt that I feel from not being
in a position where I, I can die
with them, while at the same time wanting to
be as far away as I can from it.

—Paul Watson in conversation with
Dr. Joseph LeDoux, January 2006

146

1: Fresh Air

PAUL: My name's Paul Watson.

PAUL: I'm Paul Watson.

TERRY GROSS: This
is Fresh Air,

TERRY GROSS: I'm Terry Gross. Remember
that famous 1993 photo?

PAUL: I was a reporter who happened to—

DAN: Dear Mr. Watson. I don't usually
email strangers like this.

TERRY GROSS: This is Fresh Air.

DAN: I was leaving Princeton.

PAUL: New Jersey?

DAN: Where
I had this fellowship.

PAUL: You had a what?

DAN: A residency—

PAUL: Which means you do what?

DAN: Well
I was supposed to write a play.

PAUL: A play.

DAN: Yes.

PAUL: About what?

DAN: Ghosts.

PAUL: Ghosts?

DAN: Yeah. Ghosts.

PAUL: What kind
of ghosts?

DAN: Historical, ghosts.

PAUL: And they pay you
for this?

DAN: Sort of. Definitely. I'm really
grateful to them—

PAUL: Is it scary?

DAN: My play?
I don't know. I hope so. To me it was.

TERRY GROSS: This is Fresh Air,

TERRY GROSS: I'm Terry Gross. Let's start
with a description of that now famous
Pulitzer prize-winning photo:

PAUL: I was
a reporter who happened to carry
a camera, a 35 mm

Nikon I bought because my editors
wouldn't buy me one.

PAUL: We were on the roof
of the Sahafi, where the journalists were
staying,

PAUL: *if* they were staying.

PAUL: You could count
on one hand who was still there.

PAUL: I'd have to
count on one hand because my other hand

PAUL: isn't really a hand at all.

PAUL: I was
born this way.

PAUL: A bunch of us were drinking
beer.

PAUL: Did you see that light?

REPORTER: What light?

PAUL: Behind
that chopper there. It just went down behind
that hill.

DAN: Chaos ensues.   *Image:*
                                                    white light.

PAUL: A 16-hour
battle raged through the night between US
Army rangers, special ops, Delta Force
and Somali militias. It started
as an arrest operation trying
to abduct commanders in Mohamed
Aideed's militia. They were trying to
track down Aideed and arrest him for
allegedly organizing attacks
on UN peacekeepers.

PAUL: When I woke up
on the hotel floor, still dressed, hung over,

PAUL: 18 American soldiers had been killed
and 75 wounded.

PAUL: Clouds of smoke
billowing up from burning tire barricades,
dead bodies in the street.

PAUL: American troops
were trying to get the rest of their force
back alive, and in so doing they'd killed
more than 600 Somalis so far,

PAUL: including women and children, huddled
in the darkness as bullets or shrapnel

pierced the tin walls of their shacks.

PAUL: Gutale's
my translator. He hurries through the gate:

GUTALE: They are shooting everything that moves now,
even donkeys!

PAUL: He gets 30 dollars
a day.

PAUL: My driver and bodyguard get
a hundred.

PAUL: That's always been the hardest
part of my job: convincing good people
who get none of a byline's ego boost
to risk their lives because I've decided
a story's worth dying for.

GUTALE: They're shooting
people on sight! Even people with no
weapons!

PAUL: Mogadishu was beautiful
once, white-painted Italianate villas
in the capitol of the most stable
state in Africa.

PAUL: Now you see women
grocery shopping with militias firing
machine guns up and down the avenue,

PAUL: children playing on the front lines, running
water and bullets beside their mothers
to keep the gunmen supplied.

GUTALE: They shot down
a Black Hawk! They are taking a soldier
with them from street to street, perhaps alive,
perhaps dead!

PAUL: They threw me in the back seat
of the car,

PAUL: a Toyota Cressida
that nobody outside of the safe zone
would recognize,

PAUL: and made me hide my face
between Gutale and my body guard
Mohamed.

PAUL: With another Mohamed
driving, and a gunman in front cradling
an AK-47,

PAUL: we drove through
the gates and crawled from street to street. Passing
the corpse-collectors, men carrying bodies

by their hands and feet, glaring at us through
the filthy windshield.

GUTALE: Has anyone seen
a captured American soldier?

PAUL: Some said,

GUTALE: They've seen him. He says he's alive, tied up
in a wheelbarrow.

PAUL: A wheelbarrow?

GUTALE: No,
this man says he's dead. He's most definitely
dead.

PAUL: I took a few pictures of some kids
bouncing up and down on a rotor blade
in the smoldering tail section of that downed
Black Hawk.

GUTALE: Have you seen the American
soldier?

PAUL: The entire crowd pointed,

GUTALE: This way.

PAUL: Each time a Black Hawk thundered past people
would shake their fists and curse at it.

PAUL: We drove
all over the city for two hours and
were about to give up,

PAUL: when the driver
makes a u-turn.

GUTALE: He sees something.

PAUL: A mob
of 200 Somalis, moving down
an alleyway.

GUTALE: What is it?

MOHAMED: This is bad,
too dangerous.

GUTALE: Go slowly.

PAUL: What's he saying?

GUTALE: He's a coward. He's worried about his
car.

MOHAMED: This guy's going to get us killed!

GUTALE: Shut up!

PAUL: Gutale gets out:

GUTALE: Gamay's in the car,
you know Gamay!

PAUL: Gamay is local slang
for cripple.

GUTALE: Little man! No hand! He's not American, he's Canadian! You know Gamay. He just wants to take some pictures. Can he?

PAUL: The crowd parts around me.

PAUL: I look down at the street:

PAUL: and I meet Staff Sgt. William David Cleveland.

GUTALE: Take the picture quickly.

PAUL: I've taken pictures of corpses before, many of them much more fucked up than this man.

GUTALE: Hurry, Paul!

PAUL: I bend over, shoulders stiff.

GUTALE: Take it now!

PAUL: With a camera in front of your eye, you cover your face and you focus only on the good shot.

PAUL: You shut everything else out.

PAUL: Everything goes quiet.

PAUL: Despite the noise of the crowd and the helicopters,

PAUL: everything goes completely silent. And I hear a voice both in my head and out:

CLEVELAND: If you do this, I will own you forever.

PAUL: I'm sorry but I have to.

CLEVELAND: If you do this, I will own you.

PAUL: I've sought psychiatric treatment in subsequent years. And my psychiatrist says it's my superego. I believe it was William David Cleveland speaking to me.

TERRY GROSS: And what did he mean?

PAUL: Well, Terry, I took it as a warning.

TERRY GROSS:	A warning of what exactly?
PAUL:	I have to do this.
PAUL:	I don't want to do this.
PAUL:	I don't want to desecrate your body.
CLEVELAND:	If you do this I will own you forever.
PAUL:	I took his picture.
PAUL:	While they were beating his body and cheering. Some spitting.
PAUL:	Some kid wearing a chopper crewman's goggles shoves his way into the frame. His face is all screwed up in rapturous glee while giving the dead man the finger.
PAUL:	An old man's raising his cane like a club and thudding it down against the dead flesh.
PAUL:	Wind's blowing dirt and the stench is making me gag.
PAUL:	For weeks I'd hated UN peacekeepers like this man, who killed from the sky with impunity.
PAUL:	But now it was us against them.
GUTALE:	Get in the car, Gamay!
PAUL:	The men holding the ropes that bind the soldier's wrists are stretching his arms out over his head.
PAUL:	They're rolling his body back and forth in the hammering morning light.
PAUL:	I feel like I'm standing beside myself.
PAUL:	I feel like I'm somebody else watching myself take these photographs,
PAUL:	somebody named Paul, doing this crazy thing,
PAUL:	shooting pictures.
PAUL:	Asking, Did I put the batteries in?
PAUL:	*Click.*

Image: Paul Watson's full-length photograph of Staff Sgt. William David Cleveland.

Image: another shot from this series.

Image: another shot from this series.

PAUL: The bullet wounds are in his legs: did they shoot him in the street, did he die before he crashed?

PAUL: *Click.*   *Image: another shot.*

PAUL: His body's so limp he must have just died.

PAUL: *Click.*   *Image: another shot.*

PAUL: Maybe he's still alive? Is that why I can hear his voice? If you do this,

PAUL: *Click. Click.*   *Image: another shot.*

PAUL: I will own you.

PAUL: *Click. Click. Click. Click.*   *Image: another shot.*

PAUL: You poor man. Who are you?

GUTALE: We must go. Let's go. They don't want us here anymore.

PAUL: The car door's shut.

PAUL: Soft idling of the engine. The muffled mob.

PAUL: It's like I've stepped out of Mogadishu into

PAUL: a wobbling canoe years ago in Sudan,   *Moving image: water at dusk.*

PAUL: drifting downriver at dusk with

ANDREW: Andrew Stawicki,

PAUL: a Polish émigré photographer who snaps a picture of boys running naked like a snake along the river's blood-red spine. That's going to be a great picture.

ANDREW: They won't print it.

PAUL: Why not?

ANDREW: The kid's dick is showing!

PAUL: In my mind's eye I see Sgt. Cleveland's Army-issue green underwear, the only clothing left on his body.

PAUL: The underwear's slightly askew, so you can just make out a piece of the dead man's scrotum.   *Image: Paul's full-body shot.*

PAUL: Open the door! Open it!

PAUL: This time I framed it better: the body from the waist up.

153

PAUL: A woman
slapping him with a flattened can.

PAUL: That boy
with the goggles shoveling his face through
the mob,

PAUL: laughing at us.

PAUL: Men with bloodshot
eyes notice me.

PAUL: It would be like squashing
a cockroach to kill me, this infidel
who can't take a hint.

GUTALE: Look, he's leaving now!
See? We're leaving for good! Thank you!

PAUL: The squeak
of the hotel gate always let me breathe
easier. As if a few sleepy guards could
actually keep us safe from everything
happening out there.

PAUL: I take the service stairs
two at a time to my room, stuff the roll
of film between the mattress and box spring,
switch on the broken AC,

PAUL: and collapse
on my bed with my eyes closed and I cry
for a very long time.

TERRY GROSS: This is Fresh Air.
The AP printed it, and so did Time
Magazine.

PAUL: That's right. AP moved the half
-body shots, which appeared in newspapers
all over the world. What Time Magazine
did, which I find fascinating, is they
digitally altered the underwear
so you can't see any genitals. But
you do see horrific desecration
of an American soldier.

TERRY GROSS: This picture
had incredible impact.

PAUL: Yes, Terry,
that's right. Because immediately the heat
was on President Bill Clinton to do
something. And that something was to announce
the immediate withdrawal of American
troops. Then, when it became time to decide
whether or not the United States should

Image: Paul's famous half-body shot.

154

lead an intervention in Rwanda,
where 800,000 people were killed
in a hundred days, President Clinton
decided not to use the word genocide
so we wouldn't be *forced* to intervene.
And we know without a doubt Al-Qaeda
was there in Mogadishu. It says so
on indictments in US Federal Court,
bin Laden's bragged about it, his minions
have bragged about it. But what disturbs me
the most is that Al-Qaeda learned a lot
from the propaganda impact of that
photograph. 18 American soldiers
were killed that day. Which is nothing compared
to what used to happen on a bad day
in Vietnam. And it's only relatively
bad compared to what's still happening these days
in Iraq, or Afghanistan. I think
it's safe to say, take all of the events
that happened, but remove the photograph,
and Al-Qaeda would not have chased us out
of Somalia, bin Laden would not have
been able to say to his followers, Look
we're able to do this, we only need
small victories to defeat history's greatest
military. After my photograph:
9/11, and this never-ending
war on terror.

TERRY GROSS: My guest today has been
war reporter Paul Watson. His new memoir
about reporting from war zones is called
Where War Lives.

TERRY GROSS: We'll talk more after a break.

2: Who Was He Talking To

Google map:
Princeton, NJ.

DAN: I was listening to this podcast. Writing
my play about historical ghosts. Packing
up all our things. It was the very end
of August. It was the end of New York
for us. It was the end of something else,
what? our youth? In Princeton. Which is just so
beautiful this time of year. Every time
of year, really. All the trees and leaves. All
the squirrels. All of the privileged children,
including myself, in some ways. I was

sad to leave. It had been a rough few years.
I'd walk around the campus late at night
and feel almost good about myself. Smart.
Of value. And of course I felt guilty
too, to have had this library. These trees
and squirrels. The beautiful young women
to watch. Unlimited laser printing.
While you're off in Iraq, Paul. Or Kabul.
Or Jakarta, that's where you live, Paul, right?

Google map: Jakarta.

And Jakarta's in Indonesia. Right?
There was this hangar-sized Whole Foods nearby,

Video image: verdant window in Princeton.

lots of Priuses, and bumper stickers
celebrating the date when Bush would leave
office. I'd go running in thunderstorms
sometimes. I'd sit on the back porch sipping
vodka, cooking meat on a charcoal grill.
Watching swallows swoop out of a twilit
sky into my maple tree. And your voice
got to me. It's your voice:

PAUL: I tend to be
solitary.

DAN: This is you speaking, though
it might as well be me.

PAUL: I like to stay
home with my wife and son.

DAN: Dinner parties?

PAUL: I tend to stay away. I've spent enough
time around people who do what I do,
and in my opinion, and I include
myself foremost in this group, we're a bunch
of misfits, people who are seeking self
-esteem through risk.

DAN: I felt you could have been
talking about playwrights. Without any
real risk. You were mad:

PAUL: I'm sick of being
lied to. And I take it as a challenge
to make sure nobody's lying to me.

DAN: I felt like I knew you. Or I was you
in some alternate reality.

PAUL: Men
start wars because it helps them to make sure
that women aren't laughing at them.

DAN: You
were funny. Sort of.

PAUL: I'm more comfortable
with the weak than I am the powerful,
growing up in this condition.

DAN: We should
talk about that, your hand.

PAUL: Should we?

DAN: Why not?

PAUL: It's helped me out a lot. In Kosovo
in food lines, they'd think I was a wounded
war vet and give me all kinds of free stuff.

DAN: And as I'm packing and listening to you
I'm wondering if I feel so moved because
you sound so messed up,

PAUL: If something's risky
and we probably shouldn't do it, I'll say,
Don't worry about me, I'm already
dead.

DAN: Or because you scare me. The haunted
often sound like ghosts, in my experience.

PAUL: I just have this sense I've already lived
much longer than I should have.

DAN: You poor man,
who are you?

3: Q&A. Or, Got To Go

PAUL: I have no idea who my father was.

DAN: He was a soldier, right?

PAUL: I've got to go.
Take care. Paul.

DAN: I just wanted to say thanks
for writing me back. I got your email
on my wife's BlackBerry halfway across
the country, at this tumbleweed rest stop
on an Indian reservation somewhere
outside Tulsa.

PAUL: Dear Dan, I just got back
from Kabul. Where I found out it's easy
to buy stolen US military
flash drives at an Afghan bazaar outside
Bagram air base. And these flash drives are full
of classified information, social
security numbers of soldiers, maps
of Taliban and Al-Qaeda targets
in both Afghanistan and Pakistan.

Image: Paul Watson preparing to take a photo; his deformed hand is prominent. (Andrew Stawicki)

Photo: Watson Family photo, 1960; Paul is in the baby stroller.

157

Google map: Kabul.

Images: ID photos of US soldiers, maps of air strikes in Afghanistan and Pakistan, 2008.

DAN:	Wow.
PAUL:	Sorry, what were we talking about?
DAN:	Your dad.
PAUL:	Stormed the beach at Normandy. Died a few days shy of my second birthday.
DAN:	And you were born when?
PAUL:	1959. How old are you, Dan?
DAN:	I'm younger than you. I could be your nephew, or a younger brother maybe.
PAUL:	My father didn't die in the war though.
DAN:	Of course not. How did he?
PAUL:	He had PKD, or Polycystic Kidney Disease.
DAN:	Which is what?
PAUL:	Like it sounds: cysts start growing all over your kidneys till eventually you die. I have it too.
DAN:	Will it kill you?
PAUL:	I've got pills for it.
DAN:	So, what you mean when you say you don't know who your dad was, is you don't remember him?
PAUL:	Do you?
DAN:	Do I remember my dad?
PAUL:	Do you know who he is?
DAN:	What do you mean?
PAUL:	What did you think I meant?
DAN:	He was around. I mean my father was always around, every day. He never spoke to us. If he did, well then it was just to tell you how fucking stupid you were.
PAUL:	Is he dead?
DAN:	I don't know.
PAUL:	You don't know?
DAN:	Wait why are you asking *me* questions?
PAUL:	I've got to get back to Kabul. I'll email you.

158

DAN: I'm staying
in this condo in a renovated
schoolhouse. Sometimes I hear ghostly children
laughing. This gland in my neck is swollen
and aches. I'm Googling the symptoms. Let's Skype
or Facebook. Are you on Facebook?

PAUL: I don't
know why but I'd rather keep emailing
like this. I don't know why. But it's almost
like a conversation.

DAN: Yeah but it's not
a conversation.

PAUL: Yeah but it's almost.
Are you in LA?

DAN: I'm in Madison,   *Google map:*
Wisconsin.   *Madison, WI.*

PAUL: What? Why?

DAN: Teaching.

PAUL: And writing
about ghosts?

DAN: Sure. Still.

PAUL: Is it snowing there? *Moving image:*

DAN: It hasn't stopped snowing since I touched down *falling snow.*
in January. Cars are abandoned
in the middle of highways. I don't leave
the condo much.

PAUL: I'm home in Jakarta, *Moving image:*
in case you're wondering. There's a thunderstorm *lightning, rain.*
and my little boy's asleep. He's always
asking me, How long will you be gone, Dad?
He's seven, so he doesn't understand
time just yet. Few weeks back we were lying
in bed together and he asked me, When
you're dead will you still be watching me? Where
were we?

DAN: We were talking about fathers.   159

PAUL: So then Ray enlisted at 17,

DAN: You call him Ray?

PAUL: faked his eye test. He was,

SOMEONE: Tall. Splendid physique.   *Image: family*

PAUL: That's what someone wrote *photo again;*
about him, in one of his files. It said,   *Paul's tall*
Ray is: *father.*

SOMEONE: Frank. Pleasant manner. Decisive
style of thinking.

PAUL: This one story I know,
there's only one story I know for sure,
they were taking a medieval city
in France, twisted streets, churches and houses   *Map: Villons-*
made of stone. My father takes a bullet   *les-buissons,*
in his thigh. Watches one of his soldiers   *France, 1944.*
trapped in the long grass. Ray can't do a thing
but watch his friend die. Each time this man cries
out for help, a Nazi sniper shoots him
till he's dead.

DAN: How do you know this?

PAUL: Research.
My mother told me.

DAN: Yes. Good. What's she like?

PAUL: She's the strongest woman I know.

DAN: Okay,
fine. What else?

PAUL: They were sitting together
on a streetcar. The bang of a pothole
and he's gone. She gets off at the next stop
and walks home, and sits down on the front step.
And waits for him.

DAN: Sounds like PTSD.

PAUL: I've got to cut this one short.

DAN: Can we talk
about your hand again?

PAUL: My hand?

DAN: You know,
your lack of a hand.

PAUL: I'll be in Sulu,
in the Philippines.

DAN: Outside my window   *Moving*
a freight train rolls past every night. Its bell   *image:*
tolls over and over again,   *snow falling.*

PAUL: Seven
civilians have been killed by Philippine
troops, including two children.

DAN: as the snow
piles higher on Lake Monona, burying
the sign Obama stuck in the ice: *Yes
We Can!*

PAUL: Reading glasses, check. Sensible
shoes, check.

DAN:	Spring break.

DAN: Spring break.

Image: bright light.

PAUL: —Hey, Dan! You were asking
about my hand. It doesn't bother me
much. My mother used to always tell me,
Nobody's perfect!

DAN: How'd it get that way?

PAUL: The kids would crowd around me at recess
and the bravest ones would reach out and touch
my stump,

KID: How'd it get that way, Paul? Huh? Huh?

PAUL: This was when I remember first thinking:
This is not me.

PAUL: This, that body belongs
to somebody else.

PAUL: The day I was born
I had these nubbins instead of fingers

*Image: that
picture again
of Paul
preparing
to take a
photograph.
(Stawicki)*

PAUL: and the doctor just snipped them off.

PAUL: The hand's
attached to a wrist that bends, with a palm
no bigger than an infant's.

DAN: Did your mom
take thalidomide?

PAUL: Everyone thinks that,
but no she didn't. It's a mystery,
something in the DNA.

DAN: Is that why
you're like this?

PAUL: Like what, Dan?

DAN: Oh I don't know,
a war reporter?

PAUL: iPod, check. Satellite
phone, check. Laptop, check. Endless tangles of
cable, check.

DAN: Two people have been murdered
near where I'm staying,

161

PAUL: Some bars of Dettol,
disinfectant soap for microbes.

*Image:
Joel Anthony
Marino.*

DAN: a man
my age. A girl. On different days.

PAUL: Check.

DAN: Both
were stabbed repeatedly. In the middle
of the day, at home. I go out running
on the icy roads past their stained faces

*Image:
Brittany
Zimmermann.*

THE BODY OF AN AMERICAN

PAUL:
on telephone poles. Just like I used to
jog past the makeshift morgue outside Bellevue
that long-ago September.

PAUL: Sorry, Dan,
I've been out of touch. I was in Christchurch
on vacation. Where were we?

DAN: Your perfect
childhood.

PAUL: Yes, my street was Princess Margaret
Boulevard, my school was Princess Margaret
Public School.

DAN: Who's Princess Margaret again?

PAUL: We had a milkman, mailman, paperboy.

DAN: How many siblings did you have?

PAUL: Four. You?

DAN: Five.

PAUL: Wow, you really are Irish!

DAN: Nothing
bad happened in your childhood? other than
your absent father and your absent hand
that never bothered you?

PAUL: My brother Jim
liked to take my father's old Lugar out
of hiding. Sometimes he'd let me hold it
and I'd imagine myself as the man
who'd once held his finger on that trigger.

DAN: You mean your father?

PAUL: No, the dead Nazi
he got it from!

DAN: Did you have any friends?
You sound lonely. You sound kind of like this
really lonely kid.

PAUL: I was in a band
called Eruption? I was the manager
of the band, because of my hand. We did
a shitload of drugs: Purple Microdot,
California Sunshine—

DAN: What's that, acid?

PAUL: My best friend Richard and I listening
to *Dark Side of the Moon* in the middle
of this circle we'd burnt into a field
of grass behind my house, high as two kites.
Richard turned me on to Camus. We'd chew
peyote before gym class

*Google map:
Princess
Margaret
Blvd.,
Etobicoke,
Ontario,
Canada.*

*Music:
Pink Floyd's
"Brain
Damage."*

*Image:
Paul Watson as
a teenager in
the '70s:
plaid bow tie,
plaid pants.
Long hair.*

162

PAUL: and get off
          on the psychedelic rainbows trailing
          behind high-jumpers and kids doing flips
          off balance beams.

PAUL: Oh, I remember one
          thing that was somewhat disturbing: our friend
          Andy blew his brains out at his parents'
          summer cottage.

DAN: Just somewhat disturbing?

PAUL: It was hardly surprising. He was stuck
          outside himself.

DAN: Were you, Paul?

PAUL: I hung out
          with this dealer, he must've been 30.
          At a motel he pulls out a bottle
          and a baggie full of pills. Up or down,
          my choice. I wash down a few with a belt
          of whiskey.

DRUG DEALER: You took some heavy downers,
          man.

PAUL: Who cares?

DRUG DEALER: That's the trouble with chicks, right?

PAUL: Right!

DRUG DEALER: Hells yeah!

PAUL: An hour later he's carving
          his arm with his knife.

DRUG DEALER: Bitches always want
          perfection!

PAUL: Then he's slinging my body
          over his back like I'm some medevaced
          soldier on TV in Vietnam. Dumping
          me in a taxi.

DRUG DEALER: He's my little bro,
          man. Just take him home.

PAUL: Alone and puking
          through the chain link of a construction site
          as the taxi spits gravel.

DAN: You were fucked
          up, Paul. Maybe you were depressed. Maybe
          you were low on some brain chemical like
          serotonin, dopamine, whatever,
          and this kind of crazy behavior was
          your way of feeling normal.

163

*Image: close-up
of that photo
of Paul as a
teenager in
the '70s.*

PAUL: But I was
also having fun. Didn't you have fun
in high school, Dan?

DAN: Sorry, I've got to go
teach. My students are trying to learn how
to write with conflict and stakes and something
remotely real.

PAUL: I had this one teacher
I loved. He took us all on a field trip
once. There we were floating in our canoes   *Moving*
in Algonquin Provincial Park, under   *image:*
a canopy of stars. With my classmate   *river at*
Stephen Harper, future Prime Minister,   *night. Stars.*
no kidding, paddling behind. Thinking, Who
could *not* love Albert Camus? And that's how
I ended up winning the Pulitzer.

DAN: Wait. What? I don't get it—
PAUL: I've got to go,
this time it's an emergency. Turn on   *Google Map:*
your TV and you'll see.   *Burma.*

DAN: I've got to say,
Paul, I can't help feeling you're not being
entirely honest with me here. I mean,
I don't mean that you're lying, per se. But
everything has this kind of Hemingway
patina to it. This kind of old school
journalistic swagger. It's like you're trying
to impress me.

PAUL: I got into Burma
on a tourist visa. With the Tribune
execs measuring the column inches
we produce, not getting into Burma
to cover the cyclone devastation
would've been career suicide. Hiding
by day in the hull of a riverboat
in the Irrawaddy Delta. Among
the hundreds of corpses bobbing at dusk
in the sea-soaked paddies is the body
of a child. In pajama bottoms with   *Image:*
teddy bear cartoons on them. The bleached skin's *this image.*
like rotting rattan. The leg bones are green.
The stench is unbearable, but the people
on shore don't seem to notice. My fixer
explains that Buddhists believe the body   *Moving*
FIXER: is nothing more than an empty vessel,   *image:*
                                              river at night.
                                              Stars.

and the soul has already been reborn
as someone new.

PAUL: After several stiff drinks
that night I lay on the roof of our boat
staring up at the universe,

PAUL: listening
to Laura Bush give forth with earnest pleas
to the junta on Voice of America,

PAUL: and I imagined myself as nothing
more than a passenger on this rotting
vessel of my body. And it felt good,
I felt free.

DAN: That freight train's approaching fast,
its headlamp swallowing the churning snow.
The chiming bell, the shrieking horn—

PAUL: Dear Dan,
I've been meaning to say: you sound kind of
depressed. Don't let that get ahold of you.
Trust me. Maybe you should talk to someone
besides me? Or take a pill. Has it stopped
snowing yet?   *Moving*

DAN: Nope.   *image:*
PAUL: Medication. Calculate   *falling snow.*
estimated time away, multiply
by seven pills a day for depression,
blood pressure, PKD. Toss in extra
in case I get kidnapped. Check.

DAN: Where are you
going this time, Paul?

PAUL: A few chocolate bars:
85 percent cocoa, for the dose
of flavonoids the TV doctor says
will give me an extra 3.5 years
and fight heart plaque.

DAN: Where are you now?
PAUL: My son   165
is sleeping. It's the rainy season here
again and lightning's lighting up his face
like a strobe. I lean in close to his ear
and whisper,

PAUL: Don't be afraid.
PAUL: I'll come back
home soon.

PAUL: Do not be afraid.

PAUL: Japanese
green tea for the antioxidants. Corkscrew
for the cheap Bordeaux I'll purchase en route
at Duty Free,

DAN: I've got some more questions
for you, Paul—

PAUL: more antioxidants and
some liquid courage to help ease the pain
of these five-star hotel room blues.

4: The Ghosts Are Getting Closer

But I'm whining, Dan.

DAN: Okay, let's get back
to the story. You win the Pulitzer
Prize.

PAUL: I was in Rwanda when I heard
the news. As everybody's aware now,
300 Tutsis an hour were being
beaten to death with these large wooden clubs
with bent nails and heavy spikes sticking out
of them. Real prehistoric shit. Homemade
machetes. Just a few thousand UN
soldiers with air support could've washed all
those maggots away.

PAUL: We were getting high   *Moving*
on the bridge over Rusumo Falls.   *image, sound:*

PAUL: We   *waterfall.*
is not the royal we, we is someone
I don't want you to meet just yet.

PAUL: Khareen
and I watching refugees spill over
the border to Tanzania. Watching
corpses spill over the waterfall down
into this brown whirlpool, smashing against
the rocks.

PAUL: In a house we found children piled   *Sound:*
like sandbags on a bed.   *flies buzzing.*

PAUL: There's a baby
down at the bottom. Its tiny hand is
bloated, its severed head cracked open like
an eggshell. Did the older children try
to hide him in here?

PAUL: Outside the back door
I slipped on a bunch of school books. One book
had been covered neatly with a color

publicity shot of the *Dynasty*
TV show cast. With John Forsythe's fucking
grinning face.

PAUL: The ghosts are getting closer.

PAUL: In Gahini, a 16-year-old named
François Sempundu sat on the grimy
brown foam of his hospital bed.

TRANSLATOR: He says
Hutus hacked up his mother and siblings.
He says he hid beneath the kitchen sink
for a week, beside his family's rotting
corpses.

PAUL: François Sempundu was speaking
so calmly.

TRANSLATOR: He says, By then if someone
had come to kill me I wouldn't have cared
much.

PAUL: At a church near Nyarubuye   *Sound:*
we pushed open a gate on a courtyard   *cicadas,*
like Auschwitz. Like Sarajevo. They'd come here   *crickets.*
hoping God would protect them somehow, but
it only made things that much easier
to get butchered.

PAUL: In Zaire a girl stands
at the roadside. Rows of buzzing corpses.

PAUL: At a Rwandan refugee camp.

PAUL: She's
looking for the toilet,

PAUL: which was a field
where a hundred thousand people would shit
and piss and die.

PAUL: This girl stumbles barefoot
into a ditch of bodies, some rolled up
in reed mats. She's looking everywhere and
now she begins to cry.

PAUL: As if hoping   *Sound: this*
somebody will help her.   *child crying,*
                                                      as if far
PAUL: But nobody's   *away.*
coming.

PAUL: I thought to myself, This would make
a great picture.

PAUL: This is a beautiful
picture, somehow.

167

THE BODY OF AN AMERICAN

PAUL: I raised my camera, stepped
backwards to frame her with more corpses and
I stepped on a dead old woman's arm.

PAUL: It
snaps like a stick.

PAUL: Then a few days later
I'm at Columbia University's
Low Memorial Library. In this room
like the Parthenon and the Pantheon
confused. Cornucopias of hors d'oeuvres
on aproned banquet tables, wearing tight shoes
and a navy blazer, wool slacks picked out
this morning at Brooks Brothers. John Honderich,
my boss at the *Star*—

HONDERICH: Watson, you don't look
so hot.

PAUL: I guess I just feel bad about
that soldier's family.

HONDERICH: Have you thought about
finding his wife, or his mother? hunting
them down?

PAUL: Had I?

PAUL: Had I?

PAUL: Kevin Carter,
who just last month was snorting Ritalin
off the floor of my apartment before
rocketing off into the townships,

PAUL: wins
for feature photography:

PAUL: a vulture
waiting for a Sudanese girl to die.

PAUL: Always a popular category.

PAUL: Carter comes back to the table:

CARTER: Hear that
applause, Watson? I kicked your arse!

PAUL: Two months
later I'm back in Rwanda. Honderich
calls me on my satellite phone:

HONDERICH: Carter
killed himself last night. Parked his pickup truck
in Johannesburg, duct-taped a garden hose
to the tail pipe. Left a suicide note

PAUL: that I'll paraphrase:

CARTER: I have been haunted so
now I'll haunt you.

Image: this child lost among corpses of Rwandan refugees in Zaire.

HONDERICH:	Paul?
HONDERICH:	Paul?
PAUL:	I don't care about him.
PAUL:	—Who cares?
PAUL:	I don't care!
PAUL:	With so many people suffering all over the world who want nothing more than to live—?
PAUL:	That man is a coward!
PAUL:	If you can't do your job then get out of the way so someone else can.
PAUL:	Of course I've wanted to kill myself before. But the truth is I've always lacked the courage.
PAUL:	So I tell myself:
PAUL:	Just go someplace dangerous. Let somebody else kill you.

5: Shrinking

GRINKER:	O-kay. So. You are 35 years old, you are male. You are a reporter for the *Toronto Star*, and you're stationed here in Johannesburg.
PAUL:	You have a real talent for stating the obvious.
GRINKER:	Are you shaking?
PAUL:	Am I?
GRINKER:	You have sweat all over your face!
PAUL:	Let me just catch my breath.
GRINKER:	O-kay.
PAUL:	It's just I've never been to a psychiatrist before.
GRINKER:	And what are you scared will happen to you?
PAUL:	I'll lose my edge.
GRINKER:	What does that mean, your edge?
PAUL:	Being crazy.

Image: dark bookcase.

GRINKER: You think I could
cure you of that?

PAUL: Being somewhat crazy
is a requirement in my line of work.

GRINKER: If you leave I won't charge you anything.
You wouldn't be the first to change his mind
about psychiatry. But you called me, Paul,
and told me you've been feeling paranoid—

PAUL: That's not a psychiatric disorder,
in my opinion. People don't deserve
to be trusted.

GRINKER: You are irritable,
small things will make you cry. Interestingly
you deny nightmares. No psychiatric
history prior to this. Congenitally
deformed arm. Don't smoke. Self-medicating
with lots of alcohol, marijuana—

PAUL: Look
all I want from you is some feel-good pills
to patch me up. "O-kay"?

GRINKER: O-kay. We can
find you something, I'm sure.

PAUL: Thank you.

GRINKER: But first
you'll need to talk to me. Medication
targets symptoms: we will need to target
your soul as well. You find that funny?

PAUL: Yes.

GRINKER: What's your mother like, Paul?

PAUL: She's the strongest
woman I know.

GRINKER: And have you known many
women?

PAUL: One.

GRINKER: You've known only one woman?

PAUL: I've been in a relationship with one
woman. On and off. Khareen.

GRINKER: Careen?

PAUL: Ha!

GRINKER: What a name! Tell me, what's this Careen like?

PAUL: She loves rococo art. Homemade knödles
and beer for dinner.

GRINKER: Ha ha ha! Sounds nice!

PAUL: Her father is this German bureau chief,

and one time she was sitting on his lap
in front of me, smiling, with her bare arm
up around his neck, like this. She's the one
who needs some therapy, don't you think? She flashed
her tits at me once down this long hallway
in her father's condo—I don't know why
I feel the need to keep talking about
her father. She's blonde. Great body. Sexy
voice. Calls me Paulie. She doesn't let me
have sex with her though. We share a house but
I pay the rent. I live in a closet
-sized room off the kitchen. I'm happiest
on her leash, so to speak. I like to sit
with her when she takes a bath or lying
in bed with candles lit, drinking wine or
smoking a joint, while she gets herself off
beneath the covers. It's not sex, she says.
It's only for comfort, Paulie. She likes
to tell me that. One time she let this guy
into our yard to watch through the window
while she fucked this other guy. She described
this at breakfast, in great detail. She wants
to be a war reporter, so we went
to Rwanda where we met this handsome
aid worker named Laurent. Who was building
latrines for refugees. And there I was
with my camera in my one hand. Shooting
pictures. By that evening she was lying
in his tent, under his netting, writing
in her diary. He got a hotel room
underneath ours. With grenades exploding
in the shanties and the death squads spreading
through the streets, I call downstairs. She answers
laughing,

KHAREEN: Paulie?
PAUL: We have to go.
KHAREEN: Not now,
Laurent.
PAUL: They're killing people outside.
KHAREEN: Get
off me please, Laurent!
PAUL: He's living with us
here in Johannesburg. They fight and then fuck
all the time.
GRINKER: Why don't we stop for the day.
I'm going to write you a prescription for

	450 milligrams of
	moclobemide.
PAUL:	Okay. Is that good?
GRINKER:	No,
	that is bad. You're clinically depressed and

GRINKER: you have post-traumatic stress disorder.
It's good that you've come. Do you have someone
at home? Besides that sick woman, of course.
These drugs will take some time to change your brain
chemistry, and we don't want you killing
yourself in the meanwhile.

PAUL: —Do you believe
in ghosts, Dr. Grinker?

GRINKER: Well, I believe
people are haunted.

PAUL: What if I told you
I came to you in the first place because
I'm haunted. Cursed.

GRINKER: I'd ask you some questions
to rule out schizophrenia.

PAUL: I told him
about the picture.

GRINKER: It's famous. It's yours?

PAUL: Then I told him what Cleveland's voice told me.

CLEVELAND: If you do this,

CLEVELAND: I'll own you forever.

GRINKER: That was your superego. Your mind was
simply speaking to itself.

PAUL: I know what
my own mind sounds like. This was somebody
else.

GRINKER: The soldier?

PAUL: I've felt him next to me,
feared his presence.

GRINKER: Is he here with us now?

PAUL: He is. He's here when I wake up, he's there
when I'm asleep. He's with me whenever
I'm happy, when I'm having fun or sex
or watching TV, as if he's saying,
This can not last. And of course he's with me
whenever things go wrong. He's happiest
when I'm in pain. He'll never go away
till he gets what he wants from me.

GRINKER: And what
does he want from you, Paul?

6: Iraq

PAUL: This was in Mosul in Northern Iraq
at the beginning of the war. A boy
was throwing some pebbles at a marine
humvee, whose .50 caliber machine gun
was whipping and twisting like a fire hose
spraying death. And as I'm taking pictures
a gang of students comes rushing by with
another student bleeding from a deep
gash in his face. Somebody makes that sound,
you know, *click*, like, Take his picture! And while
I'm switching lenses you can see the switch
go on in somebody's head. Like, He's white,
what the hell's he doing here? I'm lifted
off the ground, tossed around, stoned. Somebody
slides his knife in my back and I'm feeling
the blood pooling in my shirt. I'm holding
onto my camera while they're stretching out
my arms, like this, till I'm floating on top
of the mob. And I'm not trying to be
cinematic here, but it was like Christ
on the cross. Cause I had absolutely
no sense of wanting to live. Or fighting
back. Protesting my innocence. Crying
out for mercy. I had this sense of, Well
we knew this was coming. And here it is.
But the truth of these places is always
the same. A dozen people, a dozen
against a multitude, formed a circle
around me. And we were close to this row
of shops that were closing, and these people
simply pulled the shutters up and shoved me
under. That's when I realize my camera's
gone, the hand's empty, the mob is pounding
on metal. The tea shop owner says, Look
you know I'd really like to help you but
would you mind leaving my tea shop soon? So
I end up in the street again kneeling
in the dirt at the order of some pissed
-off marines, and somehow I convince them
to take me back behind the wire. That's why
I know it's not just my brain, Doctor. Or
my father dying when I was two. Or
this hand. It would be poetic justice to
get ripped apart by a mob. Remember

what Cleveland said to me: If you do this
I will own you. I just have this feeling
he's thinking, You watched my desecration,
now here comes yours.

7: Some Embarrassing Things. Or, The Plan

DAN: Dear Paul. It's been a while. Apologies.
I've finally escaped from the Wisconsin
winter, and I'm back in my strange new home, *Google map:*
LA. I've just filled my prescription for *Los Angeles.*
Zoloft. And I'm hoping you're still willing
to write this play, or whatever it is,
with me. I know it's been a long time since
I first reached out to you. Maybe sometime
I could give you a call?

PAUL: I have to go
to the Philippines, where Abu Sayyaf
the local Al-Qaeda affiliate
is on the march once again. I'm worried
my editor, who hates me for reasons
I can't even pretend to comprehend,
won't like it. It's not the sort of story
that tends to garner those coveted clicks
on the *Times'* website.

DAN: It's 75
degrees here and sunny. Women's faces
are slick masks, thanks to Botox. Some men look
embalmed and tan also. I walk my dog
four times a day. The only helicopters
I see here are LAPD circling
over Brentwood like they're still looking for
OJ's white Bronco. While I'm running up
Amalfi to Sunset the Palisades
look more like the hills of South Korea
on *MASH.* Or Tuscany. Where are you now,
Paul? What's your cell number? Can I call you?
Can I come visit you in Jakarta
soon?

PAUL: I thought you might enjoy hearing this
sound bite directly from the fetid mouth
of our paper's new owner, Sam Zell. Here's *Moving image,*
a link: http://gawker.com/ *silent: http://*
5002815/exclusive *gawker.*
-sam-zell-says-fuck-you-to-his-journalist *com/5002815/*
exclusive-sam-
ZELL: My attitude on journalism is *zell-says-fuck-*
you-to-his-
journalist

	simple: I want to make enough money
PAUL:	so I can afford you!
PAUL:	And while it's true
	I like a gutter-talking billionaire
	as much as the next guy, I do wonder
	what he's up to. Especially after
	publishing a new employee manual
	telling us all to question authority
	and "push back."
ZELL:	I'm sorry, I'm sorry but
	you're giving me the classic what I call
	journalistic arrogance of deciding
	that puppies don't count!
PAUL:	With all the chaos
	building at the gates in Afghanistan
	and Iraq, he's just the sort of leader
	I'm not willing to die for.
ZELL:	Hopefully
	we'll get to the point where our revenue
	is so significant we'll be able
	to do both puppies *and* Iraq. Okay?
	—Fuck you!
PAUL:	So if ghostly voices ever
	figure into this script, maybe this clip
	will make a good one.
DAN:	Don't you think it's strange
	you've never heard my voice, Paul? I've heard yours
	on *All Things Considered*, the *LA Times'*
	website. Let's set this trip up now! I won
	a grant to come visit you.
PAUL:	Hey, congrats
	on the grant! I've got a rusted RV
	in Bali, we can watch the surf and drink
	and discuss genocide. Only problem is
	I finally got fired. And my RV
	just got crushed by a tree. But have no fear!
	I've got an idea.
DAN:	My wife's an actress
	on a TV show that flopped. We're not sad
	about it at all, but everyone thinks
	we should be. It's winter, but it's sunny
	and warm. Every season's the same: sunny
	and warm. I have trouble remembering what
	season it is without thinking. The days
	get shorter or longer but the sun stays

Moving image: water at mid-day.

the same. I go out running on the beach
at dusk. It's beautiful. It's beautiful.
It's beautiful.

PAUL: I'm going to move back home
to Canada, where the plan is I'll work
for the *Toronto Star* again. Covering
the Arctic aboriginal beat. Shooting
pictures, writing stories, blogging about
life in the midnight sun. Or the noontime
moon. In any case I've been waking up
thankful each morning I won't have to write
another sentence about Al-Qaeda
ever again. Unless Zawahiri's
hiding in some ice cave.

*Google
terrain map:
Canadian
Arctic.*

DAN: You have no clue,
Paul, how happy this makes me! You have no
idea how much the ice-and-snow-and-wind
speaks to me, so much more so than the sun
of LA, or Bali. My entire life
I've been obsessed with nineteenth-century
polar exploration. Trapped in the ice
for months, sometimes years. Scurvy, insanity,
cannibalism. It helps me relax
and fall asleep. So maybe I could come
visit you there this winter? And who knows
maybe the Arctic will be the second
act of our play? Cause I have this deadline
coming up—

PAUL: What kind of deadline?
DAN: It's mine
and it's soon. The end of winter. So when
will you give me your God damned phone number
so I can plan this trip?

PAUL: What are they like,
Dan?

DAN: What?
PAUL: Your plays.
DAN: I don't know. Historical,
like I said. I prefer things in books.

PAUL: Why?
DAN: I like things that have already happened
to other people, a long time ago.

PAUL: Why?
DAN: I don't know. I have some ideas but—

PAUL:	Like what?
DAN:	Well the truth is I'm insecure around you, Paul. You intimidate me terribly. You're like this mythic figure, with your hand, your constant returning to the underworld of the most nauseating things in history. Recent history. You've looked at that which the rest of us won't look at, or can't look at. You're the type of writer I've always wished I were. Engaged with life, people.
PAUL:	You don't engage much with people?
DAN:	No. I like to seclude myself. Like you I like to stay away. Sometimes I lay my head against my dog's head and I think, You're my best friend. You're my only friend. If you get sick I'll get a second mortgage for you. Even though we don't have a first mortgage yet. We're just renters. I even like my obsessions but I don't know why I do. Like I said, I have my theories but I think they'd be boring to someone like you.
PAUL:	Try me.
DAN:	I'm like you, like I said. Like you I'll sometimes cry for no reason at all. Or I don't cry for months and months and months. Like you I see flashbacks. I'm scared to change that part of me that's craziest, because if I'm not crazy anymore how will I do what I do? I'm the same age you were in Mogadishu, the same age Sgt. Cleveland was that day. I'm cursed too, just like you are.
PAUL:	But you won't tell me what's cursing you?
DAN:	Because it can't compare to what you've been through!
PAUL:	After my memoir came out, I'd hear from strangers who'd tell me the most intimate things about themselves. Embarrassing. About their lives. They saw that just like them I had these internal conflicts. Except you, you didn't confess anything. Which is probably why I wrote

177

you back. Do you know that quote of Camus'
where he says he's solved the mystery of where
war lives? It lives in each of us, he said.
In the loneliness and humiliation
we all feel. If we can solve that conflict
within ourselves then we'll be able to
rid the world of war. Maybe. So tell me,
Dan: where does war live in you?

DAN: My family
stopped talking to me, several years ago,
and I have no idea why. That's not true,
I have many ideas but none of them
make sense. I was about to get married
but it wasn't like they didn't approve
of my wife. It had something to do with
the fact that nobody would be coming
from my family because they have no friends.
I mean literally my parents don't have
any friends. They can barely leave the house
and whatever's left of their own families
won't speak to them for reasons I've never
understood. And I'd just written a play
that was the closest I'd come to writing
autobiography. And my brother
was in the hospital again, for God
knows what exactly, depression mostly.
He hadn't spoken to any of us
in years. Which was mostly okay with me
cause like everyone else in my family
I suppose I just wanted to forget
he'd ever existed at all. Maybe
this was all because of him? reminding
my family of what happened years ago   *Moving*
when I was 12 and he was 17,   *image:*
one Tuesday afternoon in February   *snow falling.*
walking up the driveway when I noticed
him coming around the house with his back
all pressed with snow, the back of his head white
with snow, and I thought it was so funny
he wasn't wearing a jacket or shoes.
He was barefoot. And by funny I mean
disturbing. I've told this story thousands
of times, I hardly feel a thing. He'd jumped
out of a window, was what I found out
later, and fallen three stories without
breaking a bone. That night my mother cried

in my arms and said, This is a secret
we will take to our graves. I developed
innumerable compulsions, including
counting, hand-washing, scrupulosity
which is the fear that one has been sinful
in word or deed or thought. I was afraid
to leave the house, to touch any surface,
but I hid it so well that nobody
noticed. I was class president. I played
baseball, soccer. I wrote secret poetry.
And eventually I got out and went
to college. And things went coasting along
as well as things can in a family with
an inexplicably cruel father and
a masochistic mother who can't stop
talking about nothing. Logorrhea
is the clinical term, I think. Until
I came home one weekend for a visit
just before my wedding and my father
said I looked homeless. My beard and hair. When
in fact I looked just like other adjunct
professors of writing. But they told me
I looked like a man who'd slit his own throat
soon. They said I looked just like my father's
brother, a man who disappeared after
I was born. He was tall, he was funny,
long hair and barefoot in jeans, a hippy
and some kind of artist. The opposite
of my father. I'm the spitting image
of this man, they said. They were terrified
for this reason. There are things you don't know!
my father kept saying, without saying
what it was exactly I didn't know.
My mother and father were both screaming
together, it felt almost sexual.
There are things you don't know! I drove away
and haven't heard from them since. They are dead
to me. And I don't mean that in the way
it sounds, melodramatically. I mean
I can't remember them. And by memory
I mean I can't feel. I have no pictures
of my childhood. It's like my entire life
up until I was 33 happened
to someone else. Someone who's haunting me,
who makes me feel cursed. Makes me feel certain
that yes, they're right, I've failed, something is wrong

179

with me. I don't know what it is but yes
something is wrong. I've failed, I've failed, I've failed,
I've failed. Only writing and running helps
some. I sit at my desk like a lab rat
clicking on a button that shows me who's
visiting my website. And it doesn't
tell me who's visiting exactly but
it shows your city or town on a map
of the entire world. When I said they don't
talk to me, that wasn't true. I can tell
my mother checks my website at least once
a day. Sometimes twice. It's a compulsion,
I know, but still I like seeing those dots
on the map. But it's nothing! it's nothing
to complain about, it's the sort of thing
everybody has. And nothing compared
to the unspeakable acts of cruelty
you've seen, Paul.

PAUL: Let's get together somewhere
in the Upper Arctic, in 24
-hour darkness, this winter. The hotels there
are like dorms for racist construction crews
from the south, and the costs run high because
everything's flown in. But the ambience
will be just perfect. So let me know when
you'd like to come, and I'll put together
some kind of plan.

8: Hi What's Your Name When Are You Leaving?

DAN: Sand snow sand snow sand snow sand snow sand snow
snow snow snow.

DAN: LAX to Vancouver,
Vancouver to Yellowknife.   *Google Earth:*
                                             Yellowknife,
DAN: What the hell   *Territories,*
kind of name is Yellowknife? I've read that   *Northwest*
copper in the ground turned the Inuit's   *Canada.*
knives yellow.

DAN: Yellowknife to Kugluktuk   *Google Earth:*
by twin turboprop. How do you say that   *Kugluktuk,*
name again?   *Northwest*
                                                Territories.
DAN: Kugluktuk. But I don't know
Inuktitut.

DAN: What's that?
DAN: Their language.
DAN: Whose?

DAN: The Inuit. Which means simply people
            in Inuktitut.

DAN: I'm getting all this
            information off Wikipedia
            on my new iPhone.

DAN: The flight attendant
DAN: is an Inuit kid, gay, goth, nose ring
            and an attitude.

ATTENDANT: Does anyone want
            this last bottle of water?

DAN: The pilots
            are supposedly Inuit too, though
            the cockpit door's closed the whole way. No one
            speaks over the intercom. A black guy
            dressed all in white shares the aisle with me:

BLACK GUY: What brings you to the North, my mon?

DAN: His voice
            sounds almost Jamaican.

BLACK GUY: True dat, true dat.
            Are you done with your paper, mon?

DAN: Later
            I'll find out his name's Isaac, from Ghana,
            when Paul's interviewing him.

DAN: His family
            immigrated to Yellowknife after
            some coup in the '80s.

DAN: An old woman
            in traditional clothes, like calico
            fringed with coyote fur, her hood hiding
            her face,

DAN: doesn't say a word.

DAN: A teenaged
            girl with an iPod as we're descending
            into Kugluktuk

DAN: taps me on the arm
DAN: and asks me, smiling wide,

INUIT GIRL: Hi what's your name
            when are you leaving?

DAN: Grandma and the girl
            shuffling across the ice of Kugluktuk
            while Isaac and I fly two more hours north   *Google Earth:*
            to Ulukhaktok.   *Ulukhaktok.*

DAN: Where the airport is
            a room,

DAN:	the cab's a van gliding across
	a desert of snow.
DAN:	Sand snow.
DAN:	The cabbie's
	white, from Newfoundland, a newfy.
DAN:	Which means
	he's some kind of Canadian redneck,
DAN:	according to Wikipedia.
TAXI DRIVER:	Why
	don't you drive the taxi eh? Joe asks me.
	You know where everyone lives. Everyone
	lives in the same flipping place!
DAN:	Then he asks
	Isaac, probably because he's black:
TAXI DRIVER:	Are you
	here to teach basketball eh?
ISAAC:	No, soccer.
TAXI DRIVER:	That'll be ten dollars eh.
ISAAC:	I got it
	—welcome to the North, my mon!
DAN:	The hotel's
	a prefab one-story house, corrugated
	tin roof, windows for like six rooms.

DAN: Inside

Image:
hallway
of hotel in
Ulukhaktok.

it smells like Clorox. Inuit women
scrubbing the deep fryer.

INUIT WOMAN: Hi what's your name
when are you leaving?

DAN: I'm filling out forms
at the front desk, which is just a closet
with a desk inside it. Paul had emailed
we might have to share a room. Please God don't
make us share a room. What if he tries to
get in bed with me? What if he kills me
in my sleep? in his sleep? What happens if
he hangs himself in our shower? At least
then I'll have my second act.

PAUL: Are you Dan?
I'm Paul.

DAN: His hair's messed up. He needs a shave.
His thick wool socks are sloughing off.

DAN: Pink eyes,
unfocused.

DAN: There's a deep crease in his face,
between his eyes like it's carved.

182

DAN: He's wearing
         an old sweatshirt with a red maple leaf
         on it.
DAN: Who does this man remind me of?
DAN: He's somebody I should know.
DAN: Paul's left hand
         is a stub. Like his arm simply runs out
         of arm. But he's still got some kind of thumb
         at the end. He's rubbing his furrowed brow
         with it.
PAUL: How was Eskimo Air?
DAN: Don't look,
         Dan.
DAN: Not now.
DAN: Show what kind of man you are
DAN: by not looking at Paul's hand.
DAN: I wonder
         what I look like to him?
PAUL: You look a lot
         like Jesus. You know that?
DAN: Thanks?
PAUL: You're a real
         tight packer. Wow.
DAN: I brought dehydrated
         food. You wrote me the food sucked so I bought
         dehydrated organic lasagna
         at REI in Santa Monica?
PAUL: Ooh, I love that stuff!
DAN: Let me just finish
         with this form, and I'll swing by your room.
PAUL: Our
         room. Door's always open.
DAN: —Hey!
PAUL: Come on in,
         Dan, have a seat.   *Moving*   183
DAN: So.   *image:*
PAUL: So.   *gently*
DAN: So here we are   *snowing*
         finally!   *window.*
PAUL: Finally! I know it's not that much
         to look at. But these beds are pretty firm.
         They keep the heat so high you'll want to sleep
         on top of the blankets, but it's better

	than bunking in here with some drunk racist
	construction worker from Edmonton, right?
DAN:	Right!
PAUL:	And cell phones don't work. But the wireless
	is free. In case you want to Skype your wife.
	I Skype my wife pretty much every night,
	if you know what I mean. Ha ha ha. —So
	what do you want to do this week? Because
	we never really decided, only
	that you'd come.
DAN:	And watch you work.
PAUL:	And watch me
	interview people. You're going to get bored.
DAN:	I could interview you. You know, research
	for the play. If you want.
INUIT GIRLS:	Hi what's your name
	when are you leaving?
DAN:	Two Inuit girls
	appear in the doorway. Like *The Shining*
	or something. Selling key chains and lanyards
	made of sealskin.
PAUL:	Not now. Go away.
DAN:	Why
	are they all asking that, Hi what's your name
	when are you leaving?
PAUL:	They're just assuming
	we're leaving soon. Like every other white
	person they've ever met.
DAN:	I wish I had
	my recorder.
PAUL:	You lost it?
DAN:	I left it
	on the plane.
PAUL:	You can borrow mine. Here. Catch.
	I used it for years in Afghanistan
	and Iraq.
DAN:	How's it turn on?
PAUL:	The batteries
	are dead. You could probably buy some new ones
	at the cantina. Or just remember
	all my wise words, ha ha ha.
DAN:	Do you miss
	Afghanistan, Paul? places like that?
DAN:	Sand
	snow snow.

Image:
bright light.

DAN: Do you feel you've made a mistake
leaving war reporting behind? It's like
you've been sent away to Siberia
literally. Or is it like a respite?
a reward for everything before?

DAN: But
I don't ask him any of that. Instead
I ask:

DAN: Do you ever get bored up here,
Paul? It must get kind of lonely.

PAUL: That's right,
but I learn a lot of things too.

DAN: Like what?

PAUL: Like you shouldn't ask too many questions
about polar bear hunts, for example.
It's shamanistic. The Inuit still
believe shamans can turn themselves into
spirits, into animals like muskox
and seals and bears. That shamans can become
other people too. All in the pursuit
of exorcising ghosts—

DAN: Should I tell him
that for weeks I've been having this feeling
when I run that somebody is running
with me?

DAN: Sand sand sand.

DAN: Over my shoulder
in the sun and the sand.

DAN: Who is that man
who's running after me?

DAN: Which reminds me
of that story of Ernest Shackleton
down at the opposite pole, staggering
through a blizzard with his fellow travelers
starving, delirious,

DAN: how they kept seeing
someone with them,

DAN: how they kept asking,

DAN: Who
is that man who walks always beside you?

DAN: Is Staff Sgt. William David Cleveland
following me? And what could he possibly
want from me? I don't say any of this
to Paul.

*Moving
image:
falling snow.*

DAN:	Snow snow.
DAN:	I don't want him thinking I'm too crazy.
PAUL:	Hey, want to watch TV?
DAN:	We could try to track down a shaman.
PAUL:	Who?
DAN:	That's something we could do. This week. Maybe he could try to heal you. Ha ha ha.
PAUL:	Oh

that reminds me: I'm trying to set up
this dog sled ride with these two Inuit
hunters named Jack and Jerry. 500
dollars but I'll pay them, the *Toronto
Star* will I mean. Do you hear those huskies
howling? They're chained on the ice all their lives.
I don't know how they take it, the boredom
I mean. Because you're right, there's definitely
a lot of boredom up here. It's supposed
to snow tomorrow, but we'll go sledding
if the weather's any good.

Sound: dogs howling far away, chains, wind.

Moving image: more snow falling, becoming a blizzard of white.

9: Blizzard

Where's the remote? Do you like John Mayer?
I like John Mayer. And Ryan Adams
too. And Queen Latifah. I like to watch
TV with the sound off and just listen
to my iTunes. This okay with you? This
sucks. This sucks. There's nothing good on TV!
I usually watch just like sports, hockey
and football, sometimes entertainment news
because it's stupid but I love it when
celebrities do stupid things. It helps
me relax. And I like watching curling
as an Olympic sport. I love hearing
the women's curling team screaming, Harder!
Faster! All of these women with their brooms
that look more like Swiffer WetJets rubbing
some kind of path in the ice for the weight
or the pot or the stone or whatever
screaming, Harder! Faster! As if that does
anything, really! What about this show,
The Bachelor? Have you seen *The Bachelor*? Look,
she's pretending to cry. She's pretending
to cry! What are all these people, actors?

Light: dark Arctic noon.

Moving image: window full of snow.

Sound: Ryan Adams singing "Rescue Blues" low.

186

Strippers? She's trying so damn hard to cry
real tears! Harder! Faster! How's it look?

DAN: Looks
bad.

PAUL: It must be gusting up to like, what,
65 an hour?

DAN: My iPhone says that
it's negative 50 out there.

PAUL: Wind chill
included?

DAN: I'm not sure, let's see.

PAUL: Celsius
or Fahrenheit?

DAN: I'm Googling it.

PAUL: I think
Celsius and Fahrenheit become the same
at minus 40 anyway.

DAN: Earlier
Jack the Inuit hunter woke us up
with some coffee.   *Light:*
                                                                      dark dawn.

JACK: Morning, Paul. Morning, Dan.
Looking really bad out there.

DAN: Almost ten
and it's basically sunrise.

JACK: The next time
you come up here you bring me a brand new
skidoo. Okay? Maybe helicopter.

DAN: Before the ban on polar bear hunting
businessmen from Texas would come up here
and Jack would help them track down a mother
bear to shoot. And mount. These rich guys would leave
enormous tips, like snowmobiles.

JACK: Bad news:
can't go out sledding this morning. Jerry's
got the dogs and Jerry's at the doctor's
because he's got like this titanium plate?   187
in his forehead, from a real bad sled crash
few years back. Ha ha ha. And anyway
Elder says this snow's no good. GPS
can't see shit today. We'll go tomorrow
at nine, Inuit time.

DAN: Inuit time   *Light:*
means what, Paul?   *mid-*
                                                                      afternoon.
PAUL: At least we've got the wi-fi,

and this six-pack of Bordeaux I picked up
in Yellowknife.

*Back to the
soundless
TV screen.*

DAN: I didn't bring any
alcohol. How could I forget to buy
alcohol?

PAUL: You're not bored are you?

*iPod playing
music, John
Mayer, "Stop
This Train
(Acoustic)
(Live)."*

DAN: I was
hoping at some point we might get back to
interviewing you?

PAUL: I'm an open book,
Dan. Blank slate. No secrets.

DAN: You want to read
our play? I've got a first act but—

PAUL: I can't
figure out my story. Global warming
or the arts. Or corruption. There's something
shady going on here, I can feel it
with the white guys running this place. Kickbacks
or something. Maybe it's better not to
stir things up too much? don't want to end up
dead in a snowdrift, right?

DAN: Paul's popping pills
out of his many-chambered plastic pill
organizer—

PAUL: Depression, blood pressure,
Polycystic Kidney—

DAN: Which reminds me
to take my Zoloft.

PAUL: Oh God I love this

*Light:
evening.*

movie.

DAN: That evening it's *The River Wild.*

PAUL: Meryl Streep's on the run, on the river
actually ha ha ha, in a rafting
boat trying to escape from this psycho
-killer Kevin Bacon. Is this movie
good? or shit. It's shit but Jesus Meryl
Streep is so gorgeous.

*iPod plays
Queen
Latifah's
"Lush Life"
low.*

188

DAN: Paul, can I ask you
some questions, maybe during commercial
breaks?

PAUL: Sure. Shoot.

DAN: I'm thinking it would help me
finish our play. Which you're welcome to read
at any point, by the way—

PAUL: Do you want
a glass of Bordeaux?
DAN: Yes please.
PAUL: Go ahead.
Blank book, open slate.
DAN: What is it about
the Arctic—?
PAUL: I guess I'm just happiest
when I'm unhappy. When I'm on the phone
with one of my brothers and he's talking
about, you know, problems at work. I say,
How long we been talking? 15 minutes.
I say: Now you're 15 minutes closer
to death.
DAN: I'm sure he loves that.
PAUL: It bugs me
to the core though! that people don't notice
how quickly we die. Whether you're driving
home from work, or suntanning on a beach
in Phuket and this wave comes in and just
keeps on coming—
DAN: How can you live like that?
I mean, how can you walk around living
like you're going to die? Like back in LA
you can't be worried about the earthquake
that could erupt any second. You can't
ride the New York City subway thinking
about the likelihood of a terrorist
bomb exploding. Like on 9/11
I woke up—
PAUL: You were there?
DAN: And actually
I saw a ghost in our bedroom. Covered
in dust. Carrying his briefcase. He looked
so confused! He disappeared and I heard
the sirens. I went downstairs to find out
what was going on, and to hit Starbuck's
too. All these papers were spiraling down
from the sky. And I remember thinking
for a minute, Now all the bankers will
be humbled. I got my venti latte
and came back out in time to see the plane
hit the second tower. An old woman
sat down on the pavement and just started
sobbing. I went upstairs to get my wife

189

though we weren't married yet, and we joined
a river of people like refugees
walking uptown. While all the working men
and women were jumping. I never saw
my brother jumping out of the window
of our house, all those years ago. Maybe
there's something in that? A radio outside
a hardware store in Chinatown told us
the South Tower had come down. In a bar
somewhere in the East Village we watched as
the North Tower sank out of the blue sky
on TV. People were almost giddy
with panic, and grief. Some guys were tossing
a Frisbee in the street. I told myself,
If there's going to be a war, I will go.
I saw myself holding a machine gun
in my mind's eye, someplace bright and sandy
like Afghanistan, or maybe Iraq.
But I didn't go. Because I didn't
consider it the right war. Or because
nobody made me.

PAUL: And are you hoping
I'll forgive you?

DAN: My point is maybe not
everyone's meant to be as courageous
as you are.

PAUL: It's not courage—

DAN: It's also
altruistic. Necessary. If you
don't do what you do then none of us will
ever have any idea what's really
going on.

PAUL: When I started out it was
all for self-esteem. I'm sure you started
out the same way too. I wanted people
to say I was brave, and heroic. Then
I began to hate it but I needed
that fix of adrenalin. The third stage,
where I am now? I don't really need it
anymore. But now I see the lies, now
I see how the people doing my job
don't get it. Or if they get it they don't
talk about it. They want success, they want
a seat at the Sunday morning talk show
round table. They want their own cable show.

```
                I just want to chip away at those lies
                now. But that's a losing game. Most people
                don't care what's going on, or they don't know
                what they're supposed to do. So we just stop
                listening to the litany of evidence
                of the coups we're pulling off, the phosphorus
                bombs dropping on Fallujah in '04
                that melted the skin off children—I could
                go on and on and on and on. That's why
                I object to the word altruistic.
DAN:            Why? Because you're too angry?
PAUL:                                    I see it
                as a labyrinth: if you can find the truth
                you get out. But you don't, it just gets worse,
                you get more lost. And the harder you try
                the darker it gets. As opposed to what,
                being like you, I guess. Right, Dan? Who cares?
                Let's watch some more TV. Let's drink more wine.
                As long as I'm safe I don't need to do
                a thing!
DAN:                     I guess that's fair.
PAUL:                                 Sorry. See? This
                is why I don't like to talk to people
                besides my wife. People ask me questions
                they don't want the answers to.
DAN:                                  Do you want
                to unmute the movie?
JACK:                           Morning, Paul. Dan,
                the next time you come up here from LA
                you bring me back a black twenty-year-old
                girl. Okay?                                   Light:
DAN:                          Next morning Jack says maybe    dim sunrise.
                we'll go out on the land. Till an elder
                stands up and peers out the kitchen window
                at the snowflakes floating in a milky
                morning light.
JACK:                         Elder says,
ELDER:                                  Earth is moving
                faster now.
JACK:                  He means this weather's messed up
                cause of climate change. Says we'd better wait
                until tomorrow.
DAN:                          The snow is moving         Moving
                faster now, I can't tell if it's falling   image:
                out of the sky or up from the treeless      blizzard in
                                                            the window.
```

191

lunarscape. —Jack, do you happen to know
any shamans around here?

PAUL: Dan's thinking
it'll make a good story.

DAN: It might be,
I don't know, entertaining.

JACK: A shaman?

DAN: You know, a medicine man. A healer
of some kind?

JACK: Sure. Roger.

DAN: Roger?

JACK: Roger
Umtoq. He's a storyteller? Makes stone
sculptures, junk like that. He lives out beyond
the trap lines in Minto Inlet. Don't know
if he's still alive.

DAN: Could you ask around
for his number? or email?

PAUL: Jack told me   *Light:*
last winter one of these blizzards lasted   *evening.*
fourteen days.

DAN: Fourteen days!   *Moving*
                                                                            image:
PAUL: That's a fortnight   *blizzard in*
to Canadians.   *the window.*

DAN: Later that evening
we're getting into bed, snow is whispering
beneath the windowpanes.

PAUL: I wouldn't mind
staying here for a while. Just between me
and you, my confessor. They're refusing
to send me anywhere interesting
anymore. I don't know why.

DAN: Are you scared
you'll be fired?

PAUL: Of course. Nobody's reading
anything anymore. Are you?

DAN: Reading
newspapers?

PAUL: And nobody's clicking on
these Arctic pieces either. My expense
reports are obscene.

DAN: Why not do something
else then?

PAUL: Like what? Maybe I could become
a wedding photographer.

DAN: Why don't you
write a book?

PAUL: I already wrote a book.
Remember? I think I sold like maybe
six copies in the US. One review
on Amazon said:

AMAZON: The lesson we learn,
that war lives in all of us, is neither
original nor particularly
helpful.

AMAZON: Author Watson is at his best
whilst giving us the sights and sounds of war,

AMAZON: but his memoir suffers when he aspires
to some kind of poetry whose only
loyalty is to the truth.

PAUL: I'm paraphrasing
now, of course, but what kind of an ass-jag
uses the word whilst?

Light:
lights out.

DAN: Your book had no point
for me actually. To be completely
honest with you. I would read a chapter
or two, then have to put it down. And go
wash my hands. Because—it was all too much!
And repetitive. All these horrible
things you've lived through, I still don't understand
how you don't just surrender to profound
despair.

Sound:
wind
howling.

PAUL: Have I ever told you about
the time I met Mother Theresa?

DAN: No.

PAUL: I was stuck in Calcutta—

DAN: I'm going to
record this, okay?

PAUL: So I went over
to Mother's House. Which was this heavily
trafficked place, full of these shady-looking
characters wearing Rolex watches and
Italian business suits. There was a chair
by the door, and a sister said:

193

SISTER: Sit down,
and if she's willing she will come.

PAUL: Maybe

two or three days passed like this, till someone,
some sister comes downstairs and says,

SISTER: Mother
will see you now.

SISTER: Only for a short while,

SISTER: a moment if you're lucky.

PAUL: I turn on
my tape recorder and race up the stairs
where she's hobbling around in her knobby
crippled kind of bare feet in this small room
of hers with no doors,

PAUL: just some curtains and
I'm watching her shuffle back and forth from

PAUL: one doorway to the other,

PAUL: appearing
and then disappearing in the sunlight
and then shade.

PAUL: Never once looking at me.
Because I'd been to her treatment centers,
she didn't call them that, they're basically
places to go and die, right?

DAN: Right.

PAUL: Full of
row upon row of starving AIDS victims
and others,

PAUL: lying on these sorts of cots
very low to the ground.

PAUL: And they don't get
a lot of medical care, they get cleaned
and they get fed.

PAUL: They don't get fed a lot.

PAUL: And I was trying to be this heavy
on Mother Theresa, you know, saying,
Don't you think you should feed them some more food?

PAUL: Don't you think maybe you should be doing
this or that?

PAUL: And she said, They don't need food.
They need love. And she kept on saying that.

MOTHER: They need love. They need love. That's all. That's all.

PAUL: I was thinking, Wow, this is like shooting
ducks in a pond! This woman's a moron,
right?

DAN: Ha ha ha, right!

PAUL: So I go and write

my hit-piece about Mother Theresa.
It wasn't this blatant, but basically
what I said was that she was this harpy,
this, you know, cold-hearted nun mistreating
all these poor people. Well—bullshit. She's right.
What they *did* need was love. Because it was
respect. Either they die in the street or
they die in Mother's House. And if you die
in Mother's arms then at least you've died with
somebody loving you. And not because
they owe it to you, or because they feel
some familial obligation—they're just
doing it because they know you deserve
to be loved. You know? Maybe I'm a fool
but I think that was the point of my book
that no one bought.

DAN: So what you're saying is
war would disappear if we could all just
hold each others' hands?

PAUL: Why are you trying
to turn me into some kind of guru?

DAN: Am I?

PAUL: Like I've got some kind of answer
for you.

DAN: I don't know.

PAUL: That thing you wrote me
about your family, Dan. They disowned you
for no reason.

DAN: Right.

PAUL: And how your father
kept saying, There are things you do not know!
And how you look just like your dad's brother,
I keep thinking about that.

DAN: I do too.

PAUL: Did your father mean he's not your father?

DAN: I don't know. It's crazy, but—

PAUL: Why don't you
start asking some questions? That's what I'd do
if I were you.

DAN: Paul's laptop starts ringing.

PAUL: It's Skype. It's my wife. Stay here.

DAN: No I'll go
sit in the kitchen.

PAUL: No stay here. Hello?
Sweetness?

DAN: I hear Paul's wife's voice. I don't look
                at the screen. I go out to the hallway
                and sit by the pay phone. And try calling
                home on an empty calling card.

PAUL: Sweetness,
                I miss you so badly.

DAN: The next morning   *Light:*
                things look different.   *dawn,*
                                                                no storm.
JACK: Next time you come up here,
                Dan, you bring me back a bag of cocaine
                and an AK-47.

DAN: We step
                outside.

DAN: Snow snow.

DAN: Jerry's down on the ice
                with his sled and his dog team. The sky is
                bright, snow's drifting like pollen.

PAUL: Would you mind
                riding with Jerry, Dan? Jack can pull me
                behind his skidoo and I can shoot you
                and the dogs that way.

DAN: Jerry's middle-aged
                and mildly hunchbacked. I think I can see
                that titanium plate in his forehead.

JERRY: Guys!
                Guys! We're losing our sunlight here!

DAN: I snap
                some pictures before my camera's frozen.

PAUL: Put it inside your coat! Put it next to
                your skin!

DAN: I can't hear you!

JERRY: Hoot, hoot!

DAN: Jerry's
                beating his dogs' muzzles with a short stick.   *Moving*
                                                                image,
JERRY: No, Ghost! Bad Ghost!   *no*
DAN: You call your dog Ghost? Why? *sound:*
JERRY: I'm training him to lead. I had to sell   *Dan's*
                my old leader. But Ghost's a real scaredy   *footage*
                -cat.   *of the*
                                                                dogs.
DAN: The dogs are tangled in harnesses
                of yellow nylon cords.

JERRY: Misty wants to
                lead instead.

DAN: Who's Misty?

JERRY: The one in back.
DAN: She's cute. Smelly. Hyper. A bit dangerous.
JERRY: Real bitch.
DAN: They can't stop barking.
JERRY: Hoot! Hoot!
DAN: High
          -pitched yelps. They seem insane. Like a savage
          race of idiot wolves.
JERRY: Hoot! Hoot!
DAN: I'm missing
          my dog now. She's a miniature schnauzer
          these huskies would eat for breakfast. A few
          of them are eating their own shit. Tearing
          at hunks of meat.
JERRY: Hoot! Hoot, hoot!
DAN: Who knows what
          Jerry's trying to say?
JERRY: Sit your ass down,
          Dan! —Hoot, hoot, hoot!
DAN: And we're off. I'm sitting
          down, on my ass, on a blue plastic tarp
          with my rubber boots splayed in front, inches
          above the ice above the sea—
JERRY: Hold on
          to these ropes down here, Dan!
DAN: Jerry's kneeling
          behind my ear.
JERRY: Gee! Gee! Zaw!
DAN: Gee means right,
          I think. I've heard mushers say Haw! for left
          but Jerry says
JERRY: Zaw! —Hoot!
DAN: means faster. Paul's
          riding in a box on skis.
DAN: Jack's pulling
          him with his skidoo.
DAN: Red taillights dancing
          in a whorl of snow.
JERRY: Hoot, hoot!
DAN: You feel it
          in your spine, your neck, your skull. The grinding
          of the rusted runners on ice crystals
          like sand.

197

*Moving
image,
silent: this
dog sled
ride, Dan's
POV.*

DAN: Snow snow snow snow snow snow.

DAN: Cresting
another invisible ridge, the dogs
fan out to shit in streaks.

JERRY: Misty, no! Gee!
Gee!

DAN: We're moving onto the Arctic Sea,
and if we could only change direction
and head that way—

JERRY: Zaw! Zaw! Zaw!

DAN: If we could
only get the dogs to turn to the left
instead,

DAN: we'd be in Minto Inlet.

DAN: Where
Roger Umtoq the shaman lives.

JERRY: Misty,
no! —Zaw!

DAN: We stop at the floe's edge. The sea
is an undulating eternity
of black slush a few feet away. Seal heads
breaking through the new ice, their spectral eyes
on us.

PAUL: My feet are completely numb, Dan.

DAN: I think I bruised my tailbone.

JERRY: Hey guys! Guys!   *More*
These dogs aren't tired enough yet! Got to   *footage,*
keep going!   *no sound:*
                                               dogs barking
DAN: The dogs keep barking,   *in harness*

DAN: while Paul   *on the ice.*
sets up his tripod and shoots Jack kneeling
at the waterline,

DAN: tossing a snowball
onto the thin veneer of ice forming
on the water. It sounds like a pebble
bouncing off glass.

PAUL: Have you ever seen it
this melted before?

JACK: Usually ice floes
come down from the hill, usually springtime
like April May June?

JERRY: Hey guys! Guys! These dogs
are real worked up! Going to have to run them
some more!

198

JACK: Because that's when we get the winds?
But I've never seen it this warm before
in wintertime.

JERRY: Hey Dan.

DAN: Yeah.

JERRY: Put your weight
on this anchor.

DAN: What for?

JERRY: Just stand on this
and don't go anywhere. I need to go
drain my dragon.

DAN: The anchor's a steel claw
dug in the ice. Tied with a yellow cord
that's tied to the very last barking dog
in the team. Named Misty.

JERRY: Misty! shut up!

DAN: Jerry!

JERRY: Huh?

DAN: Do you know Roger Umtoq
the shaman in Minto Inlet?

JERRY: Old guy?
Told kids bullshit stories?

DAN: He's a healer
too.

JERRY: I don't know nothing about all that.

DAN: Can you take us out to Minto Inlet
to see him? Of course we'll pay you something,
Jerry.

JERRY: I'd like to take you to Minto
but the Roger I know out in Minto
died of heart attack last winter—

DAN: Misty
takes off,

JERRY: Misty no!

DAN: pulling the whole team,

DAN: and the sled starts sliding sideways,

DAN: I start
laughing, like I'm embarrassed,

DAN: as my boot
slips off the anchor,

DAN: as the anchor slips
out of the ice—

JERRY: What are you doing, Dan!

DAN: Me?

JERRY:	Ghost! Ghost!
DAN:	And for an instant I see the top of the world from above,
PAUL:	Hey Dan, are you okay?
DAN:	as the steel anchor wraps around my ankle and whips me up off my feet,
PAUL:	I'm so sorry.
DAN:	and the seal heads duck back under the new ice.
PAUL:	I'm feeling so guilty.
DAN:	We're back in our hotel room and I can't move.
PAUL:	How's your head?
DAN:	It's all right.
PAUL:	Do you need any more ice?
DAN:	It's my groin that's killing me.
PAUL:	We're out of wine. You sure you didn't bring anything?
DAN:	I forgot, I told you. I'm sorry.
PAUL:	—You should've seen yourself, you were sideways! You were almost inverted! I don't know how that happened, the physics of it, I mean. You don't have anything to drink? no vodka?
DAN:	I wish I had some right now.
PAUL:	This reminds me of Abdul Haq—you know who he is right?
DAN:	No.
PAUL:	He was this mujahedeen famous for defeating the Soviets in the '80s with the CIA's help, of course. After 9/11, I went to interview him in Peshawar.
DAN:	Pakistan?
PAUL:	—Here here here record this.
DAN:	Okay.

Light: Arctic night.

TV on, no sound: entertainment news.

200

PAUL:	I mean this guy looked exactly like Rob Reiner with a tan! and a bright white shalwar kameez. He hugged me! without knowing me! He was limping around on his prosthetic foot. I'm sure that's why he liked me.
DAN:	Why?
PAUL:	He was going back to Kabul so that when the US invaded he'd be an alternative to the Taliban. I'm sure he wanted revenge also, cause Talibs killed his wife and son a few years before, or maybe it was ISI—
DAN:	ISI is what again, Paul?
PAUL:	I was eating and sleeping on the floor, outside Kabul. With dried blood in the corner, bullet holes in the wall. Bathing in a bucket, with one toilet all plugged up with shit. Everybody there had dysentery. And somebody asked me, Have you heard what happened to Abdul Haq? He came over the Khyber Pass last week with 25 men, and Taliban troops ambushed him. He hid all night in the rocks calling the CIA for air support but no one came. Taliban captured him the next morning and hanged him from a tree with a metal noose. Cut off his dick and stuffed it in his mouth. Shot up his body till he was just this hanging piece of meat. I'm sorry, Dan. Sorry. I don't know why I'm thinking of him now. I don't know why I'm crying either! Maybe it's just cause you got tangled up in all that cord?

201

DAN:	Paul's staring straight ahead. He's not here. Paul's not here anymore. I get up, head spinning, groin aching.	*Moving image: snow falling.*
PAUL:	Sorry, Dan. Sorry.	
DAN:	I see who he is now, finally: sitting there in his socks, his filthy sweatshirt, his eyes are like looking down a well. His greasy	

hair's all messed up. He's my older brother
sitting at the kitchen table, the day
they brought him back home from the hospital.
I was standing in the doorway watching
him pretend to eat something. Nobody
was saying a word. I could have sat down
with him. I was scared I'd catch his disease.
I thought, Sadness is an illness you catch
if you aren't careful enough. I ran
outside to play with friends. Are you hungry,
Paul? They've left some dinner on the table
for us.

10: Yellowknife

PAUL: It's like this French bistro called *Le Frolic*
I think? just down the hill from the hotel
in Yellowknife.

DAN: That whole flight from Ulu
Paul's pitching me a TV show about
life in the Arctic:

PAUL: *Fawlty Towers* meets
White Fang!

DAN: I'm not really writing TV
shows, Paul.

PAUL: Then your wife, your wife could write it
for you!

DAN: I'm worried about the play, how
to end it.

PAUL: I'm not saying it's a good
French bistro. It's decent. I had dinner
here on my way up. I'll get a bottle
of their finest Cabernet. Do you want
some beer? vodka?

DAN: How'd you meet your wife, Paul?

PAUL: My wife?

DAN: You never mention her. Except
to say she's "changed your life," in your memoir.
Just like you've only told me your mother
is the strongest woman you've ever known.

PAUL: She's Chinese.

DAN: Your wife?

PAUL: No my mother. Yes
my wife's Chinese.

*Google
directions:
Ulukhaktok
to Kugluktuk,
Kugluktuk to
Yellowknife.*

202

DAN: She's a photographer,
        right? I read that in your book.
PAUL: I don't talk
        about her for a reason.
DAN: Is she why
        you're doing better?
PAUL: Am I?
DAN: I don't know
        what I thought would happen up here. I'm not
        saying I think I failed. Maybe I did,
        maybe I failed to get a story, but
        I don't know yet. Because in many ways
        you're just as fucked up as I'd imagined—
PAUL: Thank you.
DAN: In other ways you seem better
        than I could ever hope to be.
PAUL: You sound
        kind of disappointed, Dan.
DAN: What happened
        to the ghost of William David Cleveland?
        I kept meaning to ask—
PAUL: What do you mean
        what happened to him?
DAN: Are you still haunted
        by him? Does he follow you? Is he here
        with us now? Or was that all a story
        to sell books.
PAUL: He's here. He's gotten quieter,
        that's true. It could be the meds. I worry
        about my son, cosmic retribution
        of some kind. I don't think about myself
        anymore.
DAN: When did that change?
PAUL: I don't know
        exactly. I know you were hoping for
        an epiphany of some kind. Maybe
        an exorcism. I know you wanted
        to visit a shaman and have my soul
        cleansed—
DAN: And cleanse myself.
PAUL: That's not how it works.
        You get used to it. It just turns slowly
        into something else. It's like when I called
        Cleveland's mother—

DAN: Right that's in your book—

PAUL: No
that's just book-bullshit. When I wrote that book
I didn't understand it. I didn't
understand the conversation. You should
hear it sometime, remind me to send it
to you when I get home.

DAN: You recorded
the phone call?

PAUL: That's right.

DAN: Why?

PAUL: Flew to Phoenix,
rented a car. At the Ramada Inn
turned on the AC

PAUL: and pulled the blinds down
and picked up the phone:

Sound: answering machine beeping.

PAUL: Um yes hello ma'am
my name's Paul Watson. This is difficult
for me to say. But I took that picture
of your son that day in Mogadishu.
I've wanted to meet you for years, to speak
to you about what happened. And I hope
you might be willing to give me some time
in the next couple of days—

PAUL: Had some dinner
at the mall, back in the room the phone was—

PAUL: Hello?

BROTHER: This is William David Cleveland's
brother.

PAUL: Oh. —Hi, sir.

BROTHER: Hi. Can I ask you
never to call my mom again? She called
me crying her eyes out cause you threw her
into a really bad relapse.

PAUL: Well, sir,
it's just that I've been living with this thing
for more than a decade now—

BROTHER: You're talking
about that picture you took of my brother
drug through the streets?

PAUL: That's right. And I'm hoping
if I can understand my place in time
and his place in time, then maybe we could
bury a few things.

204

BROTHER:	Well, he was no different than all the people over there right now in Iraq and Afghanistan. Fighting for something they believe in, even when nobody else does.
PAUL:	That doesn't help me understand him as a person.
BROTHER:	That's him, that's him as a person.
PAUL:	I know him, sir, only from that moment. And for my own mental health—
BROTHER:	He was a kind of weird kid who didn't match in with nobody. But he always knew he wanted to protect people.
PAUL:	Was your father in the navy, sir?
BROTHER:	He was an engine mechanic.
PAUL:	And did your brother have a wife?
BROTHER:	Well he had a couple of them.
PAUL:	And you wouldn't know how I might go about trying to track down these women? Or other relatives?
BROTHER:	Nope.
PAUL:	He had some kids I understand.
BROTHER:	Sorry?
PAUL:	He had a few kids.
BROTHER:	—Now are you looking to do some kind of story again?
PAUL:	Sir, I just wish we could meet—
BROTHER:	I don't care to meet you at all.
PAUL:	Do you hate me, sir?
BROTHER:	What?
PAUL:	You hate me, sir, I know it!
BROTHER:	I don't hate nobody, man!
PAUL:	But—but I dishonored your brother, that's what haunts me—

BROTHER: His honor
            wasn't tarnished in the least.
PAUL: Well, sir, see
            there's a lot of people who would argue
            with you on that point.
BROTHER: They must not've been
            one of the 3,000 people crowding
            into a church that could hold only like
            a hundred for his funeral. Must not've
            been one of the 32 cars following
            us all the way to the cemetery,
            or the four helicopters with gunships
            giving him an escort all the way. They
            didn't feel he'd been dishonored.
PAUL: Others
            who know him from my picture—
BROTHER: I don't care
            about your picture! I'm not interested
            in discussing it, I'm not interested
            in meeting you, and I do apologize
            if that offends you, sir—
PAUL: Could we do this
            over email, sir?
BROTHER: No.
PAUL: Can't we just meet,
            and you can see who I am—!
BROTHER: Once again
            negative.
PAUL: Sir I have begged, I, I, I
            don't understand why—
BROTHER: You're going to have to
            deal with this on your own time.
PAUL: Your mother
            hates me, sir. I read this interview about
            that thing in Fallujah where they strung up
            the American contractors from that bridge?
            And your mother broke down crying and told
            the reporter she hated the person
            who did it then, like she hates the people
            who do it now.
BROTHER: She was talking about
            the people desecrating all of them
            bodies.
PAUL: —No, sir, she was talking about
            me, sir! I know it!

BROTHER: The thing of it was,
           when David got shot down and went missing?
           since our mom had remarried and taken
           a different name, they told his stepmother
           he'd been killed in action. We found out while
           watching Peter Jennings. When my mother
           recognized David's feet. Cause they looked like
           his dad's. If it weren't for your picture
           we might've never found out.
PAUL: You must blame
           me for that much, sir—
BROTHER: Man, you don't listen
           very well, do you?
PAUL: Do you want to know
           why I did it?
BROTHER: No.
PAUL: Why not?
BROTHER: Explaining
           don't change the fact a thing got done.
PAUL: A week
           before, another Black Hawk got shot down,
           and kids were parading the body parts
           of servicemen through the streets like pennants
           at a baseball game. And the Pentagon
           denied it. They said it didn't happen.
           Because I didn't have a picture.
BROTHER: Right.
PAUL: I wasn't a machine, I cared.
BROTHER: Right.
PAUL: And
           honestly, sir, I believe your brother
           would still be alive today if people
           . had known the truth.
BROTHER: From my own life I'd say,
           and I was in the Air Force for ten years,
           I volunteered to go to Somalia
           but they wouldn't let me go, cause of work,
           where I was. But I can honestly say
           I'd have no problem if I'd been the one
           in my brother's shoes.
PAUL: You would've wanted
           that picture taken?
BROTHER: I would've.

207

PAUL: Why, sir?
for the reason I just explained or?

BROTHER: Both,
for the reason you just said and because
you're just doing your job.

PAUL: Well I'm grateful
to you for saying that.

BROTHER: Not a problem.

PAUL: It takes a large weight off. I only wish
the rest of your family felt the same way.

BROTHER: You're going to have to take my word on that
unfortunately.

PAUL: Oh yeah no, I won't go
down that route, sir.

BROTHER: I appreciate that, sir.

PAUL: I'm just talking about the larger world
here.

BROTHER: Well the world's fucked up.

PAUL: Sure.

BROTHER: Short and sweet,
the world's a fallen place. Ha ha ha.

PAUL: And
I hope this won't upset you but one thing
that still haunts me is that I heard a voice
when I took that picture. And your brother
warned me: If you do this I will own you
forever.

BROTHER: Well how do you know David
meant something bad?

PAUL: He said I will own you
forever—

BROTHER: Maybe he meant you owe him
something now.

PAUL: Like what?

BROTHER: Look, I've got to go
pick up my boy.

PAUL: Okay sir, I forgot
to ask you your name.

BROTHER: Ray.

PAUL: Ray, that's my dad's
name.

RAY: Ha ha ha.

PAUL: Sir, please apologize
to your mother for me?

RAY:	Good night.
PAUL:	Good night.
DAN:	The phone's hung up. The hum fades out.
DAN:	Footsteps on hotel carpeting. The zipping up of a bag.
DAN:	After dinner we're struggling through blistering wind,
DAN:	sand snow,
DAN:	to the Hotel Explorer, this strangely lavish, somewhat Soviet, high-rise hotel for diplomats from the south.
PAUL:	I'm going up to Resolute soon. Where the American scientists hang out all summer long.
DAN:	—I can't hear you!
PAUL:	I said I'm doing a story about robot submarines!
DAN:	That's awesome! Maybe I'll try for a grant to go with you!
PAUL:	Great!
DAN:	We step inside the elevator.
PAUL:	I'm leaving first thing in the morning. Fuck me.
DAN:	My flight's in the afternoon. So I guess this is goodbye.
PAUL:	Here's my floor. So.
DAN:	Hey Paul, thank you for writing back to me for years now. And for writing back in the first place. It's hard to explain everything it's meant to me, to be able to leave my home and go someplace like this, with somebody like you, even for a short while.
DAN:	But I don't say any of that. I say:
DAN:	Paul, I don't know if this play's going to be any good. But I'll email it to you when I'm done.

209

PAUL: Don't
          bother, I won't read it. I can't look back
          on all this old stuff anymore, Dan. But
          I'm happy you're the one writing it. Bye
          now. Safe flight.

DAN: The elevator closes
          and I wonder if I'll ever see him   *Moving*
          again.   *image:*
                                                        snow falling.

PAUL: My deepest apologies, Dan,
          for not writing sooner. I'm in Resolute
          where I've just destroyed all my computer
          equipment, by accident, by dropping   *Google*
          my bag off the side of an icebreaker.   *terrain:*
          I simply lost my grip! as we broke through   *Resolute.*
          miles and miles of ice near Taloyoak.

DAN: I'm working on our play at a theater
          in Minneapolis, in a neighborhood
          called Little Mogadishu. Somali   *Google map:*
          refugees everywhere. Girls in hijabs   *Minneapolis.*
          walking down the sidewalk. It would be strange
          to have you with me here, Paul. I don't know
          whether you'd hate it. Or love it.

PAUL: Dear Dan,
          just between me and you, my confessor:
          the big news is I'm back in Kandahar.   *Google*
          It's summer again and the Taliban's   *Earth:*
          itching for a fight. The *Toronto Star*   *Kandahar.*
          wants its pretty thin coverage here beefed up,
          and if I want to keep my wife and son
          in new snow boots I need to make myself
          valuable to the *Star*. And Canada's
          responsible for Kandahar. Truth is
          I'm no different than all those Americans
          driving their trucks in near suicidal
          conditions in Iraq, just to pay off
          mortgages in Florida. This is what
          I've come to: I'm a mercenary and
          a desperate one at that. Just between me
          and my confessor. But there's something else:
          I feel like Cleveland's happy I've come back,
          though I don't know why yet. Maybe you'll come
          visit me sometime? Someplace relaxing
          like Kabul. Maybe there's a book in it,   *Google*
          or a play. So what do you say? Will you   *Earth:*
          come, Dan? I promise I'll keep you as safe   *Kabul*

as I can. Though of course nobody knows
what can happen out here. Talk to you soon,
your friend Paul.

END OF PLAY

HOLLY ARSENAULT's plays have been produced at Annex Theatre, Live Girls! Theater, 14/48: The World's Quickest Theatre Festival, BoxFest Detroit, and the One-Minute Play Festival. Her first full-length play, *Undo*, is the recipient of the 2013 Theatre Puget Sound Gregory Award for Outstanding New Play and the 2013 Seattle Theater Writers' Gypsy Rose Lee Award for Excellence in Local Playwriting, and was nominated for the 2014 American Theatre Critics Association new play awards. Her short play *24 Pictures of a Pilot* was a finalist for the Heideman Award at the *National 10-Minute Play Contest* at Actors Theatre of Louisville, and was published in Rain City Projects' Manifesto Series, v.2: *Vivid Impact*, edited by Steven Dietz. She is a member of the Seattle Repertory Theatre Writers Group and the Dramatists Guild of America. *Undo* will receive its southeast premiere at the Studio at Mizner Park in Boca Raton Florida, produced by Parade Productions, in January 2015. Holly has been the Executive Director of TeenTix, an arts access and engagement program for teenagers, since 2005.

Holly Arsenault

Undo

This play is dedicated to my grandmothers.

Florence Cantwell Arsenault

1909–1994

Donna Jean Miller Lamoreux

1921–2012

Hinda Feinberg Wachtel

1934–2012

A knoyl viklt zikh oykh oys
Everything comes to an end
(lit., Even a ball of thread [eventually] comes undone)

CHARACTERS

THE BOY WITH THE GLASS   just a boy, 8

JOE PFEIFFER   the husband, American and Jewish, 30

RACHEL MENDELSSOHN PFEIFFER   the wife, American and Jewish, 27

ARI GLASSMAN   Joe's best friend, American and Jewish, 28

JOAN WOLOFSKY MENDELSSOHN   Rachel's mother, American and Jewish, 49

NAOMI MENDELSSOHN   Rachel's younger sister, American and Jewish, 14

HANNAH MENDELSSOHN   Rachel's older sister, American and Jewish, 30

SIOBHAN DOYLE   Hannah's girlfriend, Irish, any ethnic background, raised Catholic, 25

ABE PFEIFFER   Joe's father, American and Jewish, 60

ADINE WOLOFSKY   Rachel's aunt, Joan's sister, American and Jewish, 60

MELITA JOHNSON   Ari's ex-girlfriend, American, any ethnic background, raised Unitarian Universalist, 26

CHARACTERS MENTIONED OR UNSEEN:

THE RABBI

OZZIE MENDELSSOHN   Rachel's father, 59

GLORIA KORNFELD PFEIFFER   Joe's mom, deceased

DEVORAH PFEIFFER   Joe's sister, 40

JEFFREY ST. CLAIR   Rachel's high school Biology teacher, age unknown

SETTING:

A suburb of Philadelphia, Pennsylvania. Sunday.

Far upstage center, a set of ornate double doors. Downstage right, a door with a wedding dress hanging on it, and a make-up table—this is Rachel's dressing room. Downstage left, a door with a suit jacket, and a sink—this is Joe's.

Scene 1—the boy with the glass

A boy enters gently carrying a cloth napkin. He sits downstage and opens the napkin, revealing a shattered glass inside. He sits, and begins carefully gluing the glass back together. He will remain here working on this project throughout the play.

A woman, Rachel, sits alone in her dressing room in her underwear doing her makeup. A man, Joe, stands alone in his dressing room in his boxers, facing his mirror.

Scene 2—the underwear

Rachel's dressing room. There is a knock on the door and then her mother enters without waiting for an answer.

JOAN: Those aren't the underwear.

RACHEL: Mom.

JOAN: Those aren't the underwear.

RACHEL: It doesn't matter.

JOAN: It does matter.

RACHEL: It really doesn't.

JOAN: You were wearing—they were those nice ones that Judy's daughter got from her friend with the fancy lingerie store.

RACHEL: No, I didn't wear those.

JOAN: I can't believe you don't remember.

RACHEL: I do remember. I didn't wear those. I got my period, remember? I bled through them and Aunt Adine went to the drug store and bought me new ones.

JOAN: No she didn't.

RACHEL: Yes. She did. You don't remember because you were yelling at the florist.

JOAN: That florist was a very dishonest man.

RACHEL: Yes.

JOAN: So, these are the underwear that Aunt Adine bought you?

RACHEL: No.

JOAN: Because those don't look like drugstore underwear.

RACHEL: They're not. These are just my underwear.

JOAN: Well, where are the Aunt Adine panties?

RACHEL: I don't know.

JOAN: You have to wear the same ones!

RACHEL: Mom.

JOAN: Rachel. You don't get to pick and choose.

RACHEL: Mom. That's your antiquated religion. Nobody cares what underwear I'm wearing.

JOAN: God cares.

RACHEL: He does not.

JOAN: If he doesn't care, then why do any of it?

RACHEL: Mom.

JOAN: No, really. Why wear the dress? Why make everybody go through—

RACHEL: Because it matters to Joe.

JOAN: What do you care what matters to Joe?

RACHEL: I care.

JOAN: You shouldn't.

RACHEL: I'm familiar with your opinion.

JOAN: You shouldn't.

RACHEL: Help me put my dress on. *(She takes the wedding dress off of its hanger.)*

JOAN: Where are the Aunt Adine panties?

RACHEL: I don't know. Gone.

JOAN: What did you do with them?

RACHEL: I don't know. Threw them out, probably. They were two-dollar drugstore underwear.

JOAN: You didn't keep them?

RACHEL: I didn't think I was going to need them.

JOAN: You kept this.

RACHEL: Yes, well. This is my wedding dress.

JOAN: Such a beautiful dress.

RACHEL: Would you help me, please?

> *Silence while she steps into the dress and turns to face the mirror.*

JOAN: *(zipping up the dress)* It still fits you perfectly. You have not gained one pound.

RACHEL: Yes.

Scene 3—the shave

> *Joe stands over the sink in his dressing room shaving his chest and crying quietly. The door is partially open. His friend Ari comes to the doorway, sees him, stops and watches for a long moment.*

ARI: Dude. What are you doing?

JOE: What does it look like?

ARI: I know but . . . why?

JOE: Because this is what I did.

ARI: Why?

JOE: Did you see my dad?

ARI: Yeah. He's out there.

JOE: How did he seem?

ARI: Fine. He seemed fine.

JOE: No he didn't.

ARI: Yeah, he's fine.

JOE: Is Dev with him?

ARI: Yeah. Is she . . .?

JOE: Yeah. I figured.

ARI: Yeah, I guess that's right.

JOE: Rachel read somewhere that that's traditional. For a sibling to take the place. If a parent is . . . not there. Or anyone who was originally involved.

ARI: Right.

JOE: It's pretty common.

ARI: Sure.

JOE: So Dev's just doing it. She's fine with it I think.

ARI: Yeah. I'm sure she's fine.

> *Joe shaves.*

JOE: You brought Melita?

ARI: Yeah. Yeah, she's out there.

JOE: Thanks for doing that, man. I know it was weird.

ARI: She gets it.

JOE: She's great.

ARI: She is not great.

JOE: What was wrong with her? Really.

ARI: She was mean to my dog. And she's unattractive.

JOE: She's fine!

ARI: She's toothy. And pear-shaped.

JOE: She was good in bed though, right?

ARI: Yeah. Yes. Very.

JOE: So, who cares if she's toothy?

ARI: She was mean to my dog.

217

JOE: Right.

    Joe shaves.

JOE: She had a magazine. Rachel. She had one of those . . . y'know . . . *Playgirls?*

ARI: Those are for gay men.

JOE: They're for women!

ARI: What women do you know who buy nudie magazines?

JOE: Rachel had this one, that's what I'm telling you.

ARI: Okay, fine. When was this?

JOE: Right before. Last time. I found it in our room.

ARI: Rachel had a *Playgirl* in your room?

JOE: Yes.

ARI: Okay.

JOE: So, I was looking at it.

ARI: Yeah.

JOE: And all the guys were, like, so smooth, y'know? Shaved-like.

ARI: Okay.

JOE: So, I figured. For our wedding night. *(He gestures to his now-shaved chest.)*

ARI: You shaved because Rachel had a *Playgirl?*

JOE: Yes!

ARI: Did she like it?

JOE: The *Playgirl* was from her bachelorette party. Joanne or somebody gave it to her as a joke.

ARI: But did she like it anyway?

JOE: I don't know. I don't remember.

ARI: Okay.

JOE: But you have to do everything the same.

ARI: Yeah. It's okay. I know.

JOE: This really fucking sucks.

ARI: I know.

JOE: Do you have any pot?

Scene 4—the gift table

    Naomi stands behind a table full of appliances, china, statuettes, etc. A sign says: "Gift table." She wears a bridesmaid dress that is two sizes too small. Abe enters.

NAOMI: Hello, Mr. Pfeiffer.

ABE: Hello. (*He stands in front of the gift table surveying the gifts. There is an awkward pause.*)

NAOMI: Which gift?

ABE: I haven't the slightest idea.

NAOMI: It's okay. I have a list.

ABE: Do you? Oh, good.

NAOMI: Vitamix.

ABE: What-a-what?

NAOMI: Vitamix.

ABE: Vitamix?

NAOMI: Yes. See, it says right here. (*She shows him.*) Vitamix.

ABE: Oh. I don't have any idea what that is.

NAOMI: Let me find it. (*She searches around the table, finds it.*) Here!

ABE: It's a blender?

NAOMI: Yes!

ABE: We got them a blender?

NAOMI: I guess.

ABE: Blender. All right. Where's the lid?

NAOMI: Um, I don't know.

ABE: What do you mean you don't know?

NAOMI: There's no lid.

ABE: I can see that.

NAOMI: It doesn't say anything on the list about a lid.

ABE: It's a blender! It comes with a lid.

NAOMI: What do you want me to do?

ABE: Find the lid!

NAOMI: I can't leave the gifts. (*Pause.*) I'm sorry there's no lid.

 Joan enters.

JOAN: Naomi. Have you seen—Oh, hello Abraham.

ABE: Hello, Joan.

JOAN: How are you doing?

ABE: Just fine, thank you.

JOAN: I'm so sorry about Gloria.

ABE: Thank you.

 Pause.

JOAN: I think Devorah is looking for you.

ABE: Ah, I'll just go find her, then.

JOAN: All right.

ABE: *(To Naomi)* **Thank you.** *(Naomi nods solemnly. Abe exits with the blender.)*

JOAN: *(watching him go)* **Terrible.** *(turning her attention to Naomi)* **What in the world are you wearing?**

NAOMI: **The dress.**

JOAN: **There is no way that is the same dress.**

NAOMI: **It is!**

JOAN: **Come over here.** *(Naomi hesitates.)* **Come over here!**

   Naomi comes out from behind the table. The dress barely covers her.

JOAN: **You look like a prostitute.**

NAOMI: **I grew! It's not my fault. It was three years ago. I was 11. Now I'm 14. I grew.**

JOAN: **Well, you can't wear that.**

NAOMI: **I have to.**

JOAN: **You do not.**

NAOMI: **Mom. Yes I do. You said I did.**

JOAN: **Well, I didn't realize that you would be flashing your tuchis at the world.**

NAOMI: **I'm not flashing. I'll stand up straight. I have to wear this. Everything must be as it was or the division cannot be sanctified.**

JOAN: *(hugging her)* **My sweet girl. Okay. Stand up very straight.**

NAOMI: **I will.**

JOAN: **Thank you. Have you seen your father?**

NAOMI: **He's over on the band thing.**

JOAN: *(turning toward the reception hall)* **Ozzie!** *(She exits.)*

Scene 5—the old people

   A hallway outside of the reception hall. Hannah and Siobhan are making out. Hannah wears the same dress as Naomi, but hers comes to her knees. She also wears a striped, pillbox hat. They are surrounded by cut flowers and vases.

SIOBHAN: *(stops kissing Hannah)* **And which one is your uncle Morty again?**

HANNAH: *(continuing to try to kiss her)* **Short wife.**

SIOBHAN: **Right, right. Uncle Morty, short wife.** *(They keep kissing.)* **Wait, wait, who is Abe? Is he one of your uncles?**

HANNAH: **No, Abe is Joe's father.** *(Keeps trying to kiss her. Siobhan is still confused.)* **Joe, Joe. Rachel's Joe.**

SIOBHAN: **Oh, right. Sorry.** *(They keep kissing.)* **So, sorry, the uncles are . . . ?**

HANNAH: **Uncle Morty . . .**

SIOBHAN: Short wife.

HANNAH: Uncle Danny . . .

SIOBHAN: Always wants to speak Spanish!

HANNAH: Right, and Uncle Dave.

SIOBHAN: Um . . . wait . . . don't tell me. *(Hannah waves her left hand in the air with the fourth finger folded in.)* Ah! Yes. Uncle Dave, bandsaw accident.

HANNAH: Yes *(tries to resume making out.)*

SIOBHAN: And you have an aunt, too, right?

HANNAH: *(sighing, relenting)* Yes, my Aunt Adine.

SIOBHAN: But I haven't met her yet.

HANNAH: Right.

SIOBHAN: Because she lives in France.

HANNAH: Right! *(They recommence making out.)*

SIOBHAN: *(stops kissing her)* Wait, do they all know?

HANNAH: Know what?

SIOBHAN: About Joe. About how he cheated on Rachel?

HANNAH: *(Hannah gives up on the making out and goes back to arranging flowers)* I don't know, but they'll all know by the end of this. They have to say it in the ceremony.

SIOBHAN: They do?

JOAN: *(off)* HANNAH!

HANNAH: Yeah mom?

JOAN: *(off)* HANNAH?

HANNAH: Yeah?

JOAN: *(off)* HANNAH?

HANNAH: In here!

JOAN: *(off)* HANNAH? *(She enters and sees Siobhan first.)* Oh. Hello Siobhan.

SIOBHAN: Hello Mrs. Mendelssohn. Can I help you with that? *(She takes some of whatever Joan is carrying.)*

JOAN: Thank you, dear. Hannah, is your Aunt Adine here yet?

HANNAH: Haven't seen her.

JOAN: Will you keep an eye out, please?

HANNAH: Sure. Wh—

JOAN: I don't want her running into Joe's father.

HANNAH: Yeah, what's the deal with that?

JOAN: What deal? There's no deal. Who said there was a deal?

HANNAH: So, why don't you want them to run into each other?

221

JOAN: I just don't want any more discomfort in this day. *(Hannah and Siobhan exchange a look.)* What? I didn't mean you.

HANNAH: Why would there be discomfort if there's no deal?

JOAN: *(sighs)* Your Aunt Adine and Joe's father, Abe, do not speak.

HANNAH: Why?

JOAN: Oh, never mind.

HANNAH: Mom!

JOAN: I honestly don't know, Hannah. They had some sort of falling out. Forever ago. When they were still kids.

SIOBHAN: Your families knew each other?

JOAN: Oh yeah, we all grew up together. Well, Joe's father—

SIOBHAN: Abe!

JOAN: Yes, and Hannah's aunt, Adine did. I'm so much younger than my sister that I didn't really know her crowd.

HANNAH: So, Abe and Aunt Adine don't speak?

JOAN: Who said that?

HANNAH: You did.

JOAN: I did not. I'm sure they would speak to each other if necessary.

HANNAH: But you don't want it to become necessary.

JOAN: Not today, please. This day is difficult enough already. *(Hannah and Siobhan exchange a look.)* I didn't mean you! You know, the two of you are very insecure about this whole lesbian thing.

HANNAH: Yeah, Mom. We're insecure about it.

JOAN: Hannah, I am delighted that you've finally found somebody who you wanted to introduce to your family. And if that had to happen this week, then, so be it.

HANNAH: We feel bathed in your warmth.

JOAN: I have to go and check on your sister. Siobhan, you are very welcome here. *(She exits.)*

SIOBHAN: Thank you, Mrs. Mendelssohn.

ADINE: *(entering)* Oh, lord, I forgot about the hat.

HANNAH: Aunt Adine! *(They hug.)*

ADINE: Hi, sweetheart.

HANNAH: You just missed Mom.

ADINE: Not by accident. *(holding Hannah at arms' length, examining the hat)* What was she thinking?

HANNAH: She thought it was important for the maid of honor to stand out.

ADINE: Well, mission accomplished, I guess.

HANNAH: Yep.

222

ADINE: Would either of you mind if I smoke?

SIOBHAN: Fine with me.

HANNAH: Yeah, go ahead. *(Adine lights a cigarette.)*

ADINE: *(To Siobhan)* You're new.

SIOBHAN: Sorry?

ADINE: You're new, are you not? You weren't here last time around?

SIOBHAN: Oh, no. I wasn't.

HANNAH: Sorry. Aunt Adine, this is my girlfriend, Siobhan.

ADINE: *(Shaking Siobhan's hand warmly)* Pleasure. My sister is allowing this?

HANNAH: She made an exception.

ADINE: I'm impressed. Things change.

HANNAH: When did you get here?

ADINE: Two days ago.

HANNAH: How come we haven't seen you?

ADINE: I went back to the old neighborhood first.

HANNAH: Oh.

SIOBHAN: Where's the old neighborhood?

ADINE: Pensy Par—   ABE: *(entering)* Pensy Park.

HANNAH: Abe!

ABE: Hi, Hannah.

HANNAH: Hi. Hi. *(Pause.)* Um . . . this is my girlfriend, Siobhan.

ABE: Lovely to meet you.

SIOBHAN: And you. I'm so sorry about your wife.

ABE: Thank you.

HANNAH: I'm sorry, too.

ABE: Thank you.

HANNAH: And you, um, know my Aunt Adine, right?

ABE: I do. Hello Adine.

ADINE: Hello.

 Silence.

SIOBHAN: Adine, could you help me bring the rest of these flowers inside?
 (There are only two flower vases left. She hands one to Adine and takes the other.)

ADINE: Sure. *(She goes to extinguish her cigarette, stops, offers it to Abe.)*

ABE: No, thank you.

ADINE: Suit yourself. *(She and Siobhan exit. Hannah and Abe watch them go in
 silence. It lingers.)*

HANNAH: Well, I should . . . *(She gestures off stage.)*

ABE: Sure.

Hannah starts to exit, stops.

HANNAH: Do you need anything?

ABE: I'm fine.

HANNAH: Should I find Devorah?

ABE: I'm sure she'll find me.

HANNAH: Okay then.

ABE: Okay.

Hannah starts to go again. Stops.

HANNAH: Abe? I really am sorry.

ABE: Thank you.

She exits.

Scene 6—the lie

Rachel's dressing room. Hannah enters.

HANNAH: Knock knock.

RACHEL: Hey. Please don't say anything about how I look.

HANNAH: If you don't say anything about how I look. *(gestures to hat)*

RACHEL: I'm so sorry. I really thought it would look chic.

HANNAH: It's fine. It works well with the whole humiliation theme.

RACHEL: What's happening out there?

HANNAH: Nothing. Just, y'know. A million people gathering to witness the most painful moment of your life.

Pause, then it becomes funny.

RACHEL: Oh God. There really are a million, aren't there?

HANNAH: No, there's, like, seventy . . . five.

RACHEL: Seventy four. Joe's mom.

HANNAH: Seventy-three, then, actually 'cause the florist was there last time.

RACHEL: It's totally fucked that Mom gets to be a tyrant about all of the rules of this thing, but then she gets to randomly decide not to use the same florist.

HANNAH: Not to use any florist. Me and Siobhan did it. Oh! Siobhan.

RACHEL: Right. So, 74.

HANNAH: Anyway, he ripped us off, that florist.

RACHEL: So? She was in here 10 minutes ago telling me "You don't get to pick and choose Rachel! God's looking at your underwear, Rachel!"

HANNAH: Well . . . she is religiously arbitrary.

RACHEL: What are you going to say?

HANNAH: In there?

RACHEL: Yeah.

HANNAH: What I said—y'know . . . what I said last time.

RACHEL: Say it.

HANNAH: Now?

RACHEL: Yes.

HANNAH: No. Why?

RACHEL: Hann!

HANNAH: Rachel! Why are you torturing yourself?

RACHEL: I'm not. Would you please just try not to pathologize me today? And just say it. Please. It's MY DAY.

HANNAH: But I don't—

RACHEL: Because if I hear it now then I won't have to listen in there and I won't, y'know . . .

HANNAH: Cry.

RACHEL: Right.

HANNAH: Fine. Okay. *(She takes a piece of paper out of her pocket and reads.)*

My sister is not a girl who's ever expected perfection. This makes her a great antidote to our mother. And it makes her a great friend. She knows that you are going to screw up, and she loves you anyway. She knows that things are not going to go the way you hope they will, and she does them anyway. This, to me, is real bravery, and real love.

My sister is not a girl who expects perfection, so she was a little disoriented when she first met Joe. I'll never forget when she called me up after their fourth date (okay, the morning after their fourth date)—

RACHEL: Pause for laughter.

HANNAH: I'll never forget when she called me up after their fourth date and gushed "He's perfect!" He's perfect. And so he is. I know it, because perfect is not a word she throws around lightly. She didn't say this reception hall was perfect (we had our Bat Mitvahs here, so . . .), she didn't say her dress was perfect (though I can't imagine anyone looking any more beautiful than she does right now), but when I saw her this morning I said "How's Joe?" and she said "He's perfect." She loves him and he loves her.

So here's to finding something perfect in an imperfect world. May we all be so lucky.

Aaand, toast.

Pause. Rachel stares off into space.

HANNAH: You didn't cry.

RACHEL: Huh.

225

HANNAH: It's kind of cheesy, actually. It's not really great. Why did we remember it being so great—

RACHEL: I'm so glad I'm not pregnant right now.

HANNAH: What?

RACHEL: I'm so glad. I would have had a big round belly by now.

HANNAH: What do you mean you would have had?

RACHEL: If I had stayed pregnant.

HANNAH: Stayed?

RACHEL: Right.

HANNAH: Are you telling me—wait—are you telling me that you were pregnant?

    Rachel looks at her.

HANNAH: Jesus, Rachel. Of all the weird ways to—when?

RACHEL: Eight months ago.

HANNAH: What happened?

RACHEL: I had an abortion.

HANNAH: What?

RACHEL: I had an abortion.

HANNAH: Why are you telling me this?

RACHEL: I thought you should know.

HANNAH: You didn't think I should know anytime in the last eight months?

RACHEL: No.

HANNAH: Rachel this is— This is— You're like— I don't even— I don't understand this behavior.

RACHEL: Do you have a tampon?

HANNAH: Did you have an abortion?

RACHEL: Yes, I just said that.

HANNAH: Rachel, this is like that freaky automaton thing you used to do to freak me out when you were little.

RACHEL: *(automoton voice)* Do you have a tampon?

HANNAH: Fuck you.

RACHEL: Hann—

HANNAH: I'm so glad I'm not pregnant, What?, Oh yeah, I had an abortion eight months ago, Do you have a tampon? What the fu—

RACHEL: Six months ago.

HANNAH: Sorry?

RACHEL: I was pregnant eight months ago. I had the abortion six months ago.

HANNAH: You were pregnant for two months?

RACHEL: Yes.

HANNAH: I can't— I don't even know where to—

RACHEL: I thought somebody should know the real reason why we're here.

HANNAH: Joe doesn't know?!

RACHEL: No, he knows. Other than Joe, I meant.

HANNAH: Are you saying that Joe is divorcing you because you had an abortion?

RACHEL: No. He forgave me.

HANNAH: Did he know that you were pregnant? Before you did it?

RACHEL: No.

HANNAH: When did you tell him?

RACHEL: After. Like, two weeks later.

HANNAH: And he forgave you.

RACHEL: Not right away.

HANNAH: When?

RACHEL: Well, pretty much right away.

HANNAH: Okay, you had an abortion without telling your husband, then you told him, then he forgave you. How does that get us to today?

RACHEL: I didn't want to have his baby.

HANNAH: Oh.

   Silence.

HANNAH: You have to tell Mom.

RACHEL: No.

HANNAH: Yes.

RACHEL: And you can't either.

HANNAH: I'm not going to because you are.

RACHEL: I'm not.

HANNAH: Yes.

RACHEL: No.

	227
HANNAH: Yes. Because you can't keep something like this from her. You can't. You'll always regret it. You're in this family and it's not how we were raised.	RACHEL: Why would I do that? I can and I already have been. I don't regret it. At all.

RACHEL: How we were raised? What? How were we raised?

HANNAH: To be honest with each other. To share our sorrows.

RACHEL: I am being honest and sharing my sorrow with you.

HANNAH: Months later.

RACHEL: Would you have supported me?

HANNAH: What don't you regret?

RACHEL: What?

HANNAH: What don't you regret? Having the abortion, or not telling mom?

RACHEL: Both. I regret neither.

HANNAH: So why did you tell me?

RACHEL: To share my sorrow.

Pause.

HANNAH: Wait. Did this happen before or after Joe cheated on you?

RACHEL: Before.

Pause.

HANNAH: What?

RACHEL: What what?

HANNAH: You said that weird.

Rachel shakes her head dismissively.

HANNAH: That doesn't make sense.

RACHEL: What doesn't?

HANNAH: You had the abortion before Joe cheated on you?

RACHEL: Yeah.

HANNAH: So, you knew you wanted to divorce Joe before he cheated?

RACHEL: Yeah.

HANNAH: But you told me. I mean, you told, you told everybody that you were getting divorced because he cheated.

RACHEL: What was I supposed to say?

HANNAH: You had an abortion, Joe forgave you, and then he cheated on you.

RACHEL: Yes.

HANNAH: For revenge?

RACHEL: Well, I don't know why he did it, Hann, you'd have to ask him.

HANNAH: You didn't?

RACHEL: Not really. I already knew I didn't want to be married to him.

Pause.

HANNAH: He didn't cheat on you.

Pause.

RACHEL: I couldn't tell—

HANNAH: Are you kidding me?

RACHEL: I couldn't tell the truth.

HANNAH: You talked Joe into saying he cheated—

RACHEL: I didn't talk him—

HANNAH: You let him take the blame—

RACHEL: He offered—

HANNAH: And you're letting him stand up in front of everybody.

RACHEL: You don't know—

HANNAH: I don't believe you.

RACHEL: Cheating is better.

HANNAH: Better? Rachel, it's a lie. A huge lie that you've imposed on your— I yelled at him!

RACHEL: I know.

HANNAH: In a parking lot. In front of, like, a bunch of people.

RACHEL: I was there.

HANNAH: I said he was worthless. I called him a fornicator!

RACHEL: (laughs) Yeah, you did.

HANNAH: This is not funny.

RACHEL: Well, I mean. It's kind of funny that you said "fornicator."

HANNAH: And he just took it.

RACHEL: As he does.

HANNAH: And now you're going to let him stand up in front of everybody you both know and take the blame—

RACHEL: He wants to . . .

HANNAH: It's a lie! In temple.

RACHEL: Oh God. Who cares about—

HANNAH: He does, Rachel! Jesus. You are . . . you are . . .

RACHEL: What?

HANNAH: You are exactly who you've always been. A selfish, self-absorbed, empathy-impaired bitch.

RACHEL: Thank you.

HANNAH: (exiting and slamming the door) You're welcome.

> A few moments go by. Rachel sits alone.

HANNAH: (re-entering) Normally I would never come back in here, but I have something time-sensitive to say. (Rachel looks at her.) You are horrible. And he loves you anyway. (She leaves.)

Scene 7—the plot

> Joe's dressing room. Joe is now dressed. He and Ari are sharing a joint.

ARI: What do you mean?

JOE: What I said.

ARI: Yeah, but, what do you mean "It's not going to happen"?

JOE: I mean that I don't think she'll go through with it.

ARI: I think you're wrong about that.

JOE: Why?

ARI: Why? Dude. She's the one who planned it. There's a room out there rapidly filling with people who she invited. And, no offense, but, between the two of you, she's the decider.

JOE: No, this isn't right. This isn't how it's supposed to be.

ARI: Joe, listen to me very carefully. This is happening.

JOE: Nope.

ARI: Is this because of your mom? Because she's not here?

JOE: It's not because of my mom.

ARI: Because nobody would blame you. I mean, you buried her two days ago. But she would want—

JOE: You're going to tell me what my mother would want in this situation?

ARI: No, I . . . just meant that . . .

JOE: My mom was alive five days ago. I had a conversation with her.

ARI: Joe, she was completely . . . out of it. I'm sorry, but—

JOE: I had a conversation with her.

ARI: Okay. What did she say?

JOE: She said to stop it.

ARI: Your mom.

JOE: Yes.

ARI: Said to stop today from happening.

JOE: Right.

ARI: Your mom did.

JOE: She wouldn't have wanted this.

ARI: Well, wait, she wouldn't have wanted it, or she didn't want it?

JOE: She—

ARI: Because those are two different things, Joe.

JOE: She—

ARI: You didn't have a conversation about this with your mom, Joe. I'm sorry, but your mom has been really really sick for a really long time. She didn't know this was happening today. She didn't have an opinion about it. I'm sorry.

JOE: Fuck you.

ARI: Okay.

230

JOE: We're stopping it.

ARI: We who?

JOE: Me and you.

ARI: No.

JOE: Yes. You have to help me.

ARI: I'm not helping you because I don't agree. I think you should go through with it. Anyway, I thought you just said Rachel's gonna stop it, so why do we have to do anything?

JOE: Because what if she doesn't? I can't have it. I can't have it.

ARI: Yes you can. You can have it. Joe, listen, I know you're, like, deep in a dark Rachel wood right now and you can't see anything beyond the trees, but, trust me, there is a meadow out there. A beautiful, sunny, lush meadow full of vaginas.

JOE: You're a poet.

ARI: I'm not saying you have to go there right away, man. Take your time. Be sad. Wander around in the woods, make camp under a mossy log, y'know . . . eat sad berries and cry in the rain and do your thing. But spring will come, dude, with its verdant pussy meadow.

JOE: You have no idea what the fuck you're talking about. This isn't like you dumping Melita for some nonsense reason because you were bored and then fucking all those Kristas.

ARI: Only two of them were named Krista. The other one was Carrie. Carlie.

JOE: Whatever. This isn't that. This is my marriage. Get it? I made a commitment. For life. No matter what.

ARI: But you didn't know when you did that that it would all turn to shit, man.

JOE: It didn't all turn to shit! I still love Rachel. I know you think she's—

ARI: A psycho bitch—

JOE: Yeah, I know. And I get why. But it was good before it went bad. I think it could be good again.

ARI: I know, I just meant—

JOE: And even if it had turned to shit, it wouldn't matter. It makes no difference what I knew or didn't know. It makes absolutely no difference. A man keeps his commitments. Period. How can I face myself if I let this happen? I can't.

> *Ari takes the joint from Joe, takes a hit, sighs.*

ARI: Okay, what do you want me to do?

231

Scene 8—the joke

Outside. Abe is smoking a cigar. Adine approaches. In a wordless exchange, she sits down next to him, and takes out a cigarette. He lights it. They smoke.

ABE: Husband and wife, married 45 years, are sitting across from each other at the breakfast table. Guy's doing the crossword. Finally, the wife looks up and says "I'm leaving you." "Why?" says the husband. "Because you're a schmuck," says the wife. "You were a schmuck when I married you, and you've been a schmuck every day for the last 45 years. You're such a schmuck, you're the world's second biggest schmuck." "If I'm such a schmuck," says he, "how come I'm only the world's second biggest schmuck?" "Because you're a schmuck!"

ADINE: Says the wife.

ABE: No.

ADINE: Yes!

ABE: How can such a smart person be so wrong about something so basic?

ADINE: How can such a funny man butcher such a simple punchline over and over and over again for forty years?

ABE: More like a fifty.

ADINE: Don't remind me.

ABE: Age is all I can think about.

Pause.

ADINE: How are you?

ABE: You disappoint me, Adine.

ADINE: How have I disappointed you, Abraham?

ABE: I thought I could count on you to be the one person who wouldn't ask me that question.

ADINE: You're right. I'm sorry.

ABE: Thank you.

ADINE: So how are you?

ABE: Well, we're here at this blessed event, my daughter would put a leash on me if it weren't unseemly, and my wife, a person with whom I have spoken every day for the last 41 years, is dead, and, as of two days ago, buried. So I am, as you can imagine, delightful.

ADINE: I saw you at the funeral.

ABE: I saw you, too.

ADINE: It was strange to go back to the old neighborhood.

ABE: We kept it the same for you.

ADINE: There never used to be a Starbucks.

ABE: Wasn't there?

Adine laughs.

ADINE: They just opened one across the street from my apartment.

ABE: In Paris?

ADINE: I don't live in Paris.

ABE: I thought you live in France.

ADINE: I do live in France, but there are other cities in France besides Paris.

ABE: Oh. And which one do you live in?

ADINE: Marseille.

ABE: And where's that?

ADINE: In the South. On the water.

ABE: Paris is on water.

ADINE: Paris is on a river. This is the Mediterranean Sea.

ABE: Is that right?

ADINE: Are you winding me up?

ABE: All those years in Paris have not done wonders for your sense of humor, my dear.

Pause.

ADINE: Didn't you ever want to leave?

ABE: Never. Every day.

ADINE: I cannot even begin to imagine what my life would have been like if I'd spent it there.

ABE: Sure you can. You would've married Max Morgenstern, had seven kids, and thrown yourself off of a bridge at the age of 35.

ADINE: How did you do it?

ABE: How'd I do what?

ADINE: Stay. There. Live in the same place your entire life. Live your entire life with the same person.

ABE: I just did.

ADINE: Yeah, but how . . . I mean— (you used to talk about traveling the world)

ABE: What was that song you used to sing?   233

ADINE: Which?

ABE: The one—you know—the one about the . . . the the the Coney Island one.

ADINE: *Goodbye My Coney Island Baby.*

ABE: That one, yes.

ADINE: That's the song.

ABE: What?

ADINE: *Goodbye My Coney Island Baby.* That's the song I used to sing. To answer your question.

ABE: Sing it.

ADINE: I'm sorry?

ABE: Sing it now.

ADINE: What are you talking about?

ABE: Sing!

ADINE: That is a song for a barbershop quartet.

ABE: Which you used to—

ADINE: Which I have not sung for 40 years and I couldn't even remember the lyrics if I had a—

ABE: Sing. Sing!

ADINE: Maybe lat—

ABE: You used to sing that song around our house. While you hung up the laundry. I know because you did that right outside the window, and I used to put down my reading and listen to you.

ADINE: You did no—

ABE: There were times when the only other sound I heard around the house for weeks it seemed like was my mother trying to breathe. Remember that sound?

ADINE: I do.

>   *Pause.*

ADINE: Abe . . .

ABE: What?

ADINE: I really want to know.

ABE: What?

ADINE: What your life was like. How you made it.

ABE: Have I made it?

ADINE: I've been thinking about this question all the way across the Atlantic. I've been thinking about it longer than that.

ABE: You might think me inarticulate.

ADINE: But?

ABE: I honestly can't answer.

ADINE: It's all right to tell me you loved Gloria.

ABE: You're saying I have your permission to mention that I loved my wife?

ADINE: You don't need my permission.

ABE: You don't say.

ADINE: Don't give your anger to me.

234

ABE: You're asking me how? How on earth did I manage to muddle through my wretched existence? I loved my wife. I loved my children. I worked for them.

ADINE: I didn't say it was wretched.

ABE: It's all wretched. Yours wasn't?

ADINE: It was, it was. Wonderfully wretched. Why are we talking about our lives in the past tense?

ABE: How did you make it? Did you have anyone? Do you?

ADINE: No, Abe. I've been celibate since the age of 19.

A moment passes in reflection. Adine lights another cigarette.

ABE: Let's not talk about it.

ADINE: I was about the say the same thing.

ABE: Sing that song!

ADINE: *(singing)* Goodbye, my Coney Island baby/Farewell, my own true love/I'm gonna go away and leave you/Never to see you any/Never gonna see you any/I'm gonna sail upon that ferry boat/Never to return again/Return again/So goodbye/Farewell/So long forever/Dee hi/Goodbye my Coney Isle/Dee ho/Goodbye my Coney Isle/Dee hi/Goodbye my Coney Island/Bye my Coney Island baby.

Silence.

ABE: My daughter is looking for me.

Abe exits. Adine lights another cigarette.

Scene 9—Gloria

Abe turns a corner and runs into Joe.

ABE: Joe.

JOE: Dad.

They hug.

JOE: Are you okay?

ABE: Sure. Sure.

JOE: Where's Dev?

ABE: She's inside.

JOE: She should be with you.

ABE: I snuck away.

JOE: Dad—

ABE: I was just going to find her.

JOE: *(smelling him)* Were you smoking?

ABE: No!

JOE: Why do you smell like smoke?

ABE: Joseph.

JOE: Sorry. Are you okay?

ABE: I'm supposed to be asking you that.

JOE: I'm fine.

ABE: I know you don't believe this, but you actually will be.

JOE: Okay.

ABE: It's true.

JOE: How do you know?

ABE: I know.

JOE: What about you?

ABE: Me too.

JOE: Is it weird that I wish Mom was here?

ABE: Well, you're a weird person.

JOE: Dad—

ABE: No, it is not weird. Of course you wish she were here. I wish she were here. She, however, does not wish she were here.

JOE: I guess not.

ABE: You did a good job, Joey. It's better that she didn't know. You did good.

JOE: I tried to tell her.

ABE: When?

JOE: Tuesday.

ABE: This past Tuesday?

JOE: Yeah.

ABE: And what did she say? *(Joe shakes his head. He starts to cry. Abe holds him.)* She would have been proud of you.

JOE: What are you talking about? I'm a failure.

ABE: Everybody's a failure, Joe. That's life. Your choice is, fail with honor, or don't. *(Pause.)* I love you.

236 JOE: I love you, too, Dad. I've gotta . . . *(He gestures down the hall.)*

ABE: Okay. *(He kisses Joe on the head.)*

JOE: Find Dev.

ABE: Okay. *(Abe exits in one direction, Joe in the other.)*

Scene 10—the last fuck

Rachel's dressing room. There is a knock on the door.

RACHEL: Come in. *(Joe enters.)* Seriously?

JOE: You look so beautiful.

RACHEL: I look sad.

JOE: Well, it's pretty much time.

RACHEL: Okay. *(She starts for the door.)*

JOE: Wait.

RACHEL: What?

Pause.

RACHEL: Oh my god. Oh my god. You've got to be fucking kidding me.

JOE: Rachel—

RACHEL: Joe, I'm doing this whole thing for you. I don't give a shit about this. I'm doing this for you.

JOE: I know.

RACHEL: If it were up to me, we could've gone to Vegas. Or done it over the internet. They have that now.

JOE: I know.

RACHEL: If you think I'm going to fuck you now, you are absolutely out of your mind.

JOE: It's just that—

RACHEL: That's what we did on that day. I know. Jesus! We did a lot of fucking things on that day, Joe, including, y'know, actually loving each other and being actually happy. God damn it. This whole ritual is completely fucked up.

JOE: This is how it's done, Rachel.

RACHEL: Well it's fucked.

JOE: Okay.

Pause.

JOE: It's not though.

RACHEL: I know.

JOE: It's part of the agreement.

RACHEL: I know.

JOE: You can't ask for the community's blessing to go in but not to come out.

RACHEL: Joe! I know. God. You think you're so much more religious than me.

JOE: I am.

RACHEL: I'm religious!

JOE: You don't believe in God.

RACHEL: Whatever. You know what? I don't want to talk about it. I'm not fighting with you today.

JOE: Okay.

> *Pause.*

JOE: We don't have to do this.

RACHEL: You just said that we do.

JOE: No, I mean. We don't have to do this. There's still time. We could tell people to go home.

RACHEL: No, we couldn't.

JOE: I don't believe that this is what you really want.

RACHEL: It is.

JOE: I don't believe it.

RACHEL: Since I'm me, and you don't actually know me that well, I'm just going to go ahead and be the judge of what I do and don't want. *(Pause.)* Is your dad out there?

JOE: Yeah.

RACHEL: He okay?

JOE: I think so. I mean, no, but—

RACHEL: Did Ari bring that Melita?

JOE: Yeah.

RACHEL: What was wrong with her?

JOE: Toothy.

RACHEL: Oh. True. *(Pause.)* Joe. The whole idea that there's a perfect way to do this. It's ridiculous. You can't clean this up.

JOE: The point is to sanctify the dissolution.

RACHEL: I know, I'm just saying. Sanctity is one thing. But it's going to take time. Don't expect yourself to feel it right away.

JOE: Did you feel it right away? After? Before, I mean.

RACHEL: *(Pause.)* No.

> *Long pause. They look at each other. Eventually, she reaches over and kisses his neck. They begin having sex in their wedding clothes. Fade to a spot on The Boy.*

238

SCENE 11—the boy with the glass

> *We spend a moment alone with the boy, watching him work.*
> *End of ACT I*

ACT II

Scene 1—the bouquet

> *Outside the reception hall. The music and the sound of a crowd can be heard within. Rachel enters, covered in dried flower bits, followed by Naomi.*

NAOMI: I'm sorry! I'm so so sorry. *(Naomi frantically tries to clean the bits off of Rachel's dress.)*

RACHEL: It's okay, Omi.

NAOMI: But . . . I . . . your dress!

RACHEL: It doesn't matter.

NAOMI: Yes it does!

RACHEL: It doesn't. Stop. STOP. *(She stops her.)* You have to relax.

NAOMI: I'm sorry.

RACHEL: And stop apologizing.

NAOMI: Sorry. Oh! Sorry. *(They sit on the floor.)*

RACHEL: You should try to keep your legs together. Who told you you had to wear that?

NAOMI: Nobody. I just knew.

RACHEL: You could have worn something else.

NAOMI: I didn't want to mess anything up. I mean, I didn't want it to be me. I wanted it to work.

RACHEL: It's not like a spell.

NAOMI: How do you know?

> *Adine enters.*

ADINE: What in the hell happened to you?

RACHEL: Naomi threw the bouquet kind of . . . at me.

ADINE: Isn't that what she was supposed to do?   NAOMI: I didn't mean to!

RACHEL: We know, Oms. It's fine. *(To Adine)* She was supposed to throw it back *to* me. *(To Naomi)* But! It's an old, dry, crumbly bouquet. This was fairly inevitable. *(To Adine)* Wait, you missed it?

NAOMI: Aunt Adine!

ADINE: Sorry.

RACHEL: Doesn't matter.

NAOMI: Does!

RACHEL: Omi, listen to me. This day is going to be terrible no matter what you or anybody else does, all right? I'm sad and Joe is sad and Mom and everybody is sad sad sad, and even if we all do everything perfectly, it's still going to be really f-ing sad. Okay? And I love you for trying so hard

239

and wearing this ridiculous dress and all that, but, I promise you, God is not watching us that carefully.

Naomi looks at Rachel for a moment, then gets on to her knees and begins to pray. Adine and Rachel watch her for a moment, then resume their conversation.

ADINE: Having a nice day?

RACHEL: You are the only person here who doesn't hate me.

ADINE: Oh, I hate you.

RACHEL: Stop it.

JOAN: *(off)* RACHEL?!

RACHEL: Oh no! I'm made.

ADINE: What's next?

RACHEL: The horrible kissing.

Adine looks at her and makes some gesture of love and compassion and sadness.

ADINE: Go! Go, go, go, before she gets out here and sees me.

Rachel exits ruefully. Adine looks after her for a moment, then goes to Naomi.

ADINE: We don't do this kid.

NAOMI: *(still in prayer)* We don't *don't* do it. It's not forbidden.

ADINE: Fair enough.

NAOMI: I asked the rabbi.

ADINE: Okay, honey. It's okay.

NAOMI: I have to do something.

ADINE: Yeah.

Adine watches her for a moment. And then kneels down next to her and joins her prayer. Inside, we hear glassware being tapped repeatedly, followed by applause. These sounds continue over this scene. After a long moment, Melita enters.

MELITA: Oh! I'm sorry. I didn't mean to interrupt.

ADINE: Give me a hand getting up.

MELITA: Oh, uh . . . sure. *(She helps Adine up from the floor. Naomi gets up, too.)*

ADINE: Thank you. You are forgiven.

MELITA: Thank you.

ADINE: Don't worry about it. I've met you, but I can't remember your name.

MELITA: It's Melita.

ADINE: Right. Sorry about that.

MELITA: Don't worry about it.

240

ADINE: *(lighting a cigarette)* You're with . . .

MELITA: Ari. But not anymore.

ADINE: I imagine that's worse for Ari than it is for you.

MELITA: Can I ask you something?

ADINE: G'head.

MELITA: Why do they make them do this kissing part? It seems cruel.

ADINE: It is.

MELITA: So why?

ADINE: My niece is the expert.

NAOMI: They have to kiss the same number of times that they kissed during their wedding.

MELITA: Somebody counted.

NAOMI: It's to prove that they really don't love each other.

MELITA: How?

NAOMI: Because it's really hard to kiss somebody who you don't love. *(Adine and Melita exchange a look.)* And if you love somebody, and you kiss them, it's undeniable.

MELITA: It's . . . ?

NAOMI: Undeniable.

ADINE: It cannot be denied!

MELITA: Got it. And they do them all in a row like this, just . . .

ADINE: To get it over with.

MELITA: And the drinking after each kiss, that's part of it, too?

ADINE: The most important part, wouldn't you say?

MELITA: Yes, yes I would. *(She pulls a flask out of her bag and shows it to Adine.)*

ADINE: You came prepared.

MELITA: Not my first rodeo. *(She offers Adine the flask.)*

ADINE: No thank you, mademoiselle.

NAOMI: We should go back.

ADINE: Okay, sweetheart. Melita?

MELITA: Oh, no thanks. I'm just going to . . . *(She makes some gesture indicating that she's going to stay outside for the moment.)*

ADINE: Fair enough.

> Adine and Naomi exit. Melita stands alone for a second. Maybe she checks her phone or something.

241

Scene 2—the nail polish

Same place, same moment. Melita notices a run in her pantyhose, pulls a bottle of bright red nail polish out of her bag, and begins applying it to the run. Siobhan enters.

SIOBHAN: Stop, I've got clear.

MELITA: You might be too late.

SIOBHAN: Oh, so I am. Well. At least it's above the hem.

MELITA: It couldn't make less of a difference anyway.

SIOBHAN: I'm Siobhan.

MELITA: **Melita.** *(She puts the cap back on the nail polish, and reaches out to shake Siobhan's hand.)* Hi.

SIOBHAN: Hi.

MELITA: You're Hannah's girlfriend.

SIOBHAN: Yes. And you're . . . ?

MELITA: I'm just here.

SIOBHAN: By yourself?

MELITA: No.

SIOBHAN: Okay.

MELITA: Sorry. I'm here with Ari. The best man? But I'm not with Ari. Anymore.

SIOBHAN: Ah. Well that's nice of you.

MELITA: It's nothing. I mean, it's important. *(She pulls an apple out of her bag.)* Want to share?

SIOBHAN: Aren't we not allowed? *(Melita takes a bite and offers it to her.)* Well, all right. Thank you. I'm starving. Did you know there wouldn't be food?

MELITA: Plenty to drink, though! It's a fasting thing. For mourning or repentance or something. Hannah didn't tell you?

SIOBHAN: No. So, you were here last time.

MELITA: Yep. There was food, though.

SIOBHAN: Can you explain the chair thing to me, then?

MELITA: The chair . . . ?

SIOBHAN: They're just sitting there in chairs staring at each other. I'm not actually allowed inside, but I peeked.

MELITA: Because you weren't here last time? *(Siobhan nods. Melita shakes her head.)* Okay. *(Siobhan offers her back the apple.)* No, you keep it. It's the least I can do. So, it's a tradition, at the wedding, for the couple to be lifted up and danced around in chairs.

SIOBHAN: So here they just have to sit in them.

MELITA: I guess. Pretty much.

SIOBHAN: Jesus, this is a perverse ritual.

MELITA: Never been to one before?

SIOBHAN: Once, back in Dublin. You?

MELITA: I've been to more than one. But I don't think it's perverse.

SIOBHAN: Don't you, now?

MELITA: No, I think it's . . . I don't know. I think it's kind of nice.

SIOBHAN: Nice?

MELITA: Yeah, it's kind of beautiful. I mean, I think it honors what you've had more than just slinking off and signing some papers.

SIOBHAN: Never been married, I take it?

MELITA: No. Have you?

SIOBHAN: I was. For eight months.

MELITA: But you didn't . . .

SIOBHAN: Do one of these jobs? No. Not for me. Weren't much there to honor, anyhow. We were just kids, and, I mean, obviously, I had no fecking idea what I was doing. But I don't see the beauty that you see here. It seems barbaric. I mean, they have to feed one another little frozen pieces of their wedding cake?

MELITA: Oh, I know. That's the best.

SIOBHAN: The best?

MELITA: You have to place a frozen piece of your own wedding cake into the mouth of the person you're divorcing and then sit there and stare at them while the cake gets all sweet and soggy in your mouth. You're literally tasting your grief. It's great.

SIOBHAN: You have a bit of a dark side.

MELITA: I guess.

    Pause.

SIOBHAN: Were they good together?

MELITA: Joe and Rachel? Yeah. I mean, I guess I didn't really know them that well. I always kind of got the feeling she's a little too, y'know *(She makes a gesture.)*—

SIOBHAN: Guarded?

MELITA: Sure, and he's kind of a little too, what's the word? Compliant? Nice? I don't know. For my taste. But they seemed to kind of balance each other out. I don't know. I thought they were happy.

SIOBHAN: Maybe they were. He cheated on her, that's it? That's the reason we're all here today?

MELITA: I guess. I can't really get my head around Joe cheating. But, I guess, y'know . . . guys.

243

SIOBHAN: Right. Guys.

MELITA: Do you know when Joe's mom died? Ari didn't say exactly and I didn't want to ask . . .

SIOBHAN: Wednesday, I believe.

MELITA: This past Wednesday?

SIOBHAN: I think so. I'm shocked they didn't postpone, actually.

MELITA: Oh, no, they couldn't've. Joe must be . . . (*shakes head or sighs or makes "ech" sound or something*). Shitty timing.

SIOBHAN: Indeed.

> *Pause.*

MELITA: Do you need a drink?

SIOBHAN: Oh, that would be lovely, actually.

MELITA: Hannah's kind of occupied in there or I'm sure she would—

SIOBHAN: No, of course.

MELITA: Okay, I have my mission. (*exiting*) Wine?

SIOBHAN: Red, please. I'll be here.

> *Melita exits, leaving Siobhan alone.*

Scene 3—the cigar

> *Outside. Abe is smoking a cigar. Naomi approaches.*

NAOMI: Excuse me, Mr. Pfeiffer?

> *Abe does not respond.*

NAOMI: Hi, Mr . . . um. Mr. Pfeiffer?

> *He turns.*

NAOMI: I'm sorry to bug you. Joe's father.

ABE: Are you asking me or telling me?

NAOMI: What?

ABE: I am Joe's father.

NAOMI: Right.

ABE: You already knew that.

NAOMI: Yes.

ABE: Because you're in my family.

NAOMI: Right. Well, sort of. I mean, not after today, I guess. How does that work?

ABE: What can I do for you?

NAOMI: They asked me to find you. My mom.

ABE: Your mother needs me for something?

244

NAOMI: I think it might be time for your toast. Thing.

ABE: Ah.

NAOMI: Or, it's coming up, I think.

ABE: I see. Thank you for finding me, then.

NAOMI: Sure.

    Pause.

NAOMI: Sir?

ABE: Abe.

NAOMI: What?

ABE: Abe. You can call me.

NAOMI: Oh, okay. You can call me Naomi.

ABE: People don't call you something else?

NAOMI: They call me Omi.

ABE: But you prefer Naomi.

NAOMI: Yes.

ABE: All right.

NAOMI: Sir—Abe?

ABE: Yes, Naomi?

NAOMI: I just wanted to say that I'm sorry that your wife—that I'm sorry
    about your wife.

ABE: Thank you.

NAOMI: I know that she died very recently.

ABE: We buried her the day before yesterday.

NAOMI: I know.

    Pause.

ABE: Was there something you wanted to ask me?

NAOMI: Aren't you sad?

ABE: Very.

NAOMI: But you're just, here. Smoking.

ABE: You don't smoke, I take it.

NAOMI: I'm fourteen.

ABE: Started when I was twelve.

NAOMI: Well . . . no. I don't.

ABE: Ever?

NAOMI: No.

ABE: Not even a puff?

NAOMI: No.

ABE: Want to?

245

Naomi stares at the proffered cigar, looks around, smooths out her dress, and takes it.

NAOMI: It's wet.

ABE: I softened it up for you.

NAOMI: What do I do?

ABE: Just put it in your mouth, and inhale. But not all at once. Little puffs. Puff, puff, puff.

She puts it in her mouth.

ABE: Don't be surprised if you cough.

NAOMI: *(cigar in mouth)* I'm not going to cough

ABE: All right.

She inhales. It goes well. She inhales some more. She smiles at him. She inhales some more, but forgets to exhale. She starts to cough. She turns away, tries to stifle the cough. It overtakes her. She doubles over, then remembers her dress, and frantically tries to smooth down the back to cover her bottom while she holds out the cigar for him to take back. He laughs. She recovers.

ABE: You okay?

NAOMI: Yes. I don't think I did it right.

ABE: You did it great.

NAOMI: Thank you.

Pause.

NAOMI: Sir?

ABE: Abe.

NAOMI: It's so awful.

ABE: What is?

NAOMI: That your wife died. And you have to be here.

ABE: Ah.

NAOMI: If my wife died—

ABE: Who is your wife?

NAOMI: Oh, I don't—I meant, if I were you.

ABE: Ah.

NAOMI: And my wife died.

ABE: Yes?

NAOMI: I think I would want to die, too.

ABE: You do, do you?

NAOMI: Yes.

ABE: Well, thank you, Naomi. That's very comforting.

246

NAOMI: I just meant—how can you be here? How can you be anywhere? Don't you want to just go somewhere and cry and cry?

ABE: Do you think that would help?

NAOMI: I don't. I'm sorry.

ABE: It's okay. You want the rest of this? (*He offers her the stub of his cigar. She takes it and tentatively puffs.*) My wife—Joe's mom—was sick for a very long time. Too long. Seeing her like that. Leaving the world in tiny, infinitesimal portions every day for years and years? That's the part that made me want to cry and cry. And I did. Seeing her die? That was a relief. More than a relief. A deliverance. My sadness about this. It's endless. Once I let it in, it's in. It will stay with me until I also die. This I know. So, I'm waiting until tomorrow.

NAOMI: Oh.

> *He starts to go.*

ABE: You coming?

NAOMI: Yes, I'll be there in a minute.

ABE: Okay.

> *He exits. She puffs tentatively at the cigar.*

SCENE 4—the punch

> *Ari enters, stumbling drunk. He's looking for somebody. He exits. Hannah enters, looking for Ari. Ari reenters, holding a bottle of red wine.*

ARI: Have you seen Melita?

HANNAH: Ari, holy shit.

ARI: Oh, right, Hannah, um, an accordion-playing monkey called. He wants his hat back.

HANNAH: (*tearing off the hat and throwing it at him*) What the fuck was that?

ARI: I speak the truth. I am a truth speaker.

HANNAH: You are an asshole.

ARI: Tell me one thing I said that wasn't true.

HANNAH: That's not the point.

ARI: What's the—

HANNAH: The point is to do it like it was done. And that's not what you said at their wedding.

ARI: Basically . . .

HANNAH: No. At their wedding you did not say that Rachel is to a cunt as a cunt is to a cunt.

ARI: Didn't I?

247

HANNAH: **Ari.**

ARI: Well she is.

HANNAH: That's not the point.

ARI: You already said that.

HANNAH: Because I can't believe you did that.

ARI: I can't believe you can't believe.

Melita enters.

MELITA: **Ari!**

ARI: **Melita. Hey.**

MELITA: Hey? What the hell?

ARI: Okay, you both need to relax. *(He offers Melita the bottle.)*

MELITA: *(refusing the bottle)* I'm good. That was spectacularly assholic.

ARI: Have a drink.

MELITA: I am plenty drunk, thank you. Not as drunk as you . . .

ARI: Listen, both of you. It was nice if you to come out here and reprimand me, but I am not sorry.

HANNAH: There are old people in there!

ARI: The old people *liked* it.

HANNAH: Really? You think Uncle Morty liked it when you said that you hope Rachel gets Chlamydia on her eyeballs?

ARI: Yes, I do.

MELITA: You're gross.

ARI: Because it's true! And the old people understand that today is about truth. If God wanted us to just go through the motions, why would he give us so much booze and nothing to eat? I am so right, and you know it, and you know i—

MELITA & HANNAH: Shut up.

Rachel enters. Everybody gets quiet. Long pause. She just looks at Ari. Joe enters.

JOE: Ari! *(Ari spins around and Joe punches him squarely in the jaw. He falls. Gasps of shock all around.)*

ARI: Fuck, dude!

JOE: Get out of here. *(To Melita and Hannah.)* Hannah, would you mind? Melita? *(All exit except Rachel and Joe. They look at each other.)*

RACHEL: What are you doing?

JOE: Defending my wife.

RACHEL: You just punched Ari.

JOE: He said you were a worse wife than Catherine the Great.

RACHEL: Yeah, I didn't get that.

JOE: She had an affair with a horse.

RACHEL: Ah. Well, he's right.

JOE: No.

RACHEL: Yes. I am the worst wife ever. I am worse than Catherine the Great.

JOE: You didn't have an affair.

RACHEL: Neither did you.

JOE: Sure I did.

RACHEL: No, Joe, you didn't.

JOE: Right, and you know that, so who cares if everybody else thinks I did?

RACHEL: That's unbelievable.

JOE: What?

RACHEL: You honestly don't mind if everybody in my family and your family and all of our friends and all of our friends' friends think that you cheated on me even though you didn't.

JOE: Not if you'll stay married to me.

RACHEL: What?

JOE: Stay married to me.

RACHEL: Is this a threat?

JOE: What?

RACHEL: If I don't stay married to you, you're going to tell? You're blackmailing me?

JOE: No, I . . . well, okay. Yeah. Yes. I am blackmailing you. Stay married to me or I'll tell everybody about your . . . thing.

Pause while she considers.

RACHEL: No you're not. You can't even say it.

JOE: ABORTION!

RACHEL: Joe! Shhh! (*She covers his mouth with her hand. He grabs it and kneels.*)

JOE: Rachel, I love you.

RACHEL: Don't . . .

JOE: I love you. I don't want to not be married to you. I don't care about your thing. 249

RACHEL: It's not just tha—

JOE: It's not? Really? Tell me you don't love me.

RACHEL: Joe—

JOE: Tell me you don't love me.

RACHEL: I don't love you.

JOE: That's a lie. You're a liar.

RACHEL: Yes. But I'm not lying about this.

JOE: We can fix it. I know we can.

RACHEL: It's not broken, Joe. It's dead.

JOE: Please please don't do this.

RACHEL: I don't deserve you.

JOE: I don't care!

RACHEL: I have to go back in. We both have to go back in, Joe. It's time for our last dance.

JOE: *(standing)* Explain to me why we're getting divorced.

RACHEL: This is ridiculous.

JOE: Explain.

RACHEL: You know why.

JOE: Tell me again.

RACHEL: Why?

JOE: Because . . . because. Because maybe I don't understand.

RACHEL: You do understand. Why are you doing this?

JOE: Why are you doing this?

RACHEL: You're just trying to hurt yourself so I'll feel sorry for you.

JOE: Look, I know the reasons that aren't the reasons.

RACHEL: What?

JOE: It's not because I cheated on you.

RACHEL: Because you didn't.

JOE: Right. And it's not because you had a . . . thing.

RACHEL: Abortion.

JOE: Because I forgave you.

RACHEL: But that's not the point.

JOE: What's not?

RACHEL: That you forgave me. You can't forgive me for that.

JOE: But I did.

RACHEL: I know. I know, I mean . . . you can't fix that. You can't fix the reasons I did it.

JOE: Why did you do it?

RACHEL: Joe . . .

JOE: Rachel, this is our divorce day. After today, we can't see each other for a year.

RACHEL: Sure we can.

JOE: No. I can't. I won't see you.

RACHEL: My bike is still at your house.

JOE: I'll have Ari bring it to you.

RACHEL: Oh. Okay. *(Pause.)* Did you make Ari do that?

JOE: No.

RACHEL: Joe.

JOE: I didn't tell him what to say.

RACHEL: What did you think, that I would stay married to you because you punched Ari?

JOE: I wanted you to see me fighting for you.

RACHEL: You're not a fighter.

JOE: And I did it anyway. I'll be whatever you need me to be.

RACHEL: I need you to get away from me.

JOE: I am your husband, Rachel. You can't just banish me.

RACHEL: I'm not trying to banish you, I'm trying to save you.

JOE: From you?

RACHEL: From us, Joe. I'll play the villain. That's fine. But you know I'm right.

JOE: You're not a villain.

RACHEL: And we don't owe anybody an explanation.

JOE: That's good, 'cause we're not giving anybody one.

RACHEL: Joe, we don't work.

JOE: And tell me that you feel something about that!

RACHEL: I can't.

JOE: Because you don't?

RACHEL: Because I'm afraid that if I tell you, you won't let go.

JOE: Well, that's the closest you've come to showing you still have feelings for me.

RACHEL: See!

JOE: I know you. I know all about you. And I still love you anyway.
    Pause.

RACHEL: There's someone else who knows you didn't cheat, by the way.

JOE: God.

RACHEL: No, I was going to say Hannah. Hannah knows. I told her. She guessed. We're supposed to be dancing right now. People are waiting. I'm going in. Come back in, okay? *(She starts to exit.)*

JOE: I'm not going back in until you tell me why you had the abortion.

RACHEL: For a lot of reasons.

JOE: What's one?

RACHEL: I thought you would break up with me.

251

JOE: What?

RACHEL: I thought you would break up with me.

JOE: You had an abortion because you thought it would make me break up with you?

RACHEL: Not only that—

JOE: And then I forgave you and screwed up your whole plan!

RACHEL: No, Joe—

JOE: God, Rachel. I'm so sorry I didn't get that you were just pulling the escape hatch! How stupid of me to forgive you!

RACHEL: No, Joe, stop—

JOE: No, no. You know what? Screw it. Let's get divorced.

RACHEL: Joe—

JOE: Go to hell. *(He exits.)*

SCENE 5—the last dance

Inside. A wedding first dance song plays. Behind a scrim, Rachel and Joe come together and dance.

SCENE 6—the confession

Ari sits slumped against a wall with a can of Coke against his eye, still holding his bottle of red wine. Joan enters from his blind side. She is lit. She sees him, saddles up alongside him, and slumps down to the floor herself. He notices her, startles, tries to get up to run away, but falls back down again.

JOAN: Don't try to run away from me. You said some very rude things about my daughter in there.

ARI: I'm sorry ma'am.

JOAN: Did Joe put you up to that?

ARI: No ma'am.

JOAN: Joe. *(makes spitting sound)* He deserves what he gets.

ARI: Yes ma'am.

JOAN: He cheated. On my Rachel.

ARI: I should— *(He goes to try to get up again.)*

JOAN: Sit down *(She pulls him back down. She gestures to his bottle. He offers it to her. She takes it and takes a slug. She keeps the bottle and continues to drink from it throughout the scene.)* Cheating on somebody. Somebody who trusts you. Is the worst. The worst. To someone who loves you. I should know. *(Ari looks around, hoping someone else will enter. No one does.)* Ask me why.

ARI: I . . .

JOAN: Ask me why.

ARI: Uh. Why what?

JOAN: Why should I know?

ARI: Oh, I don't need to—

JOAN: Ask it.

ARI: No, I don't—

JOAN: ASK.

ARI: All right. Why do you know about cheating?

JOAN: *(whispered)* Because I'm a cheat.

Ten years ago. Rachel was in her last year of high school and she was having trouble with Biology. I asked her teacher to give her some extra help. I asked him to come to our house *(She takes a slug from her bottle.)* to come to our house two afternoons a week after classes. It was innocent. I never thought . . .

ARI: I should—

JOAN: Let me speak! Please. Ari, *(She clutches his arm.)* you're the only one I can really talk to.

ARI: Oh . . . kay.

JOAN: One day he came to the house, Rachel wasn't there. I had forgotten to tell him that she was on a bus to Washington. They were doing model UN. She was Libya, of all places. Who even knew that Libya was in the UN? Not me. So there he was. Mr. St. Clair. Jeffrey. I didn't want to be rude. I invited him in for coffee. We talked. It turned out that he had grown up on the same block in Harlem that my grandmother lived on. Isn't that unbelievable? Not at the same time of course. You probably don't even know that Harlem used to be Jewish. Jeffrey told me you could still see the Star of David on top of Baptist church that his family went to . . .

ARI: Wait. Was he . . . black?

JOAN: Yes. Of course he was black. Who said he wasn't black?

ARI: Wow.

JOAN: We talked. And talked and talked. I drank more coffee that afternoon . . . and when I looked up, it was dark outside. And then it just happened. We made love. But not love. It was the first time I had ever made love with somebody I wasn't in love with.

ARI: You fucked.

JOAN: No! I would never use that word. But yes, I guess we did. And then we kept on . . .

ARI: Fucking.

253

JOAN: Every week. Tuesdays. At first it was magnificent. I felt . . . magnificent. I felt like I was living someone else's life. Then Rachel graduated, and Jeffrey St. Clair kept coming. Every Tuesday. And it started to become just another routine. Isn't it awful how something can make you feel like you're on fire and then just turn into another old habit? Damp. That happens to everything. Everything stops working eventually.

ARI: So, what happened?

JOAN: Oh, I told him to stop coming around and he said "fine."

ARI: And that was it?

JOAN: No, that wasn't it! I am a married woman who had an affair ten years ago and I never told my husband.

ARI: But it sounds like it didn't really mean anything.

JOAN: Exactly! It meant nothing. It would be one thing if I'd been in love with the man. At least I could say that I spat on my marriage vows and humiliated my husband for a good reason. Not a good reason, but something that mattered. Something worthy of sacrifice.

ARI: Love.

JOAN: Love! But it wasn't love. I didn't even particularly like him by the end. And Ozzie. Ozzie, Ozzie, my sweet husband. He has been living with a Jezebel for ten years and he hasn't even known it. And it's too late now. A marriage is a braid.

ARI: A . . . ?

JOAN: Braid. A long, long braid stretching out over the years. Jeffrey St. Clair is there. He is a strand in our braid.

ARI: A black strand.

JOAN: A black, black, black strand. Listen to me! Don't be like your friend Joe. I have to go back in. *(She turns to go.)*

ARI: Wait! Mrs. Mendelssohn! I want to tell you something that will make you feel better. *(He goes to her and holds her hands. They look at each other. Long pause while Ari tries to think of something. Finally, she releases his hands and turns. She takes another slug from the bottle of red wine as she's exiting.)*

JOAN: This isn't vodka. *(She exits.)*

SCENE 7—the escape

Outside. Rachel, in her wedding dress, runs toward the parking lot, keys in hand. She doesn't notice Abe sitting on the bench smoking.

ABE: Rachel?

Rachel stops short, but doesn't turn.

ABE: Is it over?

RACHEL: *(still not turning)* Uh . . . no.

ABE: Forget something in the car?

RACHEL: No.

ABE: Look at me, sweetheart.

RACHEL: Don't want to.

ABE: Rachel.

RACHEL: Can't.

ABE: Fine, suit yourself.

RACHEL: I'm sorry. I'm sorry I wasn't at the funeral.

ABE: I'd hoped you might come.

RACHEL: I know. I'm . . . I'm sorry.

ABE: She'll forgive you. She was very forgiving. Like her son.

RACHEL: I loved Gloria.

ABE: She was not your biggest fan.

RACHEL: What?

ABE: What, I should lie?

RACHEL: Maybe!

ABE: No, no more lies.

RACHEL: She didn't like me?

ABE: Not particularly. But she would have forgiven you, still.

RACHEL: Well, that's nice, I guess.

ABE: Yes, it is.

    Pause.

RACHEL: What did you mean that Joe was forgiving?

ABE: You don't agree?

RACHEL: No, I do. I do. I just wondered if you meant something specific, or . . . ?

ABE: I meant about your abortion.

    Rachel bursts into tears.

ABE: Who do you think told him to forgive you?

RACHEL: It was you?

ABE: No! It was Gloria.

RACHEL: But she . . . she wasn't—

ABE: Six months ago she still had a good day here and there. Joe told her. They discussed the situation.

RACHEL: So she knew this whole time?

ABE: Well, some part of her knew. But that part couldn't talk to the other parts.

RACHEL: Did she tell you?

ABE: She did, but I didn't believe her. I thought it was another one of her delusions. Maybe something she remembered from a long time ago. A girlfriend of hers, or something she saw on television.

RACHEL: So then, how did you—

ABE: You're running in a wedding dress. With car keys. You're not running away from your divorce from a man who cheated on you.

RACHEL: Why not?

ABE: Because you are not forgiving.

RACHEL: So what am I running away from? *(Pause.)* What am I running away from?

Abe says nothing.

RACHEL: Why won't you answer?

ABE: When I was a young man, my mother was very sick with emphysema. My dad was not around, my older brothers had already moved out. When she got too sick to run the house, she hired a girl from the neighborhood to come and help her.

RACHEL: I know this story. It was Aunt Adine.

ABE: Correct. It was Adine Wolofsky. She came to our house almost every day for two years, did the laundry, cooked. At the end, she bathed my mother, fed her, gave her her medicines, combed her hair, put her lipstick on. I hid in my bedroom and your aunt took care of my mother.

RACHEL: Abe, I know this story.

ABE: Sit down. *(She does, reluctantly.)* I was in love with her.

RACHEL: Who?

ABE: Adine.

RACHEL: What?

ABE: I was in love with Adine. We were in love with each other.

RACHEL What? I always thought that Adine was . . .

ABE: Gay? You kids think everybody is gay!

RACHEL: Why are you telling me this?

ABE: I asked her to marry me.

RACHEL: She turned you down?

ABE: She said yes

RACHEL: But you married Gloria.

ABE: That's right.

RACHEL: Why?

ABE: Because of Devorah.

RACHEL: What do you mean because of Dev—? Oh, no.

ABE: Oh yes.

RACHEL: You cheated on Aunt Adine with Gloria and got her pregnant?

ABE: More or less.

RACHEL: What's the less?

ABE: I was nineteen. It was the seventies.

RACHEL: Did Aunt Adine know that you were sleeping with Gloria?

ABE: No.

RACHEL: You cheated.

ABE: I'm not arguing. It was criminally stupid. I ended things with Gloria when I realized that I wanted to marry Adine. But one week after we were engaged, Gloria called me up. She was already 5 months along when she found out. I felt I had no choice.

RACHEL: So you broke up with Aunt Adine and married Gloria instead.

ABE: Right.

RACHEL: And that's why Aunt Adine moved to France?

ABE: I suppose.

RACHEL: Does my mother know about this?

ABE: Only if Adine has told her. We never announced our engagement. My mother had just died, and we wanted to wait a respectful interval.

RACHEL: So your mother never knew.

ABE: Just like Joe's mother never knew that you and Joe were getting divorced. I am grateful for that.

RACHEL: She would have wanted us together?

ABE: Of course.

RACHEL: But you just said she didn't like me.

ABE: But she knew that Joe loved you.

RACHEL: What about you?

ABE: What about me what?

RACHEL: Do you want us together?

ABE: You're asking me.

RACHEL: Yes. What?

ABE: I thought this was a done deal. I thought you'd made your decision. Isn't that why we're all here?

RACHEL: I might be having doubts.

ABE: I don't think you have doubts. I think you have guilt.

RACHEL: What am I supposed to feel guilty about?

ABE: You tell me.

RACHEL: My abortion? You can't talk to me about that.

ABE: Why's that?

RACHEL: Because. You don't know about giving up a baby.

ABE: No. I know about keeping one.

RACHEL: What are you saying that you wish Gloria had aborted Devorah?

ABE: I love my children. And I loved my wife as well as I could. We accepted one another. But there is another life running alongside the life I've lived. Sometimes it's so clear to me, it's like I could just turn the wheel and merge into it, like changing lanes on the highway. I don't want you to spend the rest of your life thinking that you're driving in the wrong lane. Not with my son in the passenger seat. But that's not what you're guilty about.

RACHEL: No?

ABE: My son is a very devoted boy.

JOAN: *(off)* Rachel?

RACHEL: Shit.

ABE: Go if you're going. I won't tell.

RACHEL: I want you to be my family still.

ABE: That's not a good enough reason.

JOAN: *(off)* Rachel?

ABE: Kid, it's decision time.

RACHEL: Just tell me what to do.

ABE: Can't.

RACHEL: What if I still love him?

ABE: Do you?

RACHEL: Maybe.

ABE: This day is designed to make you feel that way. *(Rachel scoffs.)* What? You think it's just some form of Talmudic torture, right? It's not. It's a test.

RACHEL: Of what?

ABE: Of your love. Or, rather, of your lack of love.

RACHEL: You sound like Naomi.

ABE: Smart girl.

JOAN: *(off)* RACHEL!

> Rachel lets out an impotent whine.

ABE: Rachel, grow up!

RACHEL: What does that mean?!

ABE: It means do what you came to do.

258

Joan enters, out of breath.

JOAN: Rachel, what in the hell do you think you're doing?

Rachel and Abe exchange a look.

RACHEL: I . . . nothing. I left my ring in the car. I've got it. *(She opens her fist revealing her wedding band in her palm.)*

JOAN: You left it in the car? It's supposed to be on your finger. *(Rachel puts it on and holds up her hand to show Joan.)* Fine. Come on. Everybody's waiting.

Joan regards Abe, but says nothing to him. She exits, Rachel follows. Just before exiting, she turns back to Abe.

RACHEL: I thought you weren't going to tell me what to do.

ABE: I lied.

Rachel exits.

Scene 8—the ceremony

The children's play area outside. Siobhan sits, reading and drinking from a glass. A bottle of wine is next to her. Pachelbel's Canon *can be heard from inside. Melita enters.*

MELITA: It's starting.

SIOBHAN: Aren't you supposed to be in there?

MELITA: Unh uh. *(reaching for the wine)* May I?

SIOBHAN: Sure. I don't understand.

MELITA: Last time. During the ceremony? I snuck out. Ari was the best man, he didn't notice. I was out here the whole time. And, y'know, you have to—

SIOBHAN: Do everything the way it was done. Right. *(as Melita takes a big swig from the bottle)* Well, cheers, then.

MELITA: Cheers.

SIOBHAN: So, you've been to how many of these again?

MELITA: Twelve. This is my twelfth.

SIOBHAN: But you're too young to have that many divorced friends.

MELITA: They were mostly my parents' friends. Weddings they dragged me to when I was little. But four of them have been people my age. I'm starting to think I should stop going to people's weddings. I think I might be cursed.

SIOBHAN: Oh, I'm sure you're not cursed.

MELITA: Twelve. Tw-el-ve.

SIOBHAN: Okay, you might be cursed.

259

From inside, the sound of the rabbi reciting the seven marriage blessings, in backwards order, is just barely heard. Siobhan and Melita pause for a moment and listen.

RABBI: Baruch Atah Adonai Eloheinu Melech Ha-Olam, asher barah sasson v'simcha, chatan v'kalah, gila rina, ditza v'chedva, ahava v'achava, v'shalom v're'ut *(and so on as our scene continues.)* [*This is a phonetic translation of the Hebrew.*]

MELITA: Do you want to play Celebrity?

SIOBHAN: Okay.

MELITA: Okay, um . . . he was in *Mission Impossible* . . . he was married to Nicole Kidman . . . he was married to Katie Holmes . . . *(Siobhan just looks at her blankly.)* . . . uh . . . he was in *Rain Man* . . . he's a Scientologist . . . seriously?

SIOBHAN: Oh, sorry. Am I supposed to be doing something?

MELITA: You've never played Celebrity.

SIOBHAN: Oh, no.

MELITA: Oh, okay. You just guess who the person is from the clues.

SIOBHAN: Oh, all right. Got it. Go ahead.

MELITA: Okay, same person. He flipped out on *Oprah*. He's short. He was in *Top Gun* . . . um . . . no guesses?

SIOBHAN: Antonio Banderas?

MELITA: *(shaking her head)* No.

SIOBHAN: Which one was your favorite?

MELITA: Which one what?

SIOBHAN: Of the twelve divorces.

MELITA: That seems a little callous, even for me.

SIOBHAN: You said you liked them!

MELITA: I said I thought they were a good idea. It's not schadenfreude. Okay, there was one that was a little schadenfreudy.

SIOBHAN: An ex?

MELITA: No, no. It was a friends-of-my-parents one. Their daughter— whose name was Sugaree, by the way—

SIOBHAN: Oh God.

MELITA: Yeah. My parents were hippies, in case that's not apparent. Anyway, she and I were best friends when we were little little, and then we went to different schools for elementary, and then my parents got divorced, and then we went to the same middle school, and she mocked me for having divorced parents. And she was popular and I was . . . not. She made my life hell for two years. And then her parents got divorced. I was so happy.

SIOBHAN: Was their ceremony like this?

MELITA: No. They were super Jesus-y hippies, and her father burst into tears reading some bible verse about man and woman becoming one flesh or something. And, of course, I had one of those post-middle-school revelations where you realize that the person who bullied you was actually being bullied themselves at home. The whole thing was just . . . bleak.

Another pause. A section of the Mourner's Kaddish is heard.

CONGREGATION: B'rikh hu.

RABBI: l'eila min kol bir'khata v'shirata toosh'b'chatah v'nechematah, da'ameeran b'al'mah, v'eemru:

CONGREGATION: Amein

The Kaddish continues, in its usual order and almost inaudibly, under our scene.

SIOBHAN: Let's play the game.

MELITA: Okay, why don't you go.

SIOBHAN: Ah, all right . . . um . . . ooh! Got one! Okay, he was in *The Mask of Zorro*, and *The Legend of Zorro*, and he's married to the blonde actress . . . with the lips . . .

MELITA: Is it Antonio Banderas?

SIOBHAN: YES! Wow, you're good at this.

Melita takes a swig from the bottle, passes it to Siobhan.

MELITA: This one I went to one when I was ten. They were Wiccan and it was "skyclad."

SIOBHAN: What does that mean?

MELITA: Naked. Everybody was naked. Including my mom and dad and me. I was just a baby when they got married so I didn't remember, but . . . yeah. Naked.

SIOBHAN: That's horrifying.

MELITA: I know. Like you're not vulnerable enough. It's one thing when everybody's happy and celebrating, but . . .

SIOBHAN: Oh God.

MELITA: I know. I kind of can't even think about it.

SIOBHAN: Was it in a church? Or a . . . I don't know. What do Wiccan's have?

MELITA: The woods.

They drink.

SIOBHAN: I've only been to one and it was in a church. Were most of yours in churches?

MELITA: You get kind of questiony when you're drunk, huh?

261

SIOBHAN: You don't want to talk about them. I'm sorry.

MELITA: It's just, y'know . . .

SIOBHAN: Heartbreaking.

MELITA: Yeah.

They drink.

MELITA: The one after the Wiccan one was on a boat, I guess they were no religion, then Presbyterian, um . . . not sure it was in a Mexican restaurant, Buddhist, Unitarian, Baptist, biker *(Siobhan laughs.)*—oh yeah, that one was awesome—then, something like Methodist or Lutheran I can't really tell the difference, nothing, nothing, and uh, *(She counts back to make sure she got them all.)* . . .

SIOBHAN: And that brings us to today.

MELITA: Yep.

A door opens somewhere and the low murmuring of the dissembling congregants gets louder for a moment. Ari enters.

ARI: What are you doing out here?

MELITA: What are *you* doing out here?

ARI: I came to get Siobhan.

SIOBHAN: Does that mean it's over?

ARI: It's over.

Pause.

MELITA: Everybody okay?

SIOBHAN: Are you talking about them or us?

MELITA: Whoever.

SIOBHAN: It is really sad.

ARI: It was the saddest thing I've ever seen.

Another pause while it settles on them. Melita looks at Ari.

SIOBHAN: So, what happens now?

MELITA: We go home.

SIOBHAN: *(standing up)* All right. Let's go.

Melita and Siobhan start to exit. Melita notices that Ari is just standing there. She goes back for him.

MELITA: Come on.

She tugs at his sleeve and then lets go and walks out. He follows.

SCENE 9—the lesbian and the divorcée

The hallway. Joan enters, carrying a large bag. She looks around to double check that she is alone, and then pulls out something like a boxed

Entenmann's cake. She starts shoveling the cake into her mouth. Adine enters, unnoticed by Joan.

ADINE: Don't let mom see you.

JOAN: *(looking up while stuffing cake into her mouth)* Are you kidding? She's been watching me all day.

ADINE: Give me some cake.

JOAN: *(clutching the cake)* Did you not just hear me say that Mom is watching?

ADINE: Mom would have said that sorrow goes better with soup. Or cake. *(Adine holds out her hand. Joan hands over the box, Adine eats.)*

JOAN: I'm sorry. I'm drunk.

ADINE: Don't apologize.

JOAN: I've hardly talked to you all day.

ADINE: Don't apologize.

JOAN: It's done.

ADINE: It's done.

JOAN: The lesbian and the divorcée.

ADINE: Sorry?

JOAN: My children. The lesbian and the divorcée.

ADINE: Are you feeling sorry for yourself?

JOAN: Bite me.

ADINE: Excuse me?

JOAN: You're going to drop in from your fantastic, untethered, European dream life and tell me that I'm not entitled to a little self-pity on today, of all days?

ADINE: Hannah seems happier than I've ever seen her. And Rachel . . . well, she'll survive. She's a survivor.

JOAN: So, that's a yes.

ADINE: Self-pity away, if it makes you feel better. I don't tell you what to do.

JOAN: No, you don't.

ADINE: No, I don't. *(She lights a cigarette.)*

JOAN: Don't smoke.

ADINE: Don't pity yourself.

JOAN: We are inside.

ADINE: So?

JOAN: So, people in this part of the world no longer smoke indoors. I'm sure we seem very provincial to you. *(Adine continues to smoke. Joan walks over to her, grabs the cigarette out of her hand, and stomps it on the floor.)* I said, put it out!

263

ADINE: What in the hell is the matter with you?

JOAN: When are you leaving? Tomorrow? Tonight?

ADINE: What?

JOAN: Your flight back! When is it? Tonight?

ADINE: It's tomorrow night, but I—

JOAN: That's my problem! You show up today, you leave tomorrow, and you're standing there telling me that Hannah is happy? That I should be happy? That Rachel is fine?

ADINE: Joanie, I—

JOAN: She is NOT fine! She's a stranger to me. I only hope she's talking to her sister, because for all I know she's going to leave here and throw herself off a cliff. Or join a cult! And Hannah is a 30-year-old woman who is just now getting around to bringing someone home to meet her family?

ADINE: But you knew—

JOAN: Of course we knew! We didn't discuss it at length. I never thought we needed to, and apparently, she now thinks I'm some sort of raging homophobe. I suppose she talked to you—

ADINE: Wait—

JOAN: Are she and the girlfriend going to move to Scotland—

ADINE: Ireland.

JOAN: Raise terriers? Visit you on holidays?

ADINE: She doesn't think you're a raging homophobe, whatever you said.

JOAN: Oh, and you would know. You apparently know everything about my girls. Is Naomi having sex yet? Is she doing drugs?

ADINE: No, I'm pretty sure she's doing neither.

JOAN: How can you tell?

ADINE: By looking! Joanie, *(She makes some sort of physical contact.)* you've had a hard day. Hard week. Hard month.

JOAN: You don't know from hard.

ADINE: Maybe you're right.

JOAN: You have no children, no husband, no commitments, no stress, no guilt, no worry. You do whatever you want. You come and go as you please.

ADINE: I'm sorry I wasn't here for you.

JOAN: My heart is breaking for my child. It's breaking.

ADINE: I know.

JOAN: You don't know! You have no idea how this feels.

ADINE: How could I?

JOAN: How could you?!

ADINE: Exactly. Though, the only man I ever loved has been married to someone else for the last forty years. So there's that.

    Silence.

    I'm going to smoke now. (*She lights a cigarette.*)

JOAN: I'm sorry.

ADINE: Don't be. It's an old hurt. I'm used to it. Yours is fresh.

JOAN: But being here . . .

ADINE: Being here nothing. The man's wife just died.

JOAN: Have you spoken?

ADINE: A little.

JOAN: What happened between you two?

ADINE: Not much. We just talked.

JOAN: No, I mean, back then. What happened?

ADINE: We were engaged.

JOAN: WHAT?!

ADINE: We were waiting to tell. His mother had just died. And then he phoned me up one day and said we were through. He was marrying Gloria, instead.

JOAN: He phoned you?

ADINE: I think he was afraid to tell me in person.

JOAN: You didn't know about Gloria.

ADINE: That's why they call it "cheating."

JOAN: And you never saw him again until . . .

ADINE: Rachel and Joe's wedding? Once. The night before I left. We were together. We said our goodbyes. He explained. I understood. We cried. I flew. And four months later, Devorah was born.

JOAN: So, you forgave him?

ADINE: Not exactly.

JOAN: What about now?

ADINE: What about now what?

JOAN: Have you forgiven him?

ADINE: Not exactly.

JOAN: It's been a long time.

ADINE: It feels like yesterday. Being here.

JOAN: Why did you never tell me this?

ADINE: We agreed not to tell anyone.

JOAN: Mom?

ADINE: No. Nobody.

 Pause.

JOAN: He's sorry.

ADINE: Is he? He had a life, children. I didn't.

JOAN: You had a life!

ADINE: Right, right. My "glorious, untethered" existence.

JOAN: Now who's feeling sorry for herself?

ADINE: What if I've spent my life pining after someone who just moved on?

JOAN: Adine—

ADINE: What if he never loved me to begin with? I mean, we were only nineteen—

JOAN: He loved you.

ADINE: Then why did he cheat?

JOAN: Because people do dumb shit. And then they feel bad about it. And that's the world.

ADINE: When did you get so wise?

JOAN: You've got to forgive him.

ADINE: You forgive him!

JOAN: I have to forgive other people.

ADINE: Today is the worst.

JOAN: I know.

ADINE: It doesn't get any worse than this.

JOAN: Poo, poo, poo. [*"Poo, poo, poo" is a Yiddish-ish expression, similar to spitting three times to avoid the evil eye. The three poos are said in quick succession.*]

 Pause.

ADINE: Can I ask you something?

JOAN: Sure.

ADINE: Do you still love Ozzie?

JOAN: Very much.

ADINE: You're lucky.

JOAN: You have no idea.

 Pause.

Forgive him.

ADINE: Okay.

 Joan takes a piece of cake out of the box and feeds it to Adine. They lean into each other.

HANNAH: (*off*) Mom?

SCENE 10—the real ceremony

Naomi, Hannah, Siobhan, Ari, Abe, Melita, Joan enter, carrying various things. They are leaving, Ari, barely awake, is being held up by Joan and Melita, who has a water bottle.

HANNAH: *(to Melita)* You have Ari's keys? *(Melita holds them up to confirm that she does.)*

ADINE: Where's Rachel?

JOAN: She went back to her dressing room to undress.

Rachel runs in, halfway undressed.

RACHEL: Stop.

JOAN: What is this?

RACHEL: Ari, can you get Joe? *(Ari does not respond.)* ARI!

ARI: Wha?

RACHEL: Get Joe.

JOAN: Rachel, what are you doing?

RACHEL: I need Joe. And I need you all to stay here for a minute.

JOAN: Why?

RACHEL: Just . . . will somebody please get him?

HANNAH: I'll get him.

ABE: No, I'll go. *(He goes.)*

JOAN: Rachel, I think we've all had enough of this day.

Rachel looks to Hannah.

HANNAH: Now you want my help?

JOAN: What? What's happening?

HANNAH: Mom, just let her.

Abe reenters with Joe, who is also halfway out of his wedding attire.

JOE: *(seeing Rachel)* Rachel, I told you—

RACHEL: I know—

JOE: I told you I wouldn't see you.

RACHEL: I know—

JOE: For a year. It's over now, and I won't see you for a year. I'm serious.

RACHEL: I know, I know, I'm sorry. But we haven't left the building yet. Isn't there some kind of pass?

JOE: No. The ceremony's over. It's over. And, anyway, I just really don't want to see you now.

As he starts to walk away, she grabs his sleeve. It rips.

RACHEL: Joe, I fucked up.

JOE: No shit.

267

RACHEL: I love you.

JOE: Excuse me?

RACHEL: I love you.

JOE: What are you saying that you don't want to get divorced? Now?

RACHEL: No. No, no, no. We have to get divorced.

JOE: We are divorced.

RACHEL: Right. We have to be. I love you, but not the same way you love me. I never should have married you in the first place. But you shouldn't have married me, either. Anyway, I can't do this to you. *(turning to the group)* I lied.

JOE: Rachel, you don't have to—

RACHEL: Actually, Joe lied.

JOAN: What do you mean, "Joe lied"?

ADINE: I think we already know this, honey.

RACHEL: No, you don't know.

JOE: Rachel . . .

RACHEL: I had an abortion.

NAOMI: What?!

RACHEL: I had an abortion.

ADINE: When?

RACHEL: Six months ago.

JOAN: Why would you have an abortion? You were pregnant? With a baby?

HANNAH: Mom . . .

JOAN: *(pointing to Joe)* Did he put you up to this?

RACHEL: No. He didn't even know.

SIOBHAN: Jesus.

JOAN: *(rounding on Joe)* This is your fault. She didn't want to have a baby with a cheater!

HANNAH: *(holding both of Joan's arms to restrain her from attacking Joe)* RACHEL!

JOAN: You're a filthy, baby-killing cheater!

RACHEL: *(in a torrent)* He didn't cheat he just said that to protect me so I wouldn't have to tell the truth.

Joan spins around and slaps Rachel hard on the cheek. Stunned silence.

NAOMI: Excuse me.

Naomi walks out of hall, then there is a sound of something heavy dragging along the ground. She reenters dragging a small altar table. She drags it toward the center of the group. Confused, they part to allow her through.

She hauls the table to the center of the group and then crosses to Melita, takes her water bottle, and brings to the altar.

SIOBHAN: What're you doing, love?

NAOMI: They're still married.

RACHEL: What?

NAOMI: You're still married.

ABE: She's right.

NAOMI: "We consecrate the dissolution of this covenant by an honest accounting before these here assembled of the reason or reasons that it cannot stand." *(to Rachel)* In the ceremony you said that Joe was unfaithful. You lied.

JOE: And that means we're still married?

NAOMI: Yes. Put your rings back on.

RACHEL: What?

NAOMI: *(to Hannah and Ari)* Give them back their rings and *(to Rachel and Joe)* put them back on.

JOE: Why?

NAOMI: So that you can get divorced.

RACHEL: Well we can't . . . we can't now. Everyone's gone. I thought it had to be everyone.

ADINE: Do it here.

RACHEL: What?

ADINE: Just do it right here. In front of us.

RACHEL: How? How? What do you mean? The rabbi's gone.

ABE: I'll do it.

RACHEL: But I thought it had to be everyone.

JOAN: It has to be honest.

RACHEL: No, no, no. It doesn't work like that, Mom. God requires total humiliation. Because he's a fucking asshole.

NAOMI: *(busily arranging the altar)* Rachel!

RACHEL: No, you should know this, Naomi. Your God is mean, and he will fuck you over. No matter how good you are. Actually, especially if you're good.

ADINE: Rachel—

JOAN: Let her.

RACHEL: What? It's true! Look at Joe. He's good. He's so so good. He does everything . . . everything he's supposed to do. And look what it got him. Me. I've fucked up his entire life including this divorce. And I can't fix

269

it. I can't fix it. It's over. The people are gone and I'm wearing the wrong underwear. *(to God)* Are you happy now?

JOAN: *(touching Rachel's face where she hit her)* I'm sorry. *(Rachel dissolves into Joan's arms.)*

    Pause.

JOE: I think we should do it here.

RACHEL: You do?

ADINE: Put your ring back on, honey. *(Melita—in Ari's place—brings Rachel's ring back to her. After a moment, she takes it and puts it back on. Hannah brings Joe's back to him, and he puts it back on.)*

NAOMI: Aunt Adine, can I have your scarf, please? *(Adine removes her scarf and gives it to Naomi)* Okay, Mr. Pfeifer, you stand here. *(She guides him to behind the altar.)* And you *(she takes Ari's hand)* stand here *(she guides him to one side of the altar)* and hold this *(she hands him the scarf)*, Hann, you stand here *(she guides Hannah to the side of the table opposite Ari)* and hold the other end. *(She hands her the other end of the scarf.)* Rachel, you're here *(she guides Rachel to her spot)* and Joe, you're here. *(She guides Joe to his.)* Lift your arms up. *(Ari has started to fall asleep. She claps her hands in his face.)* LIFT your arms up. *(They do, the scarf creates a makeshift chuppah downstage of the altar. She guides the rest of the group into a semi-circle around the altar. She reaches for the hand of the person next to her and grasps it. Everyone else in the semi-circle follows suit until they all holding hands.)* Okay. Go.

ABE: All right. Of course, I don't know the exact words . . .

JOAN: You don't have to talk. We all know the truth now. Do it in silence.

ABE: Naomi?

NAOMI: I think it will be more holy that way.

ABE: Okay then. *(He makes a gesture of prayer, and then nods towards the space between Rachel and Joe. They clasp hands. They kiss. They unclasp their hands. Joe reaches up and pulls Rachel's veil back over her eyes. Rachel takes the ring from Joe's finger. Joe takes the ring from Rachel's finger. They hold out their hands and Abe pours water from the pitcher over them. It cascades over the altar and onto the floor. Over the course of this ceremony, the lights have gradually faded so that the assembled are now in silhouette. Fade to black.)*

270

Scene 11—the first dance

    In the blackness, further downstage, a cigarette is lit. Lights come up slightly on Adine, sitting on a bench, smoking. Abe enters. Wordlessly, he comes up to her, takes her hand, and pulls her to standing. She extinguishes her cigarette. They dance.

Scene 12—the boy with the glass

Upstage, lights come back up on the altar. The group has now departed. The Boy carefully glues the last piece back into the glass. He holds it up to the light to inspect his work. Satisfied, he stands and carries the glass to the makeshift altar. He places it in the center, and exits.

END OF PLAY

271

MILDRED RUIZ-SAPP

Co-Founder and core member of UNIVERSES—Playwright/Actor/Vocalist. Theater credits include: *Party People* (Directed/Developed by Liesl Tommy); *Ameriville* (Directed/Developed by Chay Yew); *The Denver Project* (Director Dee Covington); *One Shot in Lotus Position* (Director Bonnie Metzger); *Blue Suite* (Directed/Developed by Chay Yew); *Rhythmicity* (Directed by Steven Sapp); *Slanguage* (Directed/Developed by Jo Bonney); *The Ride* (Directed by Steven Sapp); Alfred Jarry's *UBU: Enchained* (Director Steven Sapp). Awards/Affiliations: 2008 Ambassador of Culture: U.S. State Dept. and Jazz at Lincoln Center—Rhythm Road Tour; 2008 TCG Peter Zeisler Award; 2006 Career Advancement Fellowship from the Ford foundation through Pregones Theater; 2002–2004 and 1999–2001 TCG National Theater Artist Residency Program Award; BRIO Awards (Bronx Recognizes Its Own—Singing); Co-Founder of The Point CDC; Board Member (National Performance Network—NPN); Former Board Member (Network of Ensemble Theaters—NET); New York Theatre Workshop Usual Suspect; BARD College, BA '92—Literature/Language. Publications: *UNIVERSES—The Big Bang* (2013 release—TCG Books); *Slanguage* in *The Fire This Time* (TCG).

STEVEN SAPP

Co-Founding and core member of UNIVERSES—Playwright/Actor. Theater credits include: *Party People* (Directed/Developed by Liesl Tommy); *Ameriville* (Directed/Developed by Chay Yew); *The Denver Project* (Director Dee Covington); *One Shot in Lotus Position* (Director Bonnie Metzger); *Blue Suite* (Directed/Developed by Chay Yew); *Slanguage* (Directed/Developed by Jo Bonney); *Rhythmicity* (Director/Actor); *The Ride* (Playwright/Actor/Director); *The Architecture of Loss* (Assistant Director to Chay Yew); Will Powers' *The Seven* (Director—The University of Iowa); Alfred Jarry's *UBU: Enchained* (Director—Teatre Polski, Poland). Awards/Affiliations: 2008 Ambassador of Culture: U.S. State Dept. and Jazz at Lincoln Center—Rhythm Road Tour; 2008 TCG Peter Zeisler Award; 2002 TCG National Directors Award; 2002–2004 and 1999–2001 TCG National Theater Artist Residency Program Award; 1998 and 2002 BRIO Awards (Bronx Recognizes Its Own—Performance); Van Lier Fellowship with New Dramatists; Co-Founder of The Point CDC; New York Theatre Workshop Usual Suspect; BARD College, BA '89—Theater. Publications: *UNIVERSES—The Big Bang* (2013 release—TCG Books); *Slanguage* in *The Fire This Time* (TCG).

WILLIAM RUIZ A.K.A NINJA

Core member of UNIVERSES. Playwright/Actor. Theater credits include: *Party People* (Directed/Developed by Liesl Tommy); *Ameriville* (Actor; Directed/Developed by Chay Yew); *Slanguage* (Actor; Directed/Developed by Jo Bonney); Jack Kerouack's *Ti-Jean Blues* (Adapted/Directed by JoAnne Akalaitis); Nicole Quinn's *Tree Tails* (Directed by Shelly Wyant); Oscar Wilde's *Salome* (Directed by Nick Jones); Anthony Rivera's *Latin Howel* (Directed by Todd A. Jackson); Nicky Cruz's *Run Baby Run* (Directed by Chris Fredricks (Houston Astro-Dome, TX); and *Waiting for Gordo* (Playwright/Director—adapted from Samuel Beckett's *Waiting for Godot*). Awards/Affiliations: 2008 Ambassador of Culture: U.S. State Dept. and Jazz at Lincoln Center—Rhythm Road Tour; Founder of InVerso (poetic/musical collective based out of Puerto Rico); Member of the Network of Ensemble Theaters (NET)—UNIVERSES; BARD College, BA '89—Theater, where he studied under the tutelage of JoAnne Akalaitis and Elizabeth Smith. He also studied poetry with Bob Holman. Publications: *UNIVERSES—The Big Bang* (2013 release—TCG Books).

UNIVERSES
(Mildred Ruiz-Sapp, Steven Sapp, & William Ruiz a.k.a NINJA)

Party People

CHARACTERS:

JIMMY "PRIMO"   Nephew of Tito; A new media / visual / performing artist, who is organizing an exhibit / installation / performance inspired by the activities of the Black Panthers Party (BPP) and the Young Lords Party (YLP); He has invited members of both parties to the event.

MALIK   A Panther Cub; Collaborates with Jimmy on the BPP / YLP event; He is trying to maintain a relationship with his father, who is in prison.

TITO   Primo's uncle; a former Young Lords Party member; Retired but still involved in union organizing and a prison reentry program; Was once in a romantic relationship with Helita.

HELITA   Former Young Lords Party member; A journalist and meticulous collector of Young Lords and Black Panther historical documents. Clara's godmother.

CLARA   Daughter of Young Lords' members; Co-Raised by Helita; She wants nothing to do with a revolution that robbed her of her parents.

AMIRA   Blue's wife and former Black Panther Party member; Protects Blue and his eccentricities.

BLUE	Former Black Panther Party member; Incarcerated for involvement in a shootout that left a police officer dead but was ultimately proven not guilty.
DONNA	Widow of murdered police officer.
MARUCA	Former Young Lords Party member; She is both ruthless and romantic, and is not well accepted by others who have doubts about her past indiscretions.
MARCUS	A former young white activist affiliated with Fred Hampton's Rainbow Coalition in Chicago. A collector of memorabilia.
OMAR	Former Black Panther Party member; An Army war veteran; Seeks a public apology for having been tortured when others thought he was an informant.
SOLIAS	COINTELPRO agent provocateur infiltrating the Black Panther Party.
ROGER	COINTELPRO agent; Teaches informants how to infiltrate.
CHORUS	All cast members are the chorus.

PRODUCTION NOTES:

An opening at a performance art space for an event inspired by the activities of the Black Panther Party and the Young Lords Party of the 1960s and '70s, presents a unique opportunity for members of both groups to gather and reflect on the past and present. As those from younger generations confront party members, they wrestle with how the ideals of yesterday are reflected in the present.

Old lovers reconnect, and friends who haven't talked in 25 to 30 years reunite. Meanwhile, former frenemies and informants meet and catch up. As the evening proceeds, however, certain facts that were taken as truths come into question. Young revolutionary artists utilize performance art to reveal the inner thoughts of party leaders as well as rank and file who had contributed to the party's cause. By evening's end, history does not seem as black and white as it sometimes reads in history books.

ACKNOWLEDGEMENTS:

The authors would like to thank various people for their support and encouragement.

Among the many, Chairman Bobby Seale, Chairman Cha Cha Jimenez, Chairman Felipe Luciano, Vincente "Panama" Alba, Miguel "Mickey" Melendez, Emory Douglas, Ericka Huggins, Billy X Jennings, George Edwards, Eric Lockley, Mary Vivian, Luis Garden Acosta, David Hilliard, Iris Morales, Walter Bosque, Sal de Riviero, Omar Lopez, Obed Lopez, Carlos Flores, Jamal Joseph, Craig Kelly, Iberia Hampton, Bill Hampton, W.E. Dunbar, Gabriel Torres, Kisisay Torres, Gloria Fontanez, Billy "Che" Brooks, Mike James, Gloria Rodriguez, Alprentice Davis, Juan Gonzales, Denise Oliver, Dylcia Pagan.

The Oregon Shakespeare Festival, the New England Foundation for the Arts, The Ford Foundation, The Hemispheric Institute of Performance and Politics (NYU), Joseph Haj and PlayMakers Rep, the International Festival of Arts and Ideas, Centro de Estudios Puertorriquenos—Hunter College, Berkeley Rep, Center Theatre Group, The Public Theater, Bill Rauch, Alison Carey, Liesl Tommy, Deanna Downes, Emilio Sosa, Clint Ramos, Aaron Meicht, Daniel Baker, Pablo Molina, Simon Harding, Marcus Doshi, Millicent Marie Johnnie, Morgan Jenness, Julie Felise Dubiner, Joy Meads, Lue Douthit, Lydia Garcia, Gamal Abdel Chasten, Avery Young, Glenn Gordon, Kimberly Aileen Scott, G. Valmont Thomas, Christopher Livingston, Peter Macon, Robynn Rodriguez, Miriam Laube, Jadele McPherson, Mateo Gomez, Michael Elich, Mara Filler, Karl Alphonso, John Risser, Erin Washington, Cymry Reardon, Benajah Cobb, Jill Rendall, Kimberly Knox, RJ Maccani, Edgardo Miranda, Lisbet Tellefsen, Melisa Jimenez-Haffey, Mari Nieves Alba, Cathy Adorno-Centeno, Peter Adorno, Dominic Adorno, Deborah Lopez, Carol Lee Lopez, Freddy Calixto, Modesto, Primitivo Cruz, Israel Rodriguez, Ivan Medina, Maria E. Maso, Simon Ruiz, Quest Sapp.

275

PART I

PROLOGUE

Jimmy and Malik are on stage as the audience enters. Jimmy is editing Video interviews on his laptop while Malik watches over his shoulder. After audience is seated, Video interviews begin.

AMIRA: It was about doing whatever needed to be done.

MARUCA: Tenant's rights . . .

MARCUS: It was the SDS.

TITO: It was garbage . . .

BLUE: I was on the streets . . .

OMAR: They gave me a spatula . . .

HELITA: We opened up free clinics . . .

OMAR: They asked me, "Can you cook grits?"

MARUCA: Because no one would deal with the rats and roaches . . .

TITO: . . . picking up the garbage . . .

BLUE: . . . sellin' Panther papers for 25 cents.

MARCUS: Students for a Democratic Society

TITO: . . . it would pile up . . .

BLUE: Our newspaper was how we told our community about our programs!

HELITA: . . . got doctors to donate their time . . .

AMIRA: If it was riding on the police patrols . . .

OMAR: They asked me if I know how to change diapers.

MARCUS: It was my job to let white kids, who didn't know . . .

AMIRA: The police violence against us was out of control.

MARCUS: . . . know what was happening.

TITO: . . . mountains of it.

MARUCA: We started pest extermination programs.

AMIRA: . . . cooking breakfast . . .

TITO: So, we had to take care of it ourselves.

AMIRA: . . . teaching in the schools we created.

OMAR: There was a couple of us who was in the military.

BLUE: I spent my time in the Navy.

MARCUS: It was Vietnam, man!

TITO: If you go, you can be an American!

MARCUS: War had everybody wound up, wound up

With words "wound up" Video will begin to repeat phrases

OMAR: I ain't got no job . . .

TITO: An American!

> *Video continues with rhythmic repetition of various phrases (My time/Wound up/Vietnam/An American/No jobs).*
>
> *Actors enter the stage to confront Jimmy and Malik one-by-one as the previous video dialogue overlaps and comes to an end. Video collage bumps out at sound of Gunshots. All except Jimmy and Malik fall to the ground. BLACK OUT.*

SCENE ONE: REVOLUTIONARY SUITE

CHORUS: *(They slowly rise as they sing.)*

> *I HIDE*
> *I RISE*
> *I CRY*
> *I SURVIVE*
> *WHAT HISTORY DOESN'T TELL YOU*
> *IS THAT I BLEED RED LIKE YOU*
> *WILL YOU RISE WITH ME IN DARKEST NIGHT?*
> *ARE YOU WILLING TO SACRIFICE YOUR LIFE?*

MALIK: *(vocal riff)*

CHORUS: Hmmm, hmmm . . . *(repeats through the following)*

JIMMY: Palante, Siempre Palante

OMAR: *(BeatBox)*

JIMMY: *(DJ Scratch)*

HELITA/MARUCA:

> *LE LO LAI LE LO LE*
> *LE LO LAI LE LO LE*
> *LE LO LAI*

BLUE: I can remember it just like it was yesterday,

CLARA: I was 15,

SOLIAS: I was 16,

MALIK: I was 17,

BLUE: I was 18,

MARCUS: I was running,

TITO: I was lost,

AMIRA: I was crazy,

MALIK: I believed,

BLUE: But I remember it just like it was yesterday.

277

TITO: I heard the words.

BLUE: I saw them walk down my street.

AMIRA: I thought they were crazy.

MALIK: I wanted to stand with them but didn't dare.

BLUE: But I/But I/But I/But I

SOLIAS: Came to listen/to hear/to follow and to lead;

DONNA: To bear witness . . .

BLUE: to the bear who witnessed

TITO: The beginning of/The birth of

CHORUS: Us

DONNA: And some of us watched,

MARCUS: And some of us did not care,

CLARA: And some of us joined,

SOLIAS: And some of us died,

AMIRA: And some of us survived,

TITO: And it took all of us . . .
     to see that all we were looking for—
          Malik vocal riff.
     —was justice.

CHORUS: Justice/Just us/Justice *(repeat through following)*

HELITA:

> IT AIN'T JUST
> THAT I WOKE UP OUT THE BLUE

CHORUS:

> IT AIN'T JUST

HELITA:

> THAT I HOLD THIS GUN FOR YOU

CHORUS:

> IT AIN'T JUST

HELITA:

> THAT THIS IS LIFE AND WHAT IT DO
> YOU KNOW I DO THIS

CHORUS:

> 'CAUSE IT AIN'T JUST
> IT AIN'T JUST
> IT AIN'T JUST

> *Section above, starting with first "IT AIN'T JUST" repeats 3 more times.*

278

Guns are brought out and distributed.

JIMMY/OMAR/HELITA/CLARA:
   I'VE WALKED THESE STREETS

CHORUS:
   IT AIN'T JUST

JIMMY/OMAR/HELITA/CLARA:
   ALL MY LIFE

CHORUS:
   IT AIN'T JUST

JIMMY/OMAR/HELITA/CLARA:
   AND I AIN'T EVER SEEN CHANGE

CHORUS:
   YOU KNOW I DO THIS 'CAUSE IT AIN'T JUST,

JIMMY/OMAR/HELITA/CLARA:
   NAW I AIN'T EVER SEEN A DIME

CHORUS:
   IT AIN'T JUST

JIMMY/OMAR/HELITA/CLARA:
   I AIN'T GOT

CHORUS:
   IT AIN'T JUST

JIMMY/OMAR/HELITA/CLARA:
   NO BUTTER FOR MY BREAD

CHORUS:
   IT AIN'T JUST

JIMMY/OMAR/HELITA/CLARA:
   AND NO SHEETS ON MY BED

CHORUS:
   YOU KNOW I DO THIS 'CAUSE IT AIN'T JUST,

JIMMY/OMAR/HELITA/CLARA:
   I'D BE BETTER OFF DEAD 'CAUSE . . .

CHORUS:
   IT AIN'T JUST/IT AIN'T JUST

279

JIMMY/OMAR/HELITA/CLARA:

> *IT AIN'T JUST THE LACK OF THE HOUSING*

CHORUS:

> *IT AIN'T JUST.*

JIMMY/OMAR/HELITA/CLARA:

> *IT AIN'T JUST THE CROOKED POLICE*

CHORUS:

> *IT AIN'T JUST.*

JIMMY/OMAR/HELITA/CLARA:

> *IT AIN'T JUST THE CRACKS IN THE WALLS AND THE RATS AND
> THE ROACHES AND THE COLD AND THE MOLD*

CHORUS:

> *IT AIN'T JUST.*

JIMMY/OMAR/HELITA/CLARA:

> *IT AIN'T JUST THE BLACKS AND LATINOS*

CHORUS:

> *IT AIN'T JUST.*

JIMMY/OMAR/HELITA/CLARA:

> *IT AIN'T JUST THE BRAVE AND THE BOLD*

CHORUS:

> *IT AIN'T JUST.*

JIMMY/OMAR/HELITA/CLARA:

> *IT AIN'T JUST THE POOR*
> *THEY DO IT . . .*

CHORUS:

> *YOU KNOW I DO THIS 'CAUSE IT AIN'T JUST, IT AIN'T JUST.*

JIMMY/OMAR/HELITA/CLARA:

> *. . . TO US ALL AND I AIN'T TAKIN' IT NO MORE, I'M READY TO
> BRAWL.*

HELITA:

> *MY HEART FALLS TO PIECES*

CHORUS:

> *IT AIN'T JUST.*

HELITA:

WHEN I SEE HOW YOU LOOK AT ME.

CHORUS:

IT AIN'T JUST.

HELITA:

THERE'S MORE TO THIS THAN BLACK EYED PEAS

CHORUS:

IT AIN'T JUST.

HELITA:

THERE'S MORE TO THIS THAN RICE AND BEANS

CHORUS:

IT AIN'T JUST.

Repeat above, starting from "MY HEART FALLS TO PIECES."
PEOPLE PUT TOGETHER
A PEACEFUL DEMONSTRATION
BUT THE POLICE PUSH THE PEOPLE,
PARTY PEOPLE PUSHED TO PIECES.
POWER TO THE PEOPLE
POWER
POWER TO THE PEOPLE
POWER
POWER TO THE
POWER TO THE
POWER TO THE
POWER TO THE
PUSH
DOOBADABOOM BADADOOM DA ROOM PUSH
DOOBA ROOBA ROOM DOOM DOOM DOOM PUSH
DOOBADABOOM BADADOOM DA ROOM PUSH

Repeat DOOBADABOOM section through following.

HELITA:

ZOOBIDOOBIDOO HEY

CHORUS:

PUSH

Chorus continues under BeatBox.
JIMMY: *(BeatBox)*

PFF T P K

T KEU KPFF K
T K (X3)
PFF K PFFK PFF P K K

BLUE:

DON'T . PUSH . ME . CAUSE . I'M CLOSE . TO . THE . EDGE
DON'T . PUSH . ME . CAUSE . I'M CLOSE!

OMAR: When someone who has nothing is promised everything and paradise, they will do anything, by any means to attain it. When America promises everything and gives nothing, it should surely expect a backlash. Necessary! Civil Rights Movement, Necessary! Black Panther Party, Necessary! Young Lords, Necessary! Necessary because what we received was contrary to what we were promised. *(BeatBox stops)*

HELITA:

ZOOBIDOOBIDOO HEY

CHORUS:

BALL OF CONFUSION!

[NOTE: REFERENCE TO THE TEMPTATIONS' "BALL OF CONFUSION"]

BLUE: This ain't no history lesson.

JIMMY: Episode 1960's and 70's.

BLUE: Some names will be changed to protect the innocent and the guilty.

JIMMY: For those who need reminding.

MARUCA/CLARA/HELITA:

WHO?
HEY, HEY
WHO?
HEY, HEY.

Solias adds "and the band played on."

BLUE: The righteous and the backstabbers, they all have a part to play.

JIMMY:

WA WA WA WAWA
WA WA WOW

BLUE: Infiltrators, putting on whatever suits the moment.

OMAR: On the heels of the Civil Rights Movement, they took to the streets on foot and at the lead was M.L.K.

MALIK: In the wake of the murder of Malcolm X.

SOLIAS: In the wake of the Watts Riots.

BLUE: Here come the Panthers, black beret, powder blue shirt under a black leather jacket, the stride personified, offspring of Malcolm.

TITO: And the Young Lords followed suit, Puerto Rican soldiers, stomping boots, down city streets, where Malcolm's voice tangled with Albizu's. Black and Brown in unified redemption.

MARCUS: All they needed were 10 points and some guns to get the people's attention.

BLUE: All they needed were some pancakes, eggs and some grits to get Hoover's attention.

CHORUS: What's the number one threat in the country? Grits and gravy, grits and gravy. What's the number one threat in the country? Grits and gravy, get 'em now. (2X)

> *Then return to "Who? Hey, Hey"*

TITO: While Vietnam was ripping through the jungles, ripping through the fabric of our flag; America ripping through itself.

CHORUS: Hey, hey, LBJ, how many kids did you kill today? (4X)

TITO: The Young Lords ripped through the streets and Panthers led the charge.

BLUE: They cared to, dared to and tried to, discipline the undisciplined; organize the disorganized; those who have been conditioned to fail, conditioned to come late, conditioned to disrespect themselves, conditioned to mistrust . . .

CLARA: And flags burned.

DONNA: And police batons swung.

AMIRA: And the people wailed a loud song.

> *Jimmy stops "Wa wa."*

BLUE: Rap, Tap, Play Ball; Sing; Swing; Get High and Self Destruct; But Maaaan . . .

JIMMY/OMAR: Revolution was Necessary.

> *All music out.*

MARUCA/CLARA/HELITA:

> HEY, HEY.

BLUE: Wasn't they something?

HELITA:

> YO ME VOY PA LA CIUDAD
> CON TODA MI FAMILITA
> VOY A VENDER LA FINQUITA
> PORQUE NO PRODUCE NA (2X)

> [NOTE: REFERENCE TO ODILIO GONZALEZ' "DEL CAMPO A LA CIUDAD"]

CHORUS: *(repeats underneath the following vocals)*

[NOTE: THE FOLLOWING SECTION REFERENCES CROSBY, STILLS, NASH AND YOUNG's "CHICAGO" (REWRITE)]

DAGGA DOOGA DANG

JIMMY/SOLIAS: *(repeats underneath the following vocals)*
POM POM, POM POM

CHORUS:
THEY CAME *(4X)*
IN DROVES *(2X)*
THEY CAME

SOLIAS:
FROM OAKLAND TO SACKTOWN
THE BAY AREA AND BACK DOWN

CHORUS:
THEY CAME *(4X)*
IN DROVES *(2X)*
THEY CAME

HELITA:
AND THEY ALL WENT TO CHICAGO . . .

MARUCA:
TIME FOR CHANGE

HELITA:
TIME FOR CHANGE

CHORUS:
THEY CAME *(4X)*
IN DROVES *(2X)*
THEY CAME

MALIK/HELITA:
DOWN AND OUT, IN NEW YORK CITY

CHORUS:
THEY CAME *(4X)*
IN DROVES *(2X)*
THEY CAME

HELITA/MARUCA/AMIRA:
JUST TO CHANGE THE WORLD
REARRANGE THE WORLD

> *Omar and Jimmy begin "Hard Times instrumental."*

HELITA:

> THOUGH YOUR BROTHER'S GAGGED AND BOUND AND THEY'VE
> TIED HIM TO A CHAIR, WON'T YOU PLEASE
> COME

CHORUS:

> THEY CAME *("COME/THEY CAME" REPEATS SEVERAL TIMES)*

> *[NOTE: THE FOLLOWING REFERENCES BABY HUEY's "HARD TIMES"
> (1971)]*

MALIK:

> COLD, COLD EYES UPON ME THEY STARE
> PEOPLE ALL AROUND ME AND THEY'RE ALL IN FEAR
> THEY DON'T SEEM TO WANT ME BUT THEY WON'T ADMIT
> I MUST BE SOME KIND OF CREATURE
> UP HERE HAVING FITS
> FROM MY PARTY HOUSE,
> I'M AFRAID TO COME OUTSIDE
> ALTHOUGH I'M FILLED WITH LOVE
> I'M AFRAID THEY'LL HURT MY PRIDE
> SO I PLAY THE PART I FEEL THEY WANT OF ME
> AND I PULL THE SHADES
> SO I WON'T SEE THEM SEEIN' ME

CHORUS:

> HAVIN' HARD TIMES, IN THIS CRAZY TOWN
> HAVIN' HARD TIMES, THERE'S NO LOVE TO BE FOUND
> HAVIN' HARD TIMES, IN THIS CRAZY TOWN
> HAVIN' HARD TIMES, THERE'S NO LOVE TO BE FOUND

> *[NOTE: THE FOLLOWING REFERENCES DAVE GRUSIN's AND
> ANDREW BERGMAN's "GOOD TIMES" T.V. THEME SHOW]*

> KEEPING YOUR HEAD ABOVE WATER
> MAKING A WAVE WHEN YOU CAN (4X)

> *Malik riffs throughout.*

285

HELITA: I didn't wake up one morning and decide to become a
revolutionary; didn't wake up to wake up. Let me make it abundantly
clear, Jesus Christ didn't tell me to do this, Albizu Campos didn't tell
me to do this, Mao, Lenin and Marx didn't tell me to do this. The
contradictions in society are what made me become who I've become.
Because all you have to do is, know who you are; find yourself, human.
If you don't know what your essence is; if you don't commit yourself to
struggle, you are nobody, and then, you're a sell out. I made a choice.
I sacrificed my family for something that's much more important. The

Freedom of Our Country. That doesn't make me exceptional, it just makes me a person of conscience.

All music out.

A revolutionary.

[NOTE: THE FOLLOWING REFERENCES PROTEST SONGS OF THE 60's & 70's. INCLUDING THE PUERTO RICAN REVOLUTIONARY ANTHEM]

OMAR/BLUE/ROGER:
THE REVOLUTION HAS COME

CHORUS:
OFF THE PIGS!

OMAR/BLUE/ROGER/TITO:
IT'S TIME TO PICK UP THE GUN

CHORUS:
OFF THE PIGS!

Repeat above lines, without "OFF THE PIGS," throughout the following section. Each line in the following section also repeats several times.

TITO/JIMMY:
EL PUEBLO UNIDO JAMÁS SERÁ VENCIDO

AMIRA/CLARA/DONNA:
WE SHALL OVERCOME.

HELITA/MARUCA:
LA LIBERTAD LA LIBERTAD

SCENE TWO: MALIK & JIMMY PREPARE

Malik and Jimmy are working on exhibits. Jimmy is editing video and Malik is working on his "confessional."

286   MALIK: Motherfucker.
Motherfucker.
Motherfucker.
Used to practice saying motherfucker for hours,
how to get it to roll off my tongue,
with purpose;
how to use it as a noun, a verb, an adjective;
a predicate and a subject;
practiced my facial expressions,
staring for hours in the mirror,

getting my "I don't take no shit" look,
perfected;
practiced the face I would have
as I was being arrested,
the front page picture that would be in the paper;
practiced having my own press conferences
in front of microphones and cameras;
practiced how I would bop into the courtroom,
how I would raise my fist when I would walk in,
head held high,
the boogie man's here to put America on notice.
I watched how those brothers and sisters
carried themselves
Studied Mao, Che, and Frantz Fanon.
So I'd have my mind right,
I wanted to walk in those black shoes,
and wear that black jacket,
with that black beret on my head,
with that black crown on my head;
but heavy is the head that wears the crown.
Heavy is the head that wants to wear the crown.
And I have earned my position,
sat on the sideline
and waited to be called into the game.
I'm ready coach, put me in.
So, when I go to see my father in jail,
show him what a good boy I be,
he would take one look at me,
look me up and down for a long time,
and say,
"Boy, you ain't no Panther."
And the words tear a hole in me.
"Boy you ain't no Panther."
Making me feel like I've just been robbed.
"Boy you ain't no Panther."
Took away my birthright, and that ain't right.
Isn't this what I'm supposed to be?
Isn't this what I'm supposed to do?
Wanna be . . . like you . . .
So what do I do now?
Leave the baton where I found it?
Your fingers
holding onto it,
like a junkie holding onto his last fix.

And I can hear him say,
"Boy, you ain't no Panther."
"Boy, you ain't no Panther."
"You don't wanna walk a mile in these shoes.
You don't want this weight on your shoulders.
You don't want the blood on your hands.
This is more than a jacket and a beret,
more than fists in the air and tough talk.
This is a way of life
and there is a price to pay for this life,
sometimes more than you are ready to pay;
and you ain't got enough money
in your bank account to cover that."
So, what happens to us?
The ones who came after,
the collateral damage,
and those of us still looking for ourselves
in the mirror.
Motherfucker.

SCENE THREE: DEAR OMAR

MALIK: Boricua!

JIMMY: Yo, what up Black Power!

MALIK: Chillin'. Did you get the videos I sent you?

JIMMY: Yeah, I haven't gotten to them yet. You gotta hear some of these voicemails people left me.

MALIK: I'll listen to them later.

JIMMY: Blue and Amira RSVP'd. I think they're excited about tonight.

MALIK: Oh my god, I just got so nervous. This is for real, this just got real. We're really doing this.

JIMMY: I don't know how they'll react to everything. I don't know if they'll understand what we're saying. I don't know about this clown costume. I don't know. I don't know. I don't know.

MALIK/JIMMY:

WE DO IT FOR THE LOVE.
WE DO IT FOR THE CULTURE.
PEOPLE BETTER GET READY
FOR PRIMO AND MK ULTRA.

MALIK: Focus! First, let's check in. At 3 o'clock I have an interview with *The Village Voice*. I have not heard from Marcus with the door.

JIMMY: I spoke to him, it's all good.

MALIK: Good. Hot97 and BAI are both running the ad every hour, catering service should be here by 6:00. I just picked up the dry cleaning . . . and what have you gotten done?

JIMMY: I'm editing.

MALIK: That's it? What about the photographs for the Memory Lane segment? Nothing's up yet.

JIMMY: It's coming, it's coming. The footage is more important than anything right now.

    Omar enters.

OMAR: Hey! Can I speak to the person in charge of the event that is being presented on this flier?

MALIK: Well, he's the artist presenting this exhibit, but I'm—

OMAR: Uh-huh, so it looks like I'm talking to two motherfuckers that have no idea who they're talking to, or how shit like this is supposed to work. I've talked to some of my comrades and they told me they got interviewed. Nobody interviewed me. I am a member of the Black Panther Party, for life, and I feel offended that I was not invited to be a part of this . . . um . . . let me see here . . .

    He reads the flier.

Primo and MK Ultra present "Party People."

JIMMY: I'm Primo . . . I mean my name is Jimmy. Primo is my stage name, my show name.

    Jimmy extends his hand for a handshake. Omar ignores it.

OMAR: Show name, so you're afraid to use your real name?

JIMMY: I think I can start by saying that if I had your information I would definitely have invited you.

MALIK: I'd like to extend a VIP invitation to you. There really was no . . .

OMAR: OK, OK, OK, look, I appreciate your late "invitation." But I want some assurance that you will tell the truth about what really went down.

JIMMY: I promise I will tell as much of the truth as I know.

OMAR: Uh-huh.

JIMMY: Well, why don't you let us interview you right now?

    Indicates Malik's video camera.

OMAR: I don't just talk to anybody you know. Nowadays it looks like people are running to get in front of a camera and tell their deepest and darkest . . . well, I'm already deep and dark and I don't feel real motivated to give you an interview on my inner views.

JIMMY: If it'll make you feel more comfortable, my collaborator can do the interview with you. He's the son of a Panther.

OMAR: Uh-huh.

MALIK: Hi, I'm Malik.

Malik extends his hand for a handshake. Omar ignores it.

OMAR: Malik? Or . . .

Holding up the flier.

MK Ultra? I'm Omar. Omar Ecks. Real name.

Pause.

MALIK: Omar . . . Omar . . . Omar Ecks. I know that name. My father talked about you. He said you was a real down brother; just needed to be debriefed.

OMAR: *(Silence.)*

JIMMY: Uhhh . . . Why don't you take a seat?

Offers him a seat on a bench near the camera.

OMAR: I think I will sit . . . and no sugar for my coffee.

Omar sits on a chair instead, turning it so he can face the camera.

JIMMY: What? Oh, my bad, coffee. You want some coffee. OK, I'll go get some coffee.

Jimmy exits.

OMAR: No sugar . . .

Looks at Malik.

So, your father talked about me?

MALIK: Do you remember my father?

OMAR: Who was your father?

MALIK: My father took a stand. He threw his blackness in the air, in the form of fist and hair. And he was there when you were fighting. He was there when you were plotting underground. And he was there when you were there.

OMAR: I don't remember him.

MALIK: Same time; same town; same Chapter.
You had the same friends as my father.
Same frame and same stature.
Now as an old man,
he's been resentenced to a cell block.
Seventy-some years old
and here come the same cops.
They questioned him,
roughed him up,
cuffed him up, took my old man,
and now a new case
under the Patriot Act has opened up.
This is a hard time for me and my momma.
My parents are too old for this.

290

We thought that we'd made it through the drama.

OMAR: Malik . . .

Yeah I remember.
Same eyes, same spirit, same look as your father.
I remember.
You were born in December.
I stopped by the hospital
on the day you were born.
Your father could have swore
The night was over and that you were the dawn.
What you wanna ask? And I want a copy of this damn video!

MALIK: Tell me what I need to know . . . Just talk into the camera, slow.

SCENE FOUR: AMIRA AND BLUE PREPARE

BLUE: Hey baby! Baby!

AMIRA: Ain't no babies in here.

BLUE: Amira.

AMIRA: Yes?

BLUE: Are you sure you want to go to this thing tonight? I don't know if I really want to go.

AMIRA: Blue, I am not gonna do this with you right now. Did you RSVP and tell those boys that we're coming?

BLUE: Yes.

AMIRA: Then we're going and that is the end of that.

BLUE: You think I need to bring my gun?

AMIRA: What did you say?

BLUE: Do I need to bring my gun? You know the last time I saw some folks it wasn't on the friendliest of circumstances. I mean it got pretty heated and just because you're forgotten doesn't mean you're forgiven.

AMIRA: Are you trying to go back to jail?

BLUE: No, no, no, no, no, you're right; you're right; you're right.

AMIRA: Don't worry, you'll know when its time to knock a mother trucker out, if somebody gets out of hand.

BLUE: Oooh, look at the ghetto come out of you.

AMIRA: Huh, I'm not looking for no trouble, but I will deal with the trouble if it wants to be found.

BLUE: I hear ya soul sister, talk that talk, walk that walk.

She struts around the room.

Hahaha, that's what I'm talking about . . .

291

SCENE FIVE: ARMCHAIR REVOLUTIONARY

Tito calls Jimmy.

JIMMY: Bendición, Tío.

TITO: Tell me something, Jimmy . . . What's your problem nene? Why you so stupid? Who's gonna be at your show tonight? I heard about some people that are gonna be there. You should have asked me first.

JIMMY: Everybody's gonna be here; Marcus, Malik, Helita . . .

TITO: Wait, you invited Helita?

JIMMY: The only way I could get her to come is if I promised her that you wouldn't be there.

TITO: What? Why did you do that?

JIMMY: Because I wanted her to show up. So are you coming or not?

TITO: No. Fuck you! No.

JIMMY: What? Why?

TITO: I heard you invited Maruca. Why did you invite that woman?

JIMMY: Maruca? I had to let her know. I interviewed her for one of the pieces I did.

TITO: You shouldn't be talking to Maruca. Que sabe ella de na'? She don't know nothin' about no artwork.

JIMMY: It would be nice if you could stop being old, pathetic, and alone in your house. Come over here and see what your nephew did.

TITO: You know if some people see her there, it's gonna be problems.

JIMMY: Ok. Thanks for the heads up, but what can I do now? She's RSVP'd already. Just like everybody else. Except for you.

TITO: Dile que no venga, tell her that the party got canceled.

JIMMY: Tío, it's not a party, that's just the title of my show. And what if she still shows up anyway? Think of how stupid I would look.

TITO: Blame your stupid looks on your parents.

JIMMY: Tío! I'm trying to talk to you with respect man!

TITO: It just wasn't a good idea to let that woman know about this. You know she got a lot of history with a lot of these people, Y no todas son buenas memorias . . . Pa' que lo sepas nene.

JIMMY: Yeah, but at least she helped people. She kept busy trying to make life better for people.

TITO: What! For who? She didn't do shit for me!

JIMMY: Didn't she get you out of jail? Didn't she help in the liberation of Lincoln Hospital when Puerto Ricans needed it most? She was powerful, a leader.

TITO: Get the fuck outta here. Maruca tore us apart from the inside. I think she was a spy. Porque tienes que ser tan pendejo? She didn't take over

292

no Lincoln Hospital. WE took over Lincoln Hospital. All those bitches, boys AND girls, were sitting in the truck waiting while five of us, five bad-ass motherfuckers, took out the guards. And not just Puerto Ricans benefited from that, but all poor people from our community.

Where once there was a building for us to die in, now there is a place that ensured us longer life. But it was five of us that did that. And then "they" all rush in from the truck all like, "We takin' over!" Get the fuck outta here! And you know what else, Fedelito-Carajito-Pendejito? If you had been there, I bet you would have been one of the ones sitting in the truck waiting for us to do the dirty work . . . Pendejo.

JIMMY: Yo, fuck you then, Tío.

TITO: Cause you're an ARMCHAIR revolutionary, Jimmy, you ain't real.

JIMMY: Fuck you!

TITO: Hey fuck you too Jimmy, y que Dios te ponga verguenza. You little bitch. Ahahaha! I'm not going. Ahahaha!

Tito hangs up on Jimmy.

SCENE SIX: HELITA AND CLARA PREPARE

HELITA: Is that what you're gonna wear tonight?

CLARA: I'm not in the mood for revolution, tia Helita.

HELITA: You're going.

CLARA: Why are you even doing this? You've made it, Madrina. Why do you keep trying to go back to the ghetto? Trying to dig yourself back into the hole. I'm not trying to get sucked back in. I'm on a career path. Your loser comrades don't even know what a 401(k) is. I worked my ass off to get out the projects so I could join the 1%, and I am not about to dig myself back in.

HELITA: Clara, I'm not asking you to stand in front of an armored truck. I'm asking you to accompany me to an art gallery. You're going.

SCENE SEVEN: DEBRIEFED

Malik enters.

MALIK: Wow, man, I just got a great interview with Omar.

JIMMY: I think my heart just exploded.

MALIK: Don't die on me Jimmy. We have a plan to plan. Stuff's not on the walls yet. The footage isn't all cut. Feel sorry for yourself on your own time. You can't afford to take a break. I can't afford for you to take a break. Too much to be done. Are you listening to me? Hey Jimmy! Snapout, man! Snapout! I recruited everybody I could to come help us.

I've made phone calls! I invoked my father's name! Do you know what that means? What happens if they show up and the work just looks like scattered ideas? That's gonna reflect on me. It's gonna look like . . . I think of them as scattered. These people are like family to me, Jimmy. I know them. They are not scattered. I've got more at stake here than you. You need to get up.

JIMMY: More at stake than me? MK, don't try that shit. I will end you. My reputation is what's at stake here. Nobody knows who you are yet, and nobody's gonna care if you fuck up. If it wasn't for my reputation putting you here today you'd have nothing to worry about, right!?

MALIK: Awww, fuck you, Jimmy! Everybody knows I'm the one doing all the work here. If I didn't decide to come save your stupid ass you wouldn't be having a show to put up in the first place.

JIMMY: No, first of all your only job here is to press record for me . . .

MALIK: And run the interviews, edit the footage, invite your guests, who are all actually my guests, Jimmy! I've painted walls, mopped floors, made the calls . . . Wait . . . what do you actually do here?

JIMMY: I make shit amazing. I make you halfway interesting.

MALIK: Fuck you!

JIMMY: No, you!

MALIK: Don't push me!

JIMMY: I'll push you if I want.

They scuffle like children.

MALIK: Get off!

JIMMY: You get off!

They separate. Pause.

My Uncle's mad at me. He's not coming.

Pause.

Inviting Maruca to our opening was a mistake.

MALIK: I told you. Didn't I tell you? You don't listen. That's what's your problem. When it comes to creating new projects you always try to bite off more than you can chew, and not only that, I told you, don't make an art piece about two parties that can kick your ass. Two, motherfucker, two!

Recomposing himself.

Keep it together, keep it together, keep it together. As long as they can all find a comfortable spot in the space, everything should be fine.

JIMMY: I don't want any of them to find a nice comfortable spot anywhere. I want them uncomfortable. We want emotions. We want behavior.

MALIK: See!? And then you say shit like that! What the hell does that even mean?

JIMMY: Never mind, Malik.

    Pause.

My uncle called me an armchair revolutionary again. That shit just wrinkled my brain. But Tito's never met my alter ego. He doesn't know about Primo. Tonight I'm gonna wear a mask that will undo all of their masks. These old revolting types are always on their guard. We need to unbalance them. None of them will know how to react to Primo. Especially my uncle.

MALIK: I don't understand why you and your uncle don't get along. He's mad cool with everybody else. I think it's just you nobody likes.

JIMMY: I get along with him, we just don't get along. You know? I think my parents brainwashed me. My mother didn't like him. She made him out to be a loose cannon, said he was a criminal, a drunk, a druggie, a thief, and I thought that was so cool. I wanted to be like him, he was famous, everybody on the block knew who he was. Now he's wack. He doesn't respect my work. He doesn't see how it's revolutionary. But I don't want revolution. I don't believe revolution is enough. I want a renaissance, a paradigm shift. It's time to change the way we all think.

SCENE EIGHT: JIMMY WALKS THE STREETS

    Chorus enters. Jimmy walks to a cleared area and turns to face the camera. Malik records.

CHORUS: *(BeatBox)*

    BUDUDUMP BUMP BADUDUMP BUMPBUMP
    AND JIMMY WALKS THE STREETS
    ON THE LOWER EAST SIDE OF TOWN
    AND JIMMY PLANTS HIS FEET
    TO WATCH THEM TEAR HIS MEMORIES DOWN
    FEELS LIKE A DIFFERENT PLACE
    LOOKS FOR HIMSELF IN THE FACES
    OF THE REGULAR PASSERS BY
    AND ALL THE SIDEWALK CAFÉS
    HAVE HELPED HIS MEMORY FADE
    FLIPPED HIS ALPHABET INSIDE, INSIDE OUT

JIMMY:

    YEAH I REMEMBER THE BODEGAS
    THE JUNKIES AND ALL THE BEGGARS
    SLEEPING ON THE PARK BENCHES
    UNDER COVER OF UMBRELLAS
    THE DEALERS THEY WERE MY COUSINS
    WE COME CHEAPER BY THE DOZEN

A HUSTLER'S SONG
I'M MAKING SOMETHING OUT OF NOTHING
RISING OUT OF THE GUTTER
BLUNT PUFFING
CAUSE FUCK SUFFERING
I'D RATHER BE NUMB
THAN ANOTHER NUMBER
NO BLUFFING
I'M A
GO GETTER
DIDN'T KNOW NO BETTER
DON'T
FORGET OR I'MA PULL THE CHROME FROM THE LEATHER
WHEN COPS COCK GLOCKS
WE POP HOT SHOTS TOO
GOT AN ACCURATE CREW
WE LIFT 'EM OUT OF THEIR SHOES
WE DON'T
KNOW HESITATING
NEVER LOSE A SECOND
DON'T SLEEP
THE STREETS TOO DEEP
FOR HIGHER EDUCATION
GRADUATED FROM A SCHOOL OF HARD KNOCKS
BETWEEN A HARD PLACE
AND A PILE OF LOOSE CRACK ROCKS

CHORUS:

AND JIMMY WALKS THE STREETS
ON THE LOWER EAST SIDE OF TOWN
AND JIMMY PLANTS HIS FEET
TO WATCH THEM TEAR HIS MEMORIES DOWN
FEELS LIKE A DIFFERENT PLACE
LOOKS FOR HIMSELF IN THE FACES
OF THE REGULAR PASSERS BY
AND ALL THE SIDEWALK CAFÉS
HAVE HELPED HIS MEMORY FADE
FLIPPED HIS ALPHABET INSIDE, INSIDE OUT

JIMMY:

I GOT A DEGREE
WHEN EVERYONE WAS SURE I WOULDN'T
WENT AND PROVED THEM ALL WRONG
WHEN EVEN I BELIEVED I COULDN'T

296

MADE IT TO ANOTHER STATE OF MIND
YOUNG CRIMINAL
TO A YOUNG ADULT ALUM-NI
STUDIES DIGITAL
ARTS CRITICAL
THINK BIGGER PIC-TURE
MIX MAS-TER
SKIP CLASS-TO
FLIP SCRIP-TURE

SOLIAS/OMAR:

PREACH PAS-TOR

JIMMY:

DEBATED PROFESSORS OF ALL COLORS CREEDS AND RACES
BLEW THEM ALL AWAY
BY THE LOOKS UPON THEIR FACES
THEY HATED THE FACT THAT I WAS ACTIVELY
ATTACKING THEM WITH ISSUES AND STATS
ABOUT THEIR STATUS AND CLASS
THE CAR THAT THEY DRIVE
WORKING HARDER TO STRIVE
LIVING ON RAMEN NOODLES
STARVING MARVIN
TRYING TO SURVIVE

CHORUS:

AND JIMMY WALKS THE STREETS
ON THE LOWER EAST SIDE OF TOWN
AND JIMMY PLANTS HIS FEET
TO WATCH THEM TEAR HIS MEMORIES DOWN
FEELS LIKE A DIFFERENT PLACE
LOOKS FOR HIMSELF IN THE FACES
OF THE REGULAR PASSERS BY
AND ALL THE SIDEWALK CAFÉS
HAVE HELPED HIS MEMORY FADE
FLIPPED HIS ALPHABET INSIDE, INSIDE OUT
THE J, THE I, THE M, THE M, THE Y
THE J, THE I, THE M
IT'S JIMMY

297

JIMMY: *(Scratching)* Word up!

CHORUS:

IT'S JIMMY

JIMMY: *(Scratching)* Word up!

CHORUS:

> THE J, THE I, THE M, THE M, THE Y
> THE J, THE I, THE M
> IT'S JIMMY

JIMMY: (Scratching) Word up!

CHORUS:

> IT'S JIMMY

JIMMY: (Scratching) Word up!

> Song fades out.

SCENE NINE: DONNA PREPARES

> Donna is in her apartment. She is wearing her husband's uniform shirt. She takes it off and folds it, burying her face in it for a moment. Then she opens a cabinet, takes out her jacket, then a framed picture. She looks at the picture. After putting the shirt and picture away, she puts her jacket on and exits the apartment.

SCENE TEN: THE DOOR ARRIVES

> Jimmy edits Marcus' video interview.

MARCUS: (Video) OK, OK, OK, MLK, JFK, RFK, OK? OK. I just think that if you was white back then, and I'm talking about the 60's man, shit was happening. And if you was white and you could really see the world clear, fuck, just Leave it to Beaver and take a look at what was really happening . . . you had to get involved, man.

> Malik enters. Jimmy freezes the video.

JIMMY: Man, Marcus ain't here yet.

MALIK: I thought you were talking to him on the phone?

JIMMY: I was.

MALIK: I thought that he was close!

298

JIMMY: That's what he told me.

MALIK: He's got stuff that we need man.

He's got that door, that door, we need that door.

JIMMY: I told you he was a wild card.

MALIK: Call him.

JIMMY: Again?

MALIK: Yes, call him again.

JIMMY: I just spoke to him and I've got other shit to do.

MALIK: You know what? Just give me your phone so I can call him. Maybe he'll move faster for me.

Malik dials the phone and Jimmy returns to the video.

Uh, hello? Is this Marcus?

MARCUS: Why yes it is, and this is not Jimmy's voice. I have this number specifically saved in my phone as Jimmy, and this is not the voice I recognize as Jimmy, so before I answer any more questions who am I speaking to?

MALIK: Uh, this is Malik. *(pause)* I'm the Panther cub who originally called you about bringing your things down to this exhibit. *(pause)* I hope you remember me.

MARCUS: I remember you, but I have your number specifically saved in my phone as Malik, and since you are not calling me from that number there is no reason for me to identify your voice to this number. Man, I need things to be in the place that its supposed to be in, and if its not . . . then that really becomes a problem. And I think that that's a big problem in society, past and present. People are still trying to find their place in the world, while there are other people who feel they can just tell people where they are supposed to be. That's a problem. That's why I collect things, it gives things order.

MALIK: Marcus . . .

MARCUS: And if we don't keep things in order, the enemy can move things around, rewrite history, delete things that don't please them.

MALIK: Marcus . . .

MARCUS: Hey listen, I brought the pictures of Fred you asked for. I know I said no at first, but I changed my mind . . . I had a long time with myself to think about this, and I told me it's alright . . . and do you know how hard it was to get the door onto my truck? But I got it in there. I still can't believe they shot so many holes in that door. I can't believe the police fired so many bullets into the office, into Fred's apartment, into Fred's bedroom, into Fred . . .

Chorus softly begins "Trying Times" bass line.

My friend, Fred Hampton, Chairman of the Illinois Chapter of The Black Panther Party.

299

[NOTE: Audio OF A FRED HAMPTON SPEECH.]

FRED HAMPTON (AUDIO): "We've got to face the fact that some people say you fight fire best with fire, but we say you put fire out with water. We say you don't fight racism with racism. We're gonna fight racism with solidarity."

MARCUS: Solidarity!

[NOTE: THE FOLLOWING REFERENCES "WADE IN THE WATER"]

CHORUS:

FREE FRED HAMPTON
FREE FRED HAMPTON, *CHILDREN*
FREE FRED HAMPTON
THEY HAVE TO SET OUR WARRIOR FREE *(REPEAT)*
HE WAS ONLY 21
HE WAS ONLY 21
HAD A PLAN TO GET IT DONE
HAD A PLAN TO GET IT DONE
HE BUILT THE COALITION
RAINBOW COALITION
NEVER ASKIN' FOR PERMISSION
NEVER ASKIN' FOR PERMISSION
HE WAS SHOT THROUGH THE HEAD
SHOT THROUGH THE HEAD
WHILE SLEEPIN' IN HIS BED
WHILE SLEEPIN' IN HIS BED
CAUSE HE LOVED ALL THE PEOPLE
HE LOVED ALL THE PEOPLE
BLACK POWER TO BLACK PEOPLE
BLACK POWER TO BLACK PEOPLE
BROWN POWER TO BROWN PEOPLE
BROWN POWER TO BROWN PEOPLE
WHITE POWER TO WHITE PEOPLE
WHITE POWER TO WHITE PEOPLE
YELLOW POWER YELLOW PEOPLE
YELLOW POWER YELLOW PEOPLE
RED POWER TO RED PEOPLE
RED POWER TO RED PEOPLE
THEY WERE ALL HIS PEOPLE
THEY WERE ALL HIS PEOPLE
AND HE SERVED HIS PEOPLE
HE SERVED ALL THE PEOPLE
AND POWER
POWER
POWER
POWER
POWER
POWER
POWER
POWER
POWER
POWER
POWER

300

POWER
POWER
POWER
POWER
POWER
POWER!
POWER TO THE PEOPLE
POWER TO THE PEOPLE
POWER TO THE PEOPLE

MARCUS: The FBI, the Cook County State Attorney's office, and the Chicago Police, an unholy trinity, conspired to assassinate Fred . . . Fred . . . Fred . . . And I swear, some people don't care and some people don't know and some people just plain forget, and I'm glad you want the door. I'm glad you asked me to bring it. I know I'm talking a lot, that's just what I do when I'm excited, some people eat, some people fuck, I talk, and no I'm not on drugs. I mean, I do them but I'm not on them now . . . I just wanna make sure everything is the way it needs to be.

MALIK: Marcus, I apologize for calling you from a phone that's not mine, and disrupting your order of things, but where are you?

MARCUS: Oh, I'm almost there Malik, I told Jimmy that I was almost there, when I spoke to him on the phone. He said it was OK, just get there as fast as I can.

MALIK: Marcus, just tell me what time you're gonna get here . . . (looking at Jimmy) 'cause sometimes things can slip between the cracks, and I'm trying to make sure that you are not stuck in a crack somewhere.

MARCUS: I appreciate your concern about where I am 'cause I am carrying pieces of American history with me and when you are carrying so many important things you have to be careful . . .

MALIK: I'm glad you are being careful but we have a schedule to keep, and I'm just nervous that you're going to be a lot later than you already are.

MARCUS: And because I try really hard to be careful, I never gave you an arrival time, I told you I would get there as soon as I was able to get to you, because if you give too much information about what time you will arrive with so many important things without checking out the space on your own, mm-mmm,

Marcus arrives. He walks into the room.

and making sure the space is secure before making your presence known, is just a smart way of keeping things in order.

MALIK: Marcus?

MARCUS: Malik . . . My man Jimmy . . .

JIMMY: (*freezing video and standing to greet Marcus*) I told you he'd be here.

They all converge and move offstage together. Empty stage.

SCENE ELEVEN: SOLIAS & MARUCA PREPARE

Solias prepares.

CHORUS: *(whispers)* Snitch! / Traitor! / I know what you did! / Sell out! /
Judas! / etc

SOLIAS:

NEVER MEANT TO HURT NOBODY.
NEVER MEANT TO TURN MY BACK ON YOU.
I NEVER MEANT TO TAKE MY CROWN;
THROW IT DOWN TO THE GROUND.
NO, I NEVER MEANT TO DO THAT.
NEVER MEANT TO HURT YOU BROTHER,
NO, I NEVER MEANT TO DO THAT TOO.
NEVER MEANT TO HURT YOU SISTER,
SO I'M GOING TO DO RIGHT BY YOU.
NEVER MEANT TO TAKE THAT PLEDGE AND BREAK IT.
NEVER MEANT TO SNAP IT IN TWO.
OH NO, I NEVER MEANT TO BREAK THAT PLEDGE,
BUT THAT'S EXACTLY WHAT I'M GONNA DO.

CHORUS: *(whispers)* Snitch! / Traitor! / I know what you did! / Sell out! /
Judas! / etc

Whispers continue through next two lines

SOLIAS:

CAUSE I'M A TRAITOR, OF THE WORST KIND.
CAUSE I'M A TRAITOR, OF THE WORST KIND.

SOLIAS / CHORUS:

EVE OF DESTRUCTION, REVOLT DYSFUNCTION,
FEAR IN THE AIR, TENSION EVERYWHERE,
PEOPLE ALL OVER THE WORLD, SHOUTING END THE WAR.

SOLIAS:

AND I'M ALL ALONE.

Maruca prepares.

MARUCA: Just in case you asked me . . . Just in case you asked me to bless
. . . Just in case you asked me to bless the mic tonight . . . Just in case
you asked me to bless the mic tonight, I decided to write My Self, into
words; tell the world of my worth and all my woes; be able to stand in
the same room with friends and foes; let our stories further unfold 'til
my voice be heard and truths be told.

Time has passed and now I'm living better days and though you may
never see me in different ways, and choose to remember only who I've
been, I pray you, try to see who I am, within, and let me bring that

chapter to a close. What keeps us angry is what no one knows. Keeping secrets secret is our greatest sin.

I feel like people glare at me as I walk down the street and I'm tired of being sent home when I try to join the circle. Tonight, I hope to claim victory from defeat; make my journey complete; turn my heart back to red, from purple.

CHORUS:

CAUSE YOU'RE A TRAITOR, OF THE WORST KIND.
CAUSE YOU'RE A TRAITOR, OF THE WORST KIND.

SCENE TWELVE: ARRIVAL / MEMORY LANE

Jimmy and Malik enter to open their gallery. Attendees slowly come in, begin looking around.

[NOTE: THE FOLLOWING IS WRITTEN TO TEGO CALDERON's "EL CAMBUMBO"]

CHORUS:

SO NICE TO SEE YOU AND YOU AND YOU. THANK YOU. (3X)
HOW ARE YOU? HOW ARE YOU?
WHAT HAVE YOU BEEN UP TO LATELY?
THE YEARS JUST FLOAT AWAY. (2X: SUNG AS FIRST VERSE REPEATS)

AMIRA: Hey, how are you doing girl? It's been a long time.

HELITA: I know. You are looking great.

MARCUS: Tito, why didn't you call me and tell me you were coming?

TITO: Cause I know you don't like surprises, compadre.

CHORUS:

HOW ARE YOU? HOW ARE YOU?
WHAT HAVE YOU BEEN UP TO LATELY?
THE YEARS JUST FLOAT AWAY.

BLUE: What's up young blood? Now you know you better come show me some love.

MALIK: Hey . . . you know I was coming to see you if you didn't show up right?

MARUCA: Oh my God, you've grown into a beautiful woman. I don't know if you remember me . . . Maruca.

CLARA: Hi, you look familiar, Maruca . . . but I'm not sure.

CHORUS:

SO NICE TO SEE YOU AND YOU AND YOU. THANK YOU.

AMIRA: You see who's here don't you?

303

BLUE: I knew I should have brought my gun.

HELITA: If I knew you were going to invite undesirable members of the party, I would have reconsidered my RSVP.

OMAR: Excuse me, I don't think I remember you.

DONNA: I don't think you would remember me.

MALIK: What did Helita say to you?

JIMMY: Drama.

CHORUS:

> *COME GET A HUG.*
> *COME GET A HANDSHAKE.*
> *BETTER GET A PHOTOGRAPH.*
> *BETTER GET A BETTER RAP.*
> *(2X: Add the "HOW ARE YOU" verse second time)*

TITO: Can't we just put the past behind us?

HELITA: It's better if we just leave things alone.

TITO: Can't we spend some time at this event together? Let's show solidarity. You know all heads will turn and be amazed at how mature we are. How we can forgive and come together again, as friends, comrades. What do you say?

HELITA: The fact that we are both in the same room at the same time is enough.

> *Helita walks away.*

TITO: But enough is not good enough.

CHORUS:

> *TIME KEEPS ON SLIPPIN, SLIPPIN, SLIPPIN. (REPEATS)*
>
> *[NOTE: REFERENCES "FLY LIKE AN EAGLE" BY THE STEVE MILLER BAND]*

MARCUS: Well, look at that picture there. Reformers and revolutionaries, dreamers and doers, hillbilly nationalists, urban race rebels and black power. Yeah, man, that was it.

TITO: Ah, look at me with my purple beret. We worked for hours testing for tuberculosis on that day.

BLUE: You could see all the free grocery bags. 10,000 grocery bags, strategically packed, down to the cubic inch, and a fat healthy chicken on top of every bag, just like the Chairman wanted. And check it, that's me standing right there.

AMIRA: Where?

BLUE: Right there, that's my back.

AMIRA: Your back? Now how is anybody supposed to know that that's you standing there? That could be anybody.

BLUE: That's me, look at the lean. You know nobody else could lean like that.

AMIRA: There we are in Defremery Park. That's where we used to have our rallies.

OMAR: But we call it Lil' Bobby Hutton park now and there's Lil' Bobby, first one of us murdered by them damn pigs. He was only 17.

HELITA: Wow . . . That's Reverend Bruce and his wife, they were murdered one month before Fred . . . for supporting the original Young Lords from Chicago.

DONNA: I look at these pictures and I see people I recognize. I remember them from newspapers, screaming; and on the news, screaming. In these pictures I see people I never met, until I stepped into a court room, and there they were, screaming.

AMIRA: Now why are they gonna go there? They got pictures of cops up in here.

DONNA: Oh my god, they had the nerve to use my husband's picture.

OMAR: Isn't that, that dude Solias? There were always undercover agents around us back then; undercover agents around us now.

SOLIAS: You tryin' to say somethin' brother?

MARUCA: I can relive every moment through these.

AMIRA: I don't know, but these are making me feel old. Makes me not want to walk too far down this memory lane.

BLUE: This one here is just too full of memories.

TITO: What did we all do with our 15 minutes?

DONNA: Everything comes and goes so fast.

MARUCA: Where did I go . . . and how can I get me back?

TITO: I want to climb into these pictures. I want to live again . . . help my mind remember. I want to lose myself in past Decembers; tired of being the Great Pretender, but life betrays me, and time . . . keeps passing me by.

> [NOTE: THE FOLLOWING IS A REWRITE REFERENCING PHARCYDE's "PASSING ME BY" WHICH IS BASED ON "FLY LIKE AN EAGLE" BY THE STEVE MILLER BAND]

CHORUS:
> PASSING ME BY, PASSING ME BY.
> TIME KEEPS ON SLIPPIN, SLIPPIN, SLIPPIN.

HELITA:
> MY DEAR, MY DEAR, MY DEAR, YOU DO NOT KNOW ME. YOU DON'T KNOW ME VERY WELL. NOW LET ME TELL YOU ABOUT YOUR TIME.
> IT'S PASSING YOU BY, PASSING YOU BY.

SCENE THIRTEEN: ENTER PRIMO AND MK ULTRA

Primo suddenly appears, in clown outfit, to loud musical fanfare.

PRIMO: Extra! Extra! Ladies and gents in the gravitational pull of my
blogosphere.

Here I am in the room with the in crowd;
Kings and queens
Doctors and lawyers
Scholars, convicts, and news reporters.
And here you all are in the same room with me!
Behold, the bold Primo has just appeared
Here and now,
I stand in the midst of the where and the how.
Inside the scoop
Rubbing elbows with the who's who
of what was making the news,
back, back in the day.
Back, back in the day,
they planted a brick and out popped a
civilized, mobilized,
oversized citizen's brigade.
Hate it or love it,
this brigade helped bridge the gap,
springing the trap,
trapping the cat,
making men out of mice,
and snitches of rats.
And I guess that was that.
My Uncle Tito,
is that how you remember that?
Well, is that?

Music stops.

TITO: What's that?

PRIMO: Can you recall what ignited your passion for freedom?

TITO: Freedom? This wasn't about no freedom, 'least not for me. I was
already free, I was born free, free to do what I wanted. This was about
more, this was my cause, this was a war; a war I fought and lost and
wanted no more. I lost.

PRIMO: You lost?

TITO: I lost. I lost it all, lost friends, lost love, lost hope, that's all. That's all.

PRIMO: All you lost?

TITO: Lost all there ever was. I lost trust, lost faith, lost youth. What else
was there? We knew we heard our calling. The calling was our cause.

We fought to change the future. Rebellion's in us all. We fight, because we fight.

PRIMO: Because we fight; because we fight; isn't that right? Of course that's right. You were the muscle weren't you? You loved to fight.

TITO: *(grabbing Primo by the collar, as Maruca comes between Tito and camera)* Enough! Alright? What are you doing? Tu estas tosta'o? Why you dressed like that? Why you acting like this?

PRIMO: Gather 'round cats and kittens, rats and snitches, dogs and bitches.

> *Tiny voice.*

Party To The People
Party To The People

> *Resumes regular voice.*

This one goes out to all you non-social studies political education receiving beings

Being trapped in my world wide wire tap

Pay close attention,
Make notes
Take quotes
Because I'm asking you this once

> *To an audience member.*

What's the first point of the Young Lord's program and platform?

> *Silence.*

No? Nothing?

> *To another audience member.*

What is the first point of the Black Panther Party program?

> *Silence.*

(to Helita) I hope you know the first point of the Young Lord's program and platform.

HELITA: Number one. We want self-determination for Puerto Ricans. Liberation of the Island and inside the United States.

PRIMO: I hear Puerto Ricans on that little island provide a sizeable force to the U.S. Military. True? I also hear Puerto Ricans on that little island pay as much in Federal taxes as U.S. citizens do.

HELITA: We *are* U.S. citizens.

PRIMO: For real? Then why aren't you allowed to vote for U.S. Presidents? Somebody lied to you.

(to Maruca) YOU! Tell me number two.

MARUCA: Number two. We want self-determination for all Latinos.

PRIMO: Sounds just like the first, but worked out slightly worse.

(to Tito) Mr. T, can you tell me number three?

TITO: We want liberation for all third world people.

PRIMO: *(in a mocking voice.)* Hiberahion of hird we heho . . .

> *(to Blue)* Little Boy Blue, come blow my horn. What's number five on the Black Panther platform?

BLUE: We want education for our people that—

PRIMO: FAIL! Instead of education you got yourselves some shutdown schools. Dropouts; can't read, can't count. And they don't know no history. It's no mystery this has got to be the dumbest generation. Education.

> *(to Amira)* What's number seven?

AMIRA: We want an immediate end to police brutality and murder of black people.

PRIMO: Never gonna get it.
> Never gonna get it.
> Never gonna get it.
> Never gonna get it.
> Never gonna get it. You'll never get it.

> > *[NOTE: REFERENCES EN VOGUE's "MY LOVIN' (NEVER GONNA GET IT)"]*

> You all ought to have given up
> while your game was ahead.
> But instead you chose to push on.
> And now many do lay dead.
> How does it feel to know that you all gave yourselves Post Traumatic Stress?
> How does it feel to know we took
> and lost the streets?
> How does it feel? Tell me, how does it feel?

TITO: *(slaps Primo)* How does that feel?

HELITA: Here's something you don't seem to understand: as long as the fight in you is tiny, you're gonna have no problem going out into the world fighting your tiny little fight. Nobody's gonna stand in your way; but if you are one of those whose soul burns with fire, then you've got a much greater fight to fight. We picked a fight against the powers that be, but the powers that be have been in power for so long that we couldn't even tell where their friendships ended and their deception began.

PRIMO: *(to Helita, then camera)*

> —where their friendships ended and their deception began—

(to the audience, running in a circle)

> —where their friendships ended and their deception began!

308

CHORUS: —where their friendships ended and their deception began!

Everyone locks into a gameshow seated positions on cabinets around perimeter of stage to become audience for the "Spot-That-Mole" game show.

SCENE FOURTEEN: EXHIBIT 2—SPOT THAT MOLE/AGENT PROVOCATEUR/OMAR'S REVOLUTIONARY SUICIDE

Primo becomes the host. Omar is the contestant. Full cast is game show audience.

PRIMO: Good evening and welcome to that exciting new game show "SPOT-THAT-MOLE! The Game Show."

Whenever Primo says "SPOT-THAT-MOLE" the Chorus repeats with him.

Here contestants will have a chance to sniff out informants and Feds, for BIG BIG points and paltry sums of cash.

Today we have here with us Mr . . . .

Omar begins to say his name but is cut off by Primo.

It doesn't really matter what you answer here. We know everything about you anyway! I hear

you're visiting us here today from the Windy City, lovely weather I hear by the way. How about those Cubs?

OMAR: . . . (Silence.)

PRIMO: Sho' ya' right! Well Omar, as you'll now know, I'm going to give you one opportunity to "SPOT-THAT-MOLE!" That's right. Let's get it started. Why don't we begin with a moment in your life when you may or may not have been IN-FIL-TRATED!

Chorus joins in on "IN-FIL-TRATED!"

Haha, that's right!

SOLIAS: Go get the water ready. This rat needs a nice hot bath.

MALIK: We don't have to do it like this, do we? I trust this brother. This is our comrade.

JIMMY: This is how it needs to be.

MALIK: No, this is not how it's supposed to be.

SOLIAS: You'd better fall in line unless you're trying to sit in this chair next.

Solias and Jimmy lead Omar to a chair and handcuff him to it.

MALIK: I'm going.

SOLIAS: Ok, you're gonna start by telling us your full government name.

As torture begins, Omar recites from the Ten Point Program of the Black Panthers. [Full text is printed here but on stage, it is interrupted frequently by Solias' action and dialogue.]

309

OMAR: 1—We want freedom. We want power to determine the destiny of our black community.

2—We want full employment for our people.

3—We want an end to the robbery by the capitalists of our black community.

4—We want decent housing fit for the shelter of human beings.

5—We want education for our people that exposes the true nature of this decadent American society. We want education that teaches us our true history and our role in the present day society.

6—We want completely free health care for all black and oppressed people.

7—We want an immediate end to police brutality and murder of black people.

8—We want an immediate end to all wars of aggression.

9—We want freedom for all black and oppressed people now held in U.S. Federal, state, county, city and military prisons and jails. We want trials by a jury of peers for all persons charged with so-called crimes under the laws of this country.

10—We want land, bread, housing, education, clothing, justice and peace.

After Omar recites a couple of points, Solias punches him in the groin. Omar reels in pain.

SOLIAS: You know I never did trust you Omar. I can do this to you till the day you die. Now tell me your name.

Omar continues the 10 points.

Solias punches him again.

JIMMY: Just answer the stupid question Omar. Don't make this bad on yourself.

SOLIAS: I asked for your name.

Bends Omar's fingers back.

OMAR: Ahhhhh!!

Omar continues the 10 points.

SOLIAS: Do you smoke?

Solia lights a cigarette.

OK, we're gonna try again. Your name.

Solias burns him with a cigarette.

You should listen to your friend here. Why do you want this to hurt? How long have you been an informant?

Omar continues the 10 points.

Solias punches Omar unconscious.

Malik appears with a pot of steaming water.

310

Pour it on him. Omar needs a wake-up.

MALIK: What? But this . . .

SOLIAS: And look him in the eyes when he wakes up! He needs to know he's got no allies up in here.

Omar sees Malik with the water, then gets up and walks away from the chair.

OMAR: No! No! No! No! No! Jimmy and Malik invited me to this event and what has been done to me has not been addressed. It has been 37 years, 5 months tomorrow. I want a public apology, to have been tied up, in a basement, at gunpoint with a 45 held to my head, by members of the Party, two who are here with us today. And I know we're supposed to be all polite and shit, supposed to forgive and forget, act as if shit didn't happen, but this motherfucker is telling the truth. One comrade tied my hands, the other tied my ankles. I was forced to make a tape; to admit to things . . . to things that I didn't do. Where is that tape? Who took that tape? I am a consistent victim of what was put on that tape that night, from the Central Intelligence Agency, the U.S. Military Intelligence, the F.B.I., the State Department, the Secret Service, and Homeland Security. To this very moment, from what was put on that tape . . . at gunpoint. What happened to the tape?

AMIRA: When they came in that night, I didn't know what happened to anything. I don't know what they did with the tape. I don't know what they did with the tape recorder. All I know is, that the police came into the house and took everything.

OMAR: I can still remember that basement.

AMIRA: The stairs were rickety, they moaned when you walked on them. The lights flickered nervously, like they understood what was going on in the room. The floor was concrete, cold and distant, its eyes closed, looking away.

BLUE: And he wouldn't admit it. He wouldn't come out and say it.

OMAR: I was not an agent!

BLUE: Why wouldn't you just follow orders? All we was doing was following orders.

AMIRA: There were nine of us there, some of us stayed upstairs, couldn't bear to watch. We were all scared, but there was somebody from the outside, inside, who was orchestrating. He looked like us, dressed like us, but he was not one of us. He had everything spinning, your head and your heart. We were in a play and we didn't even know what part we were playing but we were playing it.

OMAR: Where is the tape?!

BLUE: I tried to keep my mind clear. Keep it on the moment happening around me. Don't over think it. Stay focused, show the central committee of the Oakland Panthers that they can trust me. And there is

311

no room for weakness, no room for infiltrators, no room for indecision. Blood to the horses' brow, woe to those who can't swim.

AMIRA: I filled up the pots with water. I can see the pots on the stove boiling. I could see the steam rising.

OMAR: *(to Amira)* Then what did you do?!

AMIRA: The water was so hot . . .

I walked down the steps with the boiling water. Kept myself focused on my job, looking you in the eyes liked I was trained to do.

OMAR: WHAT DID YOU DO?!

BLUE: I POURED IT !!!

I POURED IT !!!

AMIRA: You screamed, like . . . I've never heard anyone scream like that . . .

OMAR: And I told them . . . I told them . . . I told them . . .

BLUE: He said everything he was supposed to say, so we let him go.

OMAR: And they had it on tape. I said all of the revolutionary, militant, subversive ideology that I could think of. Just to stay alive.

AMIRA: Who knew who would be accused next? Who could be revealed as the next pig? The next butt in the chair could be yours.

OMAR: What happened to the tape?

AMIRA: As with all victims of war, some of us healed and learned to forgive, but sometimes . . .

OMAR: Who took the tape?!

AMIRA: . . . You can't forget.

    [NOTE: THE FOLLOWING IS INSPIRED BY THE OPENING TO WAR's "SLIPPIN INTO DARKNESS"]

OMAR:

    HELP ME,
    I FEEL MY MIND . . . FADING . . . AWAY

CHORUS:

    HELP ME,
    DON'T KNOW IF I
    DON'T KNOW IF I
    DON'T KNOW IF I'LL
    MAKE IT
    ANOTHER DAY.

OMAR/BLUE/MALIK/SOLIAS:

    IN THE MORNING/HA
    'TIL THE EVENING/HA
    ALL DAY/HA

312

I'LL BE WORKING HARD
ALL DAY/HA
'TIL THE EVENING/HA
SINCE THE MORNING/HA
I'LL BE WORKING HARD (2X)
OOH LORDY LORDY
COULD YA
HELP ME HELP ME
GET MY FEET FEET
SETTLED ON SOLID GROUND

BLUE:

CAUSE TIMES IS HARD
YOU DON'T KNOW
WHICH WAY IS UP
SO WHAT
LIFE KEEPS DRAGGING YOU DOWN

OMAR:

OOCHIE WALLY WALLY
HERE COMES MR. CHARLIE
SPIES AND EYES
WATCHING ALL OVER TOWN

BLUE:

SO YA BETTER BETTER
GET OFF YA ASS
FOR YA JUST ANOTHER
COULDA WOULDA
HANGING AROUND

OMAR/BLUE/MALIK/SOLIAS:

IN THE MORNING/HA
'TIL THE EVENING/HA
ALL DAY/HA
I'LL BE WORKING HARD
ALL DAY/HA
'TIL THE EVENING/HA
SINCE THE MORNING/HA
I'LL BE WORKING HARD

OMAR: I listened to my father and grandfather talk . . . talk that beaten broken black man rabble babble . . . ranting rhythmic recitals bout chanting chain gang chatter 'bout how one day we the people, were gonna get over, before we go under. Watched them drag themselves to dead end jobs, not realizing they were already dead doing that too-tired-to-die two step. Waiting for civil rights to be civil, that true equality would be reached when you reached heaven. So all your hopes and dreams will always be just out of reach. But after you die, after the fact, when you're just an afterthought, in the afterlife, you'll get all the things you've been chasing after.

So I didn't want to waste away waiting, wanting and watching daddy. If you always do, what you've always done, you'll always get, what you've always got. Forgive them Lord, for they know not what they do, but they do it so well. Make me feel like my inferior complex is inferior but I had plans of my own. I wasn't gonna walk the plank on this slave ship. I learn to walk that Uncle Sam military mambo. Make a black man feel like he part of this country. Teach him how to march. Teach him a trade. Teach him how to kill, kill, kill. Yes sir, Yes sir. If I learn this lesson, will I be considered equal? Can our kids go to the same schools? Can I eat in the same restaurants? Drink at the same water fountain? Sit in the front of the bus? Just be able to vote without getting my ass kicked? No? Then fuck you, that's right, I said it. A little profanity to go with this insanity, 'cause I can't shake these black and blues. For the times . . . they are a changin'. And I heard the word; shot through me like a bolt of lightning. I heard Bobby Seale speak. I heard him say,

[NOTE: THE FOLLOWING IS AN Audio RECORDING—BOBBY SEALE]
Audio of Bobby Seale:

" . . . When in the course of human events. It becomes necessary for us to dissolve the political bondage which has connected us with another and to assume among the powers of the earth; among the power in your hearts, minds and soul; that if you're dedicated to liberation of the people, the liberation for the Black Community, Native Americans, Chicano People; All Power to All the People. I say we should move forward. Organize ourselves; Organize ourselves through programs; Raise our consciousness to make sure that we understand what the pig power structure and government is doing. We're gonna organize ourselves. We're gonna stand up. We're gonna arm ourselves and we're gonna walk on this racist pig-ass power structure and we're gonna say, 'stick 'em up motherfucker, we come for what's ours.'"

314

Audio ends.

Oh yeah! Blew my mind, like a shotgun blast to my brain. Did I say shotgun? Don't wanna say that? You know some folks think it was only 'bout guns, but it was more than a gun. They had police patrols. Watch them, with walkie talkies and law books. That's right, law books, Huey knew that shit. You could observe from a certain distance. Make sure that who ever was getting arrested, actually made it to the station or didn't run into a nightstick by accident; or run into a bullet by accident; and I was running, running, running from my daddy and granddaddy's ghosts . . . running from Uncle Sam's ghost. Running trying to get me some free . . . Free, free, free . . . Free Huey . . . Free breakfast for the kids in the mornings. Got a spatula in my hand . . . locked and loaded ready to fire. "Come on in little brothers and sisters, y'all can sit down and get something to eat. Y'all can get some eggs and some bacon and some grits and get yourself a cup a milk. Yeah it's got Vitamin D, it'll make your teeth strong." But we weren't strong enough, the whole shit got flipped upside down and Hoover declared war on us. Started gunning us down and we started shooting back. 28 dead party members, 14 dead policemen: who's keeping score? I'm keeping score. And we've been infiltrated, don't know who to trust. We turn against ourselves, fighting and fucking, beatings and torture and I don't wanna know; and I don't wanna know, but I know! . . . That there are ghosts looking for me, round the corner, round the block; and I gotta keep moving or niggermortis will set in. I don't wanna die before I'm dead. And I—

[NOTE: THE FOLLOWING REFERENCES PHARCYDE's "CAN'T KEEP RUNNING AWAY"]

OMAR/CHORUS:

CAN'T KEEP RUNNING AWAY . . . (REPEATS, FADING OUT)
RUNNING, RUNNING AND RUNNING, RUNNING (UNDERNEATH LYRIC)

All freeze.
BLACKOUT.
INTERMISSION.

PART TWO

SCENE FIFTEEN: CLARA'S SONG

[NOTE: THE FOLLOWING REFERENCES "LAMENTO ESCLAVO (LAMENTO AFRICANO) TRADITIONAL SONG"]

CLARA:

AVECES QUISIERA LLORAR, CABALLEROS
Y LAS LAGRIMAS SE ME SALEN YO NO SÉ PORQUÉ
VÉLENME VÉLENME VÉLENME VEN
VÉLENME VE VEN VELEN VEN VÉLENME
QUIZÁS ES PORQUE TENGO SENTIMIENTO
CUANDO DEL ÁFRICA LLEGUÉ
YO, TRAJE MIS CARACOLES
CUANDO DEL ÁFRICA LLEGUÉ,
YO, TRAJE MIS CARACOLES
ME LLEVARON LOS ESPAÑOLES

EN UN BARCO CARABELA
ME QUITARON DE MI HIJO
PARA QUE FUERA ESCLAVO
AY, MI DIOS, QUE MUNDO MÁS TRAIDOR
EL AMO NO QUIERE QUE YO TOQUE TAMBOR
QUE YO TOQUE TAMBOR
QUE YO CANTE
ESTA CANCIÓN, OYE, NO
EL AMO NO QUIERE QUE YO TOQUE TAMBOR
QUE YO TOQUE TAMBOR
QUE YO CANTE
ESTE PREGÓN, OYE, NO
EL AMO NO QUIERE QUE YO TOQUE TAMBOR
QUE YO TOQUE TAMBOR
QUE YO CANTE
ESTA CANCIÓN
EL AMO NO QUIERE QUE YO TOQUE TAMBOR
EL AMO NO QUIERE QUE YO TOQUE TAMBOR

Pointing towards Omar.

I heard a man cry like that once.
I heard him scream and wail like every part of him was being unstitched.
His eyes, blood red from witnessing bloodshed.
His body beaten to a pulp.
It was dark and late at night.
I sat in my room listening to walls echoing his heartbeat.
He cried for his murdered brother,
heard him ask his maker why he made him "SO DAMN BLACK."
I looked through a crack in my door and saw my father on his knees;
pounding on the floor with his bare fist,
trying to recapture his rhythm,
but nothing came,
nothing ever came for him.
Why is it that no matter how far I run,
the rhythm finds me like a drum pounding in my head.
Why can't I live a different life?!
I'm tired of it,
tired of running;
tired of trying to reshape myself.
Is this what I'm stuck with?
Am I destined to hear the fucking screaming?
Destined to sweat when they sweat,
cry when they cry,
bleed when they bleed.
I don't want it!

I don't want to hear it anymore, but I hear
that rhythm even when it isn't there.

SCENE SIXTEEN: PRISON INDUSTRIAL COMPLEX

Omar approaches Malik to shake hands.

PRIMO: HAHA! Red light, blue light, red light, blue light, red light, blue
light one two three. Bad boys bad boys, what cha gonna do? Haha!
Busted. And you get to go to jail! And you get to go to jail! And you go
to jail! Haha! Everybody gets a cell!

MALIK: The first time I ever saw my father, he was in a prison cell; and the
last time I will see my father he will be in a prison cell. My first memory
is being on the inside. Funny ain't it? Not toys, or playing in the park.
I did those things, it's just not the first thing I remember.

Sounds of prison doors, voices.

I can hear the guards buzzing us in, the sound of cells opening; hear the
business of the visiting room; families having quick reunions; and the
smile on my daddy's face. He always had the biggest smile for his boy,
my momma never liked me being there but she wanted me to know my
father, even if it was inside of a prison. To know the person he was trying
to be, and no matter where we were, we are father and son. I used to
think that good and bad were always changing places. Switching sides
for whatever suited the moment. There were people trying to do good
and people doing bad to stop it. Or, is it bad people thinking they're
doing good and good people doing bad to survive? I've got a prison
industrial complex, and I can't shake it.

SCENE SEVENTEEN: LOCK DOWN

In this scene several members of the Chorus play Prisoners.
Solias is sitting in a chair under bright lights.

ROGER: Lights Ouuuuuuuuut!

Sound of prison cell closing.

He was a repeat offender, and a professional fuck-up.

SOLIAS: The walls of the cell are painted battleship gray. There is one long
bench where five, maybe six people can sit, there are a couple of bottles
filled with piss in the corners, and someone has burned "Off the Pigs"
and "Fuck Ronald Reagan" on the walls.

ROGER: The type of guy that you could easily get to work for you; all you
had to do was wait for him to make enough mistakes.

SOLIAS: I stole a car and went across state lines, which violated federal law.

ROGER: Now you know we have a very serious problem here, don't you? That there are a few things that we have to get straight. You really have two choices here. You can either serve your full sentence—and there is enough here for it to be a pretty extensive stay, and I will make sure you serve your full sentence—or you can help us help you.

SOLIAS: So when they asked me to join the Black Panthers, to look for any illegal activities, to report back everything I saw and heard, I understood what my role was to be.

ROGER: There is a mastery in what we do; hours and hours of research, character studies, investigative reporting.

SOLIAS: I felt: I'll be working with the FBI, that I'll be official. I could be somebody.

ROGER: FBI agents risked their lives to get this information. Follow me now . . . "Vamping ain't my bag" means: an informant I am not. "He is raking the scratch" means: he's taking Panther Party money. "Playing stud with the gray girls" means: having sexual relations with white girls. "Dig it" means: listen. "He is in some deep shit" means: his action must be dealt with. If you want to blend in I suggest you learn "how to speak black."

SOLIAS: Can you define Blackness? Is it what Webster says? Is it a definition too complicated to define? Too many skeletons in its closet. Does it cling to an afro? Wrap itself around Aretha's voice? Does it hang from a tree choking on its own blood? Does it use its blackness to gain access to high-risk neighborhoods? How black does black have to be before it shows how black it is? Does it walk with a bop? Does it have a Jheri curl, or dread locks? Is it braided or have a weave down its back? Can it dunk a basketball? Will it march and march and march asking to be considered equal and black? Is it related to Niggers, Coons, and colored folks? Does it consider suicide, when its blackness isn't enough? Does it carry a gun riding in a car looking to shoot itself? Does black even want to be black anymore? Is black still beautiful? Or is it the boogieman, boogieing late into the night, keeping the beat? Is it Miles Davis, Black? Or Barack Obama, Black? Define Black. Chitterlins, moonwalk, Panthers, Black? What is it's color? Is it Al Green, James Brown, Barry White, Black? Is it a don't ask don't tell Marvin Gaye, Black? Is it a raised fist for Black Power, Black, or is it hands in handcuffs behind your back Black? Or is Black sitting in a jail cell, wondering why there are more Blacks in prison now than there ever were slaves.

JIMMY/SOLIAS: Pfftpfftpff kch-kch-kch-kch-kch-kch

Pfftf Kch-kch-kch-kch

Pfftpfftpff kch-kch-kch-kch-kch-kch

Pfftf Kch-kch-kch-kch

OMAR/TITO/MARUCA: *(trading off)*

Huey Newton;

318

"Presente"
Fred Hampton;
"Presente"
Safya Bukhari;
"Presente"
Julio Roldan;
"Presente"
Beverly Axelrod;
"Presente"
Marilyn Buck;
"Presente"
Michael Tabor;
"Presente"
George Jackson;
"Presente"
Jonathan Jackson;
"Presente"
Warren Kimbro;
"Presente"
Bunchy Carter;
"Presente"
Geronimo Pratt;
"Presente"
Albizu Campos;
"Presente"
Oscar Collazo;
"Presente"
Griselio Torresola;
"Presente"
Dolores "Lolita" Lebrón Sotomayor;
"Presente"
Irving Flores;
"Presente"
Andrés Figueroa Cordero;
"Presente"
Eldridge Cleaver.
"Presente"

PRISONER 1 (HELITA):

> *[NOTE: REFERENCES NINA SIMONE's "MISSISSIPPI GODDAM"]*

HOUND DOGS ON MY TRAIL;
SCHOOL CHILDREN SITTIN' IN JAIL
BLACK CAT CROSSED MY PATH
I THINK EVERYDAY IS GONNA BE MY LAST

CHORUS:

ALL I CAN SAY IS . . . OHHH (2X)

BLUE: This is no place to be. I reminded myself every day for the 25 years that I was incarcerated that this is no place to be. Within the first week of being locked up, some kid stole something from me. I don't even remember what it was but everybody was watching; trying to see if I was a punk! So I beat him, and beat him and I felt my humanity slipping away. And I did my time, the way time gets done . . . slowly. Watching new kids come through, younger and angrier and those of us who were political prisoners understood that even on the inside, there needed to be proper conditions. That you couldn't just throw us in, lock the door and forget about us. And just when I thought I was disappearing, I got a letter from a young Panther cub, Malik. Who reminded me of who I was and that there was my wife who loved me. That there was something for me on the outside, and that I still had work to do.

PRISONER 1 (HELITA):

[NOTE: REFERENCES CARMEN SANABRIA's "EN HORAS DE AFLICCION"]

Singing continues through the dialogue that follows.

DIOS MIO, DIOS MIO
AYUDAME A VIVIR,
APLIADATE DE MI,
TE LOS SUPLICO.
MIRA, QUE CRUEL DESOLASCION
ME HIERE EL CORAZON,
BENDITO
TU SABES
LO AMARGO QUE ES VIVIR
EN MEDIO DEL SUFRIR
INTERMINABLE
MI DOLOR ES TORTURANTE
Y NADE SE APIADA DE MI
ESTO ES ALGO IMPERDONABLE.
HE LLORADO TANTO TANTO
QUE YA NO ME QUEDA LLANTO
Y ESO BIEN LO SABES TU.
Y EN MI AMARGO DESCONSUELO,
NECESITO UN CIRINEO
QUE ME AYUDE CON LA CRUZ (LAST VERSE 2X)

CHORUS:

ALL I CAN SAY IS . . . OHHH

PRISONER 2 (AMIRA): Don't nobody wanna be locked up

Locked down
Locked in
Locked out

PRISONER 4 (TITO): I was set free and now they want me back, yesterday's
COINTELPRO is today's Patriot Act. The judge dropped the charges on
his way out of court that day but he two-stepped and doubled back 40
years later just to find me guilty, today. They want me back . . . forever.

PRISONER 2 (AMIRA): Who wanna trade places tonight?
Trade lives
Trade truths
Trade lies
I'll talk to you, but don't ask me if I did it.

PRISONER 3 (OMAR):

[NOTE: REFERENCES PRINCE' "ELECTRIC CHAIR"]

IF A MAN IS CONSIDERED GUILTY
FOR WHAT GOES ON IN HIS MIND
THEN GIVE ME THE ELECTRIC CHAIR
FOR ALL MY FUTURE CRIME, OH.

MALIK: You want it straight from the horse's mouth? Horses that have
galloped and have run far? Refused to be broken or ridden? There is a
voice asking questions about a person they haven't been in a long time.
Wanting them to tell the stories of when they were super heroes but
those heroes have gotten old. Hero is in the eye of the beholder. Where's
their cape? Some of them were locked up and stripped of that cape; and
some of them were forced to take flight. Incarceration behind bars or in
exile. Stolen from us in the night; and I still try to visit; and I still write
you letters; and I still want to save you from the belly of the beast; no
man or woman left behind; 'cause I still want to find you, no matter
where you hide.

ROGER: Lights Ouuuuuuuuuut!

Sound of prison cell closing.

SCENE EIGHTEEN: BLUE AND DONNA

321

DONNA: My husband and I were together
for one thousand
three hundred
and seventeen days
and married for
nine hundred and fifty two of those days
and you took him from me in 30 minutes.

BLUE: Excuse me, uh . . . who are you?

DONNA: I am the wife . . .
    of the cop . . .
    that was murdered . . .
    a victim no one wants to hear about.

    Long pause.

    My husband was one of the cops at your "shooting."

BLUE: Excuse me, lady, I didn't shoot anybody.

DONNA: Were you there?

BLUE: I did not shoot anyone.
    I just want to make that clear.

DONNA: That's the story you want to stick to.

BLUE: That's the truth, I want to stick to the truth.

DONNA: I have a truth too . . .
    Now . . . were you there?

BLUE: OK, listen to me now.
    I was tried in a court of law,
    in front of people who were not my peers,
    who are a part of a racist power structure which has a history of legalized
    lynchings, and sent to jail for 25 years.
    Twenty-five years . . .
    Seventeen days . . .
    and 6 hours of my life . . .
    and had my conviction overturned
    because of evidence that was withheld by the prosecution
    because the District Attorney had a hard-on for an articulate,
    revolutionary black man who believed in empowering his community.
    And after sitting through appeal after appeal I was released.
    Now, I will admit that I was there,
    I never denied that,
    but I didn't shoot no pig . . .

DONNA: Did you just use the word PIG?

BLUE: A cop . . . any cop.
    Your husband.

DONNA: How dare you use that word
    in the same sentence as my husband.
    I was there at the trial every single day,
    I heard every single testimony,
    I saw every single piece of evidence.
    I have every single moment of the case ringing in my ears . . .
    I know everything that happened
    and there is nothing
    anyone can say that will change

322

what I know . . .
Now you may have fooled some people,
maybe even convinced yourself,
but you will not fool or convince me . . .
And you honestly don't remember me?

BLUE: Well, I'm sorry
if I don't remember every single thing,
my mind isn't so good at
holding on to some things nowadays.

DONNA: How convenient for you . . .
To not remember things . . .
I remember . . .
I remember the knock on the door,
tapping gently on the front door,
but it sounded so loud . . .
the time was 4:08 am.
There were three police officers standing outside my door:
two men and one woman.
I remember my knees going weak.
I've heard that saying before,
but my knees literally went weak
and I had to hold myself up . . .

BLUE: Lady, I don't have time for this.

DONNA: Make time.

I want you to know what I remember.

I can remember the ride in the police car to the hospital, and how all
the traffic lights seemed to turn green all the way there. I remember the
look on the doctor's face when I came through the emergency door, and
that was all I needed to see to know that my husband was gone. I can
remember our last breakfast together before he went on his shift, our last
kiss as he left, I remember looking at you in the courtroom, seeing your
face, I remember you even looking back at me, with those eyes, and you
were not sorry. I remember, I remember . . . how I wish I could forget.
But I will not let people forget him. He was not just some cop, or pig as
you would call them, he was a good man, with a family who loved him,
my husband . . . and I will not let anyone forget him, including you.

BLUE: It was a crazy time then. We were at war, even if you didn't know
it . . . Do you know what I remember, I remember looking at people in
my community struggling. I remember seeing despair as people were
trying to make ends meet. I remember watching these same people being
treated like second-class citizens in their own country. Being terrorized,
brutalized, murdered by a police that was supposed to protect and serve.
I remember.

323

DONNA: Do you pray?

BLUE: I try to.

DONNA: I need to, it gives me strength when I need it . . . like now. It gave me strength to sit in that courtroom day after day, to have your supporters glare at me, curse at me, spit at me, for just being there. For just being a wife. To hear the word "guilty" echo in that room.

BLUE: You know, when I heard the word "guilty" the room started spinning, and all of the sound disappeared. It wasn't until I turned around and saw my wife's face that the sound came back.

DONNA: My husband is gone, my father is gone, and my brothers and sisters are gone, and you have outlived them all.

BLUE: I'm going to keep on living . . . so should you.

DONNA: I did not come here out of hate, I came here out of love for my husband, to remind you that Kevin Michael Shanley was not just some cop.

SCENE NINETEEN: A PLACE SETTING FOR ME

Amira approaches Blue. They hold hands briefly. He sits in silence.

AMIRA: Look at us, and what a glorious mess we are. How beautiful scars can be and how ugly they can make us feel. When I look at our men, I see it, the pain of his manliness, his fight to stand up straight, his need to be with his brothers, friends, comrades. I feel his heat, his sex, how it defines him . . . Gives him his strut; his cock-a-doodle-doo, and the world is his hen house. But what does he see when he looks at me? His maid? His momma? His partner? Some pussy? A warm place to lay his head, when his head needs to be laid? Do I stand with him or behind him? Do I let myself move past him, or will it upset the order of things? Can I still be a woman, without waiting for his approval? But I can't waste my time thinking about that. I am not the sassy sidekick, the soprano to his bass. I am nobody's lap dance or lap dog, waiting for somebody to throw me a bone. I have seen some things; seen mothers struggle not to be just mammies; mothers who gotta raise their kids the best way they know how, whether daddies are there to be daddies or not. And me, being a pretty plum, in the fruit basket of life, sweet, a different flavor from the apple, orange, banana . . . Plums with something to say; who will be plucked when we want to, heads straight, eyes focused. Look at me when I talk to you! Loving, woman, dangerous, will take my place at the table even when I know that no one has put a place setting for me.

324

SCENE TWENTY: COINTELPRO

Primo, at his video console, starts a Young Lords video.

PRIMO: Alright ladies
Time to get your hair did
Nails done, face waxed
Get pretty like God intended
But first
Don't forget to feed the babies
Change the diapers
Make my breakfast
Do the dishes, scrub the floors
Iron clothes, fold my drawers
And then you can massage my feet
The way God intended
Machismo, a cultural standard
Our way of life
The women wanted to fix us
But the Federales liked us just the way we were

Video interviews begin showing. As video plays, Omar, Primo, and Solias begin a beat that Helita and Maruca use to challenge each other to a flamenoo dance.

HELITA: Machismo was written into the Young Lords' program and platform. And the women had to fight that.

MARUCA: We would no longer be submissive.

HELITA: Rebuilding ourselves was not enough, we had to actually rebuild our men as well. We fought to have women in leadership.

MARUCA: It takes a long time to build a leader.

HELITA: The male leadership began to fall apart.

MARUCA: The sisters took the drivers seat.

HELITA: It probably was the Young Lords' move to Puerto Rico that marked the beginning of the end. She was from there, but I was from here. And that was what made us a divided nation, and it depleted all of our resources.

MARUCA: "We" believed in the liberation of Puerto Rico and still do. Those that didn't join that struggle were traitors. If you were a real Puerto Rican, a real sister in the struggle, you would have fought with me.

HELITA: But we weren't all Puerto Rican. We also had black, Cuban, Dominican, Panamanian members, you name it. We started fighting about who spoke better Spanish, whose hair was straighter, and whose skin was lighter; and those people who were not Puerto Rican, of Puerto Rican descent: They were told to be quiet. They had no voice in this

325

conversation. When we started to question the leadership, they accused us of factionalism and they hunted us down.

MARUCA: What do you think this is? This is what we were trained to do. We needed to identify the internal threat and cut them out.

HELITA: Some of us looked for the weakest link and tried to mend it.

MARUCA: Some of us identified the weakest link and tried to remove it.

HELITA: We were kidnapped, tortured, and betrayed.

MARUCA: "Be resolute, fear no sacrifice, and surmount every difficulty to win victory."

HELITA: For her it seems so easy; she abandoned her own family.

MARUCA: I left my kids with their father. I wanted them to be safe from the war I was about to fight.

HELITA: And then you married an agent?

MARUCA: I was, myself, infiltrated, and betrayed by the very people I fought for.

HELITA: I'm gonna let history by your judge, my sister.

Video sequence ends with a rhythmic series of random phrases (sisters/traitors/weakest link/agent/victory/real Puerto Rican/infiltrated/etc.)

MARUCA: There were infiltrators, agitators and masturbators. Who rose to all sorts of power; and you blame me for our demise? We were all to blame. We should have never watered the seeds CoIntelPro planted; should have never laid in those beds we made; put ourselves to shame.

CHORUS: Dear Mrs. So-and-So . . .

COINTEL AGENT 1 (CLARA): Hey Girl,

COINTEL AGENT 2 (SOLIAS): Hey Man,

COINTEL AGENT 1 (CLARA): It pains me to write this note, . . .

COINTEL AGENT 2 (SOLIAS): I don't know if you've noticed, but that new dude, . . .

COINTEL AGENT 1 (CLARA): I have to tell ya, I just saw yo man . . .

COINTEL AGENT 2 (SOLIAS): . . . you know, so-and-so, . . .

COINTEL AGENT 1 (CLARA): . . . walking out of so-and-so's apartment.

COINTEL AGENT 2 (SOLIAS): well, he be giving yo girl too much airtime.

COINTEL AGENT 1 (CLARA): I've seented him there often . . .

COINTEL AGENT 2 (SOLIAS): Can't let no New Nigger steal you shit!

COINTEL AGENT 1 (CLARA): . . . and I had to tell ya yo no soy chismosa.

COINTEL AGENT 2 (SOLIAS): You gotta have that shit on lock!

COINTEL AGENT 1 (CLARA): I Luvs ya, Corazon.

COINTEL AGENT 2 (SOLIAS): I got you!

COINTEL AGENT 1 (CLARA): Signed, Your Girl

PRIMO: And today's word of the day is . . .

CHORUS/PRIMO:

> C.O.
> I.N.T.
> E.L.
> P.R.O.!
> COUNTER
> INTELLIGENCE
> PROGRAM

> *Continues repeating through the following dialogue.*

PRIMO: Come one, come all,
> Take a step through the door.
> Transformed you will be
> From the truth that's in store.
> This beautiful 20th century factory-crafted door was brought to us today
> by my main man Marcus.
> And now we begin the healing process.

> *C.O.I.N.T.E.L.P.R.O. chant ends.*

> I'm going to ask you to step through this door.
> Leave your burdens behind.
> Give thanks to the fallen comrades
> Who paid the price with their lives.

> *All walk slowly through door and have varied emotional experiences,*
> *as Malik films them. Solias, last to reach door, pauses.*

> This was Fred's door.
> Bullet-riddled by government assassins.
> Keepers of the peace
> Unloaded their pieces.
> Walls shredded to pieces
> By Chicago Polices.

> *Just as he is about to enter, cast point their guns at Solias.*

> *Sustained gunshots.*

> *Solia backs up and closes door. The following is his semi-cognitive emotional* **327**
> *experience.*

SOLIAS: You killed him.

ROGER: I did not kill anybody.

SOLIAS: Come on man, you're gonna stand there and tell me that you—

ROGER: Wait a minute Solias, let's not let our emotions run wild. I
understand—

SOLIAS: You understand what? Do you understand how I felt when I walked
in that house? Saw all the blood, the bullet holes. I knew right then and

there I had been betrayed, by you. I made this happen. I was head of his security, man. And Fred was clean. I spent a lot of time with him, man . . . he didn't drink or smoke, he was dedicated to the struggle. He didn't have no side illegal shit going on. Wasn't fucking people on the side. The older folks were proud of him, the street cats loved him cause he didn't take no shit, the only high he wanted, was to get high off the people. The motherfucker was clean, and y'all could still go in and gun him down like that. I don't understand what happened. I've done everything you asked me to do. I've given you names, told you how things worked, drew up the floor plans of the house.

ROGER: And you were paid for that. Look I've seen this before. People go undercover, and they develop an attachment to the people that they are supposed to be watching. I mean all that Panther talk can be very seductive . . .

SOLIAS: Come on, don't talk that agent talk to me . . . I don't wanna hear that, we never talked about killing anybody . . . I've been to your house man, sat at your dinner table with your wife, held your son in my arms, and you're gonna talk to me . . . like this?

ROGER: I had to get to know you, you seemed like you needed a family environment to help you trust me and talk to me.

SOLIAS: Well I did trust you, more than my own family . . . more than I trusted myself. Cause when I would question what I was doing, I knew I could talk to you, and you made me feel like one of the good guys. And you used your own family to get me to trust you. What kind of man are you?

ROGER: I have a deep love for this country. And it is because of this love, that I do this work everyday with purpose. To do my job it takes knowledge, skills, commitment, and intestinal fortitude. My parents believed in the spirit of this country, the very idea of life, liberty, and the pursuit of happiness defined everything about them. And they passed that on to me. So I consider myself a patriot. I admire Hoover and what he has asked me and my fellow agents to do. We are the only ones who know what is good for the country, and we are the only ones who can do anything about it . . . Now I will tell you this. Between me and you, kid, Fred was clean . . . but obviously somebody higher up wanted him dead. There was talk in the bureau of him possibly becoming a black messiah and you see what happens to messiahs.

SOLIAS: So what happens to me now . . .

ROGER: We can take care of you, put you in our witness protection pro . . .

SOLIAS: What happens to me now?!

Chorus begins to encircle Solias as Roger exits.

CHORUS/PRIMO:

C.O.
I.N.T.
E.L.
P.R.O.!
COUNTER
INTELLIGENCE
PROGRAM

Chant repeats through following dialogue.

SOLIAS: I lost.
I lost mine
When I lost my mind
My little light went out
Although I swore to let it shine
And, once your lights are put out
The spark is gone.
Pohhhho *(reverb)*
And who's supposed to bring me back?
Bring me back that
That
That spark
That
That burn
That yearn
That
That fire
That makes you feel free

C.O.I.N.T.E.L.P.R.O. chant ends.

NEVER MEANT TO HURT NOBODY.
NEVER MEANT TO TURN MY BACK ON YOU.
I NEVER MEANT TO TAKE MY CROWN;
THROW IT DOWN TO THE GROUND.
NO, I NEVER MEANT TO DO THAT.
CAN'T RUN FROM ALL THE GUILT INSIDE ME
IT'S TEARING ME IN TWO
DEATH IS MY ONLY WAY
SO THAT'S EXACTLY WHAT I'M GONNA DO

Whispers of "TRAITOR," etc., from Chorus as Omar gives Solias a handgun.

I WAS A TRAITOR OF THE WORST KIND
I DIED A TRAITOR OF THE WORST KIND

Gunshot.

329

OMAR: You're asking questions about . . . about the FBI.

BLUE: I have done time.

AMIRA: I have been followed . . .

OMAR: We don't talk about shit like that.

BLUE: Time that I shouldn't have done.

OMAR: It ain't nothing' to . . . ain't nothin' to play with, man.

MARUCA: The man in the Party I fell in love with . . .

AMIRA: I've had my mail opened . . .

BLUE: . . . time that is gone forever . . .

AMIRA: . . . phones tapped . . .

MARUCA: . . . had children with . . .

BLUE: They still watch me.

AMIRA: . . . had my little mother harassed and terrorized . . .

MARUCA: ..turned out to be an agent.

OMAR: When you ask questions like that . . . I don't . . . I don't wanna talk about that.

AMIRA: I watched my husband go to jail for over 20 years for something he didn't do, so when you ask this question . . .

BLUE: They still follow me.

MARUCA: So that tells you about me and the FBI.

OMAR: . . . *(Silence.)*

AMIRA: . . . *(Silence.)*

    Video sequence ends.

MARCUS: And these are the victims of COINTELPRO
    The walking wounded, who you'll never know
    Who wear deep scars
    buried in their skin like tattoos
    And would dare you to walk
    a mile in their shoes
    And they all did the best
    that they could
    While they were misused
    Misrepresented
    Misled
    Misunderstood

SCENE TWENTY-ONE: DESTRUCTION SUITE

MALIK: All I heard growing up is that when my time comes, I'd better be ready. I watched, and listened, a little soldier in training, but then it was all torn apart, and all the peoples I knew as my uncles and aunties were gone. All of the excitement of watching things happen, people putting things into action, were gone; trading their names for a prison number, gone; hunted down, set up, murdered, or guilty as charged, gone; or they ran from this country to another, in exile, gone; into the dance of drugs, gone; losing themselves in the get high, gone; and my life got quiet for a long time.

CHORUS:

> DON'T PUSH ME CAUSE I'M CLOSE . . .
> DON'T PUSH ME CAUSE I'M CLOSE . . .

MALIK/JIMMY:

> HERE COME THE DRUGS
> HERE COME THE DRUGS
> HERE COME THE DRUGS
> HERE COME THE DRUGS
> NO MATTER WHAT YOU DO NOW
> HERE COME THE DRUGS
> FEELS REAL GOOD/LIKE A HAND IN A GLOVE
> HERE COME THE DRUGS
> HERE COME THE DRUGS
> COINTELPRO IS DOING ITS THING
> GOT YOU LIKE A PUPPET ON A STRING
> THROW YOU SOME BAIT ON A HOOK
> GAME OF CHESS/PAWN/ROOK
> GIVE EACH OTHER THE SILENT TREATMENT
> WHILE HE PREYS ON YOUR WEAKNESS
> SEX, DRUGS AND ROCK AND ROLL
> TO SEX, DRUGS AND YOUR SOUL
> THIS PARTY MEMBER ROBBED A MARKET
> AND THIS PARTY MEMBER STAYED HOME
> AND THIS PARTY MEMBER STOLE MONEY
> AND THIS PARTY MEMBER HAD NONE

CHORUS:

> HERE COME THE DRUGS
> HERE COME THE DRUGS
> EVERYBODY SAY NOW

BLUE: I felt on edge, what I knew as the Party was over, and I found myself in far off places, crack houses of many shapes and sizes. Looking to get my fix when the movement couldn't be fixed and I was at war; screaming at the top of my lungs for justice, with some young bloods who only saw me as a customer; but I had been a regular customer, gave them good business and they won't give me credit, won't hook me up. I'm good for it.

MALIK:

> HERE COME THE DRUGS
> HERE COME THE DRUGS
> EVERYBODY SAY NOW
> HERE COME THE DRUGS
> TURN A PANTHER INTO A THUG
> HERE COME THE DRUGS
> HERE COME THE DRUGS
> GOT THAT WEED
> TRUE INDEED
> GONNA
> GIVE YOU EVERYTHING YOU NEED
> HEROIN
> SLIPPING IN
> MAKING IT FEEL REAL GOOD TO SIN
> HANDS SHAKING
> LATE NIGHT SWEATS
> MISAPPROPRIATED CHECKS
> DROPPING DIMES
> COCAINE LINES
> RIGHT TO THE UNEMPLOYMENT LINES
> DRUG ENFORCEMENT AGENCY
> AND THE CIAAAA
> RAISING MONEY FOR THE CONTRAS
> SPREAD CRACK IN THE USAAAA
> BLOODS, BLOODS
> CRIPS AND BLOODS
> SOLD COCAINE TO THE
> CRIPS AND BLOODS
> GUN YOU DOWN
> WITH A HOLLOW POINT SLUG

MALIK/CHORUS:

> HERE COME THE DRUGS
> HERE COME THE DRUGS
> HERE COME THE DRUGS
> HERE COME THE DRUGS
> INHALE/INHALE
> EXHALE/EXHALE

332

SPOTLIGHT/SPOTLIGHT
LIMELIGHT/LIMELIGHT

MALIK:

CULT OF PERSONALITY
BRINGING OUT THE WORST OF ME
I TRY TO RUN
I TRY TO HIDE
FROM THIS
REACTIONARY SUICIDE

MARUCA: Some of us were looking for a crutch, looking for a place to lay
our burdens down, to turn off the noise. We were having a hard time
facing the fact that what we had dedicated our lives to wasn't what we
thought it was. And women rose to power. Some say we fucked our way
there. They couldn't stand to have a woman telling them what to do.
They couldn't stand to march in rhythm to our beat.

PRIMO:

COME ON BABY
LET ME GET ONE FUCK
LOVE YOU LONG TIME
FUCK MY LUCK
LET YOU LICK ME
LIKE A LOLLI-POP THAT
JUICY PUSSY UH!
PUSSY KILLED THE PARTY
BITCHES CAME AND FUCKED IT UP
THEM BITCHES PLAYED THAT COUP D'ETAT
THAT PARLEZ VOUS MENAGE A TROIS
SHE GAVE ME TEEPEE PEEPEE
I WAS DONE LIKE 1,2,3 . . . 3
WE NEED NOT BE GREEDY
BUT SHE NEEDED ME TO LEAVE
INDEEDY
I GOT UP OUT OF THERE
I TUCKED THAT TAIL AND RAN
SHE SAID THAT DISCIPLINE
WOULD FIX THIS LADY LOVING MAN
BUT SHE WAS WRONG AND RIGHT
CAUSE I WAS UP ALL NIGHT
JUST THINKING OF SOME PUSSY
I COULD FIND AND CRAWL INSIDE
PUSSY KILLED THE PARTY
AIN'T NO DOUBT ABOUT THE FACT
PUSSY KILLED THE PARTY

GAME OF MOUSE AND PRETTY KITTY CAT
PUSSY KILLED THE PARTY
PUSSY KILLED THE PARTY
WHAT'S IT KILLED THE PARTY?
GUSHY PUSSY KILLED THE PARTY

PRIMO/MK ULTRA:
CRACK HEAD
SHAKE, SHAKE
COOK AND CUT THAT CAKE, CAKE
MANTECA
QUE TECATO
ESA AGUJA PUYA BRAZO
YOU LIKE TO BE SO HIGH
AIN'T THAT HOW HUEY DIED?
AND YOU AIN'T GOT NO PARTY
WITH HIM DIED THE PANTHER PRIDE
EVERYBODY HAD THE BOP
THAT SHOULDER LEAN THEY LOCK AND POP
THEY GO SO LOW BUT NEVER DROP
UNTIL THE FUCKIN' PARTY STOP, STOP

CHORUS:
STOP!

SCENE TWENTY-TWO: RECKONING

MARCUS: *(to Malik and Jimmy)* Oh, what, you brought people down here to . . . to insult them? Like one of them god-damn reality shows? Let's get some old activists together who might—or might not—have post-traumatic stress, and push a few buttons? Fuck this!

MARUCA: Helita, how many times have we heard our "comrades" say that "Pussy Killed the Party"?

TITO: I never said that.

AMIRA/MARUCA/HELITA: Oh, please!

AMIRA: I was a member of the party until 1982. The party did not end when the male leadership collapsed.

HELITA: Yes, the women held on, tooth and nail. And just because we were the last "man" standing, it doesn't mean that we killed the party.

OMAR: Hahahaha, we're getting to the real shit now. I don't know how they got it or where they got it, but these two motherfuckers here are trying to tell the truth. Just because some of y'all didn't experience certain things doesn't mean that they didn't happen. Hahahahaha.

TITO: Jimmy, when we were young we were fighting for something, not just pointing out what was wrong, but showing the world what could be right. I know the armchair revolutionary thing bothers you, but I—

JIMMY: Stop. We have something to add to the revolutionary conversation, but y'all told us that it can't be done the way y'all did it. With the guns and the militancy. This is a new time with new technology. The revolution can be televised, and tweeted, it can have its own website, have its own blog, have a Youtube clip with a million hits. Have its own brand.

MALIK: How is the next generation gonna look at all this, what happened before us, what you did for us and remix that shit; not be afraid to look deep in its eyes, deconstruct it, analyze, optimize, finalize, cut and paste it, Photoshop it back together again and then click share!

AMIRA: Young man, young man, come here. Listen to me close, you all are part of a generation who watches Jon Stewart for the news. It's safe, because it has a punch line, and an audience that hides behind irony just like your Primo the Clown. They feel like they make political statements by posting something on their Facebook page. But don't lose yourself behind a "brand," or get so wrapped up in the selling and marketing of something without understanding that "the people" are the ones who make things happen.

JIMMY: We are the people, where do you think we come from?

MALIK: We come from the people.

JIMMY: From the time we were 13, we were told we would die a violent death before we hit 21.

MALIK: Heard it like lullaby that rocked us to sleep. I couldn't wait until I turned 21 because then I would be safe. The sound of gunshots in my neighborhood didn't bother me. Abandoned buildings far as my eyes could see didn't bother me. It was just the landscape. Didn't all neighborhoods have local number runners who came early in the morning screaming up to windows for people to throw down their bets for the day? Didn't all neighborhoods have local drug dealers who set up shop and operated like it was a community service? People would line up for blocks to get that hit.

JIMMY: And as kids we knew to walk on the other side of the street. We learned to submit to the cops when they stopped and frisked us in the park; learned to never put our hands in our pockets when they approached us. Learned that we were guilty first in their eyes. As we got older, we saw a world that didn't make sense. That my family, friends, and neighbors were all part of something that we couldn't escape.

MALIK: The rules were fixed and the only way to beat the rules was to work twice as hard as any white kid. That was drilled in my head. Even when someone was trying to give you advice it was always wrapped around how inferior you were. Death was always around the corner. I was just another project niggah who would maybe get a city job if I was lucky. Maybe rent the roach-infested apartment I grew up in, after my parents died.

JIMMY: My parents raised me the best way they knew how, but I knew I needed more. I couldn't stay stuck . . . how arrogant that made me feel. Like what they gave me may not be enough to survive in this world.

MALIK: And I can remember sitting on the roof of my building, staring out at everything around me, and wanting to die. How I felt trapped by something that was bigger than me, like there was no way out. Like I could see the injustice, clear as day but no one else could.

JIMMY: Like everything I had learned to accept wasn't right.

MALIK: I would sit on that roof and cry because I was too much of a punk to jump. So I didn't jump, and another day turned into another day. And I learned to walk with my head up. And I learned how to speak clearly.

I can remember sitting in my dorm room in college for the entire first month waiting for someone to knock on my door to say that they had made a mistake.

JIMMY: That there was a computer glitch and that my name was selected by accident. That I was taking someone else's slot.

MALIK: And to this day, I still sit and wait for that knock on the door—

JIMMY: —waiting for someone to tell me that my entire life is someone else's slot—

MALIK: —when really I should still be sitting on that project roof, daring myself to jump.

CLARA:
I'VE WALKED THESE STREETS
ALL MY LIFE
AND I AIN'T EVER SEEN CHANGE
NAW I AIN'T EVER SEEN A DIME
I AIN'T GOT
NO BUTTER FOR MY BREAD

Jimmy joins in.

336

AND NO SHEETS ON MY BED
I'D BE BETTER OFF DEAD
'CAUSE IT AIN'T JUST
Malik joins in.

IT AIN'T JUST THE LACK OF THE HOUSING
IT AIN'T JUST THE CROOKED POLICE
IT AIN'T JUST THE CRACKS IN THE WALLS AND THE RATS AND
THE ROACHES AND THE COLD AND THE MOLD
IT AIN'T JUST BLACKS AND LATINOS

IT AIN'T JUST THE BRAVE AND THE BOLD
IT AIN'T JUST THE POOR
THEY DO IT TO US ALL AND I AIN'T TAKIN' IT NO MORE,
I'M READY TO BRAWL.

CLARA: *(Chorus adds "IT AIN'T JUST" after each line that follows)*

MY HEART FALLS TO PIECES
WHEN I SEE HOW YOU LOOK AT ME
THERE'S MORE TO THIS THAN BLACK EYED PEAS
THERE'S MORE TO THIS THAN RICE AND BEANS *(2X)*

OMAR: Civil Rights Movement; necessary! Black Panther Party; necessary! Young Lords; necessary! Revolution in the 21st century . . .

JIMMY/MALIK/CLARA: Necessary!

Omar begins clapping a rhythm that begins the next song.

EPILOGUE

MARUCA:

LIFE, HOME, LAND, BREAD

CHORUS:

LIFE, HOME, LAND, BREAD

Chorus repeats lyrics as they take turns thanking and embracing Jimmy and Malik.

HELITA:

ES LARAZON QUE PELEO

CHORUS:

LIFE AND HOME AND LAND AND BREAD

Helita and Chorus repeat their lines throughout first verse of Jimmy's rap.

JIMMY:

I AM AN AMERICAN
I'M AS AMERICAN AS APPLE PIE
AS AMERICAN AS SLAVERY
I'M AS AMERICAN AS SMALLPOX
CRAZY HORSE, SITTING BULL, GERONIMO, MALCOLM X AND THE
TRAIL OF TEARS
BASEBALL, HAMBURGERS AND GAS-GUZZLERS
LIVIN' OFF THE SWEAT OFF SOMEONE ELSE'S BACK
THAT'S THE AMERICAN WAY
AND I'M THAT

337

FIGHTING FOR THE FREEDOM TO SPEAK
THE RIGHT TO BEAR ARMS
PATROLLING THE STREETS
I'M THAT
BORN THAT, DIE THAT
NEVER GONNA CHANGE
LEFT A FEW BLOODY BODIES
MAKING HOME ON THE RANGE
THE AMERICAN WAY
NATION OF BRUTE STRENGTH
MADE A NATIONAL PASTIME
OF RATTLING CLIPS
WE LET THE CANONS EXPLODE
HOT ROCKETS RED GLARE
TOO MANY MEN IN THE TOWN
LOCKED IN THOUSAND YARD STARES

CHORUS:

GIVE ME LAND, BREAD, HOUSING
GIVE ME JUSTICE, GIVE ME PEACE

JIMMY:

ALL AMERICAN
HOMELESS VETERANS
RETURNING WITH LESS LIMBS
CAN'T GET A JOB
CAN'T KEEP IT TOGETHER
AND AFTER ALL THAT THEY'VE GIVEN US
THEY DESERVE TO GET BETTER
CHEDDAR FROM THE GOVERNMENT
CAN'T GET A CRUMB IN A CRUMBLING ECONOMY
AYO I SOLEMNLY PROMISE
TO TAKE A STAND WHEN I CAN
I'M BURNING RUBBER ON THE ROAD
LIKE THE MICHELIN MAN
I GOT A DREAM NOT A PLAN
BUT THE PLAN IN MY DREAM
INCLUDES HOUSING AND LAND
WITH A POCKETFUL OF SHELLS
AND A LIST OF DEMANDS
I'M A PATRIOT
HATE ME AND YOU HATE
WHAT IT MEAN TO BE . . .
AN AMERICAN
FUCK THE POLICE

338

FROM TIERRA DEL FUEGO IN CHILE
TO MEXICO'S STREET
GREENLAND
PANAMA, BRAZIL
CUBA
CANADA
OUT ON THE TUNDRA
WE ALL AMERICANS
JOSE CAN YOU SEE
SIMÓN BOLÍVAR WAS AS AMERICAN AS ME
WE THE PEOPLE
GET UNITED UNDIVIDED WE CAN STAND
LINE 'EM UP AND KEEP 'EM POPPIN'
LIKE AN M-1 GARAND
I GOT A MESSAGE FROM THE FAM
AND IT'S ADDRESSED TO UNCLE SAM
FUCK YOU
FUCK YOUR WEALTH
AND FUCK THE MAN
I'M AN AMERICAN
ALL AMERICAN

CHORUS:

GIVE ME LAND, BREAD, HOUSING
GIVE ME JUSTICE, GIVE ME PEACE

JIMMY:

I'M AN AMERICAN
ALL AMERICAN

CHORUS:

GIVE ME LAND, BREAD, HOUSING
GIVE ME JUSTICE, GIVE ME PEACE

BLACKOUT.

339

APPENDIX: PRODUCTION INFORMATION

THE WHALE received its world premiere in January 2012 at the Denver Center Theatre Company in Denver, CO (Kent Thompson, Artistic Director), directed by Hal Brooks. It was then produced in October 2012 at Playwrights Horizons in New York, NY (Tim Sanford, Artistic Director), directed by Davis McCallum. It was subsequently produced in March 2013 at South Coast Repertory in Costa Mesa, CA (Marc Masterson, Artistic Director) directed by Martin Benson, and in April 2013 at Victory Gardens in Chicago, IL (Chay Yew, Artistic Director), directed by Joanie Schultz. This script reflects the version produced in Chicago.

UNCLE HO TO UNCLE SAM was first developed at the Ojai Playwrights Conference (Robert Egan Producing Artistic Director) summer 2011. It had its world premiere fall 2012 at Seattle ACT: Performed by Trieu Tran, directed by Robert Egan. Scenic Design by Carey Wong. Costume Design by Rose Pederson. Lighting Design by Rick Paulsen. Sound Design by Brendan Patrick Hogan. Associate Media Design by Lara Kaminsky. Stage Manager: JR Welden. Production Assistant: Ruth Eitemiller

Kirk Douglas Theatre, fall 2013: Performed by Trieu Tran, directed by Robert Egan Scenic Design by Takeshi Kata. Lighting Design by Lap Chi Chu. Original Sound Design by Brendan Patrick Hogan. Projection Design by Lara Kaminsky. Stage Manager: Elle Aghabala

TORSO received its world premiere in March 2012, produced by Printer's Devil Theater in partnership with Theatre Off Jackson in Seattle. It was directed by David Bennett with scenic design by Jake Nelson, lighting design by Robert J. Aguilar, music composed by John Ackermann, sound design by Michael Hayes, costume design by Sarah Harlett. Production manager : Tim Crist. Stage manager: Stacey Plum.

Sarah Rudinoff – Daphne Maas
John Q. Smith – Eddie Campillo, Ted Daniels, Dr. Brandenburg, Palmer Prewitt
Emily Chisholm – Waitress, Ceil Maas, Tina Shackley, Reporter
Susanna Burney – Marlo Roy, Eleanor Stone
Stephen Hando – Director, Sammy, Dominick Roy, Dr. Mellis, Chris Jacobs

THE BODY OF AN AMERICAN was first produced at Portland Center Stage in Portland, Oregon on October 2nd, 2012. The performance was directed by Bill Rauch, with sets and costumes by Christopher Acebo, lighting by James F. Ingalls, sound by Casi Pacilio and Eamonn Farrell, projections by Eamonn Farrell. The Production Stage Manager was Jeremy Eisen. The Play was commissioned and developed with support from The Playwrights' Center's 2009-2019 McKnight Commission and Residency Program, Minneapolis, MN.

William Salyers – Paul
Danny Wolohan – Dan

UNDO premiered at Annex Theatre in Seattle, Washington, January 18 – February 16, 2013. Directed by Erin Kraft, assistant directed by Kaytlin McIntyre, costume design by Doreen Sayegh, lighting design by Michael Chinn, set design by Catherine Cornell, stage manager: Christa Luckenbach.

Ian O'Malley – The Boy with the Glass
Ashton Hyman – Joe Pfeiffer
Sydney Andrews – Rachel Mendelssohn Pfeiffer
Nick Edwards – Ari Glassman
Barbara Lindsay – Joan Wolofsky Mendelssohn
Tom Fraser – Ozzie Mendelssohn
Samantha Leeds – Naomi Mendelssohn
Jillian Vashro – Hannah Mendelssohn
Amy Hill – Siobhan Doyle
Mark Waldstein – Abe Pfeiffer
Marty Mukhalian – Adine Wolofsky
Zoey Cane Belyea – Melita Johnson

NOTE: The character Ozzie was cut subsequent to the Annex production.

PARTY PEOPLE was developed and directed by Liesl Tommy, with scenic design by Clint Ramos, costume design by ESosa, lighting design by Marcus Doshi, video design by Pablo N. Molina, dramaturgy by Julie Felise Dubiner, voice & text direction by David Carey, choreography by Millicent Johnnie, fight directon by U. Jonathan Toppo, stage Manager: Mara Filler.

G. Valmont Thomas – Blue
Mildred Ruiz Sapp – Helita
William Ruiz, aka Ninja – Jimmy
Jadele McPherson – Clara
Mateo Gomez – Tito
Peter Macon – Solias
Steven Sapp – Omar
Michael Elich – Marcus
Kimberly Scott – Amira
Robynn Rodriguez – Donna
Christopher Livingston – Malik
Miriam Laube – Maruca

Chay Yew

As a playwright, his plays include *Porcelain, A Language of Their Own, Red, Wonderland, Question 27 Question 28, A Distant Shore 17* and *Visible Cities*. His other work includes adaptations, *A Winter People* (based on Chekhov's *The Cherry Orchard*) and Lorca's *The House of Bernarda Alba*, a musical *Long Season* and theatre works, *Vivien and the Shadows, Home: Places Between Asia and America* and *A Beautiful Country*. His work has been produced at the Public Theater, Mark Taper Forum, Manhattan Theatre Club, Long Wharf Theatre, La Jolla Playhouse, Intiman Theatre, Wilma Theatre, Portland Center Stage, East West Players, Dallas Theatre Center, Cornerstone Theatre Company, Group Theatre, Studio Theatre, Perseverance Theatre, Smithsonian Institute, North Carolina Performing Arts, amongst many others. Overseas, his work has been produced by the Royal Court Theatre (London, UK), Fattore K and Napoli Teatro Festival (Naples, Italy), La Mama (Melbourne, Australia), Four Arts (Kuala Lumpur, Malaysia), Singapore Repertory Theatre, Toy Factory, Checkpoint Theatre, TheatreWorks Singapore, to name a few. He is also the recipient of the London Fringe Award for Best Playwright and Best Play, George and Elisabeth Marton Playwriting Award, GLAAD Media Award, Made in America Award, AEA/SAG/AFTRA 2004 Diversity Honor, and Robert Chesley Award. His plays *The Hyphenated American Plays* and *Porcelain* and *A Language of Their Own* are published by Grove Press. He is recently edited a new anthology *Version 3.0: Contemporary Asian American Plays* for TCG Publications.

His directing credits include the Public Theater, Playwrights Horizon, New York Theatre Workshop, Humana Festival at Actors Theatre of Louisville, Kennedy Center, Mark Taper Forum, Goodman Theatre, American Conservatory Theatre, Berkeley Repertory Theater, Denver Theater Center, Victory Gardens Theater, Huntington Theatre, Oregon Shakespeare Festival, Cincinnati Playhouse, Woolly Mammoth Theatre Company, Northlight Theatre, Empty Space, Roundhouse Theatre, Portland Center Stage, Cornerstone Theatre, Geva Theater Center, East West Players, Singapore Repertory Theatre, amongst others. His opera credits include the world premieres of Osvaldo Golijov's and David Henry Hwang's *Ainadamar* (co-production with Tanglewood Music Center, Lincoln Center for the Performing Arts and Los Angeles Philharmonic) and Rob Zuidam's *Rage D'amors* (Tanglewood). He is also a recipient of the OBIE and DramaLogue Awards for Direction.

An alumnus of New Dramatists, he has served on the Board of Directors of Theatre Communications Group and is presently on the Executive Board on the Society of Stage Directors and Choreographers. He is also the Artistic Director of Victory Gardens Theater in Chicago since July 2011.